D1759124

Housing in Ireland

Lorcan Sirr

About the Author

Dr Lorcan Sirr is a senior lecturer in housing at Technological University Dublin. He is widely published on a broad range of real estate, planning and housing issues, and is editor of *Dublin's Future: New Visions for Ireland's Capital City* (Liffey Press, 2009) and *Renting in Ireland: The Social, Voluntary and Private Sectors* (IPA, 2014). Lorcan has also written for most major Irish publications, including the *Sunday Times*, where he was a housing columnist, and is a regular speaker at international and national conferences. He provides analysis for major media outlets such as RTÉ, CBC (Canada), BBC and Bloomberg. Lorcan has an MA from the Katholiek Universiteit Leuven and an MA and PhD in Planning and Development from the University of Manchester.

Housing in Ireland

The A–Z Guide

Leabharlann Thír an Iúir
Terenure Library
Tel: 01 222 8700
terenurelibrary@dublincity.ie

Lorcan Sirr

ORPEN PRESS

- 6 JUL 2019

Published by
Orpen Press
Upper Floor, Unit K9
Greenogue Business Park
Rathcoole
Co. Dublin
Ireland
email: info@orpenpress.com
www.orpenpress.com

© Lorcan Sirr, 2019

Paperback ISBN 978-1-78605-076-2
ePub ISBN 978-1-78605-077-9

A catalogue record for this book is available from the British Library. All rights reserved. No part of this publication may be reproduced, stored in a retrieval system or transmitted in any form or by any means, electronic, mechanical, photocopying, recording or otherwise, without the prior, written permission of the publisher.

This book is sold subject to the condition that it shall not, by way of trade or otherwise, be lent, resold, hired out, or otherwise circulated without the publisher's prior consent in any form of binding or cover other than that in which it is published and without a similar condition including this condition being imposed on the subsequent purchaser.

Printed in Dublin by SPRINTprint Ltd

Acknowledgements

Thanks to the sponsors of this book: Savills; Maeve Hogan of the Property Services Regulatory Authority; Pat Davitt of the Institute of Professional Auctioneers and Valuers; and David Silke and John O'Connor of the Housing Agency.

Also many thanks to: Shane McCloud, Irish Association of Self Builders; Elaine Harley-Gunning; Mercy Law Resource Centre; Residential Tenancies Board; Beauchamps Solicitors; Irish Human Rights and Equality Commission; Kim Bakkers and Raphaël Ingelbein of Katholiek Universiteit Leuven; Melanie Robinson of Napier University, Edinburgh; Terry Sheridan, Department of Housing, Planning and Local Government; Jeff Colley, *Passive House+*; Rosalind Carroll, Residential Tenancies Board; Dermot O'Leary, Goodbody; Napier University; John Mark McCafferty, Threshold; David Hall, Irish Mortgage Holders Association; Nathalie Weadick, Irish Architecture Foundation; Helen Murray-O'Connor and Sarah Rock, Technological University Dublin; Rory Hearne of NUI Maynooth; Wayne Stanley and Mike Allen, Focus Ireland; Rory O'Donnell and Noel Cahill of NESC; Simon Brooke, Clúid Housing; Maya Healy; Mel Reynolds; Orla Hegarty, UCD; Deirdre Ní Fhloinn, barrister; Emma Gilleece; Rhona McCord; Hugh Brennan, Ó Cualann Cohousing Alliance; Declan Redmond and Brendan Williams, UCD; James Nugent of Lisney; Josh Ryan-Collins (UCL), Laurie Macfarlane (Open Democracy) and Toby Lloyd (housing policy advisor, Downing Street); Robert Somerville-Woodward; Joe O'Connor of Forsa; Karl Deeter; John McCartney. And very special thanks to Suzanne and Elizabeth Meade.

Explanatory Note

Entries are presented in alphabetical order. Within each entry, words in ***italic bold*** refer to the fact that this topic has its own separate entry in the book. At the end of certain entries, there are suggestions for related topics that have their own entries. Footnotes indicate relevant additional material or the source of the information in the entry. A footnote at the entry heading indicates that the entire entry came from this source. The bibliography at the end of the book is an alphabetical list of all the literary sources used in the book.

Preface

This is a book that has been simmering on the back burner for a long time. During that time, the topic of housing has become increasingly complex. The process of housing people has also evolved with new policies, players, business models, regulation, ideology and so on. Today, we have a framework of regulations (e.g. the Central Bank lending limits), policies (tenure neutrality), organisations (Dublin Tenants' Association), legislation (Rent Pressure Zones), and socioeconomic realities (homelessness) that were not on the national radar ten or fifteen years ago. We also have a commensurately expanded housing vocabulary.

Politicians deal with these new realities and their new terminologies. It is fair to say that housing people is a goal of every party. The political differences lie in how that is achieved (state intervention, leaving it to the market, or a combination of both); what kind of housing is to be provided (rented or owned); and who is worthy of support (is it to be the poor, the developer, the first-time buyer, the refugee, the banks). Varying emphases on different components over time have resulted in housing oversupply, housing undersupply, homelessness, emigration, a banking crisis, ghost estates, families living in hotels and tourists in houses, and numerous other impacts too many to mention here. Politically, housing suffers from the same barriers to success as other areas, including poor policy decisions, policy indecision, outsourcing, regulatory capture, occasional hubris and a blindness to policy and market failure.

The extremes in the supply of housing of recent decades would be less damaging if our socioeconomic system was not reliant on home ownership as both a physical and financial asset to see us through life. There is, therefore, a national vested interest in seeing everyone owning their own home, but also, rather perversely, in the value of these same houses perpetually rising. That is what happens when homes become assets. It is a difficult model to sustain as the cost of home ownership spirals away from those who need it.

The topic of housing in Ireland has fallen between many stools, becoming a sub-set of politics, economics, architecture, sociology and real estate, each with their own particular take on it. This book provides the reader (journalists, academics, built environment professionals, politicians, and the general public) with the information and vocabulary to further their knowledge of housing in Ireland across all disciplines. *Housing in Ireland* should act as a guide for anyone interested in the legislation around housing (e.g. Residential

Tenancies Acts), housing policies (*Rebuilding Ireland*), technical specifications (access and use), regulations (Fire Safety Notice), descriptions (accessory dwelling unit), and broader analytical terms (asset-based welfare). It is a digest for the informed and the uninformed, but mostly for those who want to be better informed.

Foreword

The last twenty years have seen considerable change in Ireland. The economy has been on a rollercoaster with GDP growth of up to 10.5 per cent in the early 2000s giving way to a painful contraction during the crisis years and a remarkable rebound in more recent times. The human side of this story is most clearly seen in the migration and labour market statistics. After an unprecedented period of employment growth and inward migration, some 389,000 people lost their jobs in the four years between January 2008 and March 2012, while 107,800 people left the country. Unsurprisingly, such economic turbulence was accompanied by political disorder. Parties of all colours and creeds (some of which no longer exist) have found themselves in government over the last two decades. And even today, with the economy once again performing strongly, Ireland's political landscape remains fragmented. The country has also seen huge demographic change. Between 2007 and 2012 Ireland experienced the biggest baby boom in its history, with 440,400 children being born. And other aspects of the population age structure have also shifted dramatically; the number of 20-somethings has collapsed from 781,900 in 2008 to 580,400 a decade later – a 26 per drop. Conversely, rapid growth in our elderly population over the same period has almost offset this decline.

Given everything that Ireland has been through it might seem strange that housing has been an ever-present topic of public debate. But each of the phases in our recent history has presented very specific housing-related challenges. At times these have been polar opposites. A booming economy and strong population growth in the late 1990s and early 2000s made increasing supply and containing house price inflation the main priorities. Indeed, these themes have re-emerged strongly in recent years with the economic recovery. In the intervening period, however, oversupply, vacancy and deflationary spirals were the key issues.

Given knock-on implications for the stability of our banking system and the Exchequer, the financing of residential construction and home ownership has also been hotly debated. Out of urgent necessity structures, policies and institutions were introduced to deal with housing-related over-indebtedness during the economic crisis. These ranged from the establishment of NAMA to the Code of Conduct on Mortgage Arrears. But preventative measures were also introduced to make the regulatory regime more resistant to future housing-related debt crises – the Central Bank's macro prudential rules being an obvious example.

In the years ahead housing will remain a hot topic of debate in Ireland. Inevitably some of the discussion will echo debates of the past. But new issues will also emerge. Ireland currently has the lowest median age of all countries in the EU (36.9 years compared with an average of 42.8) and the highest proportion of persons under 20 (27.5 per cent compared with 20.9 per cent). But the size of our elderly population is now rising. This will continue and will ultimately present new housing challenges – and opportunities. There has been a pronounced tenure shift towards private renting in recent years. The permanence of this is yet unknown, but any long-term departure from the model of home ownership is likely to highlight issues around the funding of housing costs in later life. Reflecting the current need to raise housing supply, apartment design standards have been reduced to control building costs, improve the viability of construction and increase supply. But given the demographic changes mentioned above – many more children who tend to live in large households and far fewer 20-somethings who tend to form smaller households – it remains to be seen whether the development of smaller apartments aligns with our population's age structure. Indeed the answer to this question may only be discovered when supply and demand become more evenly balanced and occupiers have more freedom of choice.

A meaningful debate about these issues requires some basic conditions to be in place. First and foremost there is a need for good quality data on the indicators that matter. Deficiencies in this area contributed to catastrophic misjudgements by players on all sides of the Irish housing market in years gone by. But thanks to the pressure being exerted by some analysts – not least the author of this book – the situation is improving. However, known deficiencies remain in our housing data and this work needs to continue. A second requirement is that all stakeholders should have a voice in the debate. In addition to better data, such an open and inclusive conversation needs a common language and a shared comprehension of key concepts. That is where this book comes in. By providing definitions of more than 600 terms that are critical to the housing discussion, *Housing in Ireland* provides us with a common lexicon to underpin meaningful debate. Of course, with multiple stakeholders the ensuing discussions are not guaranteed to generate consensus. But thanks to this book any disagreements are more likely to reflect genuine divergence on substantive issues rather than simple definitional misunderstandings.

Dr John McCartney is Director of Research at Savills and is on the editorial board of the Journal of Property Research.

Contents

A

Abhaile	1
Absorption rate	1
Access and use (houses)	1
Accessory dwelling unit (ADU)	2
Active land management	2
Adverse possession	4
Advised letting value	5
Advised market value	5
Affordability	6
Affordable Homes Partnership	6
Affordable housing	6
Affordable housing schemes	7
AirBnB	8
Airtightness	9
ALONE	9
An Bord Pleanála	11
An Foras Forbartha	12
Anglo Irish Bank	13
Annual percentage rate (APR)	13

An Taisce	13
Anti-social behaviour	13
Apartment	14
Apartment design standards	14
Apartment Owners' Network	16
Approved housing bodies	16
Aquinas, Thomas	17
Arbitration	17
Architectural Conservation Area	18
Area of Special Amenity	18
Arrears	19
Asset-based welfare	19
Asset management (housing)	20
Assigned certifier	21
Assignment of a lease	22
Auction	22
Auctioneer	23
Availability arrangements	23

B

Bacon reports	24
Balanced regional development	24
Balcony	25
Ballymun – history	25
Banking crisis	27
Basement	28
B&B (bed and breakfast)	28
BC(A)R	29
Bedsit	29
'Big House', the	29
Boarding house	30
Boundary	30
Bridging loan (bridging finance)	31
Brise soleil	31
Brownfield site	31
Bubble (housing)	31

Buchanan, Colin	33
Building Control (Amendment) Regulations [BC(A)R]	33
Building control authority	35
Building Control Management System (BCMS)	36
Building Energy Rating Certificate	36
Building envelope	37
Building Information Modelling (BIM)	37
Building regulations	37
Building society	38
Build-to-rent	38
Bungalow	39
Bungalow Bliss	39
Buy-to-let	39

Contents

C

Cadastre	40
Capital acquisitions tax	40
Capital Advance Leasing Facility (CALF)	41
Capital Assistance Scheme	41
Capital gains tax	42
Capital value	42
Carbon monoxide	43
Caretaker agreement	43
Catholic Church	43
Cavity block	45
Cavity wall	45
Central Bank of Ireland	45
Central Statistics Office	45
Certificate of Compliance on Completion (CCC)	46
Charter of Fundamental Rights	46
Chartered Institute of Housing	46
Choice-based lettings	47
Circle Voluntary Housing Association	47
Citizens' Information Board	47
Clawback	48
Clúid Housing	48
Code of Conduct on Mortgage Arrears (CCMA)	48
Cohabitation	50
Combi boiler	51
Commencement Notice	51

Commission on the Private Rented Residential Sector	52
Common areas	52
Commune	53
Community	53
Community land trust	53
Commuter belt	54
Compulsory Purchase Order (CPO)	54
Condominium	55
Consumer protection, building	55
Consumer Protection Code 2012	56
Constitution of Ireland (Article 40.3.2, Article 43)	57
Construction Industry Federation	57
Construction Industry Register of Ireland (CIRI)	57
Contracts	58
Conveyancing	58
Cooperative housing	59
Co-operative Housing Ireland	59
Cost rental	59
Cottage	60
Council housing	60
Covenant	63
Credit servicing firm	63
Credit unions	63
Criminal Law (Defence and the Dwelling) Act 2011	64
Crisis (and housing)	65
Curtilage	65

D

Daft.ie	65
Data – housing output issues	66
Davitt, Michael	69
Daylight standards	69
Deasy's Act 1860	69
Debt (household)	70
Debt-to-income ratio	70
Deed	70
Deed map	71
Default (mortgage)	71
Defects	71
Density, housing	72

Density, population	72
Department of Housing, Planning and Local Government	73
Deposit (booking)	74
Deposit (rent)	74
Deposit protection scheme (rent)	75
Derelict Sites Act 1990	76
Design certifier	77
Detached house	77
Determination Order	77
Developer	78
Development (property)	78

Development contribution scheme 79
Development Contribution Rebate
  Scheme 79
Development control 80
Development lag 80
Development land 80
Development levy 80
Development plan 81
Differential rents 82
'Digs' 82
Direct provision 83
Disability Access Certificate 83
Disabled access 84
Discrimination 84

District heating 87
Downsize 87
Dry lining insulation 87
Dual aspect 87
Dublin Artisan Dwellings Company 88
Dublin Civic Trust 88
Dublin Housing Supply
  Coordination Task Force 88
Dublin Region Homeless Executive 89
Dublin Simon Community 89
Dublin Tenants' Association 89
Duffy, Charles Gavan 90
Duplex 90
Dwelling 90

E

Easement 91
Economic growth and housing 91
Eircode 92
Emergency accommodation 92
En suite 92
Energy Efficiency – Retrofitting
  Measure 92
Enforcement, planning 93
Enhanced HAP 93
Enhanced Leasing Initiative 93
Environmental Impact Assessment/
  Environmental Impact
  Assessment Report 94
Environmental Protection Agency 95
Equity 95
Equity of tenure 95

Equity release 95
Equity sharing 95
Estate 95
Estate agent 96
European Convention on Human
  Rights 96
European Housing Rights Law 96
European Investment Bank (EIB) 96
European Social Charter 97
Eurostat 97
Eviction/illegal eviction 97
Exclusive possession 100
Exempted development 100
Existing use value 100
Extension of planning permission 100

F

Fair Deal Scheme – (Nursing
  Homes Support Scheme) 100
Fast-track planning 101
FEANTSA 101
Fee farm grant 102
Fee simple 102
Feudal system 102
FIDH (International Federation
  for Human Rights) 102
Financial Contribution Scheme 103

Financialisation of housing 104
Fire Safety Certificate 105
Fire Safety Notice 105
Fixed rate mortgage 105
Fixed term tenancy 106
Flat 106
'Flipping' 106
Focus Ireland 106
Fold Housing Association 107
Foreclosure 107

Forward Planning	107	Freehold interest	108
Four-stage process for social		Fuel poverty	108
housing	107	Further Part 4 tenancy	108

G

Gap site	109	Ghetto	112
Garden city	109	Ghost estates	113
Garden flat	110	Goodbody BER Housebuilding	
Gazump	110	Monitor	113
Gazunder	110	Granny flat	113
Geddes, Patrick	110	Green belt	113
General Boundary Rule	111	Greenfield site	114
Generation Rent	111	Greywater	114
Gentrification	111	Ground rent	114
GeoDirectory	112		

H

Headship rate	114	Housing associations	133
Health and housing	115	Housing cost overburden	133
Height	115	Housing demand	134
Help to Buy	117	Housing estate	135
High-rise	118	Housing Europe	135
Holiday homes	119	Housing Finance Agency	135
Home Building Finance Ireland	120	Housing First	135
Home insurance	121	Housing (Miscellaneous Provisions)	
Home ownership	121	Act 2009 (Part 5) Regulations	
Home Renovation Incentive	124	2019	136
Homebond	124	Housing Needs Assessment	137
'Homeless HAP'	124	Housing policy	138
Homelessness – definition	124	Housing rights approach to	
House – structural components	125	housing	138
Houseboat	126	Housing (Standards for Rented	
Household	127	Houses) Regulations 2008	139
Household Budget Survey	128	Housing (Standards for Rented	
Household Charge	128	Houses) Regulations 2017	139
Household Means Policy	128	Housing (Standards for Rented	
Households (number)	129	Houses) Regulations 2019	142
Households (size)	129	Housing stock	146
Housesitting	130	Housing strategy	147
Housing Act 1966	130	Housing (Traveller	
Housing and Sustainable		Accommodation) Act 1998	148
Communities Agency, The	130	Howard, Ebenezer	148
Housing Alliance, The	131	Hubs	148
Housing Assistance Payment	132		

I

iCare	148	Investment	153
Improvement Notice	149	Investment value	154
Imputed rent	149	Irish Association of Self Builders	154
Infill site	149	Irish Collective Asset-management	
Infrastructure	149	Vehicle (ICAV)	154
Inheritance tax	150	Irish Council for Social Housing	155
Inner City Helping Homeless	150	Irish Georgian Society	155
Institute of Professional Auctioneers		Irish Home Builders Association	156
and Valuers	150	Irish Mortgage Holders Association	156
Institutional landlord	150	Irish Planning Institute	156
Inter-authority transfer	150	Irish Strategic Investment Fund	
Interest rate	151	(ISIF)	157
International housing law		Iveagh Trust, The	157
instruments	151		

J

Joint tenancy	157	Joint ventures	157

K

Kenny Report (1973)	158	Key worker housing	159

L

Labour mobility	159	Letting agent	167
Land	160	Licence	167
Land and Conveyancing Law		Lien	170
Reform Act 2009	161	Loan-to-income	170
Land and Conveyancing Law		Loan-to-value	170
Reform Act 2013	161	Local area plan	170
Land annuity	162	Local authorities (role in housing)	171
Landbank	162	Local Authority Extensions	
Land Commission	163	Scheme	172
Land Development Agency	163	Local government	172
Land hoarding	164	Local Government Management	
Landlord	165	Agency (LGMA)	173
Land Registry	165	Local Infrastructure Housing	
Land value tax	165	Activation Fund (LIHAF)	173
Latent defects insurance	165	Localism	174
Lease	166	Local Property Tax	174
Leasehold interest	167	Lodger	174
Lessee	167	Long-term leasing arrangement	174
Lessor	167	Low Cost Sites	175

M

Maisonette	175	Money laundering	181
Managing agent	176	Mortgage	182
Marino – garden city	176	Mortgage Allowance Scheme	182
Market rent	176	Mortgage Arrears Resolution	
Market value	177	Process (MARP)	182
McQuaid, John Charles	177	Mortgage broker	183
Memorial	177	Mortgagee	183
Mercy Law Resource Centre	177	Mortgage interest tax relief	183
Mews	178	Mortgage lending rules	184
Micro-home	178	Mortgage to Rent Scheme	185
Millfield Manor fire and report	178	Mortgagor	186
Minister for Housing	179	Multi-family housing	186
Mobile home	180	Multi-Unit Developments Act	
Modular housing	181	(MUD) 2011	186
Money Advice and Budgeting			
Services (MABS)	181		

N

National Asset Management		National Oversight and Audit	
Agency (NAMA)	187	Commission	190
National Asset Residential		National Planning Framework	191
Property Services (NARPS)	188	National Spatial Strategy 2002–2020	192
National Association of Building		National Treasury Management	
Cooperatives	188	Agency	193
National Association of Tenants'		National Vacant Housing Reuse	
Organisations (NATO)	188	Strategy 2018–2021	193
National Building Agency	188	Natural property rights theory	193
National Development and		Negative equity	194
Finance Agency	189	Neoliberalism in Ireland	194
National Development Plan		New Dwelling Completions	195
2018–2027	189	NIMBY	196
National Economic and Social		Notice of termination	196
Council (NESC)	189	Notice periods	197
National Housing Strategy for		Notice to treat	197
People with a Disability		Nyberg Report, The	198
2011–2016	190	nZEB (near zero energy buildings)	198

O

Obsolescence	198	Overcrowding	202
Ó Cualann Cohousing Alliance	199	Overholding	203
One-off housing	200	Owner-occupied	203
Open House	201	Owners' management company	
Open plan	202	(OMC)	203
Overburden	202		

P

Parnell, Charles Stewart 205
Part 4 Tenancy 205
Part 8, Planning and Development
  Regulations 2001 205
Part V social housing 206
Party wall 208
Passive house 208
Pathway Accommodation and
  Support System (PASS) 209
Payment and Availability (P&A)
  Agreement 209
Peppercorn rent 209
Personal insolvency arrangement 209
Personal insolvency practitioner 210
Peter McVerry Trust 210
Pied à terre 210
Piketty, Thomas 210
Place Finder Scheme 211
Planning and Development Act
  1963 211
Planning and Development Act
  2000 212
Planning and Development
  (Housing) and Residential
  Tenancies Act 2016 212
Planning and Development
  Regulations 2001 213
Planning authority 213
Planning gain 213
Planning permission 214
Planning system 217
Plot ratio 218

Policy, housing 219
Politically exposed person (PEP) 225
Population 225
Practical completion 225
Pre '63 226
Prescribed body 226
Pre-planning 227
Price 227
Principal private pesidence 227
Priory Hall 227
Private rented sector 228
Private Residential Tenancies Board 229
Private treaty 229
Procurement 230
Profit à prendre 230
Prohibition Notice 231
Property cycle 231
Property management 231
Property Registration Authority 232
Property services providers 232
Property Services (Regulation)
  Act 2011 233
Property Services Regulatory
  Authority 233
Protected structure 234
Protective Certificate 234
Public housing 234
Public–private partnership (PPP) 234
Purpose-built student
  accommodation (PBSA) 235
Pyrite Resolution Board 236

Q

Quality of life 237
Quantitative easing 238

R

Radon 238
Rapid build housing – Poppintree 238
Real estate investment trusts
  (REITs) 239
Rebuilding Ireland 240
Rebuilding Ireland Home Loan 243
Record of Protected Structures 245

Record of qualified households 245
Redemption, mortgage 245
Refurbishment 245
Regional development 246
Registry of Deeds 246
Regulatory capture 247
Reinstatement value 247

Renoviction   247
Rent   247
Rental Accommodation Scheme
    (RAS)   248
Rent allowance   249
Rental sector – strategy   249
Rent-a-Room Scheme   249
Rent book   250
Rent control   250
Rent Index (Residential Tenancies
    Board)   251
Rent Pressure Zone   252
Rent review   254
Rent review notice   254
Rent review period (rent certainty)   255
Rent Supplement   255
Repair and Leasing Scheme   256
Replacement cost   257
Repossession   257
Reserve price   259
Residential care   259
Residential Landlords Association
    of Ireland   260
Residential property   261
Residential Property Price
    Register   261

Residential Tenancies Act 2004   261
Residential Tenancies (Amendment)
    Act 2015   262
Residential Tenancies (Amendment)
    Act 2018   262
Residential Tenancies Board   263
Residual value   264
Residualisation   265
Respond   265
Retention planning permission   265
Retention withholding money   266
Retirement housing   266
Retirement village   266
Retrofit   267
Rezoning   267
Right of way   267
Right to buy   268
Right to housing   268
Rockwool   269
Rough sleeping   269
Royal Institute of the Architects of
    Ireland, The (RIAI)   269
Rural housing   269
Rural Resettlement Ireland   270
Rus in urbe   270

S

Safe Home Ireland   271
Scheme dwelling   271
Seaside Resorts Scheme   271
Section 10 funding   272
Section 23 relief   272
Section 28 – 'mandatory
    guidelines'   272
Securitisation   273
Security of tenure   273
Self-build   273
Self-certification, house-building   274
Semi-detached house   275
Septic tank   275
Service charge – MUD Act 2011   276
Serviced Sites Fund   277
Shared ownership   278
Sheltered accommodation   279

Short-term leasing for social
    housing   279
S.I. 9 ('BCAR')   279
S.I. 365 (opt out)   279
Simms, Herbert   280
Single leaf   281
Sinking fund – MUD Act 2011   281
Site coverage   283
Site farming   283
Site value tax   283
Slum housing   284
Snag list   284
Social exclusion   284
Social housing   285
Social Housing Capital Investment
    Programme (SHIP)   288

Social Housing Current Expenditure
    Programme (SHCEP)   289
Social Housing Leasing Initiative
    (SHLI)   290
Social housing related programmes
    – summary   290
Social housing waiting list   291
Social justice   292
Social Justice Ireland   292
Society of Chartered Surveyors
    Ireland   293
Speculation   293
Split mortgage   295
Squatters' rights   295
Squatting   295
Stamp duty   295
Standards for rented houses   296

Step-down housing   296
Strategic Development Zone
    (SDZ)   296
Strategic Environmental
    Assessment   297
Strategic Housing Developments   298
Student housing   299
Studio apartment   299
Subletting   299
Sub-prime mortgage   299
Substantial change   299
Suburb   301
Suburbanisation   301
Succession of local authority house 301
Surrender Grant   302
Sustainable Energy Authority of
    Ireland   303

T

Take in charge   303
Technical guidance documents   304
Tenancy   305
Tenancy in common/Joint tenancy   305
Tenant   305
Tenant purchase   306
Tenant Right League   308
Tenement   308
Tenure   309
Tenure neutrality   310
Termination of a lease   311
Terraced house   312
Thermal bridge   312
Three Fs   313
Threshold   313
Timber-frame housing   313

Title   314
Title plan   314
Townhouse   315
Tracker mortgage scandal and
    examination   315
Tracker rate mortgage   316
Trade down   316
Transfer list   316
Transitional housing   317
Transport and housing   317
Transport poverty and equity   318
Traveller housing   318
Túath Housing   319
Turnkey   320
Tyrrelstown Amendment   320

U

U-value   321
Unauthorised development   322
Underfloor heating   322
Unfinished estates   322
United Nations Special Rapporteur
    on the Right to Adequate
    Housing   324

Urban regeneration   324
Urban Regeneration and Housing
    Act 2015   325
Urban Regeneration Development
    Fund   326
Urban sprawl   326

V

Vacancy rate	326	Valuer	332
Vacant dwellings	327	Variable rate	332
Vacant possession	328	Vesting Certificate	332
Vacant Sites Register and Levy	328	Voids	332
Valuation	330	Vulture funds	333
Value	331		

W

Wayleave	334	Welfare state	335
Wealth	334	Windfall gain	336
Wealth inequality	335	World War I housing	337

X

X-inefficiency	337

Y

Y-value	338	YIMBY	338
Yield	338		

Z

Zoning	339

A

Abhaile is a service to help homeowners find a resolution to home *mortgage arrears*. It provides vouchers for free financial and legal advice and help from experts, which are available through the **Money Advice and Budgeting Services** (MABS). The aim of Abhaile is to help **mortgage** holders in arrears to find the best solutions and keep them wherever possible in their own homes.

Abhaile is funded and supported by the Department of Social Protection and the Department of Justice and Equality with the support of the Insolvency Service of Ireland, the Legal Aid Board and the Citizens' Information Board.

See also: **Code of Conduct on Mortgage Arrears (CCMA); Mortgage Arrears Resolution Process**

Abhaile[1]

The absorption rate is the rate at which newly constructed homes can be sold into the local market without materially disturbing the market price. According to the *Independent Review of Report of Build-Out Rates* (in the UK) by Sir Oliver Letwin,[2] published in 2018, 'the fundamental driver of build out rates once detailed **planning permission** is granted for large sites appears to be the "absorption rate"'.[3] In other words, housebuilders are not going to supply the market with more houses than they can sell but will strategically drip-feed the housing market in order to maintain a house sales price that meets their needs. This absorption rate is the main cause of delay of new housing coming to the market, the Letwin Report found.

The absorption rate is also different depending on the types of **tenure**. According to the Letwin Report, the absorption rate of the '*affordable* homes' and 'social rented housing' on large sites is regarded universally as additional to the number of homes that can be sold to the open market in a given year on a given large site.[4]

See also: **Irish Home Builders Association**

Absorption rate

Since the introduction of the Disability Act in 2005, there has been a shift away from access for people with disabilities to access for all and the principle of 'universal design'. Part M of the **Building Regulations** 2010 focuses on

Access and use
(houses)[5]

---

[1] See: https://www.mabs.ie/en/abhaile/abhaile_about.html

[2] Letwin, O (2018) *Independent Review of Build-Out Rates*, Ministry of Housing, Communities and Local Government: London

[3] See: http://www.rtpi.org.uk/briefing-room/news-releases/2018/june/letwin-review-report-on-build-out-rate-published/

[4] *Ibid.*

[5] Society of Chartered Surveyors Ireland (2014) *Disability Access in Buildings – Part M of the building regulations*, SCSI: Dublin

Leabharlanna Poiblí Chathair Baile Átha Cliath
Dublin City Public Libraries

ensuring that adequate provision shall be made for all people (not just people with disabilities) to access and use a building, its facilities and its environs. Some main areas covered include:

- On-site setting-down areas
- On-site car parking
- Internal lobbies
- Ambulant disabled stairwells where a lift is proposed in a new building
- Effective clear width of internal doors (800mm)
- Accessible signage

Accessory dwelling unit (ADU)

Accessory dwelling units comprise various types of smaller residences, usually within or on the grounds of a large dwelling or between dwellings, such as a basement or garage flat, or *granny flats*.
See also: *infill site; garden flat; micro-home; mews*

Active land management

Active land management refers to the strategic management of landed resources to optimise their productivity, minimise their cost, bring market stability and certainty, and ultimately, in the case of land for housing, affordability for consumers. Active land management can also ensure that value uplifts from infrastructure projects funded by the taxpayer accrue to the taxpayer, and not merely adjacent landowners.

It refers to interventions by public bodies beyond normal zoning and land-use planning that seek to shape the way in which land is used. Needham describes the type of land-use planning that is adopted in most countries as 'passive planning'. With passive planning the ***planning authority*** identifies what type of development will be permitted in an area and decides whether or not to grant permission for particular developments. This is classified as passive 'because the planning agency itself – the municipality – takes no initiative to change the land use. Nothing changes unless someone applies for a development permit'.[6] In contrast, with proactive planning the planning agency takes active measures to realise its plans.

The need for active land management arises from characteristics of the land market and property ***development***. A conceptual approach to understanding land supply was set out[7] and drawn upon in a number of National Economic and Social Council (NESC) reports.[8] The availability of land for urban development is both uncertain and variable. First, landowners may

---

[6]   Needham, B (2014) *Dutch Land-use Planning: The Principles and the Practice*, Routledge: Oxon
[7]   See: Evans, A (2004) *Economics, Real Estate and the Supply of Land*, Blackwell Publishing: Oxford
[8]   National Economic and Social Council (2004) *Housing in Ireland: Performance and Policy*, NESC: Dublin; and National Economic and Social Council (2018) *Urban Development Land, Housing and Infrastructure: Fixing Ireland's Broken System*, NESC: Dublin

have motives other than maximising the current income from their land. Second, *speculation* on future increases in development land values may lead to land being used in a way that does not maximise current income. Third, the market for urban development land is characterised by information inefficiencies and uncertainty. Planning is needed to achieve an orderly pattern of development but the planning system reinforces the power of the owners of the land most suited to development.[9]

An approach to active land management in Ireland was set out in a 1973 report to government known as the *Kenny Report* (Committee on the Price of Building Land, 1973). This report recommended that local authorities be given the power to acquire designated land at its existing-use value plus 25 per cent. Following the servicing of this land by the local authority, it would then be sold or leased for housing and other development. These proposals were not adopted at the time or subsequently.

The *National Economic and Social Council* (NESC) identified elements of active land management in a number of aspects of Irish policy in place at that time.[10] These included *affordable housing schemes*, *Strategic Development Zones* and urban development entities such as the Dublin Docklands Development Authority. The recently introduced *Vacant Sites Register and Levy* is another instrument of relevance to active land management.

NESC have also detailed the main features of active land management, whereby:[11]

- It typically involves close collaboration between public urban development bodies, private owners of urban development land, development enterprises and not-for-profit housing entities.
- It depends on the existence of highly skilled and respected public agencies capable of managing land, and driving urban development and infrastructure investment.
- Incentivisation of productive engagement between the public and private actors depends on framework conditions, in particular the status of the urban development bodies, their planning powers and a credible system of compulsory purchase of urban development land at below full development value, used as a last resort and under judicial supervision.

It is argued by NESC[12] that Ireland needs to change its system of urban development to incorporate stronger arrangements for more effective land

---

[9] Evans, A (2004) *Economics, Real Estate and the Supply of Land*, Blackwell Publishing: Oxford
[10] National Economic and Social Council (2004) *Housing in Ireland: Performance and Policy*, NESC: Dublin
[11] National Economic and Social Council (2018) *Urban Development Land, Housing and Infrastructure: Fixing Ireland's Broken System*, NESC: Dublin
[12] *Ibid.*

management. NESC have made the following seven recommendations in the context of housing provision:

1. Ireland must change its system of urban development, land management and housing provision.
2. Build affordability into policies that are designed to increase the supply of housing, starting with land and *cost rental*.
3. Give public institutions a strong developmental mandate, political authorisation and executive capacity to drive sustainable urban development.
4. Use publicly owned land to increase the supply of housing, ensure affordability and create quality residential developments.
5. Work with private holders of urban development land to ensure the delivery of affordable housing and sustainable urban development.
6. Use the potential of locational value creation and sharing to help fund strategic infrastructure, particularly public transport infrastructure.
7. Adopt an ambitious national programme of specific, understandable and socially accepted flagship projects.

See also: *Land Development Agency; affordability; asset management; compulsory purchase*

Adverse possession

Adverse possession (colloquially known as *squatters' rights*) allows a third party to claim a right over *land* which is registered in the name of another person on the basis that they have occupied the land continuously for twelve years or more with the intention of excluding others, including the registered owner of the land. It is possession of land inconsistent with the title of the true owner.[13]

Under section 13 of the Statute of Limitations Act 1957, a claim for adverse possession requires twelve years continuous physical occupation of the land, or six years if the registered owner has died; in the case of state lands, it is thirty years. If the registered owner still uses the land during those twelve years, even on an occasional basis, then the application for adverse possession will fail. It also must be very clear to the registered owner that adverse possession is occurring.

Applicants can apply for the lands they are claiming possession of adversely to the *Property Registration Authority*.

The most common form of adverse possession arises where encroachers inadvertently assume ownership of parts of neighbouring land because there are no physical boundaries or the maps on title are inadequate.[14] It should be noted that a person cannot be in adverse possession to his/her spouse.

---

[13] Walsh, K (2015) 'What are squatters' rights, exactly?', *Irish Examiner*, 22 January
[14] *Ibid.*

See also: *easement; right of way; profit à prendre; General Boundary Rule*

Advised letting value is covered by section 55(2) of the ***Property Services (Regulation) Act 2011***. Advised letting value, in relation to land valued for letting by a licensee, means the licensee's reasonable estimate, at the time of such valuation— **Advised letting value**

(*a*) of the amount that would be paid by a willing tenant on appropriate letting terms in an arm's length transaction after proper marketing where both parties act knowledgeably, prudently and without compulsion, or

(*b*) of the relevant price range within which would fall the amount that would be paid by a willing tenant on appropriate letting terms in an arm's length transaction after proper marketing where both parties act knowledgeably, prudently and without compulsion.

In the definition, 'relevant price range' means a price range where the difference between the upper limit of such valuation and the lower limit of such valuation is not more than 10 per cent of such lower limit.

See also: ***property services provider; value; valuer; advised market value***

Advised market value is covered by section 55(1) of the ***Property Services (Regulation) Act 2011***. **Estate agents** involved in selling property must provide the vendor with a Statement of Advised Market Value (AMV). Agents are not permitted to advertise the property at a price lower than the AMV. They must also retain evidence of how they arrived at the AMV. **Advised market value**

Advised market value, in relation to land valued for sale by a licensee [e.g. an **estate agent**], means the licensee's reasonable estimate, at the time of such valuation—

(*a*) of the amount that would be paid by a willing buyer in an arm's length transaction after proper marketing where both parties act knowledgeably, prudently and without compulsion, or

(*b*) of the relevant price range within which would fall the amount that would be paid by a willing buyer in an arm's length transaction after proper marketing where both parties act knowledgeably, prudently and without compulsion.

In this definition, 'relevant price range' means a price range where the difference between the upper limit of such valuation and the lower limit of such valuation is not more than 10 per cent of such lower limit.

See also: ***property services provider; value; advised letting value; valuer***

Affordability

There is no universally accepted definition of 'affordability', although there are three main ways of measuring it:

1. The ratio approach – this considers the proportion of **household** income devoted to housing costs.
2. The benchmark approach – this considers what is affordable by reference to some fixed level of expenditure that is assumed to be reasonable.
3. The residual approach – this considers the financial resources that remain available to a household once the **rent** or **mortgage** payment and other housing costs have been met.[15]

Ideas of measuring affordability started in the nineteenth century and studies of household budgets in the US and Belgium. The general premise then was 'one week's work for one month's rent', meaning about 25 per cent of income, although this included bills. Mortgage lenders began to use this to create an income-to-expenditure model to minimise repayment risk. Over years, the percentage of what is deemed 'affordable' has crept upwards. These percentages are no more than rules of thumb, however, but became normalised in the US and Europe during the 1980s. With no legitimacy, this became the appropriate level of expenditure for housing with few people noticing. Over the same time, research into household budgets and expenditure moved from casual observations about what households 'tend' to pay, to measures and rules of what households 'ought' to pay. In Ireland too, any measure of affordability (between 30 and 40 per cent of net household income) is nothing more than a generalised assumption of what households should be paying for their housing needs.

See also: ***housing cost overburden***

Affordable Homes Partnership

The Affordable Homes Partnership was a government initiative to assist those outpriced and unable to get onto the property ladder. It was aimed at fast-tracking the provision of cheaper housing. All liabilities of the Affordable Homes Partnership (AHP) at 31 December 2010 were taken over by the ***Department of Housing, Planning and Local Government***.[16]

Affordable housing

The phrase 'affordable housing' is often used fairly loosely to mean housing that people in low-paid employment can afford to rent or own.[17]

The ***Planning and Development Act 2000*** defines affordable housing as housing or building land provided for those who need accommodation and who otherwise would have to pay over 35 per cent of their net annual income

[15] Garnett, D (2015) *The A–Z of Housing (Professional Keywords)*, Macmillan: London
[16] The Housing Agency (2017) *Annual Report 2016*, The Housing Agency: Dublin
[17] Garnett, D (2015) *The A–Z of Housing (Professional Keywords)*, Macmillan: London

on mortgage payments for the purchase of a suitable dwelling. In reference to eligibility for **affordable housing schemes**, section 84(2)(*b*) of the Housing (Miscellaneous Provisions) Act 2009 makes reference to 'whether the income of the household is adequate to meet the repayments on a mortgage for the purchase of a dwelling to meet the accommodation needs of the household because the payments calculated over the course of a year would exceed 35 per cent of the annual income of the household net of income tax and pay related social insurance'.

Irish legislative definitions have been formulated in the context of **affordable housing** for purchase but could be extended to a more general definition of affordable housing as that in which housing costs absorb no more than 35 per cent of net household income, while also meeting a minimum acceptable standard.[18]

See also: **affordability; affordable housing schemes**

There have been several schemes to help lower-income households purchase their own housing. The most well-known is the Affordable Housing Scheme, where councils provided the land on which the affordable houses would be built and sold. Discounts of up to 40 per cent of the sales price of the house were possible. The scheme commenced in 1999 and was discontinued in 2011.

> **Affordable housing schemes**

Applicants for such affordable housing had to meet several criteria, including on income. The income limits varied from council to council, but in general eligibility followed the criteria below:

- Single-income household: If the applicant's gross income (before tax) in the last income tax year was between €25,000 and €58,000, they might be eligible.
- Two-income household: If the applicants' joint income was €75,000 or less, they might be eligible.

To prevent eligible applicants selling their affordable houses for profit, a '**clawback**' clause was included with the property. This meant that if the house was sold within 20 years a certain proportion of any uplift in value (the difference between the sales price and the market value at subsequent sale) would be returned to the council. For years 1–10, 100 per cent of any uplift was returned to the council from which the house was acquired. After year 10, this percentage reduced by 10 per cent per annum until after 20 years' ownership the property could be sold without clawback and any uplift retained. If the property was sold at a loss to the owner, then no clawback liability was due to the council.

---

[18] National Economic and Social Council (2018) *Urban Development Land, Housing and Infrastructure: Fixing Ireland's Broken System*, NESC: Dublin

Another affordable housing scheme was connected to **Part V** of the **Planning and Development Acts 2000**–2002, under which developers had to set aside up to 20 per cent of new developments of five or more houses for social or affordable housing. Applicants were eligible to buy an affordable house provided under **Part V** of the **Planning and Development Acts 2000**–2002 if 35 per cent of their income was not sufficient to enable them to buy a house. This scheme is no longer in operation as the Part V criteria have since been altered.

Other schemes included the Affordable Housing Initiative, Mortgages for Affordable Homes and the Mortgage Subsidy Scheme. All of these were stood down in 2011.

In 2019, another affordable housing scheme was launched by the **Minister for Housing, Planning and Local Government** under part 5 of the Housing (Miscellaneous Provisions) Act 2009, which is targeted at first-time buyers and offers discounts of up to 40 per cent on the market price of a house.

See: **Housing (Miscellaneous Provisions) Act 2009 (Part 5) Regulations 2019**

See also: **affordability; affordable housing**

AirBnB

AirBnB is an internet-based accommodation-finding service for travellers and 'hosts'. In late 2018, there were 6,729 listings for Dublin on AirBnB; 47 per cent (3,163) of these were for the entire home or apartment, and the remainder for a private room in a property. The average price per night was €104. Over 43 per cent of hosts (2,944) had more than one listing.[19]

Whilst AirBnB has been almost revolutionary in the way it has reshaped the short-term accommodation market, it has also had other impacts on local communities and cities (as well as the traditional hotel sector). The largest impact is the amount of entire properties that may otherwise be let on the open market in the **private rented sector** that are being reserved for use on AirBnB. In cities where there is a shortage of accommodation to rent for inhabitants, any further loss of housing stock can only be harmful. There are also issues over apartments for rent on AirBnB being in breach of their **owners' management company** rules and if their apartment insurance is thereby invalidated. The social impact on neighbours of multiple different parties occupying their neighbouring apartments on a regular basis has also been recorded. At a city level, AirBnB has also been accused of promoting **gentrification**,[20] and driving up rents.[21]

[19] See: http://insideairbnb.com/dublin/#
[20] McCartney, R (2017) 'Airbnb becomes flash point in the District's hot debate over gentrification', *Washington Post*, 1 November.
[21] Wachsmuth, D, Chaney, D, Kerrigan, D, Shillolo, A and Basalaev-Binder, R (2018) *The High Cost of Short-Term Rentals in New York City*, Urban Politics and Governance Research Group School of Urban Planning, McGill University

Many cities have regulated AirBnB in their jurisdictions (e.g. Sydney, Barcelona, Berlin and Amsterdam). In 2018 new regulations were introduced for short-term letting operations in Ireland (including AirBnB), taking effect on 1 July 2019. Short-term letting is only permitted in the host's principal residence for a maximum of 90 days per annum and no more than 14 consecutive days at a time. Short-term letting was defined as 'the use of a bedroom or bedrooms in a home as paid overnight guest accommodation for a continuous period of up to two weeks.' All short-term letting hosts are required to register with their local authority. The use of a second property for short-term letting will require special planning permission (unlikely to be granted in areas of high housing demand). AirBnB hosts could also be subject to wastewater and potable water charges (€3.12 per 1,000 litres), and councils may decide to charge commercial rates on the property. The **Rent-a-Room Scheme** and **B&B**s are exempt from these regulations.[22]

Airtightness is typically measured in two units: air changes per hour (ACH) and air permeability ($m^3/hr/m^2$). For a typical building, there is usually little difference in the two figures. The smaller the airtightness figure the better. Under Irish **building regulations** new homes must have an airtightness of 10 $m^3/hr/m^2$. The 'Passivhaus' standard demands an airtightness of 0.6 ACH or less.

     See also: ***passive house; U-value; Y-value; thermal bridge***   **Airtightness**[23]

ALONE was founded by Dublin fireman Willie Bermingham. ALONE provides housing with support, support coordination and befriending services, and campaigns for change for hundreds of older people every week who are homeless, socially isolated, living in deprivation or in crisis. ALONE Housing with Support provides homes to older people who are homeless or at risk of homelessness, and need a level of support. It has 101 residents living independently with supports.   **ALONE**[24]

     ALONE also produces a series of research reports. In 2018, ALONE published *Housing Choices for Older People in Ireland: Time for Action*, which explored the various housing options that a 'spectrum of housing' for older people should include. The report showed the type and amount of housing needed as follows.

---

[22] McConnell, D (2019) 'Extra charges set for Airbnb homes in clampdown on regulations', *Irish Examiner*, 12 April

[23] See: https://passivehouseplus.ie/glossary

[24] ALONE (2018) *Housing Choices for Older People in Ireland: Time for Action*, ALONE: Dublin

Housing Type	Response	Potential	10-year Indicative Requirements	Relevant Considerations
Dedicated social housing for older people	Supportive housing	Large	41,564 units	Limited examples in Ireland. Needs investment and the development of a supportive housing model to ensure consistency across schemes
	Housing with supports	Large	4,341 units	Model needs to be further developed and implemented in Ireland, needs investment and promotion as an alternative to nursing homes
Dispersed housing	Making existing homes more age-friendly	Large	€84.5 million per annum	Cost effective and supportive of ageing in place
Shared housing in the community	Retirement villages	Medium	6,778 units	Potential for more private sector development
	Older persons' co-housing communities	Medium	6,778 units	Potential for private and social enterprise sectors
	Home sharing	Small	1,000 units	Needs promotion and regulation
	Split housing	Small	1,000 units	Can help in dealing with current general housing crisis
	Boarding out	Small	750 people	Requires promotion and regulation
Residential nursing care units	Quality nursing homes developed as part of multi-purpose complexes	Medium	36,987 places	Necessary for some; demand can be reduced through more high-support housing and Home Care Packages

See also: **retirement housing; retirement village**

An Bord Pleanála is the statutory planning appeals body in Ireland. It is quasi-judicial in nature and politically independent. An Bord Pleanála was established in 1977 under the Local Government (Planning and Development) Act 1976. It is responsible for the determination of appeals and certain other matters under the ***Planning and Development Act 2000***, as amended, and associated legislation, and determination of applications for strategic infrastructure development including major road and railway cases. It is also responsible for dealing with proposals for the compulsory acquisition of land by local authorities and others under various enactments. The Board also has functions to determine appeals under the Local Government (Water Pollution) Acts and the Building Control Acts. Under European Regulation No. 347/2013, which deals with trans-European energy infrastructure, An Bord Pleanála is the competent authority for projects of common interest.

    In general, An Bord Pleanála deals with appeals and referrals under various planning and development, and strategic infrastructure development legislation. It also has functions under the ***Urban Regeneration and Housing Act 2015***, ***Building Control Acts*** 1990 and 2007, Water Pollution Acts 1977 and 1990, Air Pollution Act 1987, Harbours Act 1966, Air Navigation and Transport (Amendment) Act 1988, Gas Act 1976, Public Health (Ireland) Act 1878, Derelict Sites Act 1990 and the Housing Act 1966.

    Appeals under section 37 of the Planning and Development Act 2000, as amended, ('normal planning appeals') account for most of the decisions made by the Board. These appeals arise from decisions by planning authorities on applications for permission for the development of land and fall into four categories:

- First-party appeals against decision of planning authorities to refuse permission
- First-party appeals against conditions proposed to be attached to permissions by planning authorities
- First-party appeals against financial contribution conditions
- Third-party appeals, which are normally against decisions of planning authorities to grant permission

In some cases, there may be both first-party and third-party appeals against a decision of a ***planning authority***. In addition to the parties to an appeal, other persons may make submissions or observations to the Board in relation to an appeal (known as 'observers').

    The Board currently has ten members. The chair of the Board is normally appointed for a period of seven years by the Government from a list of candidates selected by an independent committee in accordance with section 105 of the 2000 Act, chaired by the President of the High Court. Eight of the members are appointed by the ***Minister for Housing, Planning, Community and Local Government*** from among persons selected from four groups of organisations:

- Professions or occupations that relate to physical planning, engineering and architecture
- Organisations concerned with economic development, the promotion and carrying out of development, the provision of infrastructure or the development of land or otherwise connected with the construction industry
- Organisations representative of local government, farming and trade unions
- Organisations representative of persons concerned with the protection and preservation of the environment and of amenities/voluntary bodies and bodies having charitable objects/rural and local community development, the promotion of the Irish language or the promotion of heritage, the arts and culture/bodies representative of people with disabilities/bodies representative of young people

The other member is appointed by the Minister from among persons who in the Minister's opinion have satisfactory experience, competence or qualifications as respects issues relating to the environment and sustainability. These members normally hold office for a term of five years and may be re-appointed for a second or subsequent term provided that the person concerned is an outgoing member at the time of the re-appointment.

See also: ***planning permission; unauthorised development; development plan; retention planning permission; Planning and Development Act 1963***

An Foras Forbartha

An Foras Forbartha was the National Institute for Physical Planning and Construction Research in Ireland. It was established on 26 March 1964 under Minister for Local Government Neil Blaney. It was initially set up with help from the United Nations, and worked in partnership with the UN for the first five years of its existence, focusing its research on physical planning and road and building construction. It produced reports such as the *Dublin Transportation Study* (1972), *Land Use Budgeting* (1984), *Public Subventions to Housing* (1978), and a series on *Ireland in the Year 2000* (1980–1985). An Foras Forbartha reports were rigorous and independent, and their road safety research is still referenced at the highest levels today.

An Foras Forbartha was abolished on 1 August 1993 under Fianna Fáil Minister for the Environment Michael Smith when it was subsumed into the ***Environmental Protection Agency.***

See also: ***Ministers for Housing***

Anglo Irish Bank existed from 1964 until 2011 when it merged with the Irish **Anglo Irish Bank** Nationwide Building Society to form the Irish Bank Resolution Corporation. Anglo Irish Bank was a business bank and a primary lender to commercial property developers and builders. It was heavily exposed in the property downturn and had to be nationalised in 2009. The 'maverick'[25] bank is famous for its reckless lending practices, including giving 100 per cent loans which further exposed it to the crash. It also was involved in a controversial practice of borrowing funds from other banks to artificially inflate its own customer deposits, making them appear €7.2 billion stronger than they were. David Drumm, the bank's chief executive, was found guilty in 2018 of fraud and sentenced to six years in prison.

See also: ***banking crisis***

According to the Consumer Credit Act of 1995 the annual percentage rate is **Annual** 'the total cost of credit to the consumer, expressed as an annual percentage of **percentage rate** the amount of credit granted'. **(APR)[26]**

An Taisce, the National Trust for Ireland, is a membership-based charity **An Taisce** and was established in June 1948 with the mission to preserve and protect Ireland's natural and built heritage. It is the oldest environmental and non-governmental organisation in Ireland. An Taisce is also a ***prescribed body***, i.e. it must be informed of all planning applications in areas of science, beauty or high amenity significance where architectural, archaeological or environmental issues need to be considered. An Taisce's activities falls between the Environmental Education Unit (the National Spring Clean, Green Schools, Green Campus, Blue Flag Beaches and Clean Coasts), the Advocacy Unit (promoting nature and the built heritage by maintaining a Buildings at Risk Register and monitoring potentially pernicious developments) and the Properties Unit (managing fourteen historic buildings and nature reserves).

See also: ***Irish Georgian Society; Architectural Conservation Area; Record of Protected Structures***

The ***Residential Tenancies Act 2004*** provides a definition of anti-social **Anti-social** behaviour as being to: **behaviour**

a. engage in behaviour that constitutes the commission of an offence, being an offence the commission of which is reasonably likely to affect directly the wellbeing or welfare of others,

---

[25] Carswell, S (2018) 'Why David Drumm cooked the books at Anglo Irish Bank', *Irish Times*, 25 June
[26] Government of Ireland (1995) *Consumer Credit Act*, Government Publications Office: Dublin

b. engage in behaviour that causes or could cause fear, danger, injury, damage or loss to any person living, working or otherwise lawfully in the dwelling concerned or its vicinity and, without prejudice to the generality of the foregoing, includes violence, intimidation, coercion, harassment or obstruction of, or threats to, any such person, or

c. engage, persistently, in behaviour that prevents or interferes with the peaceful occupation—

   i. by any other person residing in the dwelling concerned, of that dwelling,

   ii. by any person residing in any other dwelling contained in the property containing the dwelling concerned, of that other dwelling, or

   iii. by any person residing in a dwelling ('neighbourhood dwelling') in the vicinity of the dwelling or the property containing the dwelling concerned, of that neighbourhood dwelling.

The **notice period** for evicting tenants engaging in anti-social behaviour is seven days.

Apartment In the **Department of Housing, Planning and Local Government**'s *Sustainable Urban Housing: Design Standards for New Apartments – Guidelines for Planning Authorities*, an apartment is defined as: 'a residential unit in a multi-unit building with grouped or common access'.[27] Apartments are typically laid out on one floor, although multi-floor apartments are now known.

In general, the minimum floor area of new apartments in Ireland are:

- **Studio apartment** (1 person) – 37 sqm
- 1-bedroom apartment (2 persons) – 45 sqm
- 2-bedroom apartment (4 persons) – 73 sqm
- 3-bedroom apartment (5 persons) – 90 sqm

See also: **detached house; semi-detached house; bedsit; maisonette; pied à terre; dwelling; terraced house; condominium; garden flat; duplex; micro-home; apartment design standards**

Apartment design standards The following are the minimum standards for newly built **apartments** in Ireland.[28]

---

[27] Department of Housing, Planning and Local Government (2018) *Sustainable Urban Housing: Design Standards for New Apartments – Guidelines for Planning Authorities*, Government of Ireland: Dublin
[28] *Ibid.*

Minimum overall apartment floor areas	
Studio	37 sqm
One bedroom	45 sqm
Two bedrooms (3 person)	63 sqm
Two bedrooms (4 person)	73 sqm
Three bedrooms	90 sqm

Minimum aggregate floor areas for living/dining/kitchen rooms		
Apartment type	Width of living/ dining room	Aggregate floor area of living/dining/kitchen area*
Studio	4m*	30 sqm*
One bedroom	3.3 m	23 sqm
Two bedrooms (3 person)	3.6m	28 sqm
Two bedrooms (4 person)	3.6 m	30 sqm
Three bedrooms	3.8 m	34 sqm

* Note: Combined living/dining/bedspace, also includes circulation

Minimum aggregate bedroom floor areas	
One bedroom	11.4 sqm
Two bedrooms (3 person)	13 + 7.1 sqm = 20.1 sqm
Two bedrooms (4 person)	11.4 + 13 sqm = 24.4 sqm
Three bedrooms	11.4 + 13 + 7.1 sqm = 31.5 sqm

Minimum storage space requirements	
Studio	3 sqm
One bedroom	3 sqm
Two bedrooms (3 person)	5 sqm
Two bedrooms (4 person)	6 sqm
Three or more bedrooms	9 sqm

Minimum floor areas for private amenity space	
Studio	4 sqm
One bedroom	5 sqm
Two bedrooms (3 person)	6 sqm
Two bedrooms (4 person)	7 sqm
Three bedrooms	9 sqm

Minimum floor areas for communal amenity space	
Studio	4 sqm
One bedrooms	5 sqm
Two bedrooms (3 person)	6 sqm
Two bedrooms (4 person)	7 sqm
Three bedrooms	9 sqm

See also: *detached house; semi-detached house; bedsit; maisonette; pied à terre; dwelling; terraced house; condominium; garden flat; duplex; micro-home; accessory dwelling unit*

Apartment Owners' Network

The Apartment Owners' Network (AON) is a volunteer advocacy organisation representing the views of owners of homes in managed estates. The network promotes best practice among directors of estates' *owners' management companies*. AON engages with the state, professional bodies, academia, and other parties affected by and interested in the sector.[29]

Approved housing bodies

Approved housing bodies (AHBs) can also be known as housing associations. They are independent, not-for-profit charities. AHBs need to get ministerial approval before they can operate. Section 6(6) of the Housing (Miscellaneous Provisions) Act 1992 empowers the Minister to grant approved status for this purpose.[30] There are over 250 approved housing bodies registered with the AHB regulator in Ireland and they vary widely in size and in the services that they provide. The vast majority of these AHBs are small and exist to manage their existing housing stock. There are three 'tiers' of AHB:

	Number [%]	Description
Tier 1	187 [74%]	AHB with up to 50 units and no development plans
Tier 2	48 [19%]	AHB with between 50 and up to 300 units, and/or with development plans to increase stock size (up to 300 units), and/or are applying for, or are in receipt of, loans from the **Housing Finance Agency**, private finance or other sources (for stock levels of up to 300 units)
Tier 3	19 [7%]	AHB with more than 300 units or with development plans to increase stock size (over 300 units), and/or are applying for, or are in receipt of, loans from the Housing Finance Agency, private finance or other sources (for stock levels over 300 units)

[29] Entry provided by the Apartment Owners' Network
[30] See: https://www.housing.gov.ie/housing/social-housing/voluntary-and-cooperative-housing/approved-housing-bodies-ahbs

In general, AHBs provide rented housing for people who cannot afford to pay for accommodation in the *private rented sector* or buy their own homes, or for particular groups, such as older people, people with special needs or homeless people. As well as providing affordable rented housing, they aim to encourage community development.

In April 2016, approved housing bodies were brought under the remit of the *Residential Tenancies Board* (RTB) and must register their tenancies with the RTB. Approved housing bodies now have the same rights and obligations as private *landlords* and their *tenants* have the same rights and obligations as private tenants under the *Residential Tenancies Act 2004*, with some exceptions.

See also: *Respond; Tuath Housing; Clúid Housing; Irish Council for Social Housing; FEANTSA; Housing Alliance, The; Ó Cualann Cohousing Alliance*

Thomas Aquinas was an Italian theologian who lived from 1225 to 1274. He **Aquinas, Thomas** argued that God gave the earth to mankind in common rather than individually and that it was justified for man to seize land for his own needs and, once seized, it was unjust to deprive him of that property. The state was to uphold these property rights, but it could expropriate land under extreme circumstances once the owner was properly compensated (see also: *compulsory purchase order*).[31] For Aquinas, only God has lordship over material things, including property, but he gives human beings the right to use these things for their benefit. Property is justified but the rights of property are always trumped by the basic rights of human beings according to natural law.[32]

Arbitration is a dispute resolution procedure whereby two parties in dispute **Arbitration**[33] agree (an arbitration agreement) to be bound by a decision of an independent third party (the arbitrator). Arbitration is private and often informal. The role of an arbitrator is similar to that of a judge save that, on principle of 'party autonomy' (whereby the parties can agree procedural and evidential matters), the procedure can be less formal. An arbitrator is usually an expert in his/her own right.

An arbitrator should be able to:

• Act fairly and impartially using his/her general knowledge of the subject matter

---

[31] Ryan-Collins, J, Lloyd, T and Macfarlane, L (2017) *Rethinking the Economics of Land and Housing*, Zed Books: London

[32] Tuininga, M (2012) 'Aquinas and Calvin believed property rights were subject to the rights of the poor', *Christian in America*, 19 September, available at: https://matthewtuininga.wordpress.com/2012/09/19/aquinas-and-calvin-believed-property-rights-were-subject-to-the-rights-of-the-poor/

[33] See: https://www.scsi.ie/dispute_resolution/role_an_arbitrator

- Reach a fair decision based on the evidence and arguments submitted by the parties
- When appropriate take the initiative in ascertaining the facts and law

Arbitration is carried out within a legislative framework with the current Act, being the Arbitration Act 2010, which has replaced the Arbitration Acts 1954–1998.

The arbitrator's decision, which is called the 'award', is final and binding. An arbitrator's award has the same status as a judgment or order of the High Court and it is enforceable as such. It is not possible to appeal an arbitrator's award and there are limited grounds for challenge.

Architectural Conservation Area[34]

An Architectural Conservation Area (ACA) is a place, area, group of structures or townscape that is of special architectural, historical, archaeological, technical, social, cultural or scientific interest, or that contributes to the appreciation of a protected structure.

Buildings falling within the boundaries of an ACA can be both protected structures and non-protected structures. Protection generally relates to the external appearance of structures and features of the streetscape; it does not prevent internal changes or rearrangements provided that these changes do not impact on the external appearance of the structure. Generally any works that may have a potential impact on the exterior would require planning permission, such as changes to the original roofing material, windows, boundary walls, etc. The aim of ACA designation is not to prevent development, rather to guide sensitive, good quality development, which will enhance both the historical character of the area and the amenity of those who enjoy it.

See also: ***development plan; protected structures; Record of Protected Structures; Planning and Development Act 2000; An Taisce***

Area of Special Amenity

An Area of Special Amenity is a designation for a landscape of national importance for its aesthetic/recreational value. Planning authorities are empowered (under section 202 of the Planning and Development Act 2000), to make a Special Amenity Area Order (SAAO) for reasons of outstanding natural beauty or its special recreational value and having regard to any benefits for nature conservation. The purpose is to preserve/enhance landscape character and to prevent/limit development. All SAAOs in Ireland are in Dublin – North Bull Island, Howth Head and Liffey Valley.[35] No compensation is

---

[34] See: http://www.dlrcoco.ie/en/heritage/conservation/architectural-conservation-areas
[35] See: http://www.dublincity.ie/main-menu-services-recreation-culture-dublin-city-parks-visit-park-north-bull-island-unesco/national

payable in respect of refusal of planning permission in an area to which an SAAO relates.[36]

See also: ***development plan; Architectural Conservation Area; An Taisce***

A mortgage is classified as in arrears if it is greater than 90 days past due on its payments.

The Central Bank keeps a record of the number of mortgages in arrears for both principal dwelling houses (PDH) and investment residential properties (***buy-to-lets***). For example, at end-September 2018, there were 728,075 private residential mortgage accounts for principal dwellings held in the Republic of Ireland, to a value of €98.2 billion. Of this total stock, 64,510 accounts were in arrears. Some 45,178 accounts (6.2 per cent) were in arrears of more than 90 days.[38]

At end-September 2018, 87 per cent of restructured PDH accounts were deemed to be meeting the terms of their arrangement. This means that the borrower was, at a minimum, meeting the agreed monthly repayments according to the current restructure arrangement.

At the same time, there were 116,129 residential mortgage accounts for ***buy-to-let*** (BTL) properties held in the Republic of Ireland, to a value of €20.3 billion. Some 20,579 (18 per cent) of these accounts were in arrears. Of the total BTL stock, 17,032 or 15 per cent were in arrears of more than 90 days. The outstanding balance on all BTL mortgage accounts in arrears of more than 90 days was €4.6 billion at end-September 2018, equivalent to 18 per cent of the total outstanding balance; the number of BTL accounts that were in arrears of more than 720 days was 12,424 (60 per cent of all BTL accounts in arrears).

See also: ***Mortgage Arrears Resolution Process***

The principle underlying an asset-based approach to welfare is that, rather than relying on state-managed social transfers to counter the risks of poverty, individuals accept greater responsibility for their own welfare needs by investing in financial products and property assets which augment in value over time. In theory, these assets can later be tapped to supplement consumption and welfare needs when income is reduced, for example, in retirement, or used to acquire other forms of investment such as educational qualifications.

Arrears[37]

Asset-based welfare

---

[36] See: http://buckplanning.blogspot.com/2006/11/areas-of-special-amenity-and-irish.html

[37] Central Bank (2018) *Residential Mortgage Arrears and Repossessions Statistics: Q3 2018*, Central Bank: Dublin

[38] The figures published here represent the total stock of mortgage accounts in arrears of more than 90 days reported to the Central Bank of Ireland by mortgage lenders and credit service providers. They include mortgages that have been restructured and are still in arrears of more than 90 days, as well as mortgages in arrears of more than 90 days that have not been restructured.

In effect, the potential wealth tied up in owner-occupied housing has been assumed to be a solution to the fiscal difficulties involved in the maintenance of welfare commitments, and through that, the 'asset' in asset-based welfare has frequently become property or a housing asset.[39, 40]

Embedded in this idea of housing as welfare are two contentious assumptions about how households hold assets and accumulate wealth over 'the lifecycle'. Firstly, a first-time homebuyer is supposed to be relatively young, making mortgage payments throughout the first half of his or her working life until the mortgage is paid off; then, when earning potential is at its highest later in working life, the mortgage is paid and income can be invested in a wider portfolio of assets. When an individual retires, the home can then be sold as a one-off cash windfall to fund retirement. However, this assumes that:

1. the lifecycle assumes a balance between income, assets, savings and debt changes across an adult's lifetime (more problematically, it assumes stable economic growth, low unemployment, stable working careers and a numerical balance between birth cohorts); and
2. households can know and control the housing market, which they cannot, so whether a householder gains or losses from house price fluctuations is, ostensibly, luck. This means that some households who buy at the right time can realise significant wealth gains, while other households purchased highly leveraged assets in the middle of a bubble and were consequently exposed to external factors such as liquidity in global credit market; other households are priced out of housing altogether.[41]

See also: ***wealth; wealth inequality; Piketty, Thomas***

Asset management (housing)

In Old French, the word 'asez' means 'enough' and it is from this that the word 'asset' derives.[42] Asset management concerns the running, maintenance, improvement, disposal and optimisation of value of the tangible assets of an organisation or authority. For example, in council housing, local authorities and ***approved housing bodies*** should have regard to:

- The profile, type and age of their housing stock
- The current and future expected demand for social housing

---

[39] Doling, J and Ronald, RJ (2010) 'Home Ownership and Asset-based Welfare', *Housing and the Built Environment*, Vol. 25, No. 2, pp. 165–173

[40] Doling, J and Ford, J (2007) 'A Union of Home Owners, Editorial', *European Journal of Housing and Planning*, Vol. 7, No. 2, pp. 113–127

[41] Montgomerie, J (2015) 'Housing-based welfare strategies do not work and will not work', *LSE Blog*, 30 January, available at: http://blogs.lse.ac.uk/politicsandpolicy/homeownership-and-the-failures-of-asset-based-welfare/

[42] Garnett, D (2015) *The A–Z of Housing (Professional Keywords)*, Macmillan: London

- How to match supply and demand
- The specific location of all their houses
- Projected expenditure on new stock or maintaining existing stock versus income
- The potential for new development alone or with partners
- Maintenance and energy efficiency
- Issues of history and conservation

Councils and AHBs should also have regard to both strategic and operational aspects of asset management. The strategic component concerns developing medium- to long-term plans for making decisions around maintaining, disposing, developing and improving properties. The operational component of asset management is more concerned with the day-to-day aspects of delivering on the strategy and occasionally responding to unexpected events.

See also: ***active land management***

The assigned certifier is appointed by the building owner to certify the works **Assigned certifier** carried out in accordance with the ***building control regulations***. They undertake to inspect and to coordinate the inspection activities of others during construction, and to certify the building or works on completion. The role of assigned certifier does not include responsibility for the supervision of any builder. They may or may not be a member of the design team.

Assigned certifiers should:

a. Provide and sign the relevant statutory certificates – the form of undertaking at commencement and the ***Certificate of Compliance on Completion***;
b. Coordinate the ancillary certification by members of the design team and other relevant bodies for the Certificate of Compliance on Completion;
c. Identify all design professionals and specialists, in conjunction with the builder, from whom certificates are required;
d. Identify all certificates required and obtain them;
e. Coordinate and collate all certification of compliance for completion in conjunction with the builder;
f. In consultation with the members of the design team, plan and oversee the implementation of the inspection plan during construction;
g. Prepare the preliminary inspection plan and oversee adherence to this plan, and on completion provide the inspection plan as implemented;
h. On termination or relinquishment of their appointment make available to the building owner all certification prepared and inspection reports carried out;
i. Act as the single point of contact with the ***building control authority*** during construction;

j. Seek advice from the building control authority, in respect of compliance matters relating to the building or works where disputes or differences of opinion arise between the parties to the project, and maintain records of inspection.[43]

An assigned certifier can only be:

1. Architects on register pursuant to part 3 of the Building Control Act 2007; or
2. Building surveyors on register pursuant to part 5 of the Building Control Act 2007; or
3. Chartered engineers on register pursuant to section 7 of the Institution of Civil Engineers of Ireland (Charter Amendment) Act 1969

'Registered surveyor' means registered building surveyor and does not include registered quantity surveyors or other *Society of Chartered Surveyors Ireland* members.

See also: *Building Control (Amendment) Regulations [BC(A)R]; building control authority; Building Control Management System; self-certification*

Assignment of a lease

Assignment is where a *tenant* transfers his or her entire interest in a *tenancy* to a third party. The original tenant then ceases to have any interest or involvement in the tenancy and the assignee becomes the tenant who now deals directly with the *landlord*. Assignment can only take place with the consent of the landlord. Where a landlord refuses an assignment of a fixed term tenancy, a tenant can serve a *notice of termination* on the landlord. Tenants of *approved housing bodies* are not permitted to assign or *sublet* the tenancy.

See also: *Residential Tenancies Act 2004; security of tenure*

Auction

An auction is a public sale where the property is sold to the highest bidder. The person selling the goods is a *property services provider* and needs a licence from the *Property Services Regulatory Authority*.

Auctions are not covered by the Consumer Rights Directive and so purchasers are not entitled to a cancellation or cooling-off period. However, goods being sold at an auction must match the description given at the auction and must be fit for the purpose they are being sold for. A bid at an auction is forming a contract, and placing a bid means the *auctioneer*'s

---

[43] Department of Environment, Community and Local Government (2014) *Code of Practice for Inspecting and Certifying Buildings and Works, Building Control Regulations*, Government of Ireland: Dublin

terms and conditions have been accepted.[44] If the property has a problem with structure or title, it is the bidder's problem once the hammer goes down and it is sold. Immediately after the auction, the bidder will be asked to sign contracts and pay a non-refundable deposit.[45]

It is an offence for agents to make or accept bids on behalf of a vendor unless the residential property is subject to a court order under the Family Law Act 1995 or the Family Law (Divorce) Act 1996.

See also: *estate agent; Property Services (Regulation) Act 2011; Property Services Regulatory Authority*

An auctioneer is a licenced *property services provider* whose job it is to conduct sales by *auction*.

Auctioneer

See also: *Property Services Regulatory Authority; Property Services (Regulation) Act 2011*

Availability arrangements can be entered into between local authorities and property owners under the *Rental Accommodation Scheme* (RAS) and the *Social Housing Leasing Initiative* (SHLI). There are two common contract types. The most common is the availability type arrangement under which property owners will:

Availability arrangements[46]

- Receive guaranteed rental income from the local authority monthly or quarterly
- Receive *rent* payments for vacancy periods
- Have no rent collection or rent *arrears* obligations
- Not incur advertising or administrative overheads
- Be required to register tenancies with the *Residential Tenancies Board* (RTB)

The main differences between this and a longer-term leasing contract are that the owner will:

- Retain responsibility for day-to-day property maintenance
- Be the landlord to tenants nominated by the local authority
- Register tenancies with the *Residential Tenancies Board* (RTB)

Owners will receive a rent amount of approximately 92 per cent of the current market rent. The rent discount may vary in this arrangement and rents will

---

[44] Coffey, C (2016) 'What are your rights when you buy at auction?', *RTE*, available at: https://www.rte.ie/lifestyle/living/2016/1018/825059-what-are-your-rights-when-you-buy-at-auction/

[45] See: https://www.ebs.ie/blog/2014/12/beginners-guide-to-buying-at-auction

[46] See: http://www.sligococo.ie/housing/Accommodation/PrivateSectorProperties/LeasingPrivateAccommodation/ShortTermLeasing/

be agreed through negotiation with the local authority. The rent discount is applied to take account of the fact that the property owner is paid for vacant unoccupied periods, rent is paid in advance and the normal landlord tasks associated with filling *voids* are eliminated. Rent reviews take place every two years.

See also: *long-term leasing arrangements*

B

Bacon reports   Dr Peter Bacon produced three reports for the government on housing. All his recommendations were implemented by government (including a review of *landlord* and *tenant* legislation), but he has argued that some were reversed too soon (e.g. the cutting of *stamp duty* for investors). Bacon is also credited with the design of the *National Asset Management Agency* (NAMA).

The reports prepared by Bacon are:

- *An Economic Assessment of Recent House Price Developments – A Report Submitted to the Minister for Housing and Urban Renewal* (April 1998) (known as Bacon 1)
- *The Housing Market: An Economic Review and Assessment – A Report Submitted to the Minister for Housing and Urban Renewal* (March 1999) (Bacon 2)
- *The Housing Market in Ireland: An Economic Evaluation of Trends and Prospects – A Report Submitted to the Minister for Housing and Urban Renewal* (June 2000) (Bacon 3)

He also produced *Evaluation of Options for Resolving Property Loan Impairments and Associated Capital Adequacy of Irish Credit Institutions: Proposal for a National Asset Management Agency (NAMA) – Abridged Summary of Report* (8 April 2009).

See also: *crisis (and housing); National Asset Management Agency*

Balanced regional development   The dominant approach to regional policy in post-war Europe involved the improvement of infrastructure in assisted regions and the provision of support to firms and incentives to mobile investors. The aim was to achieve a more 'balanced' form of national economic development by redistributing investment to regions suffering from insufficient demand.[47]

In the Irish context, this concept of balanced regional development (BRD) took shape in policy form in the *National Spatial Strategy 2002–2020*, and was a key objective of the National Development Plan 2007–2013. However,

---

[47] Ward, N (2018) 'Balanced Regional Development: Issues and Insights', University of East Anglia: Kent

although balanced regional development became an important government policy, it was not clearly or consistently defined and a range of interpretations and meanings were evident.[48]

In the absence of a definition for an Irish context, BRD in general can mean the maximisation of the development potential of every region so that the benefit of overall economic growth is shared by all; or the distribution of investment in such a way that the regional rates of growth in different parts of the country are equally attained, eliminating the regional disparities prevailing in the country. BRD does not mean the equal development of every region in the country, but can mean the simultaneous development of each region.

BRD is both a social and economic concept and the concept of achieving 'balance' is very much a contested one. Many argue that BRD cannot work as Ireland does not have the resources to promote every location with a 'one for everyone in the audience' approach.[49]

See also: ***regional development; rural housing***

A balcony is an enclosed platform attached to the outside of a building and accessed from inside an individual residential unit. The word 'balcony' comes from the Italian 'balcone'. A Juliette balcony – also known as a French balcony – is a narrow enclosed balcony with no protruding platform, deck or floor. Therefore although the access windows can be opened, there is no platform to step out onto.

Balcony

Irish apartment standards require that private amenity space shall be provided in the form of gardens or patios/terraces for ground floor apartments and balconies at upper levels. Balconies should be a minimum of 1.5 metres deep and preferably primarily accessed from living rooms. Vertical privacy screens should be provided between adjoining balconies and the floors of balconies should be solid and self-draining.[50]

See also: ***apartment design standards***

In May 1964, the Department of Local Government recommended the Ballymun Housing Scheme to the City Council. The government stated

Ballymun – history[51]

---

[48] Western Development Commission (2015) 'Balanced Regional Development – what does it mean?', *WDC Insights*, 11 May, available at: https://wdcinsights.wordpress.com/2015/05/11/balanced-regional-development-what-does-it-mean/

[49] Hughes, B (2018) 'Demography Is Destiny: Strategic Planning and Housing in Ireland', in Sirr, L (ed.), *Administration – special housing edition*, Vol. 66, No. 2, pp. 163–177

[50] Department of Housing, Planning and Local Government (2018) *Sustainable Urban Housing: Design Standards for New Apartments – Guidelines for Planning Authorities*, Government of Ireland: Dublin

[51] Entry taken from: Somerville-Woodward, R (2002) *Ballymun: A History*, Volumes I and II, Ballymun Regeneration Limited: Dublin, available at: http://www.brl.ie/pdf/ballymun_a_history_1600_1997_synopsis.pdf

from the outset that this project of more than 3,000 dwellings was intended to augment the Corporation's existing house-building programme. Both the planners and architects were convinced that system building and high-rise architecture was the only conceivable solution to the housing crisis in Ireland.

The contract for developing and building Ballymun was awarded in February 1965 to the Cubitt Haden Sisk building consortium. The consortium was a frontrunner from the beginning because of its experience using the 'Balency' method of prefabricated system building. However, by the time the plans for the Ballymun Housing Scheme were completed, high-rise system-built developments were being abandoned in the United Kingdom and elsewhere in Europe. The European experience was that the 'lack of upkeep of common areas, poor workmanship, and lack of communal facilities could lead to the physical degradation of the buildings and social isolation for those who lived there. The negative image of such projects was even earning them the tag of "vertical slums"'.

The members of Dublin Corporation, when adopting the government's proposals for Ballymun, incorporated a motion calling for the 'simultaneous building of shops, public halls, a swimming pool, a library and a clinic on the site'. However, no sooner did construction work begin than the realities of the under-budgeted, under-planned and poorly designed estate became apparent to the Corporation and National Building Agency staff connected with the project. The government's inexperience in undertaking a project of Ballymun's magnitude and the dilution of the construction contract, coupled with a lack of clarity as to how Ballymun would eventually be managed, meant that the seeds of many of Ballymun's future problems had been sown from the outset. The seven towers built in Ballymun were named, in 1966, after the seven leaders of the Easter Rising of 1916: Thomas Clarke, Seán McDermott, Thomas McDonagh, Patrick Pearse, Eamonn Ceannt, James Connolly and Joseph Plunkett.

Many of the first Ballymun tenants were not chosen for the length of time they had spent on the housing list, but on the basis of interviews carried out by Dublin Corporation staff, who selected what it considered would be the most suitable tenants for Ballymun, which was viewed as a model housing estate. Those who were chosen appear to have been picked on the basis of low or no rent arrears, with a husband in full-time employment, and with two or more children. By the summer of 1969 an entire community had been 'created' miles from Dublin city with none of the amenities necessary to satisfactorily conduct their daily lives.

Many recreational and social facilities still remained unsatisfactory or incomplete into the 1970s. Problems with lifts, heating, lack of a town centre, lack of landscaping and play areas created friction in the relationship between Dublin Corporation and the tenants. By the mid-1980s Ballymun had a large unemployed and transient community. Many of the difficulties experienced were attributed to the transient nature of the area, which was beyond the control of residents.

The publication of the *Craig Gardner Report* in August 1993 marked a watershed in the history of Ballymun. The report proposed five possible approaches for the physical renewal of Ballymun and these were presented under the premise that 'to do nothing' was not tenable. In late 1996, three years after the *Craig Gardner Report* and a year after the Housing Task Force had published its response to the key recommendations, Dublin Corporation issued its own proposals for Ballymun, which recommended that the flats should be demolished and not refurbished.

In July 1997 Dublin Corporation established Ballymun Regeneration Limited (BRL) as its agent in Ballymun: to facilitate community consultation, and to develop and implement a masterplan for Ballymun's regeneration. In 2004, the Pearse tower was the first of the seven to be pulled down.

See also: ***procurement; tenements; council housing; high-rise***

The Nyberg Report (*Misjudging Risk: Causes of the Systemic Banking Crisis in Ireland – Report of the Commission of Investigation into the Banking Sector in Ireland*) describes the conditions for the banking crisis of 2007–2008 concisely: **Banking crisis[52]**

- Entry into the Euro area markedly reduced Irish interest rates.
- Globalisation of markets and EU membership increased foreign competition in the Irish financial market, putting pressure on bank margins.
- A number of new, potentially high-risk retail products were introduced to the Irish market by new entrants (for example, tracker mortgages and 100 per cent mortgages for first-time buyers).
- Last but not least, the paradigm of efficient financial markets provided the intellectual basis for the assumption that financial markets, left essentially to themselves, would tend to be both stable and efficient.

The problems causing the crisis, as well as the scale of it, were the result of domestic Irish decisions and actions, some of which were made more profitable or possible by international developments. Though eventually unsustainable financial risks were made attractive by outside factors, there simply was nobody abroad forcing Irish authorities, banks or investors to accept such risks. The way Irish households, investors, banks and public authorities voluntarily reacted to foreign and domestic developments was

---

[52] Nyberg, P (2011) *Misjudging Risk: Causes of the Systemic Banking Crisis in Ireland – Report of the Commission of Investigation into the Banking Sector in Ireland*, Government of Ireland: Dublin

probably not very different to that in other countries now experiencing financial problems. However, the extent to which large parts of Irish society were willing to let the good times roll on until the very last minute (a feature of the financial mania) may have been exceptional.

The report also notes the requirements for a systemic banking crisis to occur; at least the following factors must be present (although the last two may not be as essential as the others):

- A sufficiently large number of households and investors who, at some point, start making serious mistakes in judging the value and liquidity of their major assets, holdings and projects
- Banks that provide financing, large in relation to their own capital, for these investments without thoroughly and sufficiently evaluating their prospects and the creditworthiness of borrowers in the longer term
- Providers of funds to such banks (often banks themselves but also depositors) that do not monitor bank soundness with sufficient diligence; in the case of private providers possibly because of perceived implicit public support for at least the important banks
- A banking regulator that remains unwilling or unable to detect or prevent banks from engaging in excessively risky lending or funding practices
- A government and a central bank that remains unaware of the mounting problems or is unwilling to do anything to prevent them
- A parliament that remains unaware of the mounting problems or concentrates its attention on other things perceived to be of greater immediate importance
- Media that are generally supportive of corporate and bank expansion, profit growth and risk taking while being dismissive of warnings of unsustainable developments

See also: ***bubble (housing); speculation***

Basement   This is the floor of a house or building that is sunk partially or entirely below ground level. Basements typically had functions as storage areas or locations for housekeeping functions such as laundry, or were for accommodating housekeeping staff and servants.

    See also: ***garden flat***

B&B (bed and breakfast)   A B&B is housing in which overnight accommodation (bed) is provided with the option of a morning meal (breakfast). Nationally, there are c.3,000 B&Bs in Ireland,[53] with, in 2019, 894 of these being Fáilte Ireland-approved.

---

[53] O'Connell, S (2018) 'The full Irish: how B&Bs bounced back', *Irish Times*, 17 March

According to Fáilte Ireland, B&Bs account for 35 per cent of all tourist accommodation properties, and 5 per cent of bed spaces (hotels have 28 per cent of properties and 65 per cent of bed spaces). Kerry has the largest number of B&Bs in Ireland at 167.[54] To be approved as a B&B by Fáilte Ireland there must be at least two and no more than six guest bedrooms. The maximum number of bedrooms in the house cannot be more than nine, including the family bedrooms. In the case of houses with guest bedrooms without private bathrooms attached, there should be one bath and one shower provided for the first six persons accommodated, including the owner's family. If more than four guest bedrooms are provided, ***planning permission*** for bed and breakfast use is necessary.[55]

See also: ***AirBnB; digs; boarding house***

See: ***Building Control (Amendment) Regulations; S.I. 9 (BC(A)R)***   BC(A)R

Section 4 of the ***Residential Tenancies Act 2004*** defines bedsit accommodation as being in the form of a 'self-contained residential unit'. Bedsits were banned in 2008 by the ***Housing (Standards for Rented Houses) Regulations 2008***. There was, however, a four-year grace period until February 2013 when the new regulations came into effect to prohibit accommodation with shared bathrooms and ***landlord***-controlled heating systems (effectively, bedsits). Since 2013, all rental properties are required to have independently controlled heating systems and appliances, individual bathrooms, adequate food preparation (four-ring cooker) and storage facilities, and access to laundry facilities. These provisions had already applied to new tenancies in properties let for the first time since February 2009.   **Bedsit**

The penalties for non-compliance with the regulations are a fine of €5,000 or imprisonment for a term not exceeding six months or both, and the fine for each day of a continuing offence is €400.

See also: ***digs; boarding house***

The term 'big house' – an ambivalently derisive expression in Ireland – refers to a country mansion, not always so very big, but typically owned by a Protestant Anglo-Irish family presiding over a substantial agricultural acreage leased out to Catholic tenants who worked the land. As rural centres of political power and wealth in Ireland, most big houses occupied property confiscated   **'Big House', the[56]**

---

[54] Fáilte Ireland (2018) 'Accommodation Capacity in Ireland 2018', available at: http://www.failteireland.ie/FailteIreland/media/WebsiteStructure/Documents/3_Research_Insights/3_General_SurveysReports/Accommodation-Capacity-in-Ireland-2018.pdf?ext=.pdf

[55] See: http://www.failteireland.ie/Supports/Get-quality-assured/irish-home-b-b.aspx

[56] This is entry is from: Kreilkamp, V (2006) 'The Novel of the Big House', in Wilson Foster, J (ed.), *The Cambridge Companion to the Irish Novel* (Cambridge Companions to Literature, pp. 60–77), Cambridge University Press: Cambridge

from native Catholic families in the sixteenth and seventeenth centuries. Their presence in the landscape, unlike that of England's 'great houses', long asserted the political and economic ascendancy of a remote colonial power structure. Whereas by the nineteenth century the English country mansion could be incorporated into a triumphal concept of national heritage, for most of Ireland's population, Ascendancy houses signalled division, not community. In a colonial country, such division reflected not just the typical disparities of class and wealth between landlords and tenants, but also difference of political allegiance, ethnicity, religion and language. Thus in a speech advocating the 1800 Act of Union, Lord Clare notoriously described Irish landlords as 'hemmed in on every side by the old inhabitants of the island, brooding over their discontents in sullen indignation'.

See also: ***Tenant Right League; Duffy, Charles Gavan; Davitt, Michael; Three Fs***

Boarding house   A boarding house is a private ***dwelling*** where people pay for lodging and meals.

See also: ***household; digs; B&B***

Boundary   A boundary is a line that identifies the limits of the property. O'Reilly and Shine[57] identify two main types of boundaries: The legal boundary consists of an 'invisible line' that divides the two properties and is based on its description in the title deed and/or deed map, and as such has no width. The earliest conveyance deed and plan that describe the parcel of land whose boundary is being investigated is accepted as the source of the legal boundary. The deed map must be used to define the position of the legal boundary on site. If this legal boundary is set out on a site that already has a physical boundary, such as a wall, hedge or fence, differences in alignment frequently become apparent. The physical boundary of a property refers to the actual physical boundary on the ground, which includes fences, walls or hedges, or any other features that can be used to show physical boundaries on a map.

The ***Registry of Deeds*** retains a ***memorial***, or summary, of the deeds. It does not contain a map and occasionally contains some dimensions. The deed records and describes the legal ownership of a property and can be accompanied by a deed map. Deed maps are prepared specifically to define the extent and boundaries of land that is the subject of a legal agreement or transaction, such as a conveyance or assignment, and are prepared for attachment to the deed concerned. Surveyors preparing deed maps frequently use an Ordnance Survey Ireland map as the base or background map.

---

[57] O'Reilly, N and Shine, P (2013) 'Beyond the Bounds: Resolving Boundary Disputes', *Surveyors' Journal*, Autumn

The **Land Registry** also maintains Land Registry maps, whose purpose is identification of properties and not of boundaries. The boundary system adopted by the Land Registry under the Registration of Title Act 1964 is a non-conclusive boundary system, occasionally referred to as a general boundary system. This dispenses with the need to determine the exact location of title boundaries when registering properties. Furthermore, it will not indicate if the boundary runs along the inner or outer face of a wall or where it runs within it. In the case of boundaries located within buildings, the exact line or plane of the title boundary will also be left undetermined.

In boundary disputes, the **deed map** must be used to define the position of the legal boundary on site.

See also: **General Boundary Rule; deed; memorial; cadastre; GeoDirectory**

A bridging loan (or bridging finance) is a temporary loan that allows people to buy a new property while they are waiting for the sale of their own property to be completed. Bridging loans typically charge a higher rate of interest than mortgage rates.

See also: **downsizing**

Bridging loan (bridging finance)

A permanent structure designed to provide shade from the sun. In the northern hemisphere these are often placed on a building's south facade to help prevent glare and overheating. Some innovative approaches to *brise soleil* include planting deciduous climbers to provide extra summer shading and more passive solar gain in winter.

See also: **balcony**

Brise soleil[58]

A brownfield site is land within the urban area on which development has previously taken place,[59] but which has the potential for new **development**. Brownfield sites can sometimes be contaminated through the materials that were produced or stored there (e.g. landfill) or by the buildings on the site (e.g. if they contained asbestos). In these cases, the costs of decontaminating the site will form part of the costs in the **residual** valuation.

See also: **greenfield site; infill**

Brownfield site

Economists disagree on how to define a bubble, or even whether bubbles exist. Intuitively, a bubble exists when the price of an asset is over-inflated relative to some benchmark; however there is difficulty finding agreement on what that benchmark should be. The benchmark may be an estimate of the asset's value based on a collection of variables that plausibly affect its supply,

Bubble (housing)

---

[58] See: https://passivehouseplus.ie/b
[59] See: https://www.eea.europa.eu/help/glossary#c4=10&c0=all&b_start=0&c2=brownfield

demand and price (the so-called fundamentals). In housing, these fundamentals often include population growth, tax policy, household size, household income and many others.[60]

The term 'housing bubble' had virtually no currency until 2002, when its use suddenly increased dramatically. However, although widely used it is rarely clearly defined. Case and Shiller[61] believe that in its widespread use the term 'bubble' refers to a situation in which excessive public expectations of future price increases cause prices to be temporarily elevated. During a housing price bubble, homebuyers think that a home that they would normally consider too expensive for them is now an acceptable purchase because they will be compensated by significant further price increases. They will not need to save as much as they otherwise might, because they expect the increased value of their home to do the saving for them (see: *asset-based welfare*). First-time homebuyers may also worry during a housing bubble that if they do not buy now, they will not be able to afford a home later. Furthermore, the expectation of large price increases may have a strong impact on demand if people think that home prices are very unlikely to fall, and certainly not likely to fall for long, so that there is little perceived risk associated with an investment in a home.[62]

Prices cannot go up rapidly forever, and when people perceive that prices have stopped going up, this support for their acceptance of high home prices could break down. Prices could then fall as a result of diminished demand and the bubble bursts. A tendency to view housing as an investment, therefore, is a defining characteristic of a housing bubble. Expectations of future appreciation of the home are a motive for buying that deflects consideration from how much one is paying for housing services. A bubble is about buying for the future price increases rather than simply for the pleasure of occupying the home. And it is this motive that is thought to lend instability to bubbles, and a tendency to crash when the investment motive weakens.[63]

Regling and Watson's report on the Irish financial crisis[64] noted that the principal causes were not the proliferation of complex financial products or exposure to the US sub-prime market, but it was 'a plain vanilla property bubble compounded by exceptional concentrations for purposes related to property – and notably commercial property'.[65] The **Nyberg Report** too

[60] Henckel, T (2017) 'What economics has to say about housing bubbles', *The Conversation*, 2 April, available at: http://theconversation.com/what-economics-has-to-say-about-housing-bubbles-74925
[61] Case, K and Shiller, R (2003) 'Is there a Bubble in the Housing Market?', *Brookings Papers on Economic Activity*, Vol. 34, No. 2, pp. 299–362
[62] *Ibid.*
[63] *Ibid.*
[64] Regling, K and Watson, M (2010) *A Preliminary Report on the Sources of Ireland's Banking Crisis*, Government Publications Office: Dublin
[65] *Ibid.*

said that: 'much points to the development of a national speculative mania in Ireland during the period, centred on the property market. As in most manias, those caught up in it could believe and have trust in extraordinary things, such as unlimited real wealth from selling property to each other on credit …. When it all ended, suddenly and inexplicably, participants had difficulty accepting their appropriate share of the blame for something in which so many others were also involved and that seemed so reasonable at the time.'[66]
See also: ***windfall gain; speculation***

In 1968, Professor Sir Colin Buchanan (1907–2001) produced a report for **Buchanan, Colin** the Irish government – *Studies in Ireland: An Exercise in Regional Planning by the United Nations on behalf of the Irish Government*, published by ***An Foras Forbartha*** – that set out a National Development Strategy for Ireland and outlined his belief that the key to ending emigration and creating enough jobs to keep people in Ireland was to develop a network of cities and large towns. Buchanan had noted that since the 1940s the most rural populations had experienced the highest rates of emigration, whereas counties with large urban populations had seen much greater success in keeping their own rural populations. He recommended the creation of a hierarchy of growth centres into which a key infrastructure and amenities were to be directed. The most extreme option was to concentrate all development in Dublin. The next best alternative was to focus on development in Cork, the Limerick–Ennis–Shannon region and a limited number of regional centres, while neither encouraging nor discouraging development in Dublin. The report was submitted to government in September 1968 and not published until May 1969.[67] The report faced stiff political opposition and ended up being pigeonholed, largely because of the Irish clientelist political system, as clientelism requires that there must be 'something for everyone in the audience'. The Fianna Fáil government of the day could not bring itself to designate new growth centres. By announcing that, say, Athlone would grow clearly implied that Mullingar and Ballinasloe would not, and that was not politically palatable.[68] The rejection of the Buchanan strategy left Ireland without a spatial policy for the country until the ***National Spatial Strategy*** in 2002.
See also: ***National Planning Framework; balanced regional development***

The Building Control Regulations ['BC(A)R'] introduced a range of new reg- **Building Control** ulatory measures at the commencement, construction and completion stages **(Amendment) Regulations [BC(A)R]**

---

[66] Nyberg, P (2011) *Misjudging Risk: Causes of the Systemic Banking Crisis in Ireland – Report of the Commission of Investigation into the Banking Sector in Ireland*, Government of Ireland: Dublin
[67] Daly, M (2006) *The Slow Failure: Population Decline and Independent Ireland, 1920–1973*, University of Wisconsin Press: Madison
[68] Anon. (2001) 'Getting to grips with the chaos in planning', *Irish Times*, 7 March

of development. BC(A)R applies to new buildings, extensions, material alterations and changes of use of buildings. They promote observance of the **building regulations** by supplementing powers of inspection and enforcement given to **building control authorities**. The Building Control (Amendment) Regulations regulate:

- **Commencement Notices** and 7-Day Notices
- **Fire Safety Certificates**, Revised Fire Safety Certificates and Regularisation Certificates
- **Disability Access Certificates** and Revised Disability Access Certificates
- Maintenance of Public Registers
- Fees
- Statutory registration of building control activity

Responsibility for compliance with building regulations and the **building control** regulations rests under law with the owner of the building, the designer who designs the works, and the builder who carries out the works.
    BC(A)R introduced the following new certification:

- **Commencement Notice**
- Notice of Assignment of **Assigned Certifier**
- Certificate of Compliance (Assigned Certifier)
- Certificate of Compliance (Design)
- Notice of Assignment (Builder)
- Certificate of Compliance (Builder)
- **Certificate of Compliance on Completion**

Some of the fundamental stages in the BC(A)R process are:[69]

1. Commencement stage – validation: This is where the Commencement Notice is submitted to the building control authority along with Notices of Assignment (builder and assigned certifier), undertakings, the Design Certificate and accompanying plans and documentation. The Commencement Notice must be received by the building control authority not less than 14 days and not more than 28 days before commencing works on site.
2. Construction stage – assessment and inspection: It is expected that local authorities will inspect 12 to 15 per cent of new buildings during construction and inspections will be targeted and based on risk assessments. They are likely to be focused on multi-unit developments such as apartments.

---

[69] See: http://www.garlandconsultancy.com/assets/media/Downloads/Building%20Control%20 Amendment%202014%20-%20Garland%20Guide.pdf

3. Completion stage: Approximately three to five weeks in advance of occupying the building, the Certificate of Completion is submitted along with particulars demonstrating how the completed project has complied with the building regulations.

See also: ***Building Control Management System (BCMS)***

A building control authority is one of 31 local authorities. Building control authorities monitor compliance with ***building regulations*** in their area having regard to:

Building control authority

- The minimum requirements for the design and construction of buildings as set out in the building regulations
- Detailed ***technical guidance documents*** showing how these requirements can be achieved in practice
- Procedures set out in the ***building control regulations*** for demonstrating compliance in respect of an individual building or works

The overall role of the building control authority should be to:

- Process applications for ***Fire Safety Certificates*** and ***Disability Access Certificates*** and issue decisions on those applications
- Validate and register ***Commencement Notices***/7-Day Notices and the accompanying Certificates of Compliance (Design), notices of assignment by the building owner, and notices of undertakings by the ***assigned certifier*** and the builder
- Undertake a risk analysis of each ***Commencement Notice*** submitted in order to inform its own inspection arrangements
- Advise the assigned certifier in relation to issues of compliance relating to the building or works that are disputed by parties to the construction project
- Validate and register the Certificate of Compliance on Completion and accompanying documentation submitted in support of same
- Maintain a public register of building control decisions and activity
- Maintain records, including records of inspection

Under the Building Control Act 1990 authorities have powers of inspection, enforcement and prosecution.[70]

---

[70] Department of Environment, Community and Local Government (2014) *Code of Practice for Inspecting and Certifying Buildings and Works, Building Control Regulations*, Government of Ireland: Dublin

Building Control Management System (BCMS) The Building Control Management System (BCMS) is an electronic administration system for *building control* functions in Ireland. All statutory processes are handled by the local *building control authority* via the BCMS,[71] which is administered by the Local Government Management Association (LGMA).

The BCMS replaced a paper-based system. Typical users of the system are property owners, architects, designers, builders and assigned certifiers. Users register on the system, complete the relevant statutory forms (e.g. a Commencement Notice), upload the relevant supporting documentation and pay the required fee online.

The BCMS was developed because of a lack of consumer confidence in the building control regulatory compliance and inspection regime, as well as a lack of streamlined procedures for doing business. There was a deficit of knowledge of the fundamental and statutory requirements of, and responsibilities imposed by, the building control regulations and building regulations; and the administration of building control involved multiple over-the-counter transactions consuming resources and time.[72]

In 2017, the BCMS recorded some 8,500 dwellings completed in Ireland. This compares to 14,400 recorded by the *Central Statistics Office*. Although the BCMS is not designed to be used to count housing supply, the discrepancy in the numbers would indicate a high proportion of non-compliance with the requirement to use the system.

See also: *Certificate of Compliance on Completion; assigned certifier; Commencement Notice; data – housing output issues*

Building Energy Rating Certificate A Building Energy Rating Certificate (BER) provides an indication of a building's energy performance on a scale of A–G, with A being the most efficient and G the least. A BER rating is calculated from a combination of energy use for both hot water and space heating, lighting and ventilation for an estimated number of people likely to occupy that type of building.

A BER Certificate is compulsory for all types of home for sale or rent, including previously built but unoccupied houses. The BER rating for a building must be included in all advertisements for sale or rent (as per S.I. 243 of 2012). Certain building types are exempt from BER requirements, such as national monuments; protected structures or proposed protected structures; places of worship or buildings used for the religious activities of any religion; certain temporary buildings; industrial buildings not intended for extended human occupancy with a low installed heating capacity (≤10

---

[71] See: https://www.housing.gov.ie/housing/building-standards/building-regulations/building-control

[72] See: https://www.oecd.org/governance/observatory-public-sector-innovation/innovations/page/buildingcontrolmanagementsystembcms.htm

W/m²); non-residential agricultural buildings with a low installed heating capacity (≤10 W/m²); and stand-alone buildings with a small useful floor area (<50m²).

See also: *nZEB; Passive House; U-value; Y-value; thermal bridge; data – housing output issues; Goodbody BER Housebuilding Monitor*

The exterior shell of the building, including the external walls, windows, floor and roof.

See also: *dwelling; house – structural components*

Building envelope[78]

Building Information Modelling (BIM) is a structured process underpinning the creation and maintenance of digital data across the lifecycle of a built asset. The BIM process uses digital technologies and standardised protocols to improve construction project efficiency. Suites of BIM-enabled tools and the use of interoperable file formats have allowed project teams to seamlessly coordinate their work, the task of which is conducted in a single digital environment known as a Common Data Environment (CDE).

Building Information Modelling (BIM)[79]

By using BIM, the asset is constructed like-for-like in a virtual space using digital objects prior to any physical work done onsite. All data necessary for the design, construction, maintenance and end-of-life protocols are held within these objects. This forms a single data source – held in the CDE – from which all relevant information (graphical and non-graphical) is derived as a deliverable, e.g. drawings, schedules and documentation.

Although BIM is often synonymised with the digital transformation of the construction sector, it has only been adopted by pockets of industry. The large capital involved in adopting BIM – e.g. upskilling personnel and software and hardware costs – has resulted in this patchy uptake, particularly for SMEs. In addition, national BIM strategies usually only mandate public sector clients to require their suppliers to deliver a BIM project, resulting in a general lack of awareness in private clients.

Building regulations are a set of legal requirements for the design and construction of new buildings, extensions and material alterations to, and certain changes of use of, existing buildings.[75] The aim of the Building Regulations is to provide for the safety and welfare of people in and about buildings, conservation of fuel and energy, and access for people with disabilities.[76] The minimum performance requirements that a building must achieve are set

Building regulations

---

[73] See: https://passivehouseplus.ie/b
[74] Entry courtesy of BIM expert Dr Melanie Robinson, Napier University, Edinburgh
[75] See: https://www.localgov.ie/sites/default/files/20180305-faqs_national_building_control_project_v1.1.pdf
[76] *Ibid.*

out in the second schedule to the Building Regulations. These requirements are set out in twelve parts (classified as parts A to M),[77] known as **technical guidance documents**.

The consistent feature of effective and robust regimes is that they are properly resourced and independent of the regulated industry with sufficient profile and credibility in the sector to influence compliance. Research suggests that part of the reason for the widespread defects in the Irish housing stock is that, at least in recent years, there has not been a credible threat of enforcement of the **building regulations**. Building control authorities also have extensive formal enforcement powers that are seldom used. The evidence of the number of **defects** in Irish houses and apartments points towards a widespread and systematic disregard of the building regulations.[78]

See also: **Building Control (Amendment) Regulations; fuel poverty; access and use (houses)**

Building society A building society is a mutual institution, with no shareholders, which lends its members' funds to other members mostly to purchase or renovate/improve housing. Building societies operate with their members' interest to the fore, whereas banks must consider their shareholders' interest first. Building societies originated in Birmingham in the late eighteenth century.

See also: **credit unions**

Build-to-rent 'Build-to-rent' describes purpose-built residential rental accommodation and associated amenity space that is designed with the sole purpose of being used as long-term rental accommodation owned and managed by a professional **landlord**. Property market experts expect that the build-to-rent sector will grow exponentially in Ireland over the next few years.[79]

The attraction of build-to-rent development for large pension and insurance funds are the steady returns over many years, through the peaks and troughs of economic cycles.[80] 'Pension funds also have the capital to develop large blocks of flats, which are let out and managed long term by a single company rather than being sold to individual landlords ... which provides a fairly stable, long-term income stream.'[81] Many investors have promoted

---

[77] See: https://www.housing.gov.ie/housing/building-standards/building-regulations/building-regulations
[78] Taken from the submission to the Oireachtas Joint Committee on Housing, Planning and Local Government Pre–legislative scrutiny: General Scheme for Construction Industry Register Ireland Bill, by Dr Deirdre Ní Fhloinn, BL, October 2017
[79] MacMahon, T (2017) 'The Emergence of Build to Rent', *Eolas Magazine*
[80] Quinlan, R (2018) 'Investors have €5bn available for Irish build-to-rent housing schemes', *Irish Independent*, 1 March
[81] White, T (2018) 'Build-to-rent: how developers are profiting from Generation Rent', *The Guardian*, 11 April

build-to-rent as a solution to the housing crisis. However, build-to-rent accommodation does not come cheap, and there is a premium to be paid for occupying purpose-built, well-maintained, new properties. This in turn means that 'despite suggestions that build-to-rent will empower **Generation Rent**, these high-spec products only really seem to be an answer for affluent young professionals.'[82] The Irish government is keen to advance the development of the build-to-rent sector.[83]

A bungalow is typically a single-storey, detached house. The name comes from east India and derives from the Hindi word for Bengali (bangala) and was used to describe the high-status houses occupied by officers of the British Raj in India. Bungalows can be single-story or split-level. It is not uncommon for bungalows to have sleeping and related accommodation in the roof space, in which case they are known as dormer bungalows. The bungalow is a popular house type but the design of bungalows varies across the world in terms of size, provision of veranda, and number of levels.

    See also: ***detached house, semi-detached house; bedsit; maisonette; pied à terre; dwelling; terraced house; condominium; duplex; mews; micro-home; accessory dwelling unit; Bungalow Bliss***

Bungalow Bliss is a best-selling patternbook of house designs and plans written by Irish architect and senator Jack Fitzsimons (1930–2014). It was first published in 1972. Fitzsimons' intention was to make housing, especially through self-building, more affordable. As such, the book featured a set of low-cost plans for bungalows (including dormer and split-level) at a time when architects' fees were considered high. It also explained other related aspects of building, including how to get ***planning permission*** and how to install a ***septic tank***. The book was controversial in that it arguably promoted a proliferation of one-off houses across the Irish countryside, a phenomenon referred to as 'bungalow blitz' by former *Irish Times* journalist Frank McDonald. *Bungalow Bliss* wasn't the only such patternbook: *The Irish Bungalow Book* by Ted McCarthy was published by Mercier Press in 1979.

    See also: ***rural housing; septic tank; bungalow***

'To let' means to rent out, hence buy-to-let property is purchased with the specific intention of renting it to tenants. Buy-to-let ***investment*** is typically done with the medium- to long-term expectation of capital growth with the rental income from ***tenants*** covering the cost of attached debt (e.g. ***mortgage***) and outgoings.

Bungalow

Bungalow Bliss

Buy-to-let

---

82 *Ibid.*
83 Quinlan, R (2018) 'Investors have €5bn available for Irish build-to-rent housing schemes', *Irish Independent*, 1 March

As many residential mortgages preclude the letting of the property, certain banks offer specific buy-to-let mortgages for such investors at higher rates than residential purchases to reflect the higher risk involved (e.g. with rental income, tenants, management and so forth). During the pre-crisis years, some banks granted 100 per cent interest-only buy-to-let mortgages, which fuelled property *speculation* and led to a property *bubble*. Holders of such mortgages rely on capital gains in the property to repay the debt when the property is sold. As the interest-only periods on other buy-to-let mortgages come to an end, the mortgage holders will see significantly increased monthly repayments as they begin to pay down the capital as well as the interest on the loan.[84]

See also: *arrears; Generation Rent; investment; ICAV*

C

Cadastre

A cadastre is a register of up-to-date land/property information. It usually contains the complete authoritative legal record of interests in each individual land/property parcel (e.g. rights, restrictions and responsibilities). Generally, this record includes a unique parcel identifier, a geometric description and a cadastral map showing the legal boundaries (sometimes with reference to *boundary* corner monumentation/markers).

Cadastres may exist for fiscal purposes (e.g. *valuation* and property taxation), legal purposes (*conveyancing*), to assist in the management of land and land use (e.g. for planning, *sustainable development* and environmental protection) or for a combination of these reasons, and are organised in different ways throughout the world, especially with regard to the Land Registration component. The differences between the two concepts relate to the cultural development and judicial setting of the country, i.e. whether a country is based on Roman law (*Deeds* systems) or Germanic or common Anglo law (*Title* systems) (and is therefore linked to the history of colonisation).

Ireland does not have a property/land cadastre. Instead, legal evidence of a person's rights to land, and/or certificate of ownership is established through the existence of deeds or registration of title. Here, land and property registration differs from the cadastral system through the *General Boundary Rule*, the limitations of the boundary description in the title deed documents and the nature (and role) of the registration map (which identifies the physical but not the legal boundary).

See also: *Land Registry; Registry of Deeds*

Capital acquisitions tax

Gift and *inheritance tax* is known as capital acquisitions tax (CAT). In principle, a person may receive gifts and inheritances up to a set value over their

---

[84] Quinn, E (2018) 'Banks tap huge margin on buy-to-lets', *Irish Examiner*, 8 March

lifetime before having to pay CAT. Once due, it is charged at the rate of 33 per cent (valid from 6 December 2012).

To calculate the amount of CAT payable, the receiver of the gift or inheritance is allocated to one of three groups:

- Group A: The person receiving the gift or inheritance is a child of the person giving it, including adopted children, step children and some foster children.
- Group B: The person receiving the gift or inheritance has a family relationship with the person giving it. This includes a brother, sister, nephew, niece, grandparent, grandchild, lineal ancestor or lineal descendant of the person making the gift.
- Group C: The person receiving the gift or inheritance has a relationship with the person giving it which is not already covered in Group A or B.

CAT thresholds for inheritances or gifts are:

	Group A	Group B	Group C
On or after 10/10/2018	€320,000	€32,500	€16,250
12/10/2016 – 09/10/2018	€310,000	€30,150	€15,075
14/10/2015 – 11/10/2016	€280,000	€30,150	€15,075
06/12/2012 – 13/10/2015	€225,000	€30,150	€15,075
07/12/2011 – 05/12/2012	€250,000	€33,500	€16,750

See also: *stamp duty*

Capital Advance Leasing Facility (CALF)

The ***Department of Housing, Planning and Local Government*** offers financial support to ***approved housing bodies*** (AHBs) in the form of a long-term loan under the Capital Advance Leasing Facility (CALF) to assist with the financing of the construction or acquisition of units that will be provided for *social housing* use. This loan facility can support up to 30 per cent of the eligible capital cost of the project, where the units will be provided under *long-term lease arrangements* to local authorities for social housing use. Funding is provided to AHBs through local authorities.

See also: ***Capital Assistance Scheme***

Capital Assistance Scheme[85]

The Capital Assistance Scheme provides funding to ***approved housing bodies*** for the provision of accommodation for persons with specific categories of housing need such as homeless and older persons, people with disabilities, returning emigrants and victims of domestic violence.

See also: ***Capital Advance Leasing Facility***

---

[85] See: http://rebuildingireland.ie/install/wp-content/uploads/2018/07/Full-Report-Final.pdf

Capital gains tax   Capital gains tax (CGT) is a tax that must be paid on any profit (gain) made from the sale, gift or exchange of an asset such as:

- *Land*
- Buildings (houses, *apartments*, or commercial property)
- Shares in companies (Irish resident or non-resident)
- Assets that have no physical form such as goodwill, patents and copyright
- Currency (other than Irish currency)
- Assets of a trade
- Foreign life insurance policies and offshore funds
- Capital payments (in certain situations)

The rate of CGT depends on the date of disposal of the asset. Since December 2012, the rate has been 33 per cent.

There is an exemption for the disposal of a *principal private residence*: when an owner transfers or sells a property they will be exempt from CGT if that property was their main residence while owned. This exemption also applies to land, up to one acre around a house. If the owner let their home at any point when they owned it, then can claim a partial exemption. The *Rent-a-Room Scheme* does not affect any claim for full exemption. An owner may sell their home and the land up to one acre around it for its development value. In this case, the exemption will only apply to the value of the house or land without its development value. They may have to pay CGT on the value of the house or land over that amount.

There are also some 'reliefs' in CGT. Section 33 of the Finance Act 2017 provides that, as regards disposals made on or after 1 January 2018, gains on land and buildings acquired between 7 December 2011 and 31 December 2014 will not be subject to CGT where the land or buildings are held for at least four years and up to seven years from the date they were acquired. If the property is held for longer than seven years, relief will only apply to the portion of the gain relating to the first seven years of ownership and the balance is taxable in the normal way.

See also: *stamp duty; capital acquisitions tax*

Capital value   Capital value is the *value* of an asset. 'Capitalisation' is the process of converting an income stream (e.g. *rent* per month) from a property into a capital value (price achieved at the sale of the asset). This is normally done by using a multiplier known as 'Years Purchase (YP) in perpetuity' [forever]. The YP in perpetuity is the reciprocal of the *yield*[86] (i.e. if the yield is 8 per cent, then

---

[86]   See: http://www.rics.org/be/knowledge/glossary/investment/

the YP multiplier is 100/8 which is 12.5 – therefore the capital value of the property is 12.5 times the annual income stream).
　　See also: ***investment***

Carbon monoxide (chemical symbol CO) is a colourless, odourless, poisonous gas. Dangerous levels of CO can accumulate when fuel is not burning properly as a result of poor ventilation, a blocked chimney or flue, or damaged appliances. All rented properties must have a carbon monoxide alarm. In private housing, where a new or replacement open-flued or flueless combustion appliance, not designed solely for cooking purposes, is installed in a ***dwelling***, a carbon monoxide (CO) alarm should be provided: (a) in the room where the appliance is located; and (b) either inside each bedroom or within 5m of the bedroom door, measured along the path of the corridor.

Carbon monoxide

A caretaker agreement is an arrangement between a house owner and another to occupy the property rent-free in exchange for the performance of certain duties. These duties could be to maintain or improve the property, ensure bins are put out on time, lawns cut and so forth. As caretaker agreements are licences, they do not have to be registered with the ***Residential Tenancies Board*** (RTB). However, if a 'licence fee' is charged (which is actually a rent), and there is ***exclusive possession*** and no obligations of care for the ***dwelling***, and other incidents of a ***tenancy*** are in evidence, it may be a tenancy whatever it is called in any agreement. If it is a tenancy, then the occupier (effectively a ***tenant***) will have certain rights in law. An on-site caretaker who is paid for their work (e.g. maintaining the apartment block in which they live) has a tenancy attached to a continuance in employment or office. However, under section 25(4)(*b*) of the ***Residential Tenancies Act 2004*** this type of tenancy is exempt from rights of ***security of tenure*** (although the tenancy still has to be registered with the RTB).
　　See also: ***licence; house-sitting***

Caretaker agreement

Both directly and indirectly the Catholic Church has had considerable influence on housing delivery and policy in Ireland since the foundation of the state. Research has shown many Catholic countries had similar housing histories (rented slums), housing policies (pro-ownership) and current housing problems (limited social housing; reliance on charities).[87]
　　Almost one hundred years ago, a general fear of civil unrest regarding poor worker conditions, coupled with terrible accommodation, drove the Church to influence government policies towards developing better housing,

Catholic Church

---

[87] Sirr, L and Xerri, K (2015) 'Ireland – A Northern European Country with a Southern European Housing Ethos', paper presented at the ENHR Conference, 28 June–1 July, Lisbon

not always for welfare reasons but often for religious ones. Large families renting and living in small, cramped conditions was also a source of fear of the potential for incest. People were encouraged to turn to their families for personal help with housing themselves and not to the state as state provision of key services was seen as a form of socialism and dilution of Church control. In turn, this allowed states to gradually reduce the amount of support they provided for housing people (as well as in education and health). *Home ownership* also helped develop a strong sense of social conservatism, and reduced the potential for workers' strikes and so this was promoted by the Church, via the state. These were common trends in housing policy across many Catholic countries. In Ireland, however, the Church's influence went further.

Ellen Rowley[88] shows that when designing new housing developments in Dublin in the 1940s, the planning department of the Dublin Corporation would send their master plans to the Archbishop, John Charles McQuaid, for personal approval. If he disapproved, as was common, the plans would have to be redrafted until acceptable.

The Church was wary of living in flats as these were seen as 'communist' (there were warnings about 'the moral dangers of the common staircase'[89]), and as such the construction of houses was much preferred. With central housing plans effectively being overseen by the bishop, Church influence perpetuated the house design as well. The belief was that the lower the density of the housing, the higher the moral behaviour therein, leading to the building of thousands of small houses. Three bedrooms were required in order that male and female children could have separate rooms.

Church influence and design approval is also why many 1920s' and 1930s' *housing estates* in Dublin can be seen in cruciform shape from the air with a large church at their centre, usually adjacent the local school. This central church was the support system for mass housing. And just when Irish architects were inspired by international sources, a lot of these churches exhibited very conservative nineteenth-century design tendencies.

Between 1940 and 1965 Archbishop McQuaid approved and built 34 churches and formed 26 new parishes, many of which were built and occupied by rural migrants. Several Dublin Corporation estates also had religious names: e.g. Fatima Mansions, St Teresa's Gardens, and also the roads: St Jarleth's Road, St Eithne's Road, St Attracta Road. Dublin's streets were 'impregnated with faith' according to a New Zealand bishop who visited Dublin in 1950.

[88] Rowley, E (2015) 'The Architect, the Planner and the Bishop: The Shapers of "Ordinary" Dublin, 1940–60', *FOOTPRINT*, No. 17, Autumn/Winter, pp. 69–88
[89] Anon. (1932) *Irish Builder and Engineer*, Vol. 73, p. 110

Although the Church's influence has waned greatly since then, the development of a system centred on home ownership has remained a considerable part of Irish economic and housing policy.

See also: ***Simms, Herbert; asset-based welfare***

Cavity blocks, sometimes called 9-inch hollow blocks, were sometimes used for the construction of dwelling houses and are particularly common in the Dublin area. Dimensions are approximately 18 inches long by 9 inches wide and 9 inches high. The middle of these blocks is hollow. **Cavity block**[90]

See also: ***cavity wall***

A wall with inner and outer masonry layers (e.g. block or brick), with a cavity in between. The cavity serves as a way to drain water out of the wall. Cavities can be insulated to improve their ability to keep heat in the building. Cavity wall construction is the predominant wall type outside Dublin. **Cavity wall**[91]

See also: ***single leaf***

The Central Bank of Ireland does not have a direct role in housing, but has significant impact indirectly, for example through the imposition of ***mortgage lending rules*** on banks. The primary objectives of the Central Bank is set out in the Central Bank Reform Act 2010. Its strategic responsibilities include stability of the financial system; protection of consumers of financial services; regulation of financial institutions and enforcement actions; regulatory policy development; independent economic advice and high quality financial statistics; and recovery and resolution of financial institutions. **Central Bank of Ireland**

The Central Statistics Office (CSO) is Ireland's national statistical office, whose purpose is to impartially collect, analyse and make available statistics about Ireland's people, society and economy. Under the Statistics Act 1993 the mandate of the CSO is '[t]he collection, compilation, extraction and dissemination for statistical purposes of information relating to economic, social and general activities and conditions in the State.' The CSO is also responsible for coordinating the official statistics of other public authorities. The CSO carries out the five-yearly census in which a significant amount of housing data is gathered. This includes data on: **Central Statistics Office**

- ***Residential Property Price Index***
- ***Planning permissions***
- ***Domestic Building Energy Ratings***

---

[90] See: http://premierinsulations.com/nice-inch-hollow-blocks-faq/
[91] See: https://passivehouseplus.ie/cavity-wall

- Survey on Income and Living Conditions (SILC)
- *Household Budget Survey*
- *Household Finance and Consumption Survey*
- *New Dwelling Completions*

In late 2017, the CSO was tasked with examining the production of housing output statistics, which had been an issue of controversy for some years (see: ***data – housing output issues***). In June 2018, the CSO commenced producing revised housing output numbers using a refined version of the previous system of using connections to the electricity grid as the basic metric.

See also: ***data – housing output issues***

Certificate of Compliance on Completion (CCC)

For work coming within the scope of the ***Building Control (Amendment) Regulations*** 2014, a Certificate of Compliance on Completion must be submitted to the ***building control authority*** and be included on the statutory register (***Building Control Management System***) before the building may be opened, occupied or used. The Certificate must be signed by the ***assigned certifier*** and the builder. It certifies that the building or works have been carried out in accordance with the ***building regulations***. It is a matter for the building control authority to validate/invalidate the Certificate of Compliance on Completion in accordance with the building control regulations.[92]

See also: ***Fire Safety Certificate; Disability Access Certificate***

Charter of Fundamental Rights

The Charter of Fundamental Rights of the European Union contains the primary protection for housing rights in the EU. While there is no specific right to housing, article 34(3) on social security and social assistance provides: 'In order to combat social exclusion and poverty, the Union recognises and respects the right to social and housing assistance so as to ensure a decent existence for all those who lack sufficient resources, in accordance with the Rules laid down by Community law and national laws and practices.'

The Charter forms part of the Lisbon Treaty and has the same legal effect as the EU treaties. However, the Charter rights may only be invoked where there is an EU law dimension to the issue in question.

See also: ***housing rights approach to housing; European Convention on Human Rights; European Housing Rights Law***

Chartered Institute of Housing

The Chartered Institute of Housing (CIH) is the professional body for those who work in housing. CIH has 17,000 members worldwide, including about 150 in Ireland. According to its Royal Charter, 'the objects of the Institute

---

[92] See: https://www.localgov.ie/sites/default/files/20180305-faqs_national_building_control_project_v1.1.pdf

shall be to promote the science and art of housing, its standards and ideals and the training and education of those engaged in the Profession of Housing Practice'.[93]

See also: *Society of Chartered Surveyors Ireland; Royal Institute of the Architects of Ireland*

Choice-based letting (CBL) is a method that can be used for the allocation of *social housing*. Rather than waiting for a local authority to make an offer of support as is the case under the traditional direct letting model, CBL involves applicants having to respond to adverts and 'bid' for *dwellings* that they would like to live in. The ultimate allocation of support will still continue to be made in accordance with the priorities set down in an authority's allocation scheme. The majority of local authorities now use CBL as a way of allocating some of their social housing properties.[94]

> **Choice-based lettings**

CBL puts the onus on applicants to seek out suitable properties and 'encourages and rewards pro-active engagement, while vulnerable households are supported in the process'.[95] The perceived benefits of CBL can include greater customer choice, more transparency, increased engagement and interaction between housing providers and customers, better management of customers' expectations, tackling low demand properties/areas, better acceptance rates and more sustainable neighbourhoods. CBL also offers the potential for significant efficiencies, saving time and money.[96]

See also: *social housing waiting list*

Circle is a Tier 3 housing association (i.e. more than 300 units), founded in 2003, accommodating people in need of homes in the Greater Dublin Area, managing more than 1,700 homes. Circle works in partnership with *tenants* and statutory and community-based agencies to enable socially responsible, environmentally acceptable and sustainable communities in its developments. The development of communities is integral to ensuring that people feel involved in where they live and that their needs are reflected in their environment.

> **Circle Voluntary Housing Association**

See also: *approved housing bodies; Housing Alliance, The*

The Citizens' Information Board is the national agency responsible for supporting the provision of information, advice and advocacy on social services,

> **Citizens' Information Board**

---

[93] See: http://www.cih.org/resources/PDF/Governance/CIH%20Charter%20%20Byelaws%20-%2015%20July%202015.pdf
[94] See: http://rebuildingireland.ie/news/choice-based-lettings/
[95] Chartered Institute of Housing/Housing Agency (n.d.) *A Guide to Choice-Based Lettings*, available at: http://www.cih.org/resources/PDF/Republic%20of%20Ireland/A%20guide%20to%20choice-based%20lettings.pdf
[96] *Ibid.*

and for the provision of the ***Money Advice and Budgeting Service***. It supports the provision of information, advice and advocacy on a broad range of public and social services.

The Citizens' Information Board provides the Citizens' Information website (www.citizensinformation.ie), and supports the network of Citizens' Information Centres and the Citizens' Information Phone Service. Governed by the Social Welfare (Miscellaneous Provisions) Act 2008, the Citizens' Information Act 2007 and the Comhairle Act 2000, the Board comes under the remit of the Department of Employment Affairs and Social Protection.

The Citizens' Information Board is the most comprehensive source of housing information in Ireland.

Clawback   In housing, a clawback is a mechanism used by the providers of low-cost social or affordable housing to recoup any profit made if that house is subsequently sold. The clawback period is typically 20 years, with 100 per cent of any profit being recouped if the property is sold within the first ten years, and then a reducing percentage (90%, 80%, etc., per annum) thereafter until the twentieth year.

Clúid Housing   Clúid Housing is an independent, not-for-profit charity that provides high quality affordable rented housing for people on low incomes who cannot afford to pay market rents in the ***private rented sector*** or purchase their own home. Established in 1994, Clúid is now the largest ***approved housing body*** (AHB) in Ireland with a housing stock of 6,500 homes across the country (mid-2018). The majority of Clúid's housing is social housing for people registered on local authority ***social housing waiting lists***, but Clúid also provides ***sheltered housing*** for older people with over 700 households in this category. Clúid has a development programme that aims to deliver 2,500 new homes by 2021.

In 2018, Clúid and five other AHBs – ***Circle Voluntary Housing Association***, ***Co-operative Housing Ireland***, Oaklee Housing, ***Respond***, and ***Túath Housing*** – came together to form the ***Housing Alliance***. This collaboration of larger AHBs aims to develop improved practices and innovative solutions in relation to social housing and to promote the AHB sector as a professionally run, high quality provider of social and ***affordable*** housing.

See also: ***retirement home; local authority role in housing; social housing***

Code of Conduct on Mortgage Arrears (CCMA)   The Code of Conduct on Mortgage Arrears (CCMA), issued by the ***Central Bank of Ireland***, came into effect in 2013. The Code sets out how mortgage lenders must treat borrowers in or facing mortgage ***arrears***. This Code applies to the ***mortgage*** lending activities of all regulated entities, except ***credit unions***, operating in the state, including:

- Financial services providers authorised, registered or licensed by the Central Bank of Ireland; and
- Financial services providers authorised, registered or licensed in another EU or EEA member state and which have provided, or are providing, mortgage lending activities in the state.

The Code applies to the mortgage loan of a borrower which is secured by their primary residence. Lenders must apply the protections of the Code to borrowers in the following circumstances:

- Borrowers in arrears and in pre-arrears; and
- In the case of joint borrowers who notify the lender in writing that they have separated or divorced, the lender should treat each borrower as a single borrower under this Code (except to the extent that an action requires, as a matter of law, the agreement of both borrowers).[97]

In general, the CCMA requires lenders to wait eight months before taking legal action about mortgages in arrears. However, this requirement does not apply if a borrower is deliberately not cooperating with the lender. Regardless of how long it takes a lender to assess a case, and provided that the borrower is cooperating, three months' notice must be given before a lender can commence legal proceedings where either:

- The lender does not offer an alternative repayment arrangement for the mortgage.
- The borrower does not accept an alternative repayment arrangement offered to them.

This gives borrowers time to consider other options, such as voluntary surrender, voluntary sale or a ***personal insolvency arrangement.***

The CCMA puts certain responsibilities on lenders, who must:

- Ensure that communications with borrowers are presented in a clear and consumer-friendly manner and that the level of communications from the lender, or any third party acting on its behalf, is proportionate.
- Not make unnecessarily frequent communications.
- Ensure that communications with borrowers are not aggressive, intimidating or harassing.

---

[97] Central Bank of Ireland (2013) *Code of Conduct on Mortgage Arrears*, Central Bank of Ireland: Dublin

- Ensure that borrowers are given sufficient time to complete an action they have committed to before follow-up communication is attempted.
- Make an information booklet available to borrowers in arrears (or pre-arrears) including details on the **Mortgage Arrears Resolution Process (MARP)**, relevant contact points for arrears issues and details of websites with mortgage arrears information, such as the **Money Advice and Budgeting Service**.
- Provide a dedicated section on their website for borrowers who are in or facing financial difficulties.
- Wait at least eight months before applying to the courts to commence legal action for repossession of a property (this does not apply if the borrower is not cooperating with the lender).

In addition, lenders are not permitted to:

- Require a borrower to change from an existing tracker mortgage to another mortgage type as part of an alternative arrangement offered to the borrower in arrears or pre-arrears, unless none of the options that would allow the borrower to retain the tracker interest rate are appropriate and sustainable for the borrower's individual circumstances.[98]

Cohabitation

According to Census 2016, of the 1.22 million families in Ireland, 152,302 comprised cohabiting couples.[99]

Section 172(1) of the Civil Partnerships and Certain Rights and Obligations of Cohabitants Act 2010 sets out a definition: a cohabitant is one of two adults (whether of the same or opposite sex) who live together as a couple in an intimate and committed relationship and who are not related to each other within the prohibited degrees of relationship or married to each other or civil partners of each other.[100] Parties are deemed to be qualified cohabitants where they have lived together for at least five years, or for two years where they have a child together. Qualified cohabitants can be of the same or opposite sex.[101]

Provisions in the Family Home Protection Act 1976 and the Civil Partnership and Certain Rights and Obligations of Cohabitants Act 2010, whereby spouses must give written consent before selling the family home, do not apply to cohabiting couples, meaning that in effect one partner could lease or sell the house without the permission of the other.

---

[98] See: http://www.citizensinformation.ie/en/housing/owning_a_home/mortgage_arrears/consumer_protection_codes_and_mortgages.html#l6ce63
[99] CSO Census 2016
[100] See: http://www.irishstatutebook.ie/eli/2010/act/24/enacted/en/print
[101] See: http://familylaw.ucc.ie/relationships/cohabitation/

As cohabitants do not possess the same legal rights and obligations as married couples or civil partnerships, the Citizens' Information Board suggest that when thinking about buying a home with a partner (to cohabit), couples should consider how the property is to be owned. They advise considering the options of joint **tenancy** or **tenancy in common**:

- Joint tenancy means the whole property is owned by two people with the intention that, when one dies, the other person will automatically own all of the property. In situations where one person has paid for the property, the other person may not get 50 per cent of the proceeds if the house is sold.
- Tenancy in common means the property is owned in defined shares by two people. For example, 50/50, 75/25, 60/40, etc. Each person can leave their share of the property to whomever they wish. (They may leave their share to their partner for example, but they must make a will stating this fact.) If no will is made, the share becomes part of the estate of the deceased partner and the other partner does not have any automatic right to the share. Instead, the family (or even a separated spouse or civil partner) of the deceased person can claim this share.[102]

Combi boiler

A combi boiler is a combined domestic water heater and central heating boiler in one unit. No separate hot water cylinder is needed, and water is usually delivered at mains pressure (thereby negating the need for an extra pump).

Commencement Notice

Section 6(k) of the **Building Control** Acts 1990–2014 require the giving of notice to building control authorities. A Commencement Notice is a notification to a **building control authority** that a person intends to carry out either works or a material change of use to which the **building regulations** apply. The notice must be given to the authority not more than 28 days and not less than 14 days before the commencement of works or the change of use. Once validated by the building control authority, works must commence on site within the 28-day period.

If the works do not start within 28 days of the date of lodgement of the Commencement Notice, applicants must submit a new Commencement Notice prior to the commencement of any works taking place.

The Regulations provide for four Commencement Notice (CN) types:

I. Commencement Notice With Additional Compliance Documentation
II. Commencement Notice with Opt-Out Declaration [**S.I. 365**]
III. Commencement Notice Without Additional Documentation

---

[102] See: http://www.citizensinformation.ie/en/birth_family_relationships/cohabiting_couples/property_rights_and_unmarried_couples.html

IV. 7-Day Notice which includes for:
  a. *Fire Safety Certificate*
  b. Declaration

A 7-Day Notice is similar to a Commencement Notice and may be used for works which require a Fire Safety Certificate when the works need to start before the certificate is granted. It must be accompanied by a valid Fire Safety Certificate application and a statutory declaration. Owners of new single dwellings, on a single development unit, and domestic extensions may opt out of the requirements for statutory certification. Compliance with building regulations must still be achieved and building control procedures will still apply.

See also: *Building Control Management System (BCMS)*

Commission on the Private Rented Residential Sector

In June 1999, amid a time of rapidly rising rents and turbulence in the sector,[103] a commission was established by the then Minister for Housing and Urban Renewal to review the regulation of the sector, including:

- *Security of tenure*
- *Rent certainty*
- *A Landlord* and *Tenant* Code that balanced rights and responsibilities of landlords and tenants
- *Investment* in the private residential sector

Following the Commission's findings and report, the *Residential Tenancies Act 2004* provided for a modern system of residential landlord and tenant legislation. This included the establishment of the *Private Residential Tenancies Board* with responsibility for tenancy registration, dispute resolution, and research, information and policy advice. The Commission was chaired by Thomas A. Dunne of Dublin Institute of Technology.

See also: *private rented sector; rents; landlord; tenant; Rent Pressure Zone; Minister for Housing; Residential Tenancies Board*

Common areas

Common areas are defined in the *Multi-Unit Developments Act 2011* as including:

- The external walls, foundations and roofs and internal load-bearing walls
- The entrance halls, landings, lifts, lift shafts, staircases and passages
- The access roads, footpaths, kerbs, paved, planted and landscaped areas, and boundary walls

---

[103] O'Sullivan, E (2014) 'Bigger and Better', paper presented at the Future of Private Renting in Northern Ireland Conference, 6 November, Belfast

- Architectural and water features
- All ducts and conduits, other than those within and serving only one unit in the development
- Cisterns, tanks, sewers, drains, pipes, wires, central heating boilers, other than such items within and serving only one unit in the development
- Other areas that are from time to time provided for common use

See also: ***General Boundary Rule; boundaries; cadastre; owners' management company; managing agent; sinking fund; service charge***

A commune is a group of related or unrelated people living together in shared accommodation with shared responsibilities. There were 4,140 communal establishments in Ireland at Census 2016.[104]

> See also: ***housing stock; household; headship rate***

Commune

'Community' is a widely used term, especially in housing and planning, without having a universally agreed definition. The word derives from the Latin 'communitas' and 'referred to a quality of fellowship that embraced common interests and relations. In the medieval period it began to extend its application from a noun of quality to a concrete noun of place denoting a location that contains a "body of fellow townsmen".'[105]

Modern notions of community have both concrete and abstract meanings. Community can therefore be thought of as a group of people living in the same place or having a similar characteristic in common. Although this definition covers both location (same place) and those with interests in common who might not be in the same location (e.g. the online community), in housing terms it generally relates to locational proximity.

> See also: ***community land trust***

Community

Community land trusts (CLT) are non-profit, community-based organisations whose mission is to provide affordable housing in perpetuity.

The CLT concept is that the trust owns the land and rents it to occupiers who can then build housing on it. Since a homebuyer doesn't have to pay for the land, just the house, the purchase price is a lot cheaper.[106] The homeowner owns the house, but not the land on which it stands. In the classic community land trust model, membership is comprised of those who live in the leased housing (leaseholders); those who live in the targeted area (community members); and local representatives from government, funding agencies and the non-profit sector (public interest).[107]

Community land trust

---

[104] CSO Census 2016
[105] Garnett, D (2015) *The A–Z of Housing (Professional Keywords)*, Macmillan: London
[106] Kapila, L (2017) 'Might Dublin see its first community land trust?', *Dublin Inquirer*, 12 July
[107] *Ibid.*

The CLT model is gaining traction in the US and in the UK but has not yet appeared in any government or local authority publication in Ireland, although there is growing public interest.

See also: ***site value tax; land; speculation***

Commuter belt A commuter belt is the area surrounding a large city, from where people travel (commute) to work in the city nearby. The width of the commuter belt varies by city, but can range from 10 to 100 kms from the city centre.

See also: ***travel poverty; suburbs; suburbanisation***

Compulsory Purchase Order (CPO) A Compulsory Purchase Order (CPO) is a legal function that allows certain statutory bodies which need to take land or property to do so without the consent of the owner. The compulsory acquisition of land typically takes place to allow a public infrastructure project to go ahead for the common good.

There are several steps in the CPO process:

1. A statutory body decides to make a CPO.
2. Affected parties will be served with a notice and newspaper notices will be published stating that the Order is about to be put on public display and submitted to ***An Bord Pleanála*** for confirmation.
3. Objections can be made (valid objections are generally on planning or legal grounds only).
4. A public local enquiry is held at which affected parties can formally put their views forward (if no objections are made An Bord Pleanála can confirm, amend or reject the CPO without a public enquiry).
5. An Bord Pleanála either confirms, amends or rejects CPO and publishes details of the decisions in this regard.
6. After expiry of objection period, the CPO is operative.
7. The acquiring authority serves notice to treat on the affected parties and discussions commence regarding the level of compensation available.
8. The affected party lodges a claim for compensation. This can be made by the claimants' valuer.
9. On reaching agreement, compensation is paid, otherwise the matter may be referred by either party to the property arbitrator to assess compensation (see: ***arbitration***).
10. Acquisition is finalised, compensation paid.

In general, the assessment of compensation will fall under a number of headings of claim which can include the following:

- Value of land acquired
- Diminution in value of retained lands, if any

- Costs resulting from acquisition
- Disturbance
- Loss of profits or goodwill
- Loss or depreciation of stock in trade
- Professional fees necessary for acquisition

An agreement on compensation can often include an extensive list of accommodation works, i.e. fencing, walls, water supply, drainage, relocation of **septic tank**, double glazing, etc. It should be noted that the statutory authority has the right to enter and take possession of land before compensation is agreed and before money has been paid.[108]

A wide range of bodies have CPO powers, including Aer Rianta, Waterways Ireland, the Minister for Defence, Transport Infrastructure Ireland, ESB, Health Service Executive, Enterprise Ireland, Industrial Development Authority, Irish Water, **National Asset Management Agency** (or a NAMA group), An Post, Sport Ireland, CIE and Bord na Móna.

See also: **Constitution of Ireland (Article 40.3.2 and Article 43); Aquinas, Thomas; adverse possession; wayleave; easement; right of way**

Condominium

'Condominium' is primarily a North American term for a group of individually owned dwellings in the same complex, usually surrounded by jointly-owned **common areas**. In Ireland, this would be referred to as a multi-unit development.

See also: **Multi-Unit Developments Act 2011; owners' management company; service charge; sinking fund**

Consumer protection, building

Consumer protection is the protection of buyers of goods and services against low quality products and advertisements that deceive people.[109] Purchasers of new housing in Ireland who subsequently find serious **defects** have limited consumer protection compared to other sectors or industries.

The Joint Oireachtas Report *Safe As Houses?*,[110] outlined some of the consumer protection issues for house buyers under the current **Building Control (Amendment) Regulations** [BC(A)R]:

- Consumer protection issues such as legal actions being statute barred (in the main, six years from purchase rather than six years from date of discovery of defect), transferable warranties of quality (warranty is only valid

---

[108] Society of Chartered Surveyors Ireland (n.d.) *A Clear Guide to Compulsory Purchase Orders and Compensation*, SCSI: Dublin

[109] See: https://dictionary.cambridge.org/dictionary/english/consumer-protection

[110] Joint Committee on Housing, Planning and Local Government (2017) *Safe As Houses? A Report on Building Standards, Building Controls and Consumer Protection*, Government of Ireland: Dublin

for original owner), minimum mandatory terms for residential construction contracts, imbalance of information between sellers and buyers, and inadequate insurance cover remain unaddressed and ultimately inaccessible to purchasers of defective housing.

- Liability for defects once discovered is unclear and dispersed across multiple actors – **developer**, builder, designer, **assigned certifier**, sub-contracted certifier, planner, building control section – thus making legal remedy prohibitively complex and expensive.
- Liability for defects is disproportionately placed on certifiers rather than developer/builder.
- Lack of mandatory latent defects insurance on all new buildings and restrictive terms of existing insurance products.

By assigning liability to a certifier under BC(A)R, the impression is given that homeowners will have recourse if things go wrong. However, that recourse can only be activated through the courts – making the process expensive, unwieldy and uncertain. In addition, while certifiers are obliged to have public liability insurance, the nature of building work is that defects may not emerge for years, by which time the certifier may have ceased to practice (or gone out of business), meaning that their insurance will have lapsed, leaving the consumer with no realistic means of redress.[111]

According to Ní Fhloinn, the **Construction Industry Register of Ireland** (CIRI) legislation 'provides no remedies for consumers; it may be presented as part of a package of reforms, but those reforms do not address the most significant issues facing consumers. These include: poor legal remedies, no cost-effective access to dispute resolution procedures, and no mandatory defects insurance to cover the legal liability of insolvent builders.'[112]

See also: ***self-certification; defects; Pyrite Resolution Board***

Consumer Protection Code 2012   This Consumer Protection Code is for the treatment of personal debt other than mortgages (covered by the **Code of Conduct on Mortgage Arrears**) – credit cards, personal loans and investment borrowings for property (i.e. **buy-to-let** lending). The Code sets out how regulated entities must deal with and treat borrowers, and requires lenders to seek a resolution with the borrower that will help them deal with their debt problem.

Lenders are not permitted to initiate more than three unsolicited communications with the consumer, by whatever means, in a calendar month, other than correspondence required by the Code of Conduct on Mortgage Arrears or other regulatory requirements.

See also: ***Mortgage Arrears Resolution Process; arrears***

---

[111] See: https://passivehouseplus.ie/magazine/dispatches/out-of-control
[112] See: https://constituo.ie

Article 40 of the Constitution of Ireland concerns personal rights. Article 40.3.2 states:

> The State shall, in particular, by its laws protect as best it may from unjust attack and, in the case of injustice done, vindicate the life, person, good name, and property rights of every citizen.

Article 43 concerns private property. It states:

> 1 1° The State acknowledges that man, in virtue of his rational being, has the natural right, antecedent to positive law, to the private owner-ship of external goods.
>
>   2° The State accordingly guarantees to pass no law attempting to abolish the right of private ownership or the general right to transfer, bequeath, and inherit property.
>
> 2 1° The State recognises, however, that the exercise of the rights mentioned in the foregoing provisions of this Article ought, in civil society, to be regulated by the principles of social justice.
>
>   2° The State, accordingly, may as occasion requires delimit by law the exercise of the said rights with a view to reconciling their exercise with the exigencies of the common good.

See also: ***compulsory purchase order; housing rights approach to housing***

Constitution of Ireland (Article 40.3.2, Article 43)

The Construction Industry Federation (CIF) is the Irish construction industry's representative body. Services it provides include recruitment and training; legal and industrial relations consultation and advice; health and safety; marketing and industrial intelligence reports; engagement with gov-ernment, statutory and other industry bodies; and updates on issues affecting the construction industry.[113]
    See also: ***Construction Industry Register of Ireland; defects***

Construction Industry Federation

The Construction Industry Register of Ireland (CIRI) is a voluntary online register of competent builders, contractors, specialist sub-contractors and tradespersons who undertake to carry out construction works. Its objective is to be recognised as the primary online resource used by consumers in the public and private procurement of construction services.[114] The theory is that building quality will improve if only suitably qualified personnel from the CIRI register are used. There is a legislative proposal to make registra-tion with CIRI mandatory. However, it has been argued that locating the

Construction Industry Register of Ireland (CIRI)

---

[113] See: https://cif.ie/about/
[114] See: https://www.ciri.ie/register/

Construction Industry Register within the Construction Industry Federation 'is not independent and amounts to self-regulation'.[115]

There have been several other issues raised about the proposed mandatory nature of CIRI.[116] There are three main areas of concern.

1. ***Consumer protection***: Consumer protection in construction regulation requires good quality housing to be built, with accessible remedies for poor quality housing. The Construction Industry Register Ireland Bill provides no remedies for consumers including: poor legal remedies, no cost-effective access to dispute resolution procedures, and no mandatory defects insurance to cover the legal liability of insolvent builders, which could at least provide an 'after the event' pathway to a remedy for the homeowner.
2. Regulation: The Scheme will result in a private system to regulate builders, and a separate public system to regulate what they build. This will result in significant information gaps – for example, only the local building control authority will know of a registered CIRI member's actual record on compliance with the building regulations.
3. Conflicts of interest: The proposed system will act as a gateway to being able to work for large numbers of people, and would be a significant transfer of power from the state to a private entity. Independence cannot be ensured simply through the composition of the CIRI boards. The system will not be overseen by a regulator (as for gas and electrical contractors). There is no mention in the proposed legislation of the Freedom of Information Act, the Ethics in Public Office Act, or whether CIRI will be subject to the Ombudsman Acts. There are no requirements on any committee or board members of CIRI to disclose their own financial interests.

See also: ***data – housing output issues; Building Control Management System; defects; consumer protection***

Contracts   See: ***procurement***

Conveyancing   Conveyancing is the legal work involved in buying or selling a house and is usually undertaken by a solicitor.

See also: ***title; memorial; Registry of Deeds; Land Registry; ground rent***

---

[115] Joint Committee on Housing, Planning and Local Government (2017) *Safe As Houses? A Report on Building Standards, Building Controls and Consumer Protection*, Government of Ireland: Dublin
[116] The following points are taken from the submission to the Oireachtas Joint Committee on Housing, Planning and Local Government Pre–legislative scrutiny: General Scheme for Construction Industry Register Ireland Bill, by Dr Deirdre Ní Fhloinn, BL, October 2017

Housing cooperatives are a worldwide movement of self-help, mutually owned associations working to relieve housing need in their communities. The members of housing cooperatives are the people who use the services the cooperative provides. Members have the opportunity to become involved in the management of their cooperative and to vote on issues that are important to them. Housing cooperatives can be involved in the building, management and maintenance of houses and *apartments* across various forms of *tenure* (e.g. rental and ownership).   **Cooperative housing**

Cooperative housing in Ireland dates back to the 1950s. These were typically self-help, home ownership building cooperatives providing affordable homes for their members.

See also: ***Co-operative Housing Ireland; Ó Cualann Cohousing Alliance***

Since the 1980s, Co-operative Housing Ireland has worked with local cooperative housing societies around Ireland to help develop social rented cooperative homes. Since 1973, more than 3,500 cooperative *dwellings* for ownership have been developed and over 2,200 rented homes continue to be managed by local cooperative societies. Co-operative Housing Ireland is an *approved housing body* (AHB) and works closely with various stakeholders in the housing sector, including local authorities, government, aspiring homeowners, *tenants* and *developers*, to provide social rented and *home ownership* cooperative homes across the country.   **Co-operative Housing Ireland**

See also: ***cooperative housing; National Association of Building Cooperatives***

Under cost rental, the rent charged by the provider is no higher than the actual incurred cost of a stock of dwellings. Costs include capital costs in addition to the cost of maintenance and management of the development. Over time the real cost of debt for existing housing declines. In a cost rental system this is used to further support affordable housing.   **Cost rental**

Cost rental housing providers may be public, non-profit or private. Austria is a leading international example of how a cost rental housing sector is a critical component of an effective, affordable and stable housing system. Austria provides extensive, but modest, supply-side subsidies for housing, mainly in the form of low-cost finance, while favourable access to sites is provided in some areas. Cost rental housing in Ireland would need some form of supply-side subsidy to be viable.

A possible model for the Irish system could be that the rent to the tenant is agreed at a proportion of income (between 25 and 30 per cent, for example [see: *affordability*]). The acceptable cost rental rate is agreed between the housing provider and the state, and the difference between the cost rental and the rent received is subsidised in a form similar to the ***Payment and Availability Agreement*** used for ***social housing*** supply.[117]

Countries with an effective system of ***affordable housing*** rely significantly on cost rental and other mechanisms to secure permanent affordability. It is the overall system of land management, housing provision and secure rental that underpins affordability.[118]

See also: ***National Social and Economic Council***

Cottage

A cottage is a small, ***detached*** or ***semi-detached***, one-storey house, typically, but not always, in the countryside, where it may be the dwelling of a farmer or labourer. In urban areas, cottages were usually philanthropic endeavours built on large estates for workers, such as on the Pembroke Estate in Booterstown, or for mill or rail workers such as at CIÉ in Inchicore (built by Great and Southern Railways), or by the likes of the ***Dublin Artisan Dwellings Company***.

See also: ***mews; bungalow; semi-detached house; detached house; terraced house; micro-home; accessory dwelling unit***

Council housing

Council housing is permanent housing provided by local authorities for low-income households who would otherwise not be able to house themselves. Traditionally this was housing constructed by local authorities – or commissioned by them – for their own use. For properties leased by local authorities, see ***social housing***.

The ***National Oversight and Audit Commission*** provide a detailed breakdown of council housing stock as follows: council housing provision is delivered through the 31 local authorities who reported in 2015 that they were maintaining a housing stock of 130,603 dwellings and managing a total of 5,785 housing estates. The units comprise 106,127 houses, 23,447 flats, 770 demountable premises (non-fixed premises) and 259 other units.[119] 81 per cent of dwellings were houses. 40 per cent of units were built less than 20 years ago and a further 30 per cent of dwellings were aged between 20 and 40 years. Local authorities reported that their council housing units contained 10,355 units, or almost 8 per cent of all local authority housing, that were built specifically for older people. Authorities reported managing a total of 5,785 housing estates and that 112,811 council housing units are located in estates. (With the passage of time, the houses in many local authority estates become privately owned by virtue of successive ***tenant purchase*** schemes.) 55 per cent of all housing stock consisted of housing units with

---

[117] Cooperative Housing Ireland (2016) *Strategy for the Rented Sector*, available at: https://cooperativehousing.ie/rentalsectorstrategy/

[118] National Economic and Social Council (2018) *Urban Development Land, Housing and Infrastructure: Fixing Ireland's Broken System*, NESC: Dublin

[119] The figures do not include halting bays or other Traveller-specific accommodation

three bedrooms, 26 per cent had two bedrooms and over 10 per cent had one bedroom. There was a total of 5,768 single rural dwellings in the local authority housing stock, 54 per cent of which are located in just six county councils (Donegal, Kerry, Galway, Wexford, Mayo and Westmeath).[120] By 2018, this council housing stock figure had increased to 141,680 council houses.[121]

Hayden and Norris[122] report that, in total, local authorities have provided 365,350 council housing units since the nineteenth century, a figure that accounted for 22 per cent of total Irish housing stock in 2016. During the 1960s and 1970s, one-third of all house constructions were council dwellings. Two-thirds of all council housing stock has been disposed of by way of tenant purchase, making an important contribution to increasing *home ownership* but reducing significantly council homes available for rent. Between 1990 and 2016, 43 per cent of the 82,869 council houses built during that period were sold to tenants, in certain instances at up to 60 per cent discount on market value. Overall, Census 2016 revealed that 8.7 per cent of all households and 30.4 per cent of all renters in cities were accommodated in council housing.

The last three decades have seen a significant reduction in the traditional role of council housing as the primary source of accommodation for low-income renters however. In 1994, council housing tenants accounted for 73.2 per cent of the low-income renting households in receipt of government housing supports. By 2016, this had fallen to just 53 per cent. In part, this development reflects the decline in council housing output following the sharp contraction in the funding available to this sector after the economic crisis commenced in the late 2000s (public funding for new council housing fell by 94 per cent between 2008 and 2013). In addition, since the 1980s governments have relied increasingly on other sources of housing for low-income households. These include not-for-profit *approved housing bodies* (AHBs) and government subsidies for *private rented sector* housing such as *Rent Supplement* and *Housing Assistance Payment* (HAP).[123]

The 2018 report *The Future of Council Housing: An Analysis of the Financial Sustainability of Local Authority Provided Social Housing*,[124] analysed the system of council housing provision in Ireland and concluded that:

[120] National Oversight and Audit Commission (2017) *A Review of the Management and Maintenance of Local Authority Housing – Report No. 12*, NOAC: Dublin
[121] Kilkenny, P and O'Callaghan, D (2018) *Department of Public Expenditure and Reform – Spending Review 2018: Current and Capital Expenditure on Social Housing Delivery Mechanisms*, Department of Public Expenditure and Reform: Dublin
[122] Hayden, A and Norris, M (2018) *The Future of Council Housing: An Analysis of the Financial Sustainability of Local Authority Provided Social Housing*, Community Foundation
[123] *Ibid.*
[124] *Ibid.*

- More council housing is required, particularly in urban areas. The report indicates that council housing plays a critical role in housing low-income groups, particularly in urban areas where rents are high and housing supply limited, and subsidies for private rented housing such as Rent Supplement and HAP are difficult to operate. AHB social housing provision also plays a valuable role in housing low-income households but homelessness cannot be resolved successfully without higher rates of council housing output.

- Arrangements for funding the capital costs of council housing provision have effected an inefficient, boom–bust pattern of output. The report flagged strong concerns about the financial sustainability of the current model used to fund the capital costs of council housing provision. These costs are currently met by central government grants which cover the full costs of building or buying council housing 'up front' in a lump sum. This model is challenging for the Exchequer to afford, particularly when the public finances are under strain. As a result, council housing output has also been strongly 'pro cyclical' in recent decades – it has increased as the economy (and the housing market) has boomed and declined radically during periods of recession. This is inefficient from an economic perspective because investment in council housing reinforced rather than counterbalanced the building bust in the late 2000s. It achieves poor value for money because spending is concentrated at the peak of economic cycles when land and construction costs are likely to be higher while during recessions, when costs usually fall, funding for council housing provision also declines.

- The funding model requires the selling of council housing at a loss. Despite the severe shortage of council housing in many parts of the country, local authorities are obliged by central government to sell council housing to tenants at a discount of up to 60 per cent of market value. This study highlights significant dependence by local authorities on their income from sales to fund council housing management and maintenance – therefore they have a perverse incentive to sell council housing at a loss. The real costs of selling houses to tenants are also disguised because the market value of council housing is not recorded on local authorities' accounts and the proceeds of sales are recorded as revenue. This conveys the impression that sales actually generated a profit whereas in fact the sale price does not cover the cost of replacing these dwellings.

- Rents generate inadequate funding for council housing management and maintenance. The revenue costs of council housing management and maintenance are funded by rents which are determined on the basis of tenants' incomes. This model has significant equity and anti-poverty benefits, particularly in view of the low average incomes of tenants in this sector. However it is problematic from the point of view of the efficiency of the housing service because there is no guarantee that it will generate adequate revenue funding to manage and maintain dwellings. Indeed there is no relationship at all between rents and the costs of providing council housing.

- National housing policies for local housing problems. There was also a strong consensus among interviewees that there are significant regional differences between the needs of urban and rural authorities.

See also: ***succession of local authority house; policy, housing***

A covenant is a contract arising by a ***deed***. Covenants can be both positive and restrictive. In terms of ***land***, covenants tend to be mostly restrictive. A restrictive covenant is a promise by one person with another, for example, by a buyer of land with a seller, not to do certain things with the land, such as to build on it or use it as a shop or factory. It binds the land and not the buyer personally, and therefore 'runs with the land'. This means that the covenant continues even when the buyer sells the land on to another person. Restrictive covenants also continue to have effect even if they were made many years ago and appear to be obsolete.

Covenant[125]

See also: ***Registry of Deeds; memorial; Land Registry; conveyancing***

A credit servicing firm (CSF) is a company regulated in Ireland that manages portfolios acquired by '***vulture funds***' on their behalf, as typically these funds are not regulated to operate in Ireland. These CSFs manage the administration and servicing of loans, as well as engaging with debtors and seeking repossession of property where necessary. A mortgage holder whose debt has been bought by an international vulture fund will therefore deal locally with a CSF in Ireland. Since 2015, CSFs are bound by the ***Code of Conduct on Mortgage Arrears*** under the Consumer Protection (Regulation of Credit Servicing Firms) Act 2015.

Credit servicing firm

See also: ***Mortgage Arrears Resolution Process; mortgage; arrears***

Credit unions are financial cooperatives formed to facilitate members to save and lend to each other at fair and reasonable rates of interest. They are not-for-profit organisations with a volunteer ethos and community focus. Each credit union is governed by its members, each of whom has one vote. The membership elects individual members to the board of the credit union. Credit unions must meet the prudential requirements set by the ***Central***

Credit unions

---

[125] Society of Chartered Surveyors Ireland (n.d.) *Boundaries: Procedures for Boundary Identification, Demarcation and Dispute Resolution in Ireland*, second edition, Geomatics Guidance Note, SCSI: Dublin

Bank of Ireland in relation to reserves, minimum liquidity requirements, investments, lending and borrowing.

In 2017, as part of a pilot project, some credit unions were permitted to lend money to purchase residential property (***mortgages***). Most focused on providing mortgage lending for a number of specific purposes such as ***tenant purchase*** schemes, ***affordable housing schemes***, those trading up and first-time buyers.[126]

Criminal Law (Defence and the Dwelling) Act 2011

The Criminal Law (Defence of the Dwelling) Act 2011 came into force on 13 January 2013. The legislation clarifies the law concerning the defence of the home. Rural interest groups had been seeking clarity on the laws applying to self-protection in the home since a 2005 court case in which a Mayo farmer was found innocent of the murder of another person, who died when the farmer shot him while he was trespassing on his farm.[127]

The 2011 Act makes it clear that a person may use reasonable force to defend themselves in their home. It allows for the use of such force as is reasonable in the circumstances, to protect people in the dwelling from assault, to protect property, to prevent the commission of a crime, or to make a lawful arrest. The Act also extends the protections it contains to the curtilage of the dwelling; it explicitly provides that a person is not under an obligation to retreat from their home when subject to an intrusion in their home and provides that a person who uses reasonable force, as provided for in the Act, cannot be sued for damages by a burglar and will not be guilty of an offence.[128]

In the Act 'dwelling' includes—

(*a*) a building or structure (whether temporary or not) which is constructed or adapted for use as a dwelling and is being so used,

(*b*) a vehicle or vessel (whether mobile or not) which is constructed or adapted for use as a dwelling and is being so used, or

(*c*) a part of a dwelling;

'curtilage', in relation to a dwelling, means an area immediately surrounding or adjacent to the dwelling which is used in conjunction with the ***dwelling***, other than any part of that area that is a public place.

These provisions do not apply where a person uses force against a member of An Garda Síochána acting in the course of his or her duty.

See also: ***dwelling***

---

[126] Ryan, S (2018) 'Will 2018 be the year of the credit union mortgage?', *Irish Independent*, 20 January
[127] Cullen, P (2012) 'Law lets householders use reasonable force', *Irish Times*, 13 January
[128] See: http://www.justice.ie/en/JELR/Pages/PR12000003

The Irish economic model which prevailed between 1993 and 2007 (Celtic Tiger era) was widely heralded as a beacon of what the deep liberalisation of a small open economy might deliver. This Celtic Tiger era of economic expansion was split into two periods: the first period (1993–2002) characterised by export-led growth dominated by foreign direct investment, and the second period (2002–2007) involving a property boom mainly consisting of Irish developers capitalised by Irish banks who, in turn, were borrowing from European banks.

As the global crisis deepened, the Irish property **bubble** burst and the vast overexposure of Irish banks to toxic property loans became apparent. The collapse of the property and banking sectors led to a contraction in the wider economy, with the drying up of credit, markets and tax receipts, leading to a huge hole in the public purse; an extensive bank bailout, including the establishment of the **National Asset Management Agency** (NAMA) which acquired €74 billion of property debt from Irish banks; bank recapitalisation (Bank of Ireland) and nationalisation (Allied Irish Banks, Irish Nationwide Building Society, **Anglo Irish Bank**); massive state borrowing to service the bank bailout and the public sector spend; rising unemployment; and plummeting house prices. Given the perilous economic state, this ultimately led to the €85 billion International Monetary Fund–European Union bailout in November 2010.

See also: **neoliberalism in Ireland; economic growth and housing; land**

In the **Criminal Law (Defence of the Dwelling) Act 2011**, 'curtilage', in relation to a **dwelling**, means an area immediately surrounding or adjacent to the dwelling which is used in conjunction with the dwelling, other than any part of that area that is a public place.

In the **Planning and Development Act 2000**, curtilage, although not specifically defined, generally means the land and outbuildings immediately surrounding a structure which is currently or has been used for the purposes of the structure.

See also: **boundary; General Boundary Rule**

D

Daft.ie is a popular online search portal for rented properties and properties for sale. It was founded in 1997 by brothers Éamonn and Brian Fallon. It claims that nine out of every ten properties for sale in Ireland are advertised on Daft.ie; there are approximately 70,000 properties listed for sale or to

---

[129] Kitchin, R, O'Callaghn, C, Boyle, M and Gleeson, J (2012) 'Placing Neoliberalism: The Rise and Fall of Ireland's Celtic Tiger', *Environment and Planning A*, Vol. 44, No. 6, pp. 1302–1326

rent on the site at any one time; over 1,000 property searches per minute are carried out on the website and app; and it has 2.5 million unique users every month generating 228 million page impressions.[130] Daft.ie also produces quarterly research reports on **rent** and sales prices based on information from its website. It is important to note that this information is based on asking rents (i.e. the rent being sought); rents cited in the **Residential Tenancies Board**'s '**Rent Index**' are based on rents achieved and recorded in a lease.

DAFT is owned by Distilled SCH, which also owns Adverts.ie and DoneDeal.ie.

Data – housing output issues The issue of measuring housing output across private and public sectors has been a controversial topic.

On the private housing output front, experts had long asserted that the method used to measure new housing output was flawed. A new house was counted when it was connected to the electricity supply (ESB). However, there were several reasons why a new residential electricity connection did not mean that a new house had been completed, including for example electricity connections to farm buildings being classified as residential. There was also the issue of unfinished estates being completed and then being counted as new housing, despite the fact they may have been built some 5–10 years previously but never connected to the electricity grid. Houses vacant for two or more years must also get a new electricity connection, compounding the potential for error. Census 2016 confirmed the anomalies when only 8,800 new houses were added to the housing stock, despite over 51,000 new houses having been reported as 'completed', with **obsolescence** adding more confusion.

In the face of mounting evidence, officials and politicians continued to insist that this was the best method of counting that was available, that it had been used since the 1970s, and would continue to be used. It was also asserted that other metrics were used including the number of **planning permissions** for houses granted and **Commencement Notices**, neither of which are an accurate indicator of housing output. Indeed, between 2011 and 2017, 35 per cent (an annual average of over 4,000 units) of all residential planning permissions granted did not get built,[131] a figure consistent with the UK experience outside London, and typical in economies with high levels of land **speculation**.

Statutory indicators that were not referred to include the number of **Building Energy Rating** (BER) Certificates issued (a legal requirement for every new house since 2009) and the number of **Certificates of Compliance on Completion** recorded in the **Building Control Management System**

---

[130] See: https://www.daft.ie/about/
[131] According to data provided by Mel Reynolds (architect) in private correspondence

(BCMS). Together with the number of *S.I. 9 opt-outs* for one-off houses, these two – again, legal requirements – should have provided an accurate indicator of housing output. The figures from both the number of BERs and the BCMS indicated that housing output was less than was being claimed. Similarly, the level of *stamp duty* transactions recorded for new houses was lower than the number of new houses it was claimed were built (even allowing for a time delay).

In 2017, the task of counting new housing output was then handed to the *Central Statistics Office*. In June 2018, the CSO reported its conclusions on the number of new houses that had been built in 2017. It used a variety of measures, but is still based primarily on connections to the ESB grid, although better filtered to remove non-residential connections and reconnections (after two years' vacancy). The CSO found that contrary to the official claims of 19,184 new houses having been completed in 2017, just 14,435 had actually been built (including local authority house builds), a lesser figure by some 25 per cent. (According to the CSO, 57 per cent of the difference is accounted for by reconnections to the ESB grid, 23 per cent by dwellings in previously built, unfinished housing developments being connected to the grid, and 20 per cent by non-dwelling connections being counted as houses.) In 2016, official figures reported 14,932 houses as having been built; the CSO revised this to 9,907. In 2015, the official figure was 12,666; the CSO revised this to 7,219. From 2011 to 2017, official figures had over-reported the number of new houses being built by some 30,000 units.

The issue raised a number of important issues, especially the importance of having an independent body assess politically important data such as house-building metrics. In addition, the discrepancy between both the number of houses recorded on the BCMS (8,500)[132] and as having a BER (9,416),[133] with the CSO figure (14,435) suggests a significant level of non-compliance with what are both legal requirements. The next logical step for housing output data would be to assess net additional stock, i.e. new housing output less housing *obsolescence*.

With social housing output, there are serious issues with the way in which social housing output is presented via *Rebuilding Ireland* progress reports, with a skewing of the presentation of the figures towards maximising purported progress towards targets. In particular, the lack of specific data per quarter, instead publishing a cumulative total of houses completed since the start of *Rebuilding Ireland* (July 2016) adds unnecessary confusion and suggests greater progress than the reality. The lack of granular detail in terms

---

[132] From private correspondence with Laura Flanelly, CSO
[133] See: https://www.cso.ie/en/releasesandpublications/ep/p-ndc/newdwellingcompletionsq12018/ber/

of what gets counted as a newly built house does not help with a lack of clarity over whether *voids* brought back into use and certain acquisitions are being counted as 'newly built' housing by local authorities.

For example, in the *Rebuilding Ireland* progress report for Q1 2018,[134] the total 'site finish' number is reported as 2,964. However, this is a cumulative number from Q4 2016. What the report does not highlight is the number of houses built by local authorities in Q1 at 100 and the number of houses acquired by *turnkey* agreements at 66, or 40 per cent of all activity. Just nine local authorities built houses in Q1 2018, and just six local authorities acquired houses via turnkey agreements. It could also be argued that turnkey house is an 'acquisition' and should not be counted as a new build.

A similar picture presents itself for the total social housing output in 2017 when the official figures presented alluded to more than 2,500 social houses as having been built in 2017. However, a breakdown of this number shows of that of the 1,014 social houses that it was claimed were local authority built houses (later reduced to 780), 761 were provided through *approved housing bodies*, and 522 from *Part V* agreements. Further analysis shows that of the official figure of 780 'local authority' built houses in 2017, in fact, only 394 of these were built by councils, the remaining 384 having been acquired from developers under turnkey agreements.

The practice whereby local authority new build output figures consolidates all local authority new unit construction activity, including units delivered by traditional construction, *rapid build*, turnkey, regeneration and Part V units[135] needs more granular detail given that the cost of delivering a house under each of the headings can vary considerably.

Counting the numbers of homeless people has proved to be the most controversial, particularly when officials instructed certain local authorities to remove some homeless people from the official count, thus helping to moderate or reduce the overall total. Apparently, a number of local authorities had 'erroneously categorised individuals and families living in local authority owned or leased housing stock, including some instances of people renting in the private sector but in receipt of social housing supports, as being in emergency accommodation'.[136] The explanation of the miscategorisation 'was down to local authorities using *Section 10 funding* (which is used for homeless accommodation) to keep families in homes or social housing stock.

---

[134] See: http://rebuildingireland.ie/news/minister-murphy-publishes-social-housing-construction-status-report-q1-2018/

[135] Kilkenny, P and O'Callaghan, D (2018) *Department of Public Expenditure and Reform – Spending Review 2018: Current and Capital Expenditure on Social Housing Delivery Mechanisms*, Department of Public Expenditure and Reform: Dublin

[136] Fitzgerald, C and Murray, S (2018) 'Hundreds more people removed from homeless figures over "categorisation issue"', *TheJournal.ie*, 30 May, available at: https://www.thejournal.ie/miscategorisation-homeless-figures-4045054-May2018/

The local authorities had then categorised these families as homeless, when in fact they were in private rental accommodation or social housing, and therefore should not be called homeless.'[137]

According to Eurostat, the statistical office of the EU, high quality data is important for a couple of reasons: 'Democratic societies do not function properly without a solid basis of reliable and objective statistics. On one hand, decision-makers at EU level, in Member States, in local government and in business need statistics to make those decisions. On the other hand, the public and media need statistics for an accurate picture of contemporary society and to evaluate the performance of politicians and others.'[138]

In 2019, the CSO reported 18,072 houses were built in 2018.

See also: ***Rebuilding Ireland; homelessness; speculation; Rebuilding Ireland Home Loan***

Davitt, Michael Michael Davitt (1846–1906) was a founder of the Irish Land League (1879), which organised resistance to absentee landlordism and sought to relieve the poverty of tenant farmers by securing fixity of tenure, fair rent, and free sale of the tenant's interest,[139] commonly known as the ***Three Fs***. It is interesting that none of the Three Fs advocated for ownership, but for better conditions of tenancy.

See also: ***Duffy, Charles Gavan; Tenant Right League; Land Commission; Dublin Tenants' Association***

Daylight standards Sunlight, daylight and overshadowing assessment for proposed new developments is normally carried out with particular regard to potential impacts on the living spaces and private open spaces of residential properties, but assessments may also extend to include amenity spaces such as public spaces, parks, playing fields and playgrounds between non-domestic buildings and in streetscapes.

The Building Research Establishment's *Site Layout Planning for Daylight and Sunlight: A Guide to Good Practice*, second edition (2011) by P.J. Littlefair, is a non-statutory guide and sets out guidelines that are most commonly used in Ireland and the UK to assess the impacts of development on daylight and sunlight.

Deasy's Act 1860 The Landlord and Tenant Law Amendment (Ireland) Act 1860 amended the Landlord and Tenant (Ireland) Act 1826. It is named after the Attorney-General of Ireland at that time and promotor of the legislation, Rickard Deasy. The importance of the Act in housing terms is that it made contract law the basis for tenancies rather than the ancient feudal notion of tenure.

---

[137] *Ibid.*
[138] See: https://ec.europa.eu/eurostat/about/overview
[139] See: https://www.britannica.com/biography/Michael-Davitt

This meant that all leases over twelve months had to be in writing in order to be enforceable, effectively making a contract between the two parties. Section 4 of the Act states:

> Every lease or contract with respect to lands whereby the relation of landlord and tenant is intended to be created for any freehold estate or interest, or for any definite period of time not being from year to year or any lesser period, shall be by deed executed, or note in writing signed by the landlord or his agent thereunto lawfully authorized in writing.

Kenna notes that: 'the notion of a free contract between landlords and tenants within the contemporary laissez faire political ideology of the time was completely inappropriate in Ireland where the bargaining positions were not so much unequal but completely dependent.'[140]

See also: *lease; tenant; landlord*

Debt (household)

Household debt is the combined debt of all people in a *household*. It therefore includes personal debt such as credit cards or car loans (consumer debt) as well as *mortgage* debt.

See also: *Household Budget Survey*

Debt-to-income ratio

The debt-to-income ratio is defined as the ratio of *households*' debt arising from loans, recorded at the end of a calendar year, to the gross disposable income earned by households in the course of that year.

The debt-to-income ratio constitutes a measure of the indebtedness of households, in relation to their ability to pay back their debt's principal sum. The debt-to-income ratio is calculated on the basis of gross debt – that is without taking account of any assets held by households.[141]

Deed[142]

A deed is a writing on paper, vellum or parchment, whereby an interest, right or property passes, or an obligation binding on some person is created, or which is affirmance of some act whereby an interest, right or property has passed. Section 32 of the Registration of Deeds and Title Act 2006 sets out a list of documents that come within the definition of 'deed' including a conveyance, an assent, a *Vesting Certificate* and any other documents as may be prescribed.

See also: *boundary; General Boundary Rule; conveyancing*

---

[140] Kenna, P (2011) *Housing Law, Rights and Policy*, Clarus Press: Dublin, p.18
[141] See: http://ec.europa.eu/eurostat/statistics-explained/index.php/Glossary:Household_debt-to-income_ratio
[142] See: https://www.prai.ie/registry-of-deeds-services/

See: *boundary*

To be in default of a mortgage means to have missed one or more mortgage repayments.

See also: *arrears; Mortgage Arrears Resolution Process; Code of Conduct on Mortgage Arrears*

The Introduction of the Joint Committee on Housing, Planning and Local Government report *Safe as Houses? A Report on Building Standards, Building Controls and Consumer Protection*[143] (2017) says: 'Poor design, shoddy workmanship and improper products resulted in badly built homes in breach of building and fire safety standards (from about 1996 to 2008). Greed, dishonesty and incompetence left many homeowners and council tenants with poor quality homes and hefty repair bills. All of this was made possible by a weak regime of regulation and compliance in which *self-certification* and limited independent inspections were the order of the day. We do not know the full extent of this legacy.'

Notable extant defects from house-building in this era include:

- Mica – mica muscovite is a mineral that can weaken concrete
- Pyrite – a mineral found in stone material used in foundations, typically causing swelling
- Water ingress/leaks
- Poor ventilation/indoor air quality – regulations still permit a hole in the wall coved by a grille as 'natural' or 'background' adequate ventilation despite the fact that there is little evidence that this is an adequate solution[144]
- Condensation/mould – mould, damp and condensation problems are usually associated with ventilation issues
- Sub-standard building materials (construction products)
- *Radon* protection (lack of)
- Drainage (including *septic tanks*, ground water contamination, also surface water in estates, etc.)
- Floodplain – numerous housing estates were permitted to be developed on known floodplains (e.g. in Donegal, Meath, Longford)
- Inefficient/incorrectly installed heating and plumbing systems, chimneys and flues
- Electrical safety problems
- Structural stability problems

---

[143] Joint Committee on Housing, Planning and Local Government (2017) *Safe As Houses? A Report on Building Standards, Building Controls and Consumer Protection*, Government of Ireland: Dublin
[144] Hearne, J (2017) 'New build homes face emerging crisis', *Passive House Plus*, 6 April

- Fire safety – defects include absence of smoke seals, blocked outlets to smoke vents, and inadequate smoke ventilation. See for examples Longboat Quay, **Priory Hall**, Carrickmines Green, **Millfield Manor**
- Poor sound insulation/noise

See also: **Pyrite Resolution Board; latent defects insurance; airtightness; nZEB; passive house; self-certification, house-building; consumer protection**

Density, housing Housing density is usually measured in one of three ways:

- Number of 'bed spaces' or individuals per unit hectare (UPH)
- Quantity of floor area (in square metres) per unit land
- Number of dwellings per unit land

In an Irish context, density in housing development typically refers to the number of houses or units built on a given plot. There are three main categories: low density, typically 8–12 units per hectare (UPH); medium, typically 20–45 UPH; and high density, 45+ UPH. Density in Dublin outer suburbs is about 27 UPH; inner suburbs such as Ranelagh and Rathmines are about 45 UPH; Georgian Dublin is about 165 UPH.

Advantages of high density include:[145] more economic provision of infrastructure and services; higher likelihood of viability of local shops, facilities and amenities; social integration and diversity; better quality public transport; reduced car dependency and congestion; increased energy efficiency; reduced land consumption; and more sustainable urban neighbourhoods. The disadvantages of high density include:[146] buildings out of character with local context; urban cramming; overcrowded living conditions; loss of privacy and amenity; less landscaped open space; impact on local property values; reduced quality of life.

See also: **plot ratio; apartment design standards; rural housing**

Density, population **Population** density measures the number of persons occupying a geographical area in proportion to the size of that area. According to Census 2016, the population density of the state has increased to 70 persons per km² in 2016, up from 67 persons in 2011 and 62 persons per km² recorded in 2006. The average population density in urban areas was 2,008 persons per km², compared to 27 persons per km² in rural areas. The more densely populated areas are predominantly located within the Greater Dublin Area, or GDA,

---

[145] Yeang, LD, Alan Baxter and Associates, and studioREAL (2013) *The Urban Design Compendium*, third edition, English Partnerships: London

[146] CABE and Corporation of London (2004) *Better Neighbourhoods: Making Higher Densities Work*, CABE: London

(i.e. Dublin City, Fingal, South Dublin, Dún Laoghaire–Rathdown, Meath, Kildare and Wicklow).

The UK has a comparable population density of 273 persons per km²,[147] with Scotland having a population density of 67 persons per km²;[148] Wales 148 persons per km²; England 426 persons per km²; and Northern Ireland 133 persons per km². Other countries vary between high density (the Netherlands at 505 persons per km²; Bangladesh at 1,252 persons per km²) and low density (Australia at 3.1 persons per km²; Russia at 8.7 persons per km²).[149]

See also: *plot ratio; height; household size*

Department of Housing, Planning and Local Government

The Department of Housing, Planning and Local Government has a long history as a government department. It was created as the Department of Local Government at the first meeting of Dáil Éireann in 1919. Its headquarters are in the Custom House, Dublin 1. Both the title of the department and some of its functions have changed over the decades.

The department has been known as:

- Department of Local Government (1919)
- Department of Local Government and Public Health (1924)
- Department of the Environment (1977)
- Department of the Environment and Local Government (1977)
- Department of the Environment, Heritage and Local Government (2003)
- Department of the Environment, Community and Local Government (2011)
- Department of Housing, Planning, Community and Local Government (2016)
- Department of Housing, Planning and Local Government (2017)

The department is responsible for, among other matters:

- Housing
- The Radiological Protection Institute of Ireland
- Local authorities and related services
- The supervision of elections including general and presidential elections, and electronic voting arrangements
- Met Éireann, the weather forecasting service

---

[147] See: https://data.worldbank.org/indicator/EN.POP.DNST
[148] National Records of Scotland (2018) *Population Density, 2011*, National Records of Scotland: Edinburgh
[149] Rae, A (2018) 'Think your country is crowded? These maps reveal the truth about population density across Europe', *The Conversation*, 23 January, available at: https://theconversation.com/think-your-country-is-crowded-these-maps-reveal-the-truth-about-population-density-across-europe-90345

See also: *Minister for Housing; politically exposed person*

Deposit (booking)

A booking deposit in the house-buying process is a sum of money as part-payment in the purchasing process. The deposit does not guarantee that the house will not be sold to someone else, but is usually taken in good faith that the property will be sold to the prospective purchaser. The amount of the deposit varies – it can be a specific amount such as €5,000, or a small percentage of the offer that has been made.[150]

The legal process to buy the property may only start when the estate agent receives a deposit. This deposit is refundable up to the signing of the contract for sale which binds the parties to the completion of the sale. If a purchaser withdraws from the purchase after this contract has been signed, they may lose their deposit.[151]

See also: *gazumping; gazunder; Property Services Regulatory Authority; conveyancing*

Deposit (rent)

A deposit (sometimes known as a 'security deposit') is a sum of money that is paid by a *tenant* to the *landlord* usually before a *tenancy* commences or on the date of commencement of the tenancy. This deposit is held by the landlord and is returned at the end of the tenancy to the tenant, once no rent arrears, bills, taxes or charges are due or damage beyond normal wear and tear has occurred. The deposit is considered the lawful property of the tenant until the landlord establishes a right to it.

Surprisingly, there is no definition of deposit and no legal guidelines as to how much of a deposit a landlord may request in the *Residential Tenancies Act 2004*. This means that landlords can effectively charge what they want, although the *Residential Tenancies Board* (RTB) recommends that a deposit equal to no more than one month's rent to be paid. It should be agreed that the tenancy has begun once the deposit is paid and the keys handed over. If a deposit is exchanged but the tenancy does not begin for a number of days and a problem occurs then, as a tenancy has not begun yet, it is outside the jurisdiction of the RTB and thus its dispute resolution services.

The deposit should be agreed and a signed and dated receipt provided to both the landlord and tenant. It is recommended that a tenant only pays a deposit when they are happy with the property and the terms and conditions of the letting and are clear on everyone's rights and responsibilities. A tenant should avoid paying a deposit in cash and always get a receipt.

The deposit should be returned once the tenancy ends and the tenancy agreement has been honoured. The deposit does not have to be returned to

---

[150] See: https://www.ccpc.ie/consumers/housing/buying-home-step-by-step-guide/
[151] See: http://www.citizensinformation.ie/en/housing/owning_a_home/buying_a_home/steps_involved_buying_a_home.html

the tenant on the day they leave the accommodation; however the landlord must return the deposit promptly. Time should be allowed for an inspection at the end of a tenancy, and for any repairs/cleaning to be carried out.

The landlord can establish a right to keep the deposit in the following certain circumstances:

- Rent arrears: if at the end of the tenancy there is rent outstanding the landlord may retain part or all of the deposit to cover the rent arrears.
- Damage: deductions may be made or the deposit retained in full if there has been damage above normal wear and tear to the property. Examples of these damages could be:
  - A broken window
  - Holes in the wall
  - Leaving litter or personal items in the property
  - Leaving the property in an unhygienic or unsafe condition
  - Not returning the property in a clean manner
  - Items broken or missing from the inventory
  - Outstanding utility bills and other charges
- If the tenant owes money for utility bills, such as gas or electricity, and the utility bill is in the landlord's name, the landlord may withhold part or all of the deposit to cover these costs. The tenant should always retain a copy of the bills to ensure that payment is applicable to what is being owed.
- If a tenant provides insufficient notice of their termination of the tenancy, or they terminate a *fixed term tenancy* before the end of the agreed term[152]

Issues around the return of deposits have consistently been one of the main causes of disputes between landlords and tenants in dispute resolution.

See also: *deposit protection scheme (rent); notice of termination; private rented sector*

Deposit protection scheme (rent)

A deposit protection scheme is where the deposits of *tenants* are held not by the *landlord*, as is currently the case in Ireland, but by an independent body and returned to the tenant within a specific timeframe subject to the agreement of both parties.

There are two broad categories of deposit protection scheme. The most common of these is a custodial (security) based scheme while less common is an insurance scheme option. Custodial schemes are evident in Australia (New South Wales and Queensland), New Zealand and the UK (England and Scotland).

---

[152] See: https://onestopshop.rtb.ie/beginning-a-tenancy/deposits/

The main difference between custodial and insurance schemes is the manner in which the deposit is secured. In the insurance scheme, the landlord pays a fee to the scheme operator in order to protect the deposit. In the custodial option, the deposit is transferred to the scheme where it is ring-fenced in accordance with client money protection regulations and is pooled to earn interest income. This income is used to cover the costs of operating the scheme. There are schemes that are operated publicly while others are competitively tendered to the private sector by national governments. In the UK all deposit protection schemes are privately managed on behalf of the state. In countries like New Zealand and Australia, deposit protection schemes are operated by public bodies.[153]

The *Residential Tenancies (Amendment) Act of 2015* contains a proposal to establish a deposit protection scheme where landlords would lodge deposits with the *Residential Tenancies Board* (RTB) at the same time as they are registering the tenancy. The interest on these deposits would fund the operation of the scheme. To date, it has not been enacted.

See: *deposit (rent); tenure; private rented sector*

Derelict Sites Act 1990 The Derelict Sites Act came into effect on 27 June 1990. A derelict site is any land that 'detracts, or is likely to detract, to a material degree from the amenity, character or appearance of land in the neighbourhood of the land in question because of:

• Structures which are in a ruinous, derelict or dangerous condition; or
• The neglected, unsightly or objectionable condition of the land or of structures on it; or
• The presence, deposit or collection of litter, rubbish, debris or waste.'

The 1990 Act provides a range of enforcement mechanisms to local authorities to tackle derelict sites. The major powers contained in the Act are the following:

• Informal action (S.10)
• Notice of intention to enter on the Derelict Sites Register (S.8(2))
• Entry on the Derelict Sites Register (S.8(2)) with resultant imposition of a levy equating to 3 per cent of market value of the derelict site. Unpaid levies attract interest of 1.25 per cent per month.

---

[153] Indecon (2012) *Indecon's Assessment of the Feasibility of a Tenancy Deposit Protection Scheme in Ireland*, Indecon review submitted to the Department of the Environment, Community and Local Government/Housing Agency and the PRTB, available at: https://onestopshop.rtb.ie/images/uploads/forms/indecons-assessment-of-the-feasibility-of-a-tenancy-deposit-protection-scheme-in-ireland.pdf

- Service of a notice requiring specified works to be carried out (S.11)
- Compulsory acquisition of a derelict site (S.14 and S.17)

The Act provided that one year after its commencement all local authorities shall compile and maintain a register of all derelict sites within their area. It also places a duty on every owner and occupier of land, including statutory bodies and state authorities, to take all reasonable steps to ensure that the land does not become or continue to be a derelict site.

See also: ***Vacant Sites Register and Levy***

The design certifier is responsible for the preparation of the drawings, specification and particulars for the design of the building, and ensures that ancillary certificates are obtained for any other members of the design team.[154]   **Design certifier**

See also: ***assigned certifier; Building Control (Amendment) Regulations; Building Control Management System; Certificate of Compliance on Completion; Commencement Notice; building regulations***

A detached house is a single, standalone dwelling. The ***Central Statistics Office*** categorises ***one-off*** houses as detached. As at Census 2016, detached houses account for 715,133 dwellings (c.40%), while 28 per cent of households reside in ***semi-detached*** houses.[155]   **Detached house**

See also: ***bedsit; maisonette; pied à terre; dwelling; terraced house; condominium; apartment; garden flat; duplex; mews; townhouse***

Determination Orders are issued by the ***Residential Tenancies Board*** (RTB) following adjudication and tribunal hearings. A Determination Order gives the outcome of a case and sets out both the terms to be complied with and timescale for compliance. The compliance period runs from the date of issue of the Determination Order, which will be stated in the cover letter accompanying the order. If a Determination Order has not been complied with within the required timeframe, the RTB can be requested to enforce it. Under the RTB's Enforcement Policy, decisions on whether or not to pursue legal enforcement are made on a case-by-case basis, taking into account the Board's own limited resources, the cost of taking legal proceedings and the likely success of achieving a favourable outcome.   **Determination Order**

Some reasons given as to why Determination Orders are not enforced include the other party resides outside the jurisdiction or the RTB is unable to obtain contact details for either party.

Should the RTB decide not to proceed with enforcement then, under the Act, enforcement of the order can be sought through the courts. This will

---

[154] See John Duffy Design Group at: https://www.jddg.ie/design-certifier-assigned-certifier/
[155] See: https://www.cso.ie/en/releasesandpublications/ep/p-cp1hii/cp1hii/od/

involve getting legal representation, which can be a costly process and therefore will not always be a viable option.

Developer

A developer of property is a person (or company) whose job involves buying and selling *land* and buildings and arranging for new buildings to be built.[156] The range of people who can be classified as a developer is broad and it should be noted that not all developers are engaged in *development* for profit (e.g. hospitals, *approved housing bodies*, churches and so on).

Development projects include a variety of stakeholders with an interest in the outcome of the project (government, community, lenders, users), as well as many participants who make the project possible from inception of the idea to construction (architects, marketing consultants, land planners, contractors). In the development process the developer manages these various interests and inputs in order to meet their objectives and make sure development potential is realised. Traditional developers represent the private interests present in the process; the goals of the private sector participants are to minimise risk while maximising their personal or institutional objectives, which are primarily monetary in nature. Non-profit developers or public entities interested in real estate development usually use other criteria for measuring the success of a project.[157]

See also: *residual value; valuation; investment; land; yield*

Development (property)

The classic definition of property development is 'the continual reconfiguration of the built environment to meet society's needs'.[158] The aim of the development process is the creation of a building, which can either be rented by future unknown users or sold in the real estate market.

In Ireland, the Revenue Commissioners regard land as being developed when:[159]

- A new building is constructed
- An existing building is extended, altered or reconstructed
- An existing building is demolished
- Work which adapts the land for materially altered use is carried out. Work which is not designed to make a material alteration in the use to which land is put is not development. Therefore, no account is taken of fencing, land drainage, laying of roads for agricultural purposes and so on.

---

[156] See: https://dictionary.cambridge.org/dictionary/english/property-developer

[157] Woods, E (2012) 'Economies of Reuse', MSc Architecture thesis, University of Cincinnati

[158] Berens, G, Haney, R and Miles, ME (1996) *Real Estate Development: Principles and Process*, Urban Land Institute: Washington DC

[159] See: https://www.revenue.ie/en/vat/vat-on-property-and-construction/vat-and-the-supply-of-property/what-does-developed-mean.aspx

In relation to development:

- Maintenance and repair work does not constitute development.
- The fact that *planning permission* had been obtained for development does not, of itself, constitute development for VAT purposes.
- Where a supply of property takes place on foot of a *Compulsory Purchase Order*, Revenue will not, in general, consider the supply to be taxable solely by virtue of development work carried out by the acquiring body under its statutory powers, after the notice to treat has issued.

See also: *developer; yield; land; speculation*

Development contributions (sometimes referred to as a '*development levy*') are payments from a developer to a *planning authority*. A planning authority may, when granting a permission, include conditions for requiring the payment of a contribution in respect of public infrastructure and facilities benefiting development in the area of the planning authority and that is provided, or that it is intended will be provided, by or on behalf of a local authority (regardless of other sources of funding for the infrastructure and facilities). It is up to each individual council to determine the rate applicable to the scheme, and it may make more than one scheme for different parts of its area. The rate is normally divided into different rates for industrial/commercial development and residential development. South Dublin County Council applies the following rates:

Development contribution scheme

- Residential development – €90.42 per square metre
- Industrial/commercial development – €79.73 per square metre

Local authorities are also permitted to establish supplementary development contribution schemes for different areas under their control or for specific projects (e.g. the Luas Cross City project was subject to a supplementary development contribution scheme to capture a portion of its catchment area's enhanced property values).

See also: *planning gain; site value tax; Development Contribution Rebate Scheme*

The Development Contribution Rebate Scheme was launched in 2015. In it, builders and *developers* could apply for a refund of development contributions if they were building more than 50 units and selling them for less than €300,000 in Dublin and €250,000 in Cork. Developers could apply for a full refund if they sold *affordable* units in 2016 or 2017, meaning rebates of, on

Development Contribution Rebate Scheme

average, €500,000 were available.[160] The scheme terminated in 2017, and as of the mid-2018 no payments have been made under the scheme.

See also: ***development contribution scheme***

Development control

Development control is the process that regulates the ***development*** and use of ***land***. This includes the construction of new buildings, the extension of existing ones and the change of use of buildings or land to another use. Land-owners wishing to develop are typically required to apply to a local authority (depending on the proposal) for permission prior to commencing any development work (see: ***planning permission***). Such development control – regulating and managing what is built where, and when – allows local authorities to manage land across a large area. It allows authorities to balance competing needs – such as allocating land for farming, while accommodating the growth of cities and towns – and to protect areas with particular values.[161] Development is mostly controlled by planning and development legislation.

See also: ***unauthorised development; development plan; Commencement Notice***

Development lag

In property, a ***development*** lag is the delay between recognising that a demand exists (e.g. for housing) and the delivery of the product to satisfy the demand. The construction of houses can take between one and two years depending on specific circumstances of the ***developer*** and the land; depending on when construction starts, in this time the ***property cycle*** may have moved from one phase to another, leading to a satiation of demand and potential oversupply of housing when finally completed.

See also: ***unfinished estates; economic growth and housing; rapid build housing – Poppintree***

Development land

Development land is ***land*** with the potential for property ***development*** (e.g. housing). It can be a cleared, ***brownfield*** or ***greenfield*** site, or the site may need to be redeveloped by removing all, or substantially all, of the existing buildings and constructing new buildings.[162]

See also: ***residual value; speculation; developer; infill site***

Development levy

See: ***development contribution scheme***

[160] RTÉ (2018) 'No money paid out in State house building scheme', *RTÉ News*, 16 April
[161] See: http://www.townplanning.gov.fj/index.php/planning/aspects-of-planning/development-control
[162] Royal Institution of Chartered Surveyors (2008) *Value of Development Land*, first edition, RICS: London
[163] See: https://www.housing.gov.ie/sites/default/files/migrated-files/en/Publications/Development andHousing/Planning/NationalSpatialStrategy/FileDownLoad%2C1589%2Cen.pdf

The development plan is the main public statement of planning policies for the local community. A new plan must be made every six years. Development plans show a local authority's land use, amenity and ***development*** objectives for the sole or primary use of particular areas (e.g. residential, commercial, industrial, agricultural: see ***zoning***), for road improvements, for development and renewal of obsolete areas, and for preserving, improving and extending amenities. The plan consists of a written statement of objectives and a map or series of maps. The local authority, in making decisions on planning applications, must consider the provisions of the plan and try to secure its objectives.

Development plan[163]

All planning applications are measured against the development plan to assess their conformity with the plan's objectives and development permitted must normally be in accordance with the plan. The ***planning authority*** is obliged to secure the objectives in its development plan. While an individual planning application may not comply with the objectives of the development plan, it might still be in line with the proper planning and development of the area. The planning authority may then decide to permit it as a material contravention of the plan, following public consultation. In this case the planning authority must publish notice of its intentions in a locally circulating newspaper.

Development plans must provide objectives for:

- Zoning
- Infrastructure provision
- Conservation and protection of the environment
- Social, community and cultural requirements
- Preservation of character of landscape
- Protection of structures
- Preservation of Architectural Conservation Areas
- Development and renewal of areas in need of regeneration
- Accommodation for Travellers, use of particular areas for that purpose
- Control of new establishments having regard to the Major Accidents Directive
- Provision and facilitation of services
- Protection of linguistic and cultural heritage

The development plan process is set out in sections 9–17 inclusive of the ***Planning and Development Act 2000***.

See also: ***planning permission; development control; unauthorised development; Architectural Conservation Area; protected structures; Record of Protected Structures; unauthorised development; retention planning permission***

Differential rents Local authority rents are based on a system called 'differential rents'. This means that the amount of rent paid depends on the amount of total household income:

- If the household income is low, the rent payment will reflect this and will be low.
- If the household income increases so will the rent payment.
- The income of all household members is considered and rent calculations are adjusted accordingly.
- If the household income or the income of anyone in the household changes, tenants must inform the local authority and rent will be adjusted upwards or downwards in accordance to the change.[164]

Each local authority operates its own rent scheme with their own individual features. The rules around assessing income for determining rent are in the ***Household Means Policy***.

The system of differential rents which progressively pegs rents to the incomes of tenants gradually spread nationwide between the 1930s and 1960s. As Norris describes,[165] in an effort to make rents affordable, the municipality of Cork decoupled its tenants' rents from the cost of housing provision in the 1930s and instead linked them to their incomes. Campaigning from tenants' associations meant that this system of 'differential rents' spread nationwide and was made mandatory for local authorities in the ***Housing Act 1966***. The result was a decline in rental income for councils, and increasing difficulty in financing social house-building.

This differential rents system has encouraged better-off tenants to purchase their council houses, as the rents paid by higher earning households often exceeded the costs of servicing mortgages on houses bought from councils under highly favourable purchase terms.[166]

See also: ***cost rental; National Association of Tenants' Organisations***

'Digs' 'Digs' is a form of temporary lodging. To live in 'digs' means to rent a room in a house, with or without breakfast. Digs is a late-nineteenth-century word, 'short for diggings, used in the same sense, probably referring to the land where a farmer digs, i.e. works and, by extension, lives.'[167]

See also: ***B&B; Rent-a-Room Scheme; bedsit; boarding house***

---

[164] See: https://www.housingagency.ie/housing-information/what-is-social-housing/renting-from-my-local-authority.aspx
[165] Norris, M (2017) *Property, Family and the Irish Welfare State*, Palgrave Macmillan: London
[166] Fahey, T and Norris, M (2011) 'From Asset Based Welfare to Welfare Housing? The Changing Function of Social Housing in Ireland', UCD policy paper
[167] See: https://en.oxforddictionaries.com/definition/digs

Direct provision is a means of accommodating asylum seekers directly while **Direct provision** their claims for refugee status are being processed rather than through full cash payments. Direct provision commenced on 10 April 2000, from which time asylum seekers have received full board accommodation and, as of 2019, personal allowances of €38.80 per adult and €29.80 per child per week. Asylum seekers get accommodation on a full-board basis. The cost of all meals, heat, light, laundry, tv, household maintenance, etc. are paid directly by the state. Reception and Integration Agency (RIA) staff are not present in direct provision centres but from time to time RIA staff visit the centres to ensure that asylum seekers' needs are being met and to ensure that they have access to all relevant services. These visits include at least two unannounced inspections per year, along with regular clinics conducted by RIA staff for residents.[168]

There are approximately 4,500 asylum seekers living in 32 direct provision centres across Ireland, including approximately 1,500 children. Seven of the centres are state-owned but the majority of the centres are run on a for-profit basis by private contractors.

As of 2018, the top five countries of origin applications for declaration as a refugee were: Syria, Georgia, Albania, Zimbabwe and Nigeria.[169]

A Disability Access Certificate is a certificate granted by a **building control** **Disability Access** **authority** which certifies compliance of the design of certain works (e.g. new **Certificate** buildings except **dwelling** houses), some extensions to, and some material alterations to buildings (except dwelling houses) with the requirements of part M of the **Building Control (Amendment) Regulations** (see: **technical guidance documents**). A Disability Access Certificate is required in respect of the following works to buildings other than dwellings (but including **apartment** buildings), in so far as the requirements of part M apply and which commence or take place on or after 1 January 2010. Where a **Fire Safety Certificate** is required for any works, a Disability Access Certificate is also required. Although a Disability Access Certificate is not required for domestic dwellings, as per part M of the **Building Regulations**, all new houses must be designed to provide access for the disabled.

A Disability Access Certificate is not required prior to submitting a **Commencement Notice**. However, a Disability Access Certificate is required for non-domestic works which require a Fire Safety Certificate. A building cannot be opened, operated or occupied unless a Disability Access Certificate has been granted on the building.

---

[168] See: http://www.ria.gov.ie/en/RIA/Pages/Direct_Provision_FAQs
[169] Reception and Integration Agency (2018) *Monthly Report, June*, Department of Justice and Equality: Dublin

See also: ***Fire Safety Certificate; Fire Safety Notice***

Disabled access   See: ***Access and use (houses)***

Discrimination[170] It is unlawful to discriminate against anyone on nine specified grounds (gender; civil status; family status; sexual orientation; religion; age (over 16); race; and membership of the Traveller community). In addition, since 2016 providers of accommodation services are prohibited from discriminating against someone on the 'housing assistance ground', i.e. on the grounds that they are in receipt of:

- ***Rent Supplement***
- ***Housing Assistance Payments***
- Other social welfare payments

The housing assistance ground protects anyone who has applied for and is eligible to receive such payments and applies both to existing tenants and to those who are looking for accommodation. Discrimination on the housing assistance ground, or on any of the nine grounds, may also take the form of landlords or letting agents:

- Refusing to let someone look at the property
- Refusing to ***rent*** the property to you
- Refusing to accept Rent Supplement or Housing Assistance Payments
- Refusing to complete the necessary forms to enable the tenant to receive Rent Supplement or Housing Assistance Payments
- Including discriminatory terms or conditions in leases or other tenancy agreements, whether written down or spoken
- Refusing to renew a ***lease*** or other ***tenancy*** agreement
- Ending a lease or other tenancy agreement
- Withdrawing services related to property or making it very hard for a tenant to get these services

It is unlawful to publish or display an advertisement that indicates an intention to discriminate on any of the discriminatory grounds, including the housing assistance ground. For example, advertisements that contain any of the following phrases may indicate an intention to discriminate on the housing assistance ground:

- 'Rent Allowance/Housing Assistance Payments not accepted'

---

[170] See: https://www.ihrec.ie/your-rights/i-have-an-issue-with-a-service/i-have-an-issue-about-accommodation/

- 'Professionals only'
- 'Would suit professionals'
- 'Work/professional references required'

These are exemptions. Some of these exemptions apply to all the main grounds covered by the Equal Status Acts 2000–2015 (ESA), while others are more specific.

Anyone can be treated differently in relation to:

- A person's home: If the accommodation is in a private home, the lodger is not covered by the ESA. For example, if the homeowner found that having a lodger was disrupting their family life, they could ask the lodger to leave.
- Accommodation for a particular kind of person: For example, the law allows some accommodation to be reserved for particular people, such as older people or homeless people.
- Wills and gifts: The person making the will or gift can choose who benefits.

Other specific exemptions:

- Gender in relation to shared accommodation: This applies where privacy is an issue. For example, it is not against the law to have a dormitory just for women in a youth hostel.
- Housing authorities can treat people differently in relation to:
  - Family size
  - Family status
  - Civil status
  - Disability
  - Age
  - Membership of the Traveller community

In addition, while providers of accommodation services are prohibited from discriminating on the grounds that a person is in receipt of Rent Supplement, Housing Assistance Payment, or social welfare payments ('the housing assistance ground'), the person providing accommodation can require that the Rent Supplement is paid directly to them.

In June 2018, the Irish Human Rights and Equality Commission (IHREC) published a peer-reviewed report, *Discrimination and Inequality in*

Housing in Ireland,[171] which examined housing discrimination and inequality across the nine equality groups. The main findings of the report were:

- Gender: females are more likely than males to experience environmental deprivation but are less likely to be homeless. Lone parents, a group which is overwhelmingly female, are disadvantaged on all measures.
- Age: age is associated with all the housing dimensions considered. People under 30 years are particularly disadvantaged.
- Nationality/race/ethnicity: Non-EU nationals are found to be at greater risk of overcrowding compared to others on the same income and with the same characteristics.
- Family status: lone parents are a particularly disadvantaged group. Their situation regarding homelessness is particularly striking: 60 per cent of homeless family units (defined as either a couple with or without children or a single parent with children) are lone mother families.
- Disability: people with a disability emerge to be among the most disadvantaged groups. They experience high risks of discrimination and housing and environmental deprivation, and are particularly over-represented among the homeless population.
- Travellers: members of the Traveller community are the most at risk of being homeless – while they represent less than 1 per cent of the Irish population they make up 9 per cent of the homeless population.
- Recipients of government housing payments: Rent Supplement claimants emerge as more likely to experience housing deprivation and overcrowding.
- Housing tenure: Young people, non-Irish nationals and those of Black ethnicity are highly concentrated in the private rented sector, while those with a disability and lone parents are over-represented in local authority housing.

  Local authority renters were four times more likely to report discrimination in accessing housing than homeowners; and private renters were 4.6 times as likely to report discrimination as homeowners, net of equality group membership, education and employment status. Those in local authority housing are twice as likely as owner-occupiers to report housing deprivation, environmental deprivation and overcrowding compared to owner-occupiers. Private renters are also more likely to experience housing deprivation than owner-occupiers.
- Socioeconomic status: the results show that people with lower socioeconomic backgrounds, i.e. low-educated and unemployed individuals, are

---

[171] Grotti, R, Russell, H, Fahey, E and Maître, B (2018) *Discrimination and Inequality in Housing in Ireland*, IHREC: Dublin

more likely to experience discrimination in access to housing. Unsurprisingly, socioeconomic status, proxied by household income, is also strongly associated with housing deprivation, environmental deprivation and overcrowding.

See also: ***direct provision; Traveller housing***

A type of heating system in which heat is piped from a large central heating system (such as a boiler) to multiple units (such as houses or ***apartments***), rather than each unit having its own separate heat source. Often financed via energy service companies (ESCos), district heating systems tend to become less viable in very energy efficient buildings, given that the low space heating demand means smaller bills payable to the ESCos.
    See also: ***nZEB; passive house; Y-value; U-value; thermal bridge***

District heating[172]

To 'downsize' means to move from larger to smaller accommodation (also known as 'trading down'). Households downsizing make up about 7 per cent of the housing market. Research has found that the typical trade-down buyer wants a two-bedroom apartment with study or second living space.[173] Downsizing is considering something that retired people do as their families have grown and left and their need for space has reduced. Although the mortgage on the house for sale may be paid off, there may still be a need for a ***bridging loan*** to allow the downsizing household to purchase the smaller property whilst awaiting the sale of their own house.
    See also: ***residential care; sheltered accommodation; trade down***

Downsize

Dry lining (sometimes referred to as drywalling) is a system for cladding the internal faces of buildings, such as walls and ceilings. Plasterboard is attached to the internal faces, creating a smooth surface that finishes such as paint can be applied to directly; a 'wet' plaster finish is not required. Dry lining requires less technical expertise than traditional plastering (a 'wet' trade), hence the term 'dry' lining.

Dry lining insulation[174]

Dual aspect means that windows are on two or more walls facing in different directions. In many ***apartment*** blocks this is achieved by having the units run from the front to the back of the building with windows on both sides. It can also be achieved in corner units.
    Dual-aspect apartments, as well as maximising the availability of sunlight, also provide for cross ventilation. The amount of sunlight reaching an

Dual aspect

---

[172] See: https://passivehouseplus.ie/glossary
[173] Hynes, L (2016) 'Focus on downsizing: When small is beautiful', *Irish Independent*, 3 April
[174] See: https://www.designingbuildings.co.uk/wiki/Dry_lining

apartment significantly affects the amenity of the occupants. The minimum number of dual aspect apartments that may be provided in any single apartment scheme is 33 per cent in more central and accessible urban locations, where it is necessary to ensure good street frontage and subject to high quality design. Otherwise, it is an objective that there should generally be a minimum of 50 per cent dual aspect apartments in a single scheme.[175]

See also: ***apartment design standards; quality of life; daylight standards***

Dublin Artisan Dwellings Company[176]

The Dublin Artisans Dwellings Company was a semi-philanthropic private enterprise established in June 1876 to provide quality housing for the city's working classes, and to make a profit while doing so. The company's earliest developments were blocks of one- or two-roomed flats but it quickly concluded that flats, though cheaper to build, were less popular and therefore less profitable than individual houses. Most of the Company's schemes consisted of terraces of single-storey cottages and two-storey houses laid out in groups of parallel streets, a template readily followed by Dublin's municipal authorities and hence one that came to characterise whole areas of the city well beyond the boundaries of the company's activities. To control costs and speed of construction, a small number of common house designs was used across the company's schemes.

Between 1879 and 1933, the company built 3,600 dwellings in over thirty major schemes across Dublin city, in Dún Laoghaire and Bray, most of which survive in use to this day.

See also: ***Iveagh Trust***

Dublin Civic Trust

Dublin Civic Trust is an independent charitable organisation that works to identify, preserve and create awareness about Dublin's architectural heritage. It is an educational trust that promotes best practice repair and conservation of historic buildings and streetscapes, involving identifying and recording the city's built heritage, developing policy and skills training, and undertaking targeted acquisition and refurbishment of historic buildings as engaging demonstration projects. Dublin Civic Trust was founded in 1992.

See also: ***An Taisce; Irish Georgian Society; Record of Protected Structures***

Dublin Housing Supply Coordination Task Force

Construction 2020 committed to the establishment of a Housing Supply Coordination Task Force for Dublin. The task force was established in June 2014 and comprises the Department of Housing, Planning and Local

---

[175] Department of Housing, Planning and Local Government (2018) *Sustainable Urban Housing: Design Standards for New Apartments – Guidelines for Planning Authorities*, Government of Ireland: Dublin
[176] See: https://iarc.ie/homes-for-workers-a-house-and-home-blog/

Government, the four Dublin local authorities (Dublin City, Fingal, South Dublin and Dún Laoghaire–Rathdown), the **National Asset Management Agency** (NAMA) and other agencies.

The focus of the task force is to address supply-related issues to the delivery of housing units in the Dublin region. The groups are working together to identify housing developments that have planning permission and that are capable of delivering housing to the market. This remit includes monitoring relevant housing data on the supply of viable and market-ready approved developments.[177]

See also: **data – housing output issues; policy, housing**

Dublin Region Homeless Executive The Dublin Region Homeless Executive (DRHE) is provided by Dublin City Council as the lead statutory local authority in the response to **homelessness** in Dublin and adopts a shared service approach across South Dublin County Council, Fingal County Council and Dún Laoghaire–Rathdown County Council. DRHE established the **Pathway Accommodation and Support System** (PASS), which provides 'real-time' information in terms of homeless presentation and bed occupancy across the Dublin region. DRHE provides the placement service for all persons in emergency accommodation and publishes the homeless figures. DRHE is responsible for providing support and services to the Dublin Joint Homelessness Consultative Forum and the Statutory Management Group.

See also: **homelessness; Housing First; Inner City Helping Homeless; rough sleeping**

Dublin Simon Community Dublin Simon Community was founded by a group of Trinity and UCD students in 1969. In addition to a soup run, which still goes out 365 nights of the year, Dublin Simon Community provides many services which aim to help those who are **rough sleeping** on the streets, people who are in their own accommodation but at risk of homelessness, and those who are at any of the stages in between. There are now Simon Communities across the country, providing both medium- and high-support housing projects for people who are homeless and unable to live independently. Dublin Simon also provides independent housing for individuals, couples and families.

See also: **homelessness**

Dublin Tenants' Association The Dublin Tenants' Association (DTA) was established in 2014 in response to the crisis in the **private rented sector**. It is a tenant-led organisation that provides peer support and public education on tenants' rights and advocates

---

[177] See: https://www.housing.gov.ie/housing/construction-2020-strategy/dublin-housing-supply-task-force/housing-supply-coordination-task

for policy and political change. The association believes that the private rental sector, and especially tenants, have been ignored within Irish policy-making, particularly with regard to *security of tenure*, *rent certainty* and the standard of housing. The DTA aims to galvanise tenants to advocate for themselves at a local and national level. In recent years the DTA has participated in the consultation process around the National Rental Strategy, taken part in the trade union-led Secure Rents campaign and organised a number of successful social media campaigns and protests. It is also a member of the stakeholder committee of the *Residential Tenancies Board*. The DTA is part of a new wave of grassroots tenant organising evident in Europe in recent years, including Scotland's Living Rent, the London Renters' Union and the Tenants' Unions of Barcelona and Madrid.

See also: *National Association of Tenants' Organisations; differential rent*

Duffy, Charles Gavan Charles Gavan Duffy (1816–1903) was the founder of the *Tenant Right League* in 1849 with Frederick Lucas and others, which sought the '*Three Fs*' (Fair Rent, Fixity of Tenure, and Free Sale).

See also: *Davitt, Michael; Land Commission*

Duplex A duplex is a set of rooms for living that are divided on two floors of a building. In an Irish context, a duplex is normally to be found on the top two floors of a three-storey block where the bottom floor is a *garden flat* or *apartment*.

See also: *detached house, semi-detached house; bedsit; maisonette; pied à terre; dwelling; terraced house; condominium; mews*

Dwelling In the *Residential Tenancies Act 2004* 'dwelling' means a property let for *rent* or valuable consideration as a self-contained residential unit and includes any building or part of a building used as a dwelling and any out-office, yard, garden or other land appurtenant to it or usually enjoyed with it and, where the context so admits, includes a property available for letting but excludes a structure that is not permanently attached to the ground and a vessel and a vehicle (whether mobile or not).

See also: *detached house; apartment; semi-detached house; bedsit; maisonette; pied à terre; duplex; terraced house; Criminal Law (Defence and the Dwelling) Act 2011; curtilage*

E

An easement is a right which an owner/occupier of land has, by virtue of his ownership of his land, over the land of a neighbour, e.g. *right of way*, light, support and water. Examples of easements include rights of way, *wayleaves*, pipes and cables, right to light, and shooting and fishing rights. Easements cannot exist in gross, i.e. they cannot exist as a benefit not connected to land.

Easement[178]

See also: ***adverse possession; compulsory purchase order; Aquinas, Thomas***

The construction and use of decent housing affects economic development through its impact on employment, savings, investment and labour productivity. Since 1945, housing experts have articulated three views about the role of housing for economic development. In the early post-war decades most writers viewed housing as a social expenditure and a drag on growth. A minority argued that housing could be an important adjunct to specific development projects, usually in isolated locations. Since the 1970s, housing has increasingly come to be seen as a contributor to growth, not only because house-building is a major employer with large multiplier effects but also because housing is seen to have social consequences with diverse economic effects.[179]

Economic growth and housing

Housing contributes to **GDP** in two basic ways: through private residential investment, including construction, and consumption spending on housing services. The first is through residential fixed investment (RFI). RFI is effectively the measure of the home building, ***multi-family*** development, and remodelling contributions to GDP. It includes construction of new single-family and multi-family structures, residential remodelling, production of manufactured homes and agents' fees. The second impact of housing on GDP is the measure of housing services, which includes gross ***rents*** (including utilities) paid by renters, and owners' ***imputed rent*** (an estimate of how much it would cost to rent owner-occupied units) and utility payments. The inclusion of owners' imputed rent is necessary from a national income accounting approach because without this measure an increase in home ownership would result in a decline of GDP.[180]

Conversely, a lack of housing supply also impacts economic growth in:

- Labour markets – the lack of availability, inflexibility and unaffordability of housing prevents ***labour mobility***.

---

[178] See: https://www.prai.ie/registration-of-easements-and-profits-a-prendre-acquired-by-prescription-under-section-49a/

[179] Harris, R and Arku, G (2006) 'Housing and Economic Development: The Evolution of an Idea since 1945', *Habitat International*, Vol. 30, No. 4, pp. 1007–1017

[180] See: http://eyeonhousing.org/2018/04/housing-share-of-gdp/

- *Infrastructure* – high demand for housing leads to a strain on infrastructure, while areas of low demand often have poor infrastructure (for example, *transport*), again impacting upon labour mobility.
- Business – areas of high demand and spiralling prices make wages and rent higher for businesses. Poor housing options make it difficult to attract people with the right skills.[181]

See also: *crisis (housing); wealth*

Eircode

Eircode is Ireland's postcode system, which launched in July 2015. Eircode is a unique postcode for every postal address in the country, unlike other countries where postcodes define clusters or groups of addresses. In the alphanumeric seven-digit code (e.g. A65 B2CD), the first three entries (the routing key) relate to a postal district with the last four randomly-generated letters and numbers identifying a unique postal address point location within that area.

See also: *GeoDirectory; cadastre*

Emergency accommodation

Emergency accommodation for homeless people is usually provided in dedicated hostels or *bed and breakfasts* on a night-to-night basis.

See also: *homelessness; Pathway Accommodation and Support System (PASS)*

En suite

Typically used in housing to refer to a bathroom immediately adjoining a bedroom.

Energy Efficiency – Retrofitting Measure

Under the *Social Housing Investment Programme* (SHIP), local authorities are allocated capital funding each year in respect of a range of measures to improve the standard and overall quality of their *social housing* stock. The programme includes a retrofitting measure aimed at improving the energy efficiency of older *apartments* and houses by reducing heat loss through the fabric of the building and the installation of high-efficiency condensing boilers.

Funding of up to €15,000 per *dwelling* may be provided, depending on the energy improvement achieved, for necessary works such as attic and wall insulation, the replacement of windows and external doors, and the fitting of energy-efficient condensing boilers. In addition, €3,000 per unit may be provided for non-energy related improvement works to the dwelling.[182]

---

[181] Glossop, C (2008) 'Housing and Economic Development: Moving Forward Together', *Centre for Cities*, November, available at: http://www.centreforcities.org/wp-content/uploads/2014/09/08-11-06-Housing-and-economic-development.pdf

[182] See: https://www.housing.gov.ie/housing/social-housing/other/improvements-existing-dwellings

See also: ***Sustainable Energy Authority of Ireland; nZEB; passive house; Department of Housing, Planning and Local Government***

Planning enforcement ensures that decisions taken at the planning stage are actually carried out in the finished building or development according to the grant of ***planning permission***. It deals with those who flout the law by ignoring, or not complying with, the planning process. Local authorities are generally responsible for granting individual planning permissions and for operating an enforcement regime to deal with ***unauthorised development***. The term 'planning authorities' is often used when local authorities take decisions in relation to planning cases.[183]

(margin: Enforcement, planning)

Planning enforcement will not investigate matters which lie outside its scope, including civil matters such as: encroachment; private ***rights of way***; trespass; civil ***boundary*** disputes; noise nuisance (unless the noise breaches a condition attached to a planning permission); structural damage to private property resulting from construction works; matters related to 'private drains'; outlets associated with boilers and other gas appliances (unless same has a material visual impact from a public area); and other types of private nuisance.[184]

See also: ***retention planning permission***

See: '***Homeless HAP***'

(margin: Enhanced HAP)

In 2018, the ***Department of Housing, Planning and Local Government*** expanded the terms of its existing leasing initiative to:

(margin: Enhanced Leasing Initiative)

- Ramp-up the scale of delivery under the leasing delivery mechanism
- Target newly built or yet to be built houses and ***apartments*** for leasing to minimise competition with existing housing stock
- Target property ***developers*** and investors who are in a position to deliver housing at a reasonable scale
- Provide for ***lease*** terms that require the property owner to provide day-to-day maintenance of the properties under a schedule of management services. The expanded scope of requirements to be performed by the property owner is compensated by an increase in the proportion of the market rent payable under the enhanced lease to a maximum of 95 per cent.

---

[183] See: https://www.housing.gov.ie/sites/default/files/migrated-files/en/Publications/DevelopmentandHousing/Planning/FileDownLoad%2C31565%2Cen.pdf

[184] See: http://www.corkcity.ie/services/strategicplanningeconomicdevelopment/enforcementof planningregulations/

The main terms of the lease under this scheme are: lease is from a 'proposer' to a local authority (LA); for a term of 25 years; at 95 per cent market rent; with three-yearly index-linked *rent reviews*; and the owner can sell subject to the lease with consent of the local authority. The following are the property requirements of the scheme: new or old but not occupied for previous twelve months; minimum of twenty properties within LA area; owner satisfied *Part V* planning requirements; conditional agreement for lease.

The owner will be the landlord to the local authority and be responsible for structural repair; insurance; property taxes; *service charge*; management services; interior repair and maintenance; unilateral rent suspension and penalties for breach; and commercial termination provisions.

As a tenant to the owner, and landlord to council tenants, the local authority will supply and manage occupier; absorb any vacancy losses; carry administrative letting overheads; and collect differential rent from occupier.

See also: *social housing initiatives*

Environmental Impact Assessment/ Environmental Impact Assessment Report

Environmental Impact Assessment (EIA) is the process of examining the anticipated environmental effects of a proposed project – from consideration of environmental aspects at design stage, through consultation and preparation of an Environmental Impact Assessment Report (EIAR), to evaluation of the EIAR by a competent authority, and the subsequent decision as to whether the project should be permitted to proceed, encompassing the public response to that decision.

The assessment must be carried out in certain cases. For example, motorways, large-scale developments in agriculture, the food industry, chemical industry, infrastructure and urban developments all require an EIA.

The EIA process has several stages:

1. Screening (assessing whether an EIA is required)
2. Scoping (engaging with all relevant authorities and NGOs)
3. Consultation (with the design team and stakeholders)
4. Report preparation (Environmental Impact Statement (EIS))
5. Review
6. Monitoring
7. Editing

The EIS will include a full description of the proposed development, set out the planning policy background and report on the findings of the overall process. The EIS will also include details of the interaction of all the separate studies. Specifically, the EIA process includes a detailed analysis of the receiving environment in terms of human beings/socioeconomic, hydrology and hydrogeology, geology, flora and fauna, air, climate and noise, landscape and visual impact, cultural heritage and material assets (such as traffic and retail impact).[185]

See also: ***Strategic Environmental Assessment; An Bord Pleanála; Environmental Protection Agency***

The Environmental Protection Agency (EPA) is responsible for protecting and improving the environment as a valuable asset for the people of Ireland. Its primary responsibilities include:

- Environmental licensing
- Enforcement of environmental law
- Environmental planning, education and guidance
- Monitoring, analysing and reporting on the environment
- Regulating Ireland's greenhouse gas emissions
- Environmental research development
- ***Strategic Environmental Assessment***
- Waste management
- Radiological protection

See also: ***Environmental Impact Assessment***

The equity in a property is the ***value*** of property less the amount of outstanding debt (i.e. mortgage).

See also: ***equity release; equity sharing***

See: ***tenure neutrality***

See also: ***home ownership; private rented sector***

This is where money is borrowed secured by the amount of ***equity*** in a property.

See also: ***equity sharing***

See: ***shared ownership***

There are two meanings of relevance to estate. In the first meaning, an estate is a large area of land or property often owned by one person, family or body and typically with a large house at its centre. The second meaning is that of all the assets (bank accounts, stocks, property, etc.) of a person, usually deceased.

See also: ***Big House, the***

Margin headings:
Environmental Protection Agency[186]

Equity

Equity of tenure

Equity release

Equity sharing

Estate

---

[185] See: https://verde.ie/consultancy/environment/environmental-impact-assessment/
[186] See: https://www.epa.ie/pubs/reports/other/corporate/WhoweAredigital2016.pdf

Estate agent An estate agent is a licenced ***property services provider*** whose job it is to manage, let and sell property (commercial or residential).

See also: ***Property Services Regulatory Authority; Property Services (Regulation) Act 2011; letting agent***

European Convention on Human Rights There are several articles in the European Convention on Human Rights which, indirectly, provide protection for the right to housing:

- The right to life (article 2)
- The prohibition of inhuman or degrading treatment or punishment (article 3)
- The right to liberty and security of person (article 5)
- The right to a fair trial (article 6)
- The right to respect for family and private life, home and correspondence (article 8)
- The prohibition of discrimination (article 14)
- The right to peaceful enjoyment of possessions (article 1, protocol 1)

The European Convention on Human Rights (ECHR) was drafted by the Council of Europe in 1950. Ireland ratified the Convention in 1953. The ECHR was incorporated into Irish law in 2003 by the European Convention on Human Rights Act 2003.

See also: ***housing rights approach to housing; UN Special Rapporteur on the Right to Adequate Housing***

European Housing Rights Law There is no general right to housing in European Union law. EU law does however protect certain related rights in several ways. These include:

- Protections for migrant workers seeking housing
- The prohibition of ***discrimination*** on the basis of race, nationality, or gender
- Protections for consumers in housing purchase and rental contracts
- Protections under the Charter of Fundamental Rights of the European Union.

See also: ***Mercy Law Resource Centre; housing rights approach to housing; UN Special Rapporteur on the Right to Adequate Housing; discrimination***

European Investment Bank (EIB) The European Investment Bank (EIB) is a bank owned by European Union member states. It provides finance and expertise for sustainable investment projects that contribute to EU policy objectives. More than 90 per cent of EIB activity is in Europe. In Ireland, it provides funding for social housing projects, usually distributed as loans via the ***Housing Finance Agency*** (HFA), who can offer lending at competitive rates to ***approved housing bodies***.

The European Social Charter (Revised) ('the Revised Charter') provides a range of protections for housing and related rights. The European Social Charter is a Council of Europe treaty that guarantees fundamental social and economic rights. While the European Convention on Human Rights protects civil and political rights, the Charter protects social and economic rights. The original Charter was adopted in 1961. The Revised Charter was adopted in 1996. States that ratify the Charter are bound by the Charter. States can, under certain conditions, choose the provisions of the Charter that they are accept. Ireland ratified the original Charter in 1964 and the Revised Charter in 2000, although it has opted out of article 31, the right to housing. **European Social Charter**

The rights under the Revised Charter of relevance to housing are, in summary:

- The right to social security (article 12)
- The right of persons with disabilities to independence, social integration and participation in the life of the community (article 15)
- The right of the family to social, legal and economic protection to ensure its full development (article 16)
- The right of elderly persons to social protection (article 23)
- The right to protection against poverty and social exclusion (article 30)
- The right to housing (article 31)

Eurostat is the statistical office of the European Union, situated in Luxembourg. In 2018 Eurostat issued an important decision for Ireland on the accounting classification of borrowings of ***approved housing bodies*** (AHBs). These had been assumed to be off-balance sheet as they were arms-length organisations delivering social housing. However, Eurostat said: 'AHBs, being Non-Profit Institutions controlled by government and not being market producers, should be classified in the government sector,' thereby regarding AHBs as part of the state apparatus for several reasons, including the degree of financing, contractual agreement, special regulations and risk exposure (in particular, in the context of the new ***Payment and Availability Agreement***, via the Continuation Agreement). **Eurostat**

See also: ***Clúid Housing; social housing; data – housing output issues***

An eviction is when a person is forced to leave their housing. In the ***private rented sector***, tenants can be legally evicted under section 34 of the ***Residential Tenancies Act 2004***, whereby a valid reason must be given in a ***notice of termination*** alongside the appropriate ***notice period***. **Eviction/illegal eviction**

Eviction from local authority housing follows a different process. Article 8 of the European Court of Human Rights Act 2003 requires that even when a person's right to occupation has come to an end under domestic law, they must have access to an independent tribunal, which can determine the proportionality of the eviction.[187] Until recently, the legal basis for repossession was section 62 of the Housing Act 1966. In 2012, the Supreme Court held that this section was not compatible with the **European Convention on Human Rights** because it did not allow for an independent hearing of the merits of the proposed repossession. The Housing (Miscellaneous Provisions) Act 2014 replaced section 62 with new procedures.

The new procedures apply where local authorities want to repossess because:

- There has been a serious or repeated breach of a condition of the **tenancy** agreement, for example, **anti-social behaviour** or non-payment of rent, or
- The **dwelling** has been abandoned by the **tenant** and is occupied by a squatter, or
- The tenant has died and the dwelling is occupied by someone who is not entitled to succeed to the tenancy.

The new procedures provide that a local authority may issue a tenancy warning if there is an alleged breach of the tenancy conditions such as anti-social behaviour or non-payment of rent. If the tenant does not deal with the breach of the tenancy agreement, even after the tenancy warning, the local authority can apply to the district court for a possession order to enable it to repossess the dwelling. If a possession order is granted, it gives the date on which the local authority can repossess the dwelling. This must be no sooner than two months (and no later than nine months) after the date of the order. The tenancy will be terminated on the date that the local authority takes possession of the dwelling under the possession order.[188]

An illegal eviction is an unlawful termination of tenancy, and occurs where a landlord through force, intimidation or otherwise (such as cutting off utilities or changing locks) denies a **tenant** from accessing a rented **dwelling** or removes a tenant's belongings from the dwelling whether or not a valid notice of termination has been served.

- Section 58 of the Residential Tenancies Act 2004 provides that a **tenancy** may not be terminated by the landlord by means of a notice of forfeiture,

---

[187] Kenna, P (2011) *Housing Law, Rights and Policy*, Clarus Press: Dublin
[188] See: http://www.citizensinformation.ie/en/housing/local_authority_and_social_housing/notice_to_quit_and_eviction.html

a re-entry or by any other process or procedure not provided under part 5 of the Act. Thus, a landlord must issue a valid written notice of termination that complies with section 62, section 34 and section 66(3) of the Residential Tenancies Act.

- In the absence of such, any actions taken by the landlord on foot of an invalid notice of termination or if a notice of termination is not issued may constitute an illegal eviction.

A tenant may be deemed to be illegally evicted if:

- The landlord does not issue a tenant with a valid notice of termination
- The landlord changes the locks while the tenant is out or stops the tenant from getting into their home
- The landlord makes life so uncomfortable for the tenant that they are forced to leave their home
- The tenant is physically removed from the property by the landlord or landlord's authorised agent

There are three types of illegal eviction:

1. Actual illegal eviction – this occurs where the tenant has been evicted from the property without the landlord complying with the provisions of the Residential Tenancies Act 2004.
   - No notice of termination issued; tenant was requested to leave verbally; physically removed from the property
   - Acted on an invalid notice of termination and insisted on the tenant vacating
   - Locks changed denying the tenant access to the property
   - Tenants' belongings seized
2. Threatened illegal eviction – this is where the landlord threatens to evict a tenant without complying with the provisions of the Residential Tenancies Act 2004:
   - Threatens to change the locks
   - Threatens to act on foot of an invalid notice of termination
   - Verbally threatens to throw a tenant out of a property in the absence of a valid *notice of termination*
3. Constructive eviction – is indirect. The term refers to a landlord's attempts to make a property uninhabitable in the hope that the tenant will leave, by for example:
   - Cutting off the heating, water or electricity
   - Refusing to maintain the property to make it safe

Exclusive possession

Exclusive possession is one of the key components of a **tenancy**. The result of case law is that the concept of exclusive possession is treated by the courts as a negative criterion only.[189] Its absence in a particular case will rule out a tenancy, but its presence will not necessarily result in a ruling in favour of a tenancy. Its presence will simply be regarded as one factor, but not necessarily the determining one, pointing to a tenancy.[190]

The right to 'exclusive possession' is what the **landlord** is purporting to give the tenant in a **lease** (which is why its existence has so often been regarded as a key element of a tenancy). On that basis the obligation to honour the bargain ought to be regarded as an 'overriding' one, out of which the landlord may not contract.[191] Exclusive possession does not exist in a **licence** arrangement.

Exempted development

See: **planning permission**

Existing use value

This is the price at which a property can be sold on the open market assuming that it can only be used for the existing use for the foreseeable future.

See also: **Part V social housing**

Extension of planning permission

Section 22 of the **Planning and Development (Housing) and Residential Tenancies Act 2016** deals with large developments which have remained unfinished since the recession and provides that a further extension of the duration of a **planning permission** which has already been extended may be granted by the **planning authority** for housing developments which consist of 20 or more houses where the authority considers it necessary for the **development** to be completed. The extension must not exceed five years or extend beyond 21 December 2021, whichever occurs first.[192]

See also: **speculation**

F

Fair Deal Scheme – (Nursing Homes Support Scheme)

The Ancillary State Support Scheme (also known as the Nursing Homes Support Scheme) is more commonly referred to as the Fair Deal Scheme. It provides financial support for those in long-term nursing home care. Users pay part of their nursing home fees and the state pays the balance. This

---

[189] Wylie, JCW (2010) *Irish Land Law*, fourth edition , Bloomsbury Professional: Dublin, paragraphs 2.35–2.36

[190] Per Griffin J in the Gatien case op cit at 414. See also Barron J in *Texaco (IR) Ltd v Murphy*, High Court, 17 July 1991, at 9

[191] Law Reform Commission (2003) *Consultation Paper on General Law of Landlord and Tenant*, LRC: Dublin

[192] See: https://beauchamps.ie/publications/445

scheme applies to approved public, private and voluntary nursing homes, and where the person in nursing home care has assets including land and property. Those availing of the Fair Deal Scheme must contribute up to 80 per cent of their income and up to 7.5 per cent of the value of any assets towards their cost of care.

Under the rules, the value of a person's home is only included in the financial assessment for the first three years of their period in care. If assets include land and/or residential property in the state, the 7.5 per cent contribution based on those assets can be deferred. This means it does not have to be paid during the person's lifetime and will be collected from their estate. This is the nursing home loan element of the scheme, which is officially referred to as 'ancillary state support'.[193]

The Health Service Executive (HSE) pays the money to the nursing home on behalf of the person in nursing home care. When the loan is due to be repaid, the HSE will inform Revenue of the amount due and the date that it is due. Revenue then collects the loan on behalf of the HSE. Once Revenue receives payment within specified time limits (typically twelve months from death), no interest is charged. The estate cannot be distributed before the loan is repaid, unless prior written consent is obtained from the HSE.[194]

A significant issue with the Fair Deal Scheme is the presumption of debt-free *ownership* of a house which can then be used to pay for care. More people are remaining in the rental sector. This needs to be considered in light of the current funding model of the Fair Deal Scheme, where there is a presumption of a) reliance on the debt-free home as an asset to provide accommodation and financial support for the housing needs of older persons; and b) a substantial fraction of older persons having housing equity. By 2021 the Fair Deal Scheme is estimated to cost €1.2 billion per annum,[195] but if there are fewer assets with which to supplement, the cost to the state could be much higher.

See also: *residential care; asset-based welfare*

See: *Strategic Housing Development*

Fast-track planning

FEANTSA is the European Federation of National Organisations Working with the Homeless. Established in 1989, FEANTSA brings together non-profit services that support homeless people in Europe. FEANTSA has over

FEANTSA

---

[193] See: https://health.gov.ie/wp-content/uploads/2014/04/Frequently-Asked-Questions.pdf
[194] See: https://www.revenue.ie/en/life-events-and-personal-circumstances/nursing-homes-fair-deal-loan/index.aspx
[195] BDO (2014) *Health's Ageing Crisis: A Time for Action – A Future Strategy for Ireland's Long-term Residential Care Sector*, BDO Ireland: Dublin

130 member organisations from 30 countries, including 28 EU member states. Most are national or regional federations.

See also: ***Irish Council for Social Housing***

Fee farm grant   Fee farm grant is a type of ***freehold*** estate with characteristics of a ***leasehold*** estate such as the payment of a rent and compliance with covenants. Legislation in Ireland prohibits the creation of new fee farm grants from 1 December 2009 but does not affect fee farm grants already in existence.[196]

See also: ***fee simple; estate***

Fee simple   A fee simple is the largest estate in land where ownership is absolute.[197] Fee simple is a form of ***freehold*** estate, as is ***fee farm grant***.

Feudal system   The feudal system, or feudalism, is a land ownership structure that existed throughout much of Europe between 800 and 1400 and that revolved around a multi-level hierarchy between lords (who held land granted under ***tenure*** from the king), and their ***tenants*** (also called serfs or vassals). Related and sometimes synonymous terms are 'fief' and 'fee'. The thrust of the feudal system, as it was initially imposed on the English by the conquering Normans as of 1066, was that tenants would ***lease*** land from the lord in exchange for loyalty and goods or services, such as military assistance or money. In exchange, the vassal would be protected from attack and have exclusive use of a designated parcel of land.

FIDH (International Federation for Human Rights)   FIDH (International Federation for Human Rights) is an international human rights non-governmental organisation federating 184 organisations from 112 countries. In 2017, following a collective complaint taken by FIDH, the European Committee on Social Rights (ECSR) found that Ireland has failed to take sufficient and timely measures to ensure the right to housing of an adequate standard for many families living in local authority housing across the country.

The ECSR recognised that the conditions advanced by the complaint go to the core of adequate housing. It found that persistent dampness, mould and contaminated water experienced by tenants raised serious concerns as to both habitability and access to essential services. It particularly noted 'the high number of residents in certain estates in Dublin complaining of sewage invasions (for example the Dolphin House complex) years after the problems were first identified'.[198] The Committee also raised the impact on tenants of delays and stalling of regeneration programmes.

---

[196] See: https://www.williamfry.com/docs/default-source/ezine-print-friendly-documents/the-legal-500-real-estate-comparative-guide---ireland.pdf?sfvrsn=0
[197] See: http://fgphelan.ie/conveyancing_glossary.php
[198] See: https://www.ihrec.ie/human-rights-equality-commission-responds-european-committee-social-rights-finding-ireland-social-housing/

The decision is a result of a collective complaint, the evidence for which was gathered over five years through the work of Community Action Network working with tenants from twenty local communities, closely supported by the Centre for Housing Law, Rights and Policy at NUI Galway and Ballymun Community Law Centre. It was lodged in 2014 against Ireland on behalf of local tenants by FIDH with the support of affiliate member FLAC (Free Legal Advice Centre) along with PILA (Public Interest Law Alliance).[199]

The Financial Contribution Scheme was introduced by Dublin City Council in recognition of the fact that there are persons of 55 years and over living in the city who find their existing dwellings too large for their needs and who wish to be considered for housing by Dublin City Council, as tenants, in older persons' accommodation. The following conditions apply:

Financial Contribution Scheme[200]

- The property must be located in Dublin City Council's administrative area.
- Admission to the Financial Contribution Scheme shall only be offered to a homeowner if Dublin City Council wishes to purchase a homeowner's property and is able to source a vacancy in older persons' accommodation for the applicant.
- Applicants who may have to sell their property due to separation, divorce or family agreements shall only be able to access one dwelling per property.
- Dublin City Council cannot purchase any house with a value in excess of the price limit set out by the *Department of Housing, Planning and Local Government* for acquisitions.
- Dublin City Council shall only consider purchase of properties at a discount for homeowners who are eligible for older persons' accommodation.
- Successful applicants will be placed on the financial contributions list until a suitable vacancy arises.
- Refusal of two offers of accommodation in the applicant's area of choice will result in cancellation of the application.
- Homeowners who are housed must pay a housing rent to Dublin City Council in line with the differential rent scheme.
- The discount Dublin City Council shall apply is: 55–69 years old: 60 per cent of the market value of the property; 70 years and older: 70 per cent of the market value of the property.
- The date of acceptance on to the list is the effective date for selection for vacancies. Properties may be subject to inspection when the candidate is

---

[199] See: https://www.fidh.org/en/region/europe-central-asia/ireland/tenants-welcome-european-committee-of-social-rights-finding-that#

[200] See: https://www.dublincity.ie/councilmeetings/documents/s16415/2a.Scheme%20of%20Lettings%20-%20Draft%20Allocations%20Scheme%202018.pdf

reached for selection. If the dwelling is found unsuitable by Dublin City Council or it may require substantial repairs Dublin City Council shall not purchase the property and an applicant shall not be eligible for the Financial Contribution Scheme.

Financialisation of housing　The financialisation of housing refers to the increasing way in which housing is seen less as a home (where the value is in its use) and more as an investment vehicle (where the value is in the price inflation).

The United Nations defines the financialisation of housing as structural changes in housing and financial markets and global investment whereby housing is treated as a commodity, a means of accumulating wealth and often as security for financial instruments that are traded and sold on global markets.[201] Others see the financialisation of housing as being 'the increasing dominance of financial actors, market, practices, measurements and narratives, at various scales, resulting in a structural transformation of economies, forms (including financial institutions), states and households'.[202]

'Over the past thirty years land and housing have become increasingly "financialised"—seen as assets to hold and trade for profit, rather than as potential places to live.'[203] Instead of investing money in productive enterprises to generate greater wealth, societies have become increasingly dependent on rising property values (both land and housing) as a source of wealth.

Politicians have responded to these changing conditions by also conceptualising the housing market in financialised terms, and developing policy solutions which are pegged to this understanding. '***Help to Buy***' is a classic example. By pumping more money into the system through equity loans, the government helps push a few more people over the line into home ownership while simultaneously accelerating (rather than keeping in check) the growth of land and house prices.[204]

Less well known, but equally pernicious, is the nature of ***speculation*** in the land market. In the UK in 2018, 55 per cent of planning permissions were held by non-builders, many of whom will be speculating on the market, and benefitting from land value uplift, without ever intending to build a single home.[205]

See also: ***asset-based welfare; land***

---

[201] Human Rights Council (2017) *Report of the Special Rapporteur on Adequate Housing as a Component of the Right to an Adequate Standard of Living, and on the Right to Non-Discrimination in this Context*, United Nations General Assembly: New York
[202] Aalbers, M (2016) *The Financialisation of Housing: A Political Approach*, Routledge: London
[203] Winterburn, M (2018) 'Home Economics: Reversing the Financialisation of Housing', *Journal of Architecture*, Vol. 23, No. 1, p. 184
[204] Winterburn, M (2018) 'Home Economics: Reversing the Financialisation of Housing', *Journal of Architecture*, Vol. 23, No. 1, pp. 184–193
[205] *Ibid.*

A Fire Safety Certificate is a certificate issued by the ***building control author-ity*** which states that the works or building to which the application relates will, if constructed in accordance with the plans and specifications submitted, comply with the requirements of part B of the Second Schedule to the Building Regulations 1997 (see: ***technical guidance documents***). It is therefore a certification of the proposed fire safety design, not the fire safety design of the finished building. Individual houses do not need to obtain a Fire Safety Certificate, although apartment buildings do.

> **Fire Safety Certificate**

Usually a Fire Safety Certificate application is made by a fire safety consultant, architect or engineer who is familiar with the Building Regulations and the procedure for applying for a Fire Safety Certificate.[206]

See also: ***Fire Safety Notice***

Under the provisions of section 20(1) of the Fire Services Act 1981, fire authorities may issue a Fire Safety Notice on the owner of a building if they are of the opinion the building is unsafe. Fire Safety Notices can be issued on the person in control of buildings where people sleep (such as an ***apartment*** block, hostel or hotel), but not on individual houses. Such notices can prohibit the use of the building or parts or it; direct the owner to carry out certain fire-safety-related works (such as appropriate maintenance of fire signage, or the installation of fire extinguishers). Problems with fire detection systems, fire alarms, emergency lighting and smoke ventilation were the main reasons for Fire Safety Notices being issued in 2017, along with people using commercial properties for residential use.[207] Dublin City Council fire authority served 33 Fire Safety Notices in 2017, of which 11 were served on residential properties. It is difficult, if not impossible, to sell a residential property (apartment) if there is an outstanding Fire Safety Notice on it. Fire authorities have no powers of inspection in respect of dwelling houses occupied as single dwellings, but they can inspect apartment blocks.

> **Fire Safety Notice**

Under section 20(8) of the Fire Services Act 1981, each fire authority is also obliged to keep at its offices a register of Fire Safety Notices served by it and the register shall be open to inspection by any person at all reasonable times.

See also: ***Fire Safety Certificate***

In a fixed rate mortgage the interest rate remains the same for the term of the loan. Mortgage interest rates can also be 'fixed' for a specified period of years during a mortgage, depending on the lender.

> **Fixed rate mortgage**

See also: ***interest rate; variable rate mortgage***

---

[206] See: https://kilkennycoco.ie/resources/Fire%20Safety%20Certificates%20-%20Frequently%20asked%20questions1.pdf

[207] RTÉ (2017) '26 residential buildings served fire safety notices this year', *RTÉ News*, 4 July

Fixed term tenancy

A fixed term tenancy is a tenancy that lasts for a specific amount of time as set out in a tenancy agreement or lease. It may be for any period but is typically for a period of one year. In a fixed term tenancy:

- The **landlord** may not end the tenancy before the end of the fixed term unless the tenant has breached their obligations.
- A **tenant** may not end the tenancy before the end of the term unless the landlord has breached his obligations under it; the tenant is exercising a break clause; the tenant has got someone to replace them; or the landlord and tenant both agree to end it.

If a private landlord refuses to consent to an assignment or sublet of the tenancy, the tenant can terminate the tenancy under section 186 of the **Residential Tenancies Act 2004** (this does not apply to social housing tenants).

A 'Part 4' tenancy runs alongside a fixed term tenancy, which means that the tenant shall, after a period of six months and as in the normal course, become entitled to the provision of a 'Part 4' tenancy. A Part 4 tenancy means they can stay in the property for a further five-and-a-half years, or three-and-a-half years if the tenancy commenced before 24 December 2016, and subject to certain exceptions for **termination**. This means that irrespective of the length of a fixed term lease, a tenant has an entitlement to remain in the dwelling for up to six years and termination of a lease can only happen on limited grounds (s.34 of the Residential Tenancies Act 2004).

See: **lease; security of tenure**

Flat

A flat is a self-contained residential unit in a larger house that will typically contain more flats. Flats are typically units that have been converted and that are in older buildings. The word 'flat' derives from the fact that the residential unit was on one floor, and hence flat.

See also: **apartment; studio apartment; garden flat; mews; duplex; detached house; semi-detached house; tenements; Simms, Herbert**

'Flipping'

Flipping property involves buying and then selling property in the hope of short-term gain. It is a form of **speculation**. There are several forms of flipping, the two most common being: (a) buying and carrying out some **refurbishment** before selling on again; and (b) buying a property (including land) and doing nothing to it, but waiting until its **capital value** has risen sufficiently to sell at a profit. 'Flipping' is most prevalent in land and housing markets where values are rising quickly.

Focus Ireland

Focus Ireland is a non-profit organisation based in Dublin that provides services for homeless people. It is the largest national voluntary association in Ireland. Focus Ireland was founded by Sr Stanislaus Kennedy. Sr Stan was involved in a research project into the lives of homeless women in Dublin when she realised the importance of involving people who are or have been directly affected by *homelessness* in the development of homelessness services. In 1985, two years after the initial research, Focus Point (now Focus Ireland) opened its doors in Eustace Street, Dublin. The organisation provides 'street-work' services to young people, advice, advocacy, information and help with finding a home as well as a place to meet and have a low-cost meal.

See also: *Peter McVerry Trust; rough sleeping; Housing Act 1988*

Fold Housing Association

Fold Ireland provides apartments and houses for older people and families. In addition, the association provides supported housing with 24-hour care for frail and older people, including housing-with-care and day care for frail older people and people with dementia; *sheltered housing*; and general needs accommodation for families. Its organisational purpose is to develop partnerships with local authorities, appropriate care providers and developers in greater Dublin and in the border counties to provide social housing at these locations.

See also: *approved housing bodies*

Foreclosure

This is a legal procedure whereby property used as security for a mortgage is sold to repay the debt in the event of default in payment of the mortgage or default of other terms in the mortgage. Foreclosure passes the title in the mortgage property to either the holder of the mortgage or a third party who may purchase the property.

Forward Planning

Forward Planning sets out an overall strategy for the proper planning and *sustainable development* of all areas.[208] Forward Planning is often a specific section in Irish local authorities that works on *development plans*, *local area plans* and other strategic planning publications. In some counties, Forward Planning may also have responsibility for renewable energy strategies (e.g. Waterford).

Four-stage process for social housing

The 'four-stage process' refers to the number of stages a local authority must go through in order to get funding approval to construct social housing. This applies to projects above €2 million and for a maximum of eight units; projects over €20 million will most likely require a cost-benefit analysis and will happen on a phased basis. (For applications under €2 million, there is a one-stage approval process.) Local authorities forward design proposals and costings to the *Department of Housing, Planning and Local Government*

---

[208] See: https://www.clarecoco.ie/planning/planning-overview/

sequentially, as the local authorities advance the projects through their own planning work. The four stages are:

- Stage 1 – Capital appraisal to verify the business case and basic project suitability: this is a light presentation of information; no design and only indicative costs are required at this initial stage.
- Stage 2 – Pre-planning outline design and cost check: following site investigations, this involves the level of designs that are required for the *Part 8* planning process and a completed quantity surveyor's cost plan; detailed tender drawings and resulting costs are not needed at this stage until *planning permission* is obtained.
- Stage 3 – Pre-tender costs check: the more detailed designs and cost estimates have been prepared by the local authority design team at this stage and a cost check submitted before going to tender, but if costs are consistent with the earlier stages, then this review will be swift. Unless there have been changes to the design following Part 8 planning, or conditions to be met, the design is not reviewed.
- Stage 4 – Tender approval from Department: the tenders have been received and assessed by the local authority and again, if costs are consistent with the earlier stages, this review will be 'swift'.[209]

See also: *turnkey; data – housing output issues*

Freehold interest A freehold interest is an exclusive right to enjoy the possession and use of a parcel of land or other asset for an indefinite period. In contrast, a *leasehold* interest is for a fixed, definite period.[210]

See also: *title; Registry of Deeds; Land Registry; memorial*

Fuel poverty Fuel poverty is the experience of not being able to afford to heat one's house. Fuel poverty is defined as having to spend 10 per cent or more of a *household*'s disposable income on heating in any one year; severe fuel poverty is spending more than 15 per cent; and extreme fuel poverty is spending 20 per cent or more.[211, 212]

See also: *transport poverty and equity; welfare state*

Further Part 4 tenancy At the end of the first *tenancy* period (of four or six years), a tenant then enters a further *Part 4* tenancy.

---

[209] See: http://rebuildingireland.ie/install/wp-content/uploads/2018/07/Full-Report-Final.pdf
[210] Grimes, L (n.d.) *Limited Interests, Some Taxation Implications*, Certified Public Accountants: Dublin
[211] Department of Communications, Energy and Natural Resources (2011) *Warmer Homes – A Strategy for Affordable Energy in Ireland*, Government of Ireland: Dublin
[212] Society of St Vincent de Paul (2015) 'Energy Poverty – Experienced by One Parent Families in the Republic of Ireland', *Policy Links*, Edition No. 1, January

If a tenancy started on or before 24 December 2016, when the four-year cycle of the tenancy has ended, a new tenancy starts, known as a *further Part 4 tenancy*. This tenancy will now last six years.

If a tenancy started after 24 December 2016, the further Part 4 tenancy will start when the first six-year cycle of the original Part 4 tenancy has ended and it will last six years.

In ending a further Part 4 tenancy, the legislation originally provided that your landlord could end a further Part 4 tenancy at any time during the first six months without having to give a reason. This rule has been changed with effect from 17 January 2017 and the landlord must provide one of the valid reasons in section 34 of the *Residential Tenancies Act 2004*. If a landlord wishes to stop a further Part 4 tenancy coming into existence, they may serve a notice during the original Part 4 tenancy, with the notice period expiring on or after the end of the tenancy.

See also: *notice of termination; termination of a lease*

G

Gap site

See: *infill site*

Garden city

The housing model for social reformers in early-twentieth-century Britain and Ireland was that of the 'garden city', first envisaged by Ebenezer Howard in 1898. Howard saw the city slum as morally and physically corrupting and hoped to replace them with out-of-town suburbs, surrounded by parkland and connected to the city centre by public transport. His vision had a considerable influence on early public housing initiatives in Ireland.[213]

Howard's solution to the related problems of rural depopulation and the runaway growth of great towns and cities was the creation of a series of small, planned cities that would combine the amenities of urban life with the ready access to nature typical of rural environments. At the centre of the city would lay a garden ringed with the civic and cultural complex, including the city hall, a concert hall, museum, theatre, library and hospital. Six broad main avenues would radiate from this centre. Concentric to this urban core would be a park, a combination shopping centre and conservatory, a residential area, and then, at the outer edge, industry. Traffic would move along avenues extending along the radii and concentric boulevards.[214] His emphasis on green belt areas and controlled population densities has become an integral part of suburban and city planning as well.

---

[213] See: McCord, R (2011) 'A Garden City – The Dublin Corporation Housing Scheme at Marino, 1924', *The Irish Story*, 7 September, available at: http://www.theirishstory.com/2011/09/07/a-garden-city-the-dublin-corporation-housing-scheme-at-marino-1924/#.W3LxTC17FR0
[214] See: https://www.britannica.com/topic/garden-city-urban-planning

Letchworth (1903) and Welwyn Garden City (1930) in the United Kingdom are examples of Howard's vision turned into reality.

See also: *Marino; Howard, Ebenezer; density, housing*

Garden flat

A garden flat is a basement or ground-floor flat typically looking onto or with access to a garden or lawn. Garden flats are most common in Georgian and Victorian buildings where they would formerly have housed the storage and cooking areas and sometimes servant accommodation.

See also: *detached house; semi-detached house; mews; flat; duplex; condominium; apartment; terraced house*

Gazump

To gazump is to refuse to sell a house to someone to whom it was previously agreed, and instead to sell it to someone who had subsequently made a higher offer.

Gazumping is legal in Ireland as the sale of a house is not legally binding until contracts are exchanged. In 1999, the Law Reform Commission concluded that the current legal position, which does not confer any interest in property upon the payment of a booking deposit, generally benefits the purchaser more than the vendor. For example, it allows the purchaser to conduct the necessary preliminary investigations, whether it be in the financial, physical or legal field, before committing to an irrevocable agreement.[215]

See also: *gazunder; deposit (booking)*

Gazunder

Gazunder is where a prospective purchaser retracts their offer shortly before contracts are due to be signed and makes a lower offer instead. This is more likely to occur in weak markets, where vendors have trouble finding purchasers. As with *gazumping*, this is legal in Ireland as no legally binding contract exists until contracts are signed.

See also: *gazump; deposit (booking)*

Geddes, Patrick[216]

Sir Patrick Geddes (1854–1932) was a Scottish town planner. In the years 1911–1916 Patrick Geddes was heavily involved in the search for solutions to Dublin's acute health and housing problems. In 1914, Dublin Corporation appointed Geddes and Raymond Unwin as consultants to comment on and suggest improvements to various new housing schemes. Among their recommendations, most of which were not adopted, Geddes proposed a workers' garden village at *Marino*.

See also: *Howard, Ebenezer; garden city*

---

[215] Law Reform Commission (1999) *Report on Gazumping*, LRC: Dublin
[216] Bannon, MJ (1978) 'Patrick Geddes and the Emergence of Modern Town Planning in Ireland', *Irish Geography*, Vol. 11, No. 2, pp. 141–148; and McManus, R (2002) *Dublin, 1910–1940: Shaping the City and Suburbs*, Four Courts Press: Dublin

The General Boundary Rule means that the title to registered property is 'qualified' in that the state guarantees does not extend to boundaries. The Land Registry map identifies properties not boundaries and provides that the description of the land on the Registry map shall not be conclusive as to the boundaries or extent of the land.

General
Boundary
Rule[217]

The precise line of the property **boundary** is undetermined, and the Registry map does not indicate whether it includes a hedge, a wall or a ditch, or runs along the centre of a wall or fence or its inner or outer face or how far it runs within it or beyond it: or whether or not the land registered includes the whole or any portion of an adjoining road or stream. Where registration is made to the centre of a road or stream, the map is not to be taken as conclusive evidence that such, or any, portion of same is included in the property.

See also: **cadastre; Land Registry; Registry of Deeds**

Generation Rent refers to a cohort of people, typically born in the 1980s, who for economic reasons are more likely to rent their home than to buy it. It denotes young people who are increasingly living in the **private rented sector** for longer periods of their lives because they are unable to access **home ownership** or **social housing**[218] – this is mainly due to wages not matching house price inflation and a diminishing amount of social and/or **affordable housing** supplied from the state.

Generation Rent

Gentrification is regarded as the transformation of a working-class or vacant area of the central city into middle-class residential and/or commercial use. More literally, gentrification or 'gentry-fication' means the replacement of an existing population by a gentry.[219] The term 'gentrification' was first used by the British sociologist Ruth Glass in 1964[220] to describe some new and distinct processes of urban change that were beginning to affect inner London thus:

Gentrification

> [W]orking class quarters of London have been invaded by the middle classes—upper and lower; shabby, modest **mews** and **cottages**—two rooms up and two down—have been taken over, when their **leases** have expired, and have become elegant, expensive residences; larger Victorian houses, downgraded in an earlier or recent period—which were used as lodging houses or were otherwise in multiple occupation—have

[217] Society of Chartered Surveyors Ireland (n.d.) *Boundaries: Procedures for Boundary Identification, Demarcation and Dispute Resolution in Ireland*, second edition, Geomatics Guidance Note, SCSI: Dublin

[218] Hoolachan, J, McKee, K, Moore, T and Soaita, AM (2017) '"Generation Rent" and the Ability to "Settle Down": Economic and Geographical Variation in Young People's Housing Transitions', *Journal of Youth Studies*, Vol. 20, No. 1, pp. 63–78

[219] Lees, L, Slater, T and Wyly, E (2008) *Gentrification*, Routledge: Oxford

[220] Glass, R (1964) 'Introduction: Aspects of Change', in Centre for Urban Studies (ed.), *London: Aspects of Change*, MacKibbon and Kee: London, pp. xviii–xix

been upgraded once again…. Once this process of 'gentrification' starts in a district it goes on rapidly until all or most of the original working class occupiers are displaced and the social character of the district is changed.[221]

Smith defined gentrification as: 'the process by which working class residential neighbourhoods are rehabilitated by middle class homebuyers, landlords and professional developers'.[222] The *Dictionary of Human Geography* (2000) described gentrification as: 'the reinvestment of capital at the urban centre, which is designed to produce space for a more affluent class of people than currently occupies that space. Glass's term has mostly been used to describe the residential aspects of this process but this is changing, as gentrification itself evolves'.[223]

There were, however, previous terms for the same, or a similar, process: the 'Haussmannisation' of Paris in the time of Napoleon III; the 'brownstoning' of New York; 'homesteading' in Baltimore; 'whitepainting' in Toronto; and 'red brick chic' in San Francisco. There is widespread academic agreement that gentrification is expanding dramatically. At the same time it is mutating, so that there are now different types of gentrification, such as rural gentrification, new-build gentrification, and super-gentrification.[224]

The main criticism of gentrification (of several) is that it prices local residents out of their own property market where they may have had a reasonable expectation of being able to purchase a home where they had been raised.

GeoDirectory   GeoDirectory is Ireland's electronic register of most postal addresses (approximately 2.2 million) matched to their geographical locations. GeoDirectory is developed jointly by An Post and Ordnance Survey Ireland (OSi), and is made available under licence through a number of paid-for products. It holds the coordinates and geographical position of each building (accurate to 1m, building centre), classifies whether a building is commercial, residential or mixed residential/commercial, and, importantly, whether a building has single or multiple addresses.

See also: ***cadastre; Eircode; Land Registry; Registry of Deeds***

Ghetto   A ***slum*** area of a city, often overcrowded, poor and occupied by ethnic minorities.

See also: ***overcrowding***

---

[221] *Ibid.*
[222] Smith, N (1982) 'Gentrification and Uneven Development', *Economic Geography*, Vol. 58, No. 2, pp. 139–155
[223] Smith, N (2000) 'Gentrification', in Johnston, RJ, Gregory, D, Pratt, G and Watts, M (eds), *The Dictionary of Human Geography*, fourth edition, Blackwell: Oxford, p. 294
[224] Lees, L, Slater, T and Wyly, E (2008) *Gentrification*, Routledge: Oxford

See: *unfinished estates*

In 2017, Goodbody commenced its 'BER Housebuilding Monitor' to
measure housebuilding output. Since the 1970s, official housing statistics
utilised data on electricity connections and these were used as the proxy for
house completions in the state. The Goodbody BER Housebuilding Monitor
was created to provide a more accurate and timely gauge of new housing
supply. It utilises publicly available information from the **Sustainable Energy
Authority of Ireland** (SEAI) to count the number of new residential units
that have been issued with a **Building Energy Rating Certificate** (BER). All
units which are sold or rented in the state are required to have been issued
with a BER, but there is some level of non-compliance on this stipulation.
The creation of the BER tracker played a role in moving the responsibility for
housing statistics to the independent **Central Statistics Office**. The CSO's
data showed that housing output was being over-stated, and that new supply
was well ahead of the number of BERs issued, suggesting a larger degree of
non-compliance than was commonly assumed.
    See also: **data – housing output issues**

A granny flat is a self-contained living residential unit within or adjacent to a
family home, developed for the use of aging parent or relative.
    See also: **detached house; mews; terraced house; semi-detached house;
apartment; accessory dwelling unit; micro-home; duplex; condominium**

A green belt is an area of land protected by law from the **development** of
housing or commercial infrastructure.
    The main purpose of the green belt policy is to protect the land around
larger urban centres from urban sprawl, and maintain the designated area for
forestry and agriculture as well as to provide habitat for wildlife. Buildings for
agricultural use and sanitation facilities are usually allowed. In some cases, it
is also possible to change the use of land in a green belt and even gain permission for structures that are officially not allowed in a green belt.[225]
    When housing is in short supply, cities with green belts usually come
under pressure to allow development on them. Liffey Valley Shopping Centre
was built on lands that were controversially rezoned from partly green belt,
resulting in the establishment of the Mahon Tribunal of Inquiry into Certain
Planning Matters and Payments.
    See also: **Howard, Ebenezer; greenfield; garden city; development plan**

---

[225] See: http://www.politics-greenbelt.org.uk

Greenfield site This is land on which no urban *development* has previously taken place; usually understood to be on the periphery of an existing built-up area.[226]
See also: *brownfield site; development plan*

Greywater Greywater is all of a house's wastewater from baths, sinks, dishwashers, washing machines, etc., except that from toilets.
See also: *septic tank; rural housing*

Ground rent There is no common law definition of 'ground rent'. It is, however, accepted as a rent paid where the *tenant* has provided or constructed the buildings and the landlord has provided the ground only. The payment of a ground rent indicates that any property on it is held on leasehold only.

Owners have a right to acquire the *freehold interest* in the property for which they have been paying or owe ground rent. The Landlord and Tenant (Ground Rents) Act 1978 abolished the right of landlords to create new ground rents in respect of dwellings and brought in the Ground Rents Purchase Scheme which: 're-defined the categories of tenants given the right by law to acquire the *fee simple* interest in their premises, and empowered the Registrar of Titles: to vest the fee simple interest in such tenants, where the premises comprise a dwellinghouse; and for that purpose to arbitrate where agreement is not reached between *tenant* and *landlord*.'[227]

Property owners frequently discover they are leaseholders and not free-holders when they come to sell their property. It is also quite usual that the payment of ground rent has not occurred for many years. Even if the property is not for sale, there are good reasons for acquiring the freehold of the property, including having better *title* on the property, which itself will form a better base for borrowing and having more control over the property and its *development* potential. Modern purpose-built flats – which are owned leasehold – are conveyed to the purchaser in such a way that there is no entitlement to acquire the superior title.

In residential property, the price of buying out the ground rent is calculated using formulae which depend on whether there is more or less than fifteen years left on the lease. Applications to acquire the fee simple are made to the *Property Registration Authority*.
See also: *Registry of Deeds; Land Registry*

H

Headship rate The headship rate provides one measure of the rate of *household* formation. The headship rate is the proportion of individuals in an age cohort that

---

[226] See: https://www.eea.europa.eu/help/glossary/eea-glossary/greenfield-site
[227] See: https://www.prai.ie/ground-rents/

list themselves as 'head of household' or 'principal reference person' in the Census. Each household provides one reference person, thus an increase in the headship rate reveals an increase in the number of households.[228]

See also: ***housing demand; housing stock; population***

Health and housing

A decent, suitable home is fundamental to good health and wellbeing.[229] Research has consistently demonstrated a strong link between housing and health, with factors generally falling into four categories: housing quality, housing community, housing location, and housing affordability.

- Housing quality: Housing that is safe, dry, clean, maintained, adequately ventilated, and free from pests and contaminants, such as lead, radon and carbon monoxide, can reduce the incidence of negative health outcomes such as injuries, asthma, cancer, neurotoxicity, cardiovascular disease and poor mental health.
- Housing community: Neighbourhoods free from segregation and concentrated poverty, and in which residents have close and supporting relationships with one another, can improve physical and mental health by reducing stress and exposure to violence and crime as well as improving school performance and civic engagement.
- Housing location: Easy access to public transportation, parks and recreation, quality schools, good jobs, healthy foods and medical care can help reduce the incidence of chronic disease, injury, respiratory disease, mortality and poor mental health.
- Housing affordability: Affordable housing enables people to pay for other basic needs such as utilities, food and medical care, which can reduce the incidence of negative health outcomes such as malnutrition, diabetes, anxiety and depression.[230]

Height

The government's 2018 report *A Review of Delivery Costs and Viability for Affordable Residential Developments* found that increased structural and safety costs for high-rise buildings mean that six-storey blocks are the optimal height to make affordable apartments economically viable for ***developers*** to build. The report said that ***apartment*** buildings of a greater height do not necessarily increase the density of housing developments. It says that: 'contrary to common understanding, higher-rise development' can be 'a more expensive form of development'. This is generally due to the increased requirements from a structural and fire safety perspective. In this regard, high-rise does not

[228] Duffy, D, Byrne, D and Fitzgerald, J (2014) 'Alternative Scenarios for New Household Formation in Ireland', *Quarterly Economic Commentary*, ESRI: Dublin

[229] Care Act 2014 (UK)

[230] Pew Trusts (2014) *Links between Health and Housing*, The Pew Charitable Trusts: Philadelphia

necessarily improve matters where affordable delivery is the focus, nor does it always translate into increased density.[231]

Dublin City Council's **Development Plan** 2016–2022 has the following height guidelines:[232]

Category	Area	Height (m)
Low-rise (relates to the prevailing local height and context)	Inner City	Up to 28m (commercial)
		Up to 24m (residential)
	Rail hubs (See 3)	Up to 24m (commercial and residential)
	Outer City	Up to 16m (commercial and residential)
Mid-rise	Digital Hub	Up to 50m
	St Teresa's Gardens	
	North Fringe	
	Clonshaugh Industrial Estate	
	Ballymun	
	Pelletstown	
	Park West/Cherry Orchard	
	Naas Road	
	Oscar Traynor Road	
	National Concert Hall Quarter	
High-rise	Docklands Cluster	50m+
	Connolly	
	Heuston	
	George's Quay	

Despite the findings of the preceding report, in December 2018 the government issued revised height guidelines for local authorities (*Urban Development and Building Heights – Guidelines for Planning Authorities*). The guidelines were issued by the **Minister for Housing, Planning and Local Government** under section 28 of the Planning and Development Act 2000, as amended (see: **Section 28 – 'mandatory guidelines'**). Therefore:

> Planning Authorities and **An Bord Pleanála** are required to have regard to the guidelines and apply any specific planning policy requirements (SPPRs) of the guidelines, within the meaning of section 28(1C) of the Planning and Development Act 2000 (as amended), in carrying out

[231] Kelly, F (2018) 'Six-storey apartments "are optimal height for affordability"', *Irish Times*, 13 April
[232] See: http://www.dublincity.ie/sites/default/files/content/Planning/DublinCityDevelopment-Plan/Written%20Statement%20Volume%201.pdf

their functions. Accordingly, where SPPRs are stated in this document, they take precedence over any conflicting policies and objectives of development plans, local area plans and strategic development zone planning schemes. Where such conflicts arise, such plans/schemes need to be amended by the relevant *planning authority* to reflect the content and requirements of these guidelines and properly inform the public of the relevant SPPR requirements.[233]

In effect, 'City and county councillors will no longer be allowed impose a maximum height for residential and commercial developments.'[234] Critics of the new guidelines have called them 'misguided spurious opportunism' and also questioned the legality of the *Strategic Environmental Assessment* that accompanied them on several grounds, including that parts of it appeared to have been copied from other SEAs.[235]

See also: *density; development plan; plot ratio; speculation; high-rise*

The Help to Buy (HTB) incentive is a scheme for first-time property buyers. **Help to Buy**[236] It was designed to help with the *deposit* needed to buy or build a new house or apartment, which must then be lived in as a home.

To claim HTB, applicants must:

• Be a first-time buyer
• Buy or build a new property between 19 July 2016 and 31 December 2019
• Live in the property as their main home for five years after they buy or build it
• Be tax compliant; if self-assessed they must also have tax clearance

To qualify, applicants must not have previously bought or built a house or apartment, either on their own or jointly with any other person. If applicants are buying or building the new property with other people, they must also be first-time buyers. If applicants have inherited or been gifted a property it will not affect their eligibility.

For those buying a property, contracts must have been signed to buy that property on or after 19 July 2016. If self-building, the first part of the mortgage must have been drawn down on or after that date.

[233] See sections 1.13, 1.14 of: https://www.housing.gov.ie/sites/default/files/publications/files/urban_development_and_building_height_guidelines_for_planning_authorities_december_2018_0.pdf
[234] Melia, P (2018) 'Death of the semi-D as height limits scrapped', *Irish Independent*, 8 December
[235] Smith, M (2018) '(S)height', *Village Magazine*, December
[236] See: https://www.revenue.ie/en/property/help-to-buy-incentive/index.aspx

To qualify for HTB, the property that is built or bought must be:

- The applicant's home
- Newly built with the construction subject to Value Added Tax (VAT) in Ireland

The purchase value of a new build means the price that applicant bought it for. For self-built property, the purchase value is the approved *valuation* by the lender at the time that the mortgage was taken out. If the applicant bought the property between 19 July 2016 and 31 December 2016, the purchase price must be €600,000 or less. If bought after 1 January 2017, it must be €500,000 or less.

Mortgages must be taken out with a qualifying lender. This loan must be used only for buying or building the property and must be at least 70 per cent of the purchase value of the property. Applicants are allowed to have a guarantor on the loan.

The amount that can be claimed is the lesser of:

- €20,000
- 5 per cent of the purchase price of a new home. For self-builds this is 5 per cent of the completion value of the property
- The amount of oncome tax and deposit interest retention tax (DIRT) the applicant has paid in the four years before the purchase or self-build

See also: *financialisation of housing*

High-rise

High-rise is a nebulous term, and very much depends on its context. In the Dún Laoghaire–Rathdown *Development Plan* 2016–2022, 'high buildings' or 'higher buildings' are defined as buildings which are higher than the overall building height in any given area, whilst 'tall buildings' are defined as buildings that are significantly higher than their surroundings and/or have a considerable impact on the skyline. 'Higher buildings' can sometimes act as local or district landmarks, whilst 'tall buildings' may perform a function as strategic or citywide landmarks.[237]

More generally, a high-rise building is defined variously as a building in which:

- The number of storeys means occupants need to use a lift to reach their destination.
- The height is beyond the reach of available fire-fighting equipment.
- The height can have a serious impact on evacuation.

---

[237] See: http://www.dlrcoco.ie/sites/default/files/atoms/files/appendix9_2.pdf

Typically this is considered to include buildings of more than 7–10 storeys or 23–30m. A low-rise building is one which is not tall enough to be classified as high-rise.

Other definitions of buildings in relation to their height include:

- Mid-rise buildings of five to ten storeys, equipped with lifts
- Skyscrapers of 40 storeys or more
- Supertall buildings exceeding 300m
- 'Megatall' buildings exceeding 600m
- 'Groundscrapers' that extend horizontally over a large distance while only being of a low to medium height
- Super-slender buildings which are pencil-thin and of 50–90+ storeys[238]

See also: *height; density; plot ratio; development plan*

Holiday homes

A holiday home – sometimes referred to as a 'second home' – is housing accommodation typically in a different location to one's permanent home, which is used primarily during periods of holiday, or specifically for holidays, and which remains vacant throughout other periods. At Census 2016, there were 62,148 recorded vacant holiday homes in Ireland. This is an increase of 2,753 or 4.63 per cent on the 2011 figure of 59,395.

The international research on holiday homes reveals both positive and negative economic impacts. There is evidence that they can contribute to regional economic growth by helping to maintain existing business and employment, and encourage entrepreneurial start-ups – a contribution which is especially valuable in declining regions. However, concerns have been raised about the sustainability of employment associated with holiday homes, which is concentrated in the construction phase, and that their employment effects may be negligible when the expenditure associated with them is too low to enable specialisation in a second homes market.[239] By contrast, the international literature is broadly negative about the social impact of holiday homes, with two problems widely noted: large numbers of holiday and *vacant dwellings* undermine community structures; and a high demand for holiday homes drives up house prices, creating housing accessibility problems

[238] See: https://www.designingbuildings.co.uk/wiki/High-rise_building
[239] Hall, M and Müller, M (eds) (2004), 'Introduction: Second Homes, Curse or Blessing? Revisited', in Hall, M and Müller, M (eds), *Tourism, Mobility and Second Homes: Between Elite Landscapes and Common Ground*, Channel View Publications: Clevedon

(e.g. for local people wishing to purchase housing in their communities) and displacing households seeking principal residences.[240, 241]

See also: ***regional development; rural housing***

Home Building Finance Ireland

Home Building Finance Ireland is a company formed under the Companies Act 2014 and the Home Building Finance Act 2018, and owned by the Minister for Finance. Its purpose is to fund the construction of commercially viable residential developments – both houses and apartments – in Ireland. The target market of HBFI is small- to medium-sized developers who have experienced difficulty in accessing finance from other market lenders. HBFI has an overall budget of €750 million to lend at market rates and a target of delivering 7,500 houses over five years. Certain criteria apply to potential borrowers, including having at least applied for planning permission on a site, a proposal for a minimum of ten housing units, and having at least 20 per cent equity. HBFI plan to lend 50 to 80 per cent of the funding required.

Questions had been raised as to whether HBFI would fund remediation works in **apartment** blocks where there had been found to be **defects**. However, HBFI do not 'envisage a situation where [they] could provide funding for apartment remediation'. While there is nothing contained in the Home Building Finance Ireland Act 2018 that excludes this form of lending, the commerciality of funding such remediation is highly risky from two perspectives:

• The projected costs of such projects regularly exceed the estimates once the 'opening up' works are undertaken due to the discovery of other issues which were not evident or identified during the investigation work.
• ***Owners' management companies*** (the borrowing entity) do not generally have the ability to provide security for the sums being borrowed. The taking of personal guarantees from the individual apartment owners is not an option.

Based on the high level of risk that would pertain to such lending, it could not be considered commercial in many cases and could put HBFI in breach of its commercial remit. Any funding or resources provided for the remediation of apartments would have to be diverted from new home development.[242]

See also: ***Multi-Unit Developments Act (MUD) 2011***

---

[240] Gallent, N, Mace, A and Tewdwr-Jones, M, (2005) *Second Homes: European Perspectives and UK Policies*, Ashgate: Aldershot
[241] Paris, C (2006) 'Multiple "Homes": Dwelling and Hyper-mobility and Emergent Transnational Second Home Ownership', paper presented to the European Network for Housing Research Conference, 2–5 July, Ljubljana, Slovenia; copy available from Chris Paris, University of Ulster
[242] Personal communication with HBFI

This is a policy that covers any structural damage to a home. All mortgage   **Home insurance**
lenders require it and will want their interest noted on the policy. Often in
apartment complexes or managed property the maintenance fee will cover
the building insurance; in this case it is referred to as a 'block policy' as one
policy covers a block of apartments. This is not the same thing as 'contents
insurance'; although it is possible to have contents covered by building insurance, in the case of *apartments* it is usual to need a separate 'contents policy'
as the block policy cannot be added to by separate individuals.[243]

See also: *reconstruction cost; service charge*

Home ownership means the ownership of a home with or without a *mortgage*.   **Home ownership**
The rate of home ownership in Ireland in 2016 was 67.6 per cent, which is
below the EU-28 average of 69.3 per cent. The UK has a home ownership
rate of 63.4 per cent, and the USA 64.3 per cent.[244]

Property markets in the EU display considerable differences in relation
to tenure status – the proportion of people who rent or own their home.
Generally there has been an increase in home ownership, with a preference to
move into single-family dwellings that have more internal and external space.
According to the EU-SILC (Survey on Income and Living Conditions), 69.3
per cent of all households in the EU-28 were owner-occupied in 2016, while
30.7 per cent were lived in by tenants (renting at either a market price or a
reduced price [i.e. social tenants]). The highest home ownership rates were
recorded in the eastern EU member states and the Baltic member states: e.g.
90 per cent or more of the dwellings in Croatia, Lithuania and Romania were
owner-occupied.[245] (Note that at the end of the 1980s/start of the 1990s,
many of the former socialist countries of eastern Europe and the Baltic region
decided to transform their housing markets through privatisation schemes,
often selling housing stock to existing inhabitants at relatively low prices.)[246]
In contrast, the lowest proportions of ownership were found in Germany
(51.7 per cent), Austria (55.0 per cent) and Switzerland (42.5 per cent). See
table below.[247]

---

[243] See: https://www.mortgagebrokers.ie/mortgage-information/mortgage-definitions-mortgage-
jargon/
[244] See: https://tradingeconomics.com/united-states/home-ownership-rate
[245] See: https://ec.europa.eu/eurostat/statistics-explained/index.php?title=People_in_the_EU_-_
statistics_on_housing_conditions#Home_ownership
[246] See: https://ec.europa.eu/eurostat/statistics-explained/index.php/Urban_Europe_—_statistics
_on_cities%2C_towns_and_suburbs_—_housing_in_cities
[247] See: https://www.statista.com/statistics/246355/home-ownership-rate-in-europe/

Country	Home Ownership %	Country	Home Ownership %
Romania	96	Luxembourg	73.8
Lithuania	90.3	Cyprus	72.5
Croatia	90	Italy	72.3
Slovakia	89.5	Finland	71.6
Hungary	86.3	Belgium	71.3
Poland	83.4	Netherlands	69
Norway	82.7	Ireland	67.6
Bulgaria	82.3	Sweden	65.2
Malta	81.4	France	64.9
Estonia	81.4	United Kingdom	63.4
Latvia	80.9	Denmark	62
Czech Republic	78.2	Austria	55
Spain	77.8	Germany	51.7
Portugal	75.2	Switzerland	42.5

Approximately one-third of Europeans rented their homes in 2016. In 2016 some 42.7 per cent of the EU-28 population lived in an owner-occupied household where there was no outstanding *mortgage* or housing loan (Ireland, 29.2%), while owner-occupants with a mortgage or housing loan accounted for 26.5 per cent of the EU-28's population (Ireland, 30%). Less than 10 per cent of the population lived in an owner-occupied household with a mortgage or loan in Latvia, Croatia, Bulgaria, Romania and Slovakia; this could be contrasted with the situation in the Netherlands, where 61.0 per cent of the population were owner-occupants with a mortgage or housing loan; Sweden was the only other member state where a majority of the population were owner-occupants with a mortgage or housing loan. These high rates of owner-occupancy without mortgage or loan in the eastern member states reflect, to a large degree, privatisation policies during the early 1990s that resulted in the transfer of property rights and the widespread sale of formerly state-owned housing stock.[248]

Despite a purported policy of '*tenure neutrality*', Ireland has an ideological (and practical) predisposition towards home ownership. Policies supporting home ownership (the *Rebuilding Ireland Home Loan*, for example) implicitly also support a certain set of social and power relationships. Policies that support renting – or at least regulations that support renting – are in conflict with the larger socioeconomic system of *asset-based welfare*, of which home ownership is a crucial component. Given the advantages conferred by home

---

[248] See: https://ec.europa.eu/eurostat/statistics-explained/index.php/People_in_the_EU_-_statistics_on_housing_conditions#Home_ownership

ownership, propagating the purchase of housing also propagates these advantages: those who own their own homes are significantly better equipped in life than those who do not. Governments argue that access and choice in home ownership are imperatives.

Home ownership is seen as a hedge against risk just as the ***financialisation of housing*** via global money flows makes it even riskier and less secure. The growth of home ownership has traditionally been seen as a natural process, and the social ideal. However, it has been anything but natural given consistent government support for it over the decades. As Norris has pointed out: 'by the early 1960s ... almost 30 per cent of the cost of a standard suburban house could be recouped [from government] by the purchaser'.[249] Ireland's status as a 'home ownership society' was underpinned not only by the overwhelming dominance of this tenure, but also by the normalisation of this situation in Irish official and media discourse.[250] High home ownership rates were routinely analysed with reference to cultural factors (e.g. Byrne relates it to the search for security inspired by the appropriation of the 'native Irish' lands by colonialists[251]) and presented as the 'natural order' by policy makers (until the early 1990s all government housing policy statements identified home ownership as the 'form of tenure preferred by most people').[252]

Home ownership has also been bound up with notions of freedom and autonomy, especially in countries with a 'cultural tradition of individualism', and is historically related to land and property ownership.[253] Industrialisation and urbanisation – neither of which have ever been historically prevalent in Ireland (Ireland was a predominantly rural country until 1966) – tended to lead to the development of rental living to cope with the large increases in population coming to urban areas to work in factories.

Some countries have specifically chosen to develop their rental sectors, private and public/social. Others have chosen to concentrate on the promotion of home ownership. Some of the wealthiest and most advanced countries have some of the lowest rates of home ownership (e.g. Germany, Switzerland), whilst some of the poorest have the highest rates of home ownership

---

[249] Norris, M (2014) 'Policy Drivers of the Retreat and Revival of Private Renting: Regulation, Finance, Taxes and Subsidies' in Sirr, L (ed.), *Renting in Ireland: The Social, Voluntary and Private Sectors*, IPA: Dublin

[250] Gurney, C. (1999) 'Pride and Prejudice: Discourses of Normalisation in Private and Public Accounts of Home Ownership', *Housing Studies*, Vol. 14, No. 2, pp. 163–183

[251] Byrne, D (1999) 'Ireland: Housing and Mortgage Markets and the Single Currency', *Housing Finance International*, March, pp. 25–28

[252] Norris, M and Winston, N (2004) *Housing Policy Review, 1990–2002*, Government Stationery Office: Dublin

[253] Ronald, R (2008) *The Ideology of Home Ownership: Homeowner Societies and the Role of Housing*, Palgrave Macmillan: London

(e.g. Romania).[254] At the heart of home ownership are socio-ideological forces based on historical factors ultimately leading to contemporary policies that are arguably as symbolic as they are useful.

See also: *tenure; freehold interest; leasehold; private rented sector; policy, housing*

Home Renovation Incentive

The Home Renovation Incentive (HRI) was a relief from income tax for homeowners, landlords and local authority **tenants** who could claim the HRI tax credit for repairs, renovations and improvements to their home or rental property. It ran until 31 December 2018.

Homebond

Homebond is a company that provides structural defect cover for new houses in Ireland.

See also: *latent defects insurance*

'Homeless HAP'

Homeless HAP (**Housing Assistance Payment**) (also referred to as Enhanced HAP or the Place Finder Scheme) is a form of HAP in which local authorities will pay a **deposit** and up to two months' **rent** on a rental property up-front. In the Dublin region, HAP rates can be up to 50 per cent higher than the normal limits. The local authority must have determined that the household is homeless and has no alternative accommodation.

See also: *homelessness – definition; emergency accommodation; Pathway Accommodation and Support System (PASS); Housing Act 1988; Dublin Region Homeless Executive*

Homelessness – definition[255]

Key legislation relating to homelessness in Ireland includes the Health Act 1953 and Childcare Act 1991, the **Housing Act 1988** and the Housing (Miscellaneous Provisions) Act 2009.

The Housing Act 1988 provided the first legal definition of homelessness in Ireland. Section 2 states that a person should be considered to be homeless if:

(*a*) there is no accommodation available which, in the opinion of the authority, he, together with any other person who normally resides with him or who might reasonably be expected to reside with him, can reasonably occupy or remain in occupation of, or

(*b*) he is living a hospital, county home, night shelter or other such institution, and is so living because he has no accommodation of the kind referred to in paragraph (a), and

(*c*) he cannot provide accommodation from his own resources.

---

[254] *Ibid.*
[255] See: https://www.homelessdublin.ie/info/policy

Different types of homelessness include visible homelessness – on the streets, *rough sleeping*, in shelters; hidden homelessness – in temporary, insecure, low quality or overcrowded housing with relatives or friends; living in *bed and breakfast* accommodation; and *squatting*.[256]

While the 1988 Act does not impose a duty on housing authorities to provide housing to people who are homeless, it does clearly give responsibility to the local authorities to consider their needs and expand their powers to respond to those needs. Specifically, authorities may house homeless people from their own housing stock or through arrangement with a voluntary body. The Act also enables the local authority to provide a homeless person with money to source accommodation in the private sector.[257]

In addition to the provisions relating to direct responses to people presenting as homeless, section 10 of the Act enables local authorities to provide funding to voluntary bodies for the provision of *emergency accommodation* and long-term housing for people who are homeless (see: *Section 10 funding*).

The 1988 Act requires that local authorities carry out periodic assessments of the number of people who are homeless in their administrative area, as part of their *housing needs assessment*.

See also: *rough sleeping; data – housing output issues*

House – structural components

- Foundation – this is the base on which the house sits. There are different types of foundations depending on the condition of the land where the house is to be built and the size of the house. The nature of the ground is the more important aspect. The main types of foundations are:
  - Strip – strips of concrete laid in a narrow trench. This is the most common foundation type in Ireland.
  - Raft – this is a slab of reinforced concrete the size of the footprint of the house, and is usually used on ground that retains a lot of water.
  - Piles – pile foundations are concrete columns driven deep into the ground, and usually used in soft ground.
- *Radon* barrier – this is placed above the foundation. The radon barrier is a membrane designed to cover the footprint of the house to protect it from radon gas (a major cause of lung cancer in Ireland).
- External walls – the most common wall types in Irish houses are *cavity walls* and *single leaf*. The outer leaf of many houses is comprised of bricks with the inner (unseen) leaf of concrete blocks.
- Internal walls – these can be of brick, block or stud partition, which is a timber frame covered in plasterboard to make the walls.

---

[256] See: https://spunout.ie/life/article-amp/homelessness
[257] See: https://www.homelessdublin.ie/info/policy

- Wall finishes – plaster or dashed wall finishes are common in Ireland, as are natural stone and brick. Metal cladding (such as zinc) can also be used.
- Roof – typical roof pitches in Ireland range from 35 to 45 degrees. Roof coverings are usually of slate (natural, Bangor Blue or manmade synthetic), although they can also be made from zinc, copper, weathered copper or green roofing.
- Heating – there are many different types of heating systems used in Irish houses (boiler, heatpump, etc.), but increasingly common is the use of underfloor heating. This is a system of pipes laid under a floor to heat a house. Hot water flows through these pipes to warm up the floor. The floor effectively becomes a giant radiator. The water in the pipes can be heated by a boiler or a heat pump.[258]
- Solar panels – these are a flat panel or group of tubes which are exposed to the sun's energy, normally on a roof. They contain special fluid which heats up and circulates through the hot water cylinder in a house to heat water. Solar panels can also be photovoltaic, meaning that they generate electricity for use in the home. Although less common, they are becoming more popular in recent years.[259]

See also: *U-value; Y-Value; thermal bridge; self-build; septic tank; planning permission; nZEB; S.I. 365 (opt-out)*

Houseboat   A houseboat is a small boat on a river or canal on which people live. Some houseboats are permanently stationary and others have motors and can move from location to location.

A permit is required to stay on a houseboat. There are three types:

1. Combined Mooring and Passage Permit – All boats (unless staying fewer than thirty days in one period within twelve months) require a Combined Mooring and Passage (CMP) Permit and are permitted to pass through locks and moor at visitor moorings or any location within 500 metres of that location (that is not an extended mooring location) for up to five days in any calendar month. The permit costs €126 per annum.
2. Extended Mooring Permit – An Extended Mooring Permit grants a boat owner the right to leave their boat in one location for longer than five days. This permit will enable the holder to moor in a position allocated by Waterways Ireland on a soft bank area of navigation property for a period of up to one year. The Extended Mooring Licence costs €152 per annum.
3. Visitor Permit – Boats entering the canal system and staying under 31 days can apply on entry for a free permit. This permit can only be used

---

[258] See: http://www.renova.ie/heating-glossary-renova/
[259] *Ibid.*

once every calendar year. Boats intending to stay more than the 31 days must apply in advance for the Combined Mooring and Passage Permit and if intending to stay in one location longer than five days will also need an Extended Mooring Permit as above.[260]

In the ***Household Budget Survey*** the CSO define a household as: a single person or group of people who regularly reside together in the same accommodation and who share the same catering arrangements. The household members defined in this fashion are not necessarily related by blood or by marriage. Thus, resident domestic servants and boarders (i.e. persons paying to share the household accommodation and meals) are included. Any other individual or group of people living in the same ***dwelling*** constitute a separate household or households if they have separate catering arrangements.[261]

Household

The following criteria are applied in the survey to certain categories of persons to decide whether or not they are members of a particular household:

- Family members who permanently live and work away from home are not included in their home household even though they return on holidays (if they are visiting the home household during the survey period they are treated as visitors and excluded).
- Children away at primary and secondary boarding school are included as members of their parents' households, but older persons receiving higher education away from home (e.g. at university, teacher or Garda training college) are included as members only if they are at home for the full fourteen-day period of diary record-keeping (e.g. during vacations).
- Family members working away from home who contribute to the income of their home household are included as members of the household only if they return home at least one night each week.
- Family members who do not contribute to the income of their home household and who are regularly away from home for part of each week are included as members of the household only if they spend at least four nights at home each week.
- Boarders are included in the household only if they reside there for at least four nights a week and have at least one meal each day with the family when they are in residence.
- Family members temporarily away on holiday, on business or in hospital are included as members of the household unless they have been away continuously for more than six months prior to the interviewer's visit.

---

[260] See: https://www.waterwaysireland.org/permits
[261] See: https://www.cso.ie/en/methods/housingandhouseholds/householdbudgetsurvey/appendix1-conceptsanddefinitions/

- Visitors and temporary members of the household are included as household members only if they have resided continuously in the household for more than six months prior to the interview.[262]

For the purposes of the Census, there are additional definitions: A 'permanent private household' is a private household occupying a permanent dwelling such as a dwelling house, *flat* or *bedsit*. A 'temporary private household' is a household occupying a caravan, mobile home or other temporary dwelling and includes Travelling people and homeless persons living rough on Census night.[263]

See also: *homelessness; rough sleeping; cohabitation; household size; headship rate; Traveller housing*

Household Budget Survey

The Household Budget Survey is carried out by the *Central Statistics Office* every five years in order to 'determine in detail the pattern of household expenditure in order to update the weighting basis of the Consumer Price Index'. The survey collects data on household expenditure and income as well as a number of household characteristics, e.g. household composition, household *tenure*, accommodation type, household facilities and appliances.[264]

See also: *headship rate; household size; population*

Household Charge

The European Commission–International Monetary Fund–European Central Bank Programme of Financial Support for Ireland committed the government to the introduction of a property tax commencing in 2012.[265] The Household Charge was a €100 charge introduced by the Local Government (Household Charge) Act 2011 which was payable by owners of residential property to their local authority. It was up to owners of residential properties to register and pay the Household Charge on or after 1 January 2012 and owners were liable for the charge in 2012 only.

The Household Charge was payable by the owner of a building in respect of each unit of residential accommodation. Where the building was divided into a number of flats or bedsits, the charge applied to each flat or bedsit. The Household Charge was superseded by the valuation-based *Local Property Tax* (LPT) in July 2013.

Household Means Policy[266]

The Household Means Policy sets out the manner in which housing authorities assess the means of applicant households for the purpose of determining

[262] See: https://www.cso.ie/en/releasesandpublications/ep/p-hbs/hbs20152016/app1/
[263] See: https://www.cso.ie/en/media/csoie/census/documents/vol3_appendix.pdf
[264] See: https://www.cso.ie/en/methods/housingandhouseholds/householdbudgetsurvey/
[265] See: https://www.housing.gov.ie/housing/chargestaxes/household-charge/household-charge

the household's ability to provide accommodation from its own means and by extension its eligibility, or otherwise, for *social housing* support.

The income threshold is the basic measure of whether a household is eligible for social housing support. The determination of whether an applicant household meets the income criteria is based on a calculation of net income (i.e. gross income less income tax, Universal Social Charge, Pension-Related Deduction within the meaning of Financial Emergency Measures in the Public Interest Act 2009, and Pay-Related Social Insurance). The income of all persons aged 18 years and over included in a social housing application is assessed for the purposes of determining whether an applicant household meets the income requirements.

In assessing household income for the purposes of the Household Means Policy, a housing authority may decide to disregard income that is once-off, temporary or short-term in nature and which is outside the regular pattern of a person's annual income.

Between Censuses 2011 and 2016, the number of *households* in the country increased by 49,285, or 3 per cent. At the same time the population of the country increased by 3.7 per cent.

Households (number)

There is significant spatial variation in this growth. For example, the population of Fingal increased by 8.1 per cent, but the number of households grew by only 4.4 per cent; conversely, Donegal lost population (-1.5 per cent) yet experienced a small increase in the number of households (0.8 per cent).

See also: *households (size); headship rate; housing stock; population*

There are 1,702,289 households in Ireland. Average *household* size increased between 2011 and 2016, from 2.73 to 2.75 persons, reversing a long-term trend of declining household size.

Households (size)

Average size varies by household type. The number of households comprised of cohabiting couples with children increased by 14,068 or 25.6 per cent, while the number of persons living in those households increased by 59,196 or 28.7 per cent, resulting in the average size increasing from 3.76 to 3.85. Households comprised of unrelated persons only increased by 10.8 per cent while the number of persons living in such households increased by 15.3 per cent, resulting in the average household size increasing from 2.66 persons in 2011 to 2.77 in 2016.

Of the 1,702,289 private households in the country, a total of 1,195,467 households (70.2 per cent) contained families. A further 399,815 (23.5 per cent) were one-person households. The remaining 107,007 (6.3 per cent)

[266] Department of Environment, Heritage and Local Government (2011) *Social Housing Support – Household Means Policy*, Government of Ireland: Dublin

were non-family households. There were 73,361 family households (6.1 per cent of all family households) with persons other than family members living in them. Lone parents were most likely to share their home with others. There were 399,815 people living on their own at the time of the last census, almost evenly split between men and women with 195,519 and 204,296 respectively. The majority of those living alone were single (52.6 per cent), with just under one in four widowed. Those living alone had in general a lower social class than the overall population.

There were 107,007 non-family households in 2016, up from 102,219 in 2011, a 4.7 per cent increase; 69,359 (64.8 per cent) of these were comprised of unrelated persons only, while 37,648 (35.2 per cent) contained related persons such as siblings.[267]

See also: ***headship rate; housing demand; cohabitation; housing stock; population***

Housesitting

Housesitting is the practice of being permitted to live in a property rent-free for a specified time, usually in exchange for performing a set of duties (e.g. taking care of pets, maintaining lawns) in the absence of the owners.

See also: ***caretaker agreement; licence***

Housing Act 1966

The 1964 White Paper *Housing – Progress and Prospects* set out the government's plans for housing provision until 1970, as well as a review of existing legislation in the field of housing. In relation to legislative proposals it was envisaged that all the previous legislation would be consolidated into one Act. The Housing Act 1966 translated most of these proposals into legislation. There was a new emphasis on the role of private house-building, and in the 1960s, for the first time, the rate of private house-building was higher than that of local authority building.[268] The Act contained provisions on assistance of certain research, training and bodies; housing loans and grants, etc.; contributions by the Minister to certain annual loan charges; stamp duties; provision and management of dwellings; overcrowded and unfit houses; acquisition of land, etc.; disposal of land and dwellings; and purchase of certain cottages under the Act of 1936.

Sections of the 1966 Act are still relevant today, especially section 63, the definition of ***overcrowding***.

Housing and Sustainable Communities Agency, The

The Housing and Sustainable Communities Agency (known as the Housing Agency) was set up in May 2010 to work with and support local authorities, ***approved housing bodies***, and the ***Department of Housing, Planning***

---

[267] CSO Census 2016. See: https://www.cso.ie/en/releasesandpublications/ep/p-cp4hf/cp4hf/hhlds/

[268] Kenna, P (2011) *Housing Law, Rights and Policy*, Clarus Press: Dublin

and Local Government in the delivery of housing and housing services. The agency resulted from the merger of the Affordable Housing Partnership, *National Building Agency* and Centre for Housing Research.[269]

The services of the Housing Agency include:

- Enhanced leasing: the Housing Agency is the national coordinator of this scheme and manages and administers it on behalf of the Department
- Events: the Housing Agency runs a series of events throughout the year
- Housing management services: offering support to local authority housing practitioners and approved housing bodies in relation to all aspects of housing
- Housing Procurement Office: providing procurement support and advice in support of local authorities and AHBs in the accelerated delivery of their social housing programmes
- Housing supply services: to provide a range of solutions for improving the supply of social housing
- Pyrite Remediation Scheme: The Pyrite Remediation Scheme has been set up to remediate dwellings that have been significantly damaged as a result of pyritic heave caused by the swelling of hardcore under ground floor slabs (see: *Pyrite Resolution Board*).
- Research services: The agency's research function is to:
  - carry out research and evaluations
  - provide policy advice
  - analyse information on housing matters
  - distribute information on housing matters to housing practitioners and the wider public
- Unfinished housing developments: The agency has been considerably involved in the resolution of the issue of *unfinished estates*.

The Housing Alliance is a collaboration of six of the larger Irish *approved housing bodies* (AHBs): *Clúid Housing*, *Circle Voluntary Housing Association*, *Co-operative Housing Ireland*, Oaklee Housing, *Respond* and *Túath Housing*.

It originated in informal discussions in autumn 2016 which led to an agreed set of objectives under the broad heading of promoting the delivery of social and *affordable* housing. These objectives include: increasing the delivery of social and affordable homes; developing improved practices in the management of social and affordable housing; developing practical and innovative solutions to increase social and affordable housing; and promoting

Housing Alliance, The

---

[269] Department of Public Expenditure and Reform (2014) *A Report on the Implementation of the Agency Rationalisation Programme*, Government of Ireland: Dublin

the AHB sector as a professionally run, high quality provider of social and affordable housing.

Housing Alliance members own or manage a total **housing stock** of 19,000 dwellings, which represents two-thirds of the total AHB housing stock owned or managed by the 253 AHBs registered with the AHB regulator (the **Housing Agency**). This demonstrates the diverse structure of the AHB sector. The small number of larger AHBs with ambitious development programmes face similar challenges and opportunities in realising their objectives, which arise directly from their size. This growing awareness of shared concerns was a key driver in the establishment of the Housing Alliance.

At the same time as working collaboratively on a range of issues, Housing Alliance members explicitly retain their status as independent and autonomous organisations and have agreed a code of conduct which explicitly forbids any anti-competitive behaviour.

Housing Assistance Payment[270]

The Housing Assistance Payment (HAP) scheme is provided under Part 4 of the Housing (Miscellaneous Provisions) Act 2014. The HAP is a *social housing* support which provides access to accommodation within the *private rented sector*. In 2018, there were more than 37,000 **households**[271] in HAP accommodation at the end of 2017, with 350 being added each week.[272] There are some 21,000 separate landlords and agents currently in receipt of monthly HAP payments.[273]

The HAP scheme was introduced on a phased basis from 2014. Recipients are responsible for sourcing their own accommodation within the private rented sector. The resultant tenancy agreement is between the **landlord** and the **tenant**. The rental payment to the landlord is made directly by local authorities (LA) through a shared service centre; there is no contractual relationship between the LA and the landlord. The level of **rent** being charged for the accommodation should generally be within the limits set down for the household type in that LA's area, although there is an element of flexibility to this with LAs being able to use discretion of up to 20 per cent above rent limits (or 50 per cent for homeless households – see: **Homeless HAP**). Tenants then pay a contribution towards their rent (**differential rent**) to the LA based on their income and ability to pay. In terms of scheme eligibility, all households that qualify for social housing support (as assessed by their LA) are eligible to apply for HAP. It is a government objective that all long-term recipients of **Rent Supplement** (longer than eighteen months) will transfer to

[270] See: http://hap.ie
[271] See: https://data.gov.ie/dataset/hap-scheme-2014-2018
[272] Burns, S (2018) 'Just 8% of properties affordable for those on rental supports', *Irish Times*, 16 August
[273] See: https://www.kildarestreet.com/wrans/?id=2018-06-26a.1490

the HAP scheme on a phased basis. An important difference between HAP and Rent Supplement is that it allows recipients to work full time while Rent Supplement recipients can't work for more than 30 hours per week.[274]

The system works as follows:

1. To qualify for HAP, a household must be qualified for social housing support by their local authority, which means the household must qualify to go on the local authority *social housing waiting list*.
2. HAP tenants must find their own accommodation in the private rented market.
3. The landlord must agree to rent their property to the HAP tenant. (Under the Equal Status Acts 2000–2015, landlords are not allowed discriminate against HAP tenants. See: *discrimination*.)
4. The local authority will make a monthly payment to the landlord. This payment is made on the last Wednesday of each month. The payment is subject to terms and conditions, including rent limits and that the HAP tenant pays their rent contribution to the local authority.
5. The HAP tenant pays their rent contribution to the local authority, usually through An Post's Household Budget Scheme. If the HAP tenant does not pay this rent contribution, HAP payments to their landlord will be suspended and eventually stopped. The HAP tenant is then responsible for paying the full rent themselves.

The tenancy relationship between landlord and tenant in a HAP agreement is a *lease* and covered by the *Residential Tenancies Acts*.

HAP tenants are considered to have had their housing needs met and are taken off the social housing waiting list.

See: *approved housing bodies*

Housing associations

The housing cost overburden rate is the percentage of the population living in households where the total housing costs represent more than 40 per cent of disposable income ('net' of housing allowances).

Housing cost overburden

In 2016, 4.6 per cent of the Irish population suffered housing cost overburden – the EU-28 average is 11.1 per cent. This is broken down as:[275]

---

[274] Kilkenny, P and O'Callaghan, D (2018) *Department of Public Expenditure and Reform – Spending Review 2018: Current and Capital Expenditure on Social Housing Delivery Mechanisms*, Department of Public Expenditure and Reform: Dublin
[275] See: https://ec.europa.eu/eurostat/statistics-explained/index.php/Glossary:Housing_cost_overburden_rate

	Owner-occupied with mortgage	Owner-occupied without mortgage	Tenant in private rented sector	Local authority/ AHB tenant
Ireland	2.2%	1.5%	19.6%	4.2%
EU-28	5.45%	6.4%	28%	13%

See also: **affordability**

Housing demand A range of factors have implications for the number of houses that a country needs at any one time. In general, the following broad headings are drivers of housing demand:

- Economic growth
- Demographic developments
- Patterns of income distribution
- The level and distribution of wealth
- The cost and availability of finance
- Fiscal policy
- The level of **housing stock**[276]

More specifically, the three headings below are immediate drivers of demand for housing.

- **Headship rate**: The headship rate provides one measure of the rate of household formation. The headship rate is the proportion of individuals in an age cohort that list themselves as 'head of household' or 'principal reference person' in the Census. Each household provides one reference person, thus an increase in the headship rate reveals an increase in the number of households.[277]
- Housing **obsolescence**: this is the number of houses that fall out of use or become unusable each year. For 2017, despite 14,407 houses being recorded as completed by the CSO, the Department of Housing, Planning and Local Government added just 10,000 houses to their calculation of the national housing stock.
- **Population** growth: as emigration returns to natural levels, population growth through immigration and natural means will create demand for an extra 300 or so houses a week, or over 16,000 houses a year.

---

[276] National Economic and Social Council (2004) *Housing in Ireland: Performance and Policy*, NESC: Dublin

[277] Duffy, D, Byrne, D and Fitzgerald, J (2014) 'Alternative Scenarios for New Household Formation in Ireland', *Quarterly Economic Commentary*, ESRI: Dublin

Estimates for the number of houses that Ireland needs each year range from below 20,000 to more than 50,000 units. However, 'most analysts believe that, in the medium term, 30,000–35,000 dwellings are needed each year to cover population growth, changing household sizes, obsolescence and some "over-building" to offset previous under-construction.'[278]

See also: ***data – housing output issues; obsolescence; headship rate; housing stock; affordability***

A housing estate is a planned area of housing or a group of houses, typically built at the same time. A housing estate can be built by one or more contractors, and can take several years to complete from start to finish. It is increasingly common to find housing estates including a mixture of ***detached***, ***semi-detached***, and ***terraced housing***, as well as ***duplexes*** and ***apartments***. It is not unusual to find retail and community facilities within or close to housing estates.

See also: ***scheme dwelling; unfinished estates***

Housing estate

Housing Europe is the European Federation of Public, Cooperative and ***Social Housing***. Since 1988 it is a network of 45 national and regional federations gathering together 43,000 housing providers in 24 countries. Together they manage over 26 million homes, about 11 per cent of existing dwellings in Europe. It has a comprehensive programme of events, projects, publications and resources. Housing Europe is based in Brussels, Belgium.[279]

See also: ***FEANTSA; Irish Council for Social Housing***

Housing Europe

The Housing Finance Agency (HFA) was established in 1982 as a state-owned body. The Housing Finance Agency plc is now a company under the aegis of the ***Minister for Housing, Planning and Local Government*** of Ireland.

The HFA's function is to advance loan finance to local authorities and the voluntary housing sector to be used by them for any purpose authorised by the Housing Acts 1966–2009, and to borrow or raise funds for these purposes. In infrastructure, the HFA is empowered to lend funds to local authorities for waste and environmental capital projects under the terms of the Housing (Miscellaneous Provisions) Act 2002.[281]

See also: ***European Investment Bank***

Housing Finance Agency[280]

Housing First offers permanent accommodation to people in chronic need without requiring them to go through the formal homelessness system of

Housing First

[278] McCartney, J (2018) 'How many houses do we really need?', *Irish Times*, 1 June
[279] See: http://www.housingeurope.eu
[280] See: http://www.hfa.ie/hfa/Live/Release/WebSite/HomePage/aboutus.html
[281] Housing Finance Agency (2018) *Annual Report 2017*, HFA: Dublin

waiting lists, hostels and temporary accommodation. While models in different places may differ slightly, Housing First tends to be directed at people who are sleeping rough or have experienced repeat homelessness and have mental health and addiction problems. Under Housing First there is no requirement for the homeless person to be 'housing ready' or to have addressed their addiction problems before moving into a permanent home. Health and addiction issues are addressed after housing has been secured, and intensive, open-ended support is provided to help the person maintain their tenancy.[282]

The Housing First model operates by taking account of two key convictions:

- Housing is a basic human right, not a reward for clinical success.
- Once the chaos of homelessness is eliminated from a person's life, clinical and social stabilisation occurs faster and is more enduring.[283]

As chronic housing shortages contribute to homelessness, increasing the supply of affordable rental housing is a critical part of the Housing First approach.

Several Irish homeless charities (e.g. Depaul, **Peter McVerry Trust**) run Housing First programmes, as do Dublin City Council.

See also: **homelessness; rough sleeping**

Housing (Miscellaneous Provisions) Act 2009 (Part 5) Regulations 2019

Part 5 of the Housing (Miscellaneous Provisions) Act 2009 provides a new statutory basis for the delivery of **affordable housing** for purchase. The 2019 affordable purchase scheme is based on local authorities providing, directly or indirectly, below market price housing.

The main tenets of the scheme are as follows:

- It is targeted towards low- to middle-income first-time buyer households
- Discounts of up to 40 per cent of the market price of the property will be provided
- The local authority will place a charge against the property equal to the discount provided
- The charge is repayable and the proceeds will be placed into a centralised affordable housing fund giving the scheme long-term sustainability
- The affordable dwellings fund will be administered by the **Housing Finance Agency**

The areas in which the scheme operates are determined by economic assessments carried out by local authorities.

[282] Chartered Institute of Housing (2017) *Housing First in the UK and Ireland*, CIH: Coventry
[283] Shelter (2008) *Housing First: Good Practice*, Shelter: London

According to the *Minister for Housing, Planning and Local Government*:

The affordable housing scheme [is] open to applications according as projects are delivered. In that regard, significant delivery is to be achieved through the €310 million *Serviced Sites Fund* (SSF), under which at least 6,200 affordable homes are to be supported over the next three years. An initial ten projects have been approved for €43 million of funding under the first call for proposals under the SSF. ... The first homes are expected to be delivered in 2020.

In addition, some 2,350 affordable homes will be delivered on mainly publicly owned lands being supported through the *Local Infrastructure Housing Activation Fund* (LIHAF), while 5,600 further homes will benefit from a LIHAF-related cost reduction. The work of the *Land Development Agency* (LDA) will also be of crucial importance in terms of delivering more affordable housing; the initial portfolio of sites that the LDA has access to will have the potential, over the short- to medium-term, to deliver 3,000 affordable homes in line with the government policy of achieving 30 per cent affordable housing on state lands generally.[284]

See also: *affordability; affordable housing schemes*

Housing Needs Assessment Housing authorities were previously required to undertake an assessment of housing need in their functional areas every three years. Since 2016, this assessment has been annual. The list comprises *households* that have been approved for housing support but not yet had their housing needs met.

The criteria for being on this list are:

a. Households must be qualified for social housing support; and
b. Households currently living in local authority rented accommodation, voluntary/cooperative accommodation, accommodation provided under the *Housing Assistance Payment* (HAP) scheme, accommodation provided under the *Rental Accommodation Scheme* (RAS), accommodation provided under the *Social Housing Capital Expenditure Programme* (SHCEP) schemes or any household on a *transfer list* are not included in the net need number.

The key findings of the Social Housing Assessment 2018 were as follows:

• In total, 71,858 households were assessed as qualified for housing support as of 11 June 2018.

[284] See: https://www.kildarestreet.com/wrans/?id=2019-03-12a.1929&s=%22housing+%28miscellaneous+provisions%29%22+part+5#g1932.r

- The four Dublin local authorities (Dublin City, Dún Laoghaire–Rathdown, Fingal and South Dublin) account for 43.4 per cent of the national total.
- The majority (54.2 per cent) of those qualified for social housing support are unemployed and in receipt of social welfare payments/assistance.
- Single-person households are the predominant household grouping in need of social housing support.
- Just under 60 per cent of households qualified for social housing support are currently in the private rented sector.
- Over a quarter of all households qualified for support are waiting more than seven years for a social housing support.

As the Housing Needs Assessment excludes several categories of households (for example, those in receipt of HAP), it can be argued that the figure of 71,858 is not an accurate representation of genuine 'housing need' as those who are excluded from the Housing Needs Assessment are typically accommodated in the *private rented sector* and, as such, it is debateable that their housing needs have truly been met as they are now living subject to the lack of *security of tenure* and other market conditions that are not prevalent in local authority-owned and managed housing. A household having their 'housing needs met' may therefore be only a temporary status, being subject to the provisions in the *Residential Tenancies Act 2004*, and particularly section 34 on reasons for termination.

See also: *transfer list; social housing; council housing*

Housing policy See: *policy, housing*

Housing rights approach to housing Kenna explains the housing rights approach to housing.[285] He says both social democrat and neoliberal democratic governments accept the market as the primary provider of housing, with government intervention to regulate the excesses of the market and to intervene when the market fails. Disagreement between these two appears to merely centre around how serious that failure is and just what government should do about it. These approaches to housing can be contrasted with a right-to-housing position 'in which government's first obligation is to see that all are decently housed, and the for-profit market is managed and regulated in a way subservient to that goal'.[286] The for-profit market is the default position for neoliberal and social democratic policies, with public action limited to countering its failure. Government support for decent and affordable housing for all who need it is the default position of

---

[285] See: Kenna, P (2011) *Housing Law, Rights and Policy*, Clarus Press: Dublin
[286] See: Marcuse, P and Keating, W (2006) *The Permanent Housing Crisis: The Failures of Conservatism and the Limitations of Liberalism*, Temple University Press: Philadelphia

the right-to-housing approach, with the for-profit market functioning where it does not interfere or frustrate that provision.

See also: *UN Special Rapporteur on the Right to Adequate Housing; discrimination; neoliberalism in Ireland*

The Housing (Standards for Rented Houses) Regulations 2008 revoked the Housing (Standards for Rented Houses) Regulations 1993 (S.I. No. 147 of 1993). The main impact of these regulations was to bring in a ban on *bedsits*.

The Housing (Standards for Rented Houses) Regulations 2008 (S.I. No. 534 of 2008) and the Housing (Standards for Rented Houses) (Amendment) Regulations 2009 (S.I. No. 462 of 2009) were both revoked by the *Housing (Standards for Rented Houses) Regulations 2017*.

See also: *Fire Safety Certificate; Fire Safety Notice*

Housing (Standards for Rented Houses) Regulations 2008

These regulations require landlords of rented houses (including *flats* and *maisonettes*), with some exceptions, to ensure that such houses meet certain minimum standards. In general, the standards relate to: structural condition; provision of sanitary facilities; food preparation, storage and laundry; availability of adequate heating, lighting and ventilation; safety of oil, electricity and gas installations; fire safety; and refuse facilities. The regulations came into operation generally on 1 July 2017. All landlords have a legal obligation to ensure that their rented properties comply with these regulations and enforcement of these regulations is the responsibility of each local authority.

The *Department of Housing, Planning and Local Government* provides an overview of the main points of these standards:

Housing (Standards for Rented Houses) Regulations 2017

- Structural condition
  - All rental accommodation must be maintained in a proper state of structural repair. This means that the dwelling must be essentially sound, internally and externally, with roof, roofing tiles and slates, windows, floors, ceilings, walls, stairs, doors, skirting boards, fascia, tiles on any floor, ceiling and wall, gutters, down pipes, fittings, furnishings, gardens and common areas maintained in good condition and repair, and not defective due to dampness or otherwise.
  - There must be suitable safety restrictors attached to a window which has an opening through which a person may fall and the bottom of the opening is more than 1400mm above the external ground level. Suitable safety restrictors must secure the window sufficiently to prevent such falls. Lockable restrictors that can only be released by removable keys or other tools should not be fitted to window opening sections.

- Sanitary facilities
  - All rental accommodation must contain the following self-contained sanitary facilities:
    » Water closet with dedicated wash hand basin with hot and cold water
    » Fixed bath or shower, supplied with hot and cold water
  - These facilities must be provided in a room separate from other rooms by a wall and door and contain separate ventilation.
- Heating facilities
  - All habitable rooms must contain a fixed heating appliance which is capable of providing effective heating. The tenant must be able to control the operation of the heating appliance.
  - Where necessary, suitably located devices for the detection and alarm of carbon monoxide
- Food preparation and storage and laundry
  - All rental accommodation shall contain the following self-contained facilities:
    » Four-ring hob with oven and grill
    » Provision for the effective and safe removal of fumes to the external air by means of cooker hood or an extractor fan
    » Fridge and freezer
    » Microwave oven
    » Sink with a draining area
    » Adequate number of kitchen presses for food storage purposes
    » Washing machine within the dwelling unit or access to a communal washing machine facility within the curtilage of the building
    » In cases where the accommodation does not contain a garden or yard for the exclusive use of this accommodation, a dryer must be provided
- Ventilation
  - All habitable rooms must have adequate ventilation, maintained in good repair and working order. Kitchens and bathrooms must be provided with adequate ventilation for the removal of water vapour to the external air.
- Lighting
  - All habitable rooms must have adequate natural lighting.
  - All rooms (including every hall, stairs and landing) must have a suitable and adequate means of artificial lighting.
  - The windows of every room containing a bath and/or shower and a water closet shall be suitably and adequately screened to ensure privacy.

- Fire safety
  - Multi-unit dwellings are required to contain a fire detection and alarm system, an emergency evacuation plan and emergency lighting in common areas.
  - Rental units that do not form part of a multiple unit must have a suitable self-contained fire detection and alarm system and a suitably located fire blanket. Smoke alarms should be either mains-wired with battery back-up or ten-year self-contained battery-operated smoke alarms.
- Refuse facilities
  - The regulations require access for tenants to proper, pest- and vermin-proof refuse storage facilities. The use of communal storage facilities, where appropriate, will be considered to comply with the regulations.
- Electricity and gas
  - Installations in the house for gas, oil and electricity supply, including pipework, storage facilities and electrical distribution boxes, must be maintained in good repair and safe working order.
  - There must also be, where necessary, provision for the safe and effective removal of fumes to the external air.

The regulations apply to all rental accommodation with the exception of the following categories of housing:

- Holiday homes
- Accommodation provided by the Health Service Executive or an approved housing body containing communal sanitary, cooking and dining facilities. This kind of accommodation usually houses people with disabilities or the elderly and provides support for people with special needs who require assistance to live in the community
- Demountable (e.g. mobile homes) housing provided by a housing authority
- Accommodation let by a housing authority or an approved housing body will be exempt from the requirements for food preparation, storage and laundry purposes. In this kind of accommodation, the tenant usually provides these goods, retaining ownership of them when they move to new accommodation (all other articles of the regulations apply to both housing authorities and approved housing bodies.)

Buildings on the ***Record of Protected Structures*** are also required to meet the requirements of the regulations. The owner or occupier of a protected structure is entitled to ask the ***planning authority*** to identify works that would, or would not, require planning permission in the case of their particular building.

Local authorities and certain housing bodies have to adhere to different requirements regarding laundry, food preparation and storage facilities and must provide:

- Facilities for the installation of cooking equipment
- Sink, with a piped supply of potable cold water taken directly from the service pipe supplying water from the public main or other source to the building containing the house and a facility for the piped supply of hot water, and an adequate draining area
- Suitable facilities for the effective and safe removal of fumes to the external air by means of a cooker hood or extractor fan
- Suitable and adequate number of kitchen presses for food storage purposes[287]

Housing (Standards for Rented Houses) Regulations 2019

These regulations came into effect on 1 May 2019 and revoked previous regulations from 2017. The regulations apply to every house let, or available for letting, for **rent** or other valuable consideration solely as a house unless the house is let or available for letting—

(*a*) To a person only for the purpose of conferring on that person the right to occupy the house for a holiday,

(*b*) By the Health Service Executive or by an approved body, as accommodation with sanitary, cooking or dining facilities provided for communal use within the building which contains the house, or

(*c*) By a housing authority pursuant to any of their functions under the Housing Acts 1966–2014, and is a caravan, mobile home or a structure or a thing (whether on wheels or not) that is capable of being moved from one place to another (whether by towing, transport on a vehicle or trailer, or otherwise).

The headings are:

Structural Condition

4. (1) A house to which these Regulations apply (hereinafter referred to as 'the house') shall be maintained in a proper state of structural repair.

(2) For the purposes of Regulation 4(1) 'a proper state of structural repair' means sound, internally and externally, with roof, roofing tiles and slates, windows, floors, ceilings, walls, stairs, doors, skirting boards, fascia, tiles on any floor, ceiling and wall, gutters, down pipes, fittings, furnishings, gardens and common areas maintained in good condition and repair and not defective due to dampness or otherwise.

[287] See: https://www.housing.gov.ie/housing/private-rented-housing/inspections/minimum-standards-rented-accommodation

(3) Where a window has an opening section through which a person may fall, and the bottom of the opening section is more than 1400mm above external ground level, suitable safety restrictors shall be fitted. Safety restrictors shall restrain the window sufficiently to prevent such falls.

(4) Where necessary, adequate provision shall be made to prevent harbourage or ingress of pests or vermin.

Sanitary Facilities

5. (1) There shall be provided within the same habitable area of the house, for the exclusive use of the house:

(*a*) A water closet, with dedicated wash hand basin adjacent thereto with a continuous supply of cold water and a facility for the piped supply of hot water, and

(*b*) A fixed bath or shower with continuous supply of cold water and a facility for the piped supply of hot water.

(2) The requirements of Regulation 5(1) shall:

(i)   Be maintained in a safe condition and good working order,

(ii) Have safe and effective means of drainage,

(iii) Be properly insulated,

(iv) Have minimum capacity requirements for hot and cold water storage facilities, and

(v)   Be provided in a room separated from other rooms by a wall and a door and containing separate ventilation.

Heating Facilities

6. (1) Every room used, or intended for use, by the tenant of the house as a habitable room, and any bathroom, or shower-room shall contain a permanently fixed:

(*a*) Heat emitter,

(*b*) Heat distribution system, or

(*c*) Heat producing appliance, capable of providing effective heating.

(2) Every room referred to in Regulation 6(1) shall contain suitable and adequate facilities for the safe and effective removal of fumes and other products of combustion to the external air where a heat producing appliance is used.

(3) A heat producing appliance referred to in Regulation 6(1)(*c*) shall be so installed that there is an adequate supply of air to it for combustion, to prevent overheating and for the efficient working of any flue pipe or chimney serving the appliance.

(4) The operation of any:

(*a*) Heat emitter,

(*b*) Heat distribution system, or

(*c*) Heat producing appliance

as referred to in Regulation 6(1) shall be capable of being independently manageable by the tenant.

(5) All appliances under Regulation 6(1) shall be maintained in a safe condition and in good working order and good repair.

(6) Each house shall contain, where necessary, suitably located devices for the detection and alarm of *carbon monoxide*.

Food Preparation and Storage and Laundry

7. (1) Notwithstanding paragraph (4), paragraphs (2) and (3) shall not apply where the house is let or available for letting –

    (i)   By a housing authority under the Housing Acts 1966 to 2014,

    (ii) By a housing body approved under section 6 of the Housing (Miscellaneous Provisions) Act 1992, or

    (iii) For a minimum lease period of ten years under a tenancy agreement.

(2) Subject to paragraph (1), there shall be provided, within the same habitable area of the house, for the exclusive use of the house:

(*a*) Four-ring hob with oven and grill,

(*b*) Suitable facilities for the effective and safe removal of fumes to the external air by means of a cooker hood or extractor fan,

(*c*) Fridge and freezer or fridge-freezer,

(*d*) Microwave oven,

(*e*) Sink, with a piped supply of potable cold water taken direct from the service pipe supplying water from the public main or other source to the building containing the house and a facility for the piped supply of hot water, and an adequate draining area,

(*f*) Suitable and adequate number of kitchen presses for food storage purposes,

(*g*) Washing machine, or access to a communal washing machine facility within the curtilage of the building, and

(*h*) Where the house does not contain a garden or yard for the exclusive use of that house, a dryer (vented or recirculation type) or access to a communal dryer facility.

(3) All facilities under Regulation 7(2) shall be maintained in a safe condition and in good working order and good repair.

(4) Responsibility for maintenance of facilities under Regulation 7(2) shall rest with the landlord.

(5) Where a house is let or available for letting:

(*a*) By a housing authority under the Housing Acts 1966 to 2014,

(*b*) By a housing body approved under section 6 of the Housing (Miscellaneous Provisions) Act 1992, or

(*c*) For a minimum lease period of ten years under a tenancy agreement, there shall be provided, within the same habitable area of the house, for the exclusive use of the house:

(i)   Facilities for the installation of cooking equipment,

(ii) Sink, with a piped supply of potable cold water taken direct from the service pipe supplying water from the public main or other source to the building containing the house and a facility for the piped supply of hot water, and an adequate draining area,

(iii) Suitable facilities for the effective and safe removal of fumes to the external air by means of a cooker hood or extractor fan, and

(iv) Suitable and adequate number of kitchen presses for food storage purposes.

Ventilation

8. (1) Every room used, or intended for use, by the tenant of the house as a habitable room shall have adequate ventilation.

(2) All means of ventilation shall be maintained in good repair and working order.

(3) Adequate ventilation shall be provided for the removal of water vapour from every kitchen and bathroom.

Lighting

9. (1) Every room used, or intended for use, by the tenant of the house as a habitable room, shall have adequate natural lighting.

(2) Every hall, stairs, and landing within the house and every room used, or intended for use, by the tenant of the house shall have a suitable and adequate means of artificial lighting.

(3) The windows of every room containing a bath or shower and a water closet shall be suitably and adequately screened to ensure privacy.

Fire Safety

10. (1) Each house shall contain a suitable self-contained fire detection and alarm system.

(2) Each house shall contain a suitably located fire blanket.

(3) Each self-contained house in a multi-unit building shall contain a suitable fire detection and alarm system and an emergency evacuation plan.

(4) A suitable fire detection and alarm system shall be provided in common areas within a multi-unit building.

(5) Emergency lighting shall be provided in all common areas within a multi-unit building.

(6) Fire detection and alarm systems and emergency lighting systems required under Regulation 10(4) and 10(5) shall be maintained in accordance with current standards.

(7) In this Regulation:

'Current standards' means standards produced by the National Standards Authority of Ireland for Fire Detection and Fire Alarm Systems in Buildings and for Emergency Lighting.
'Multi-unit building' means a building that contains two or more houses that share a common access.

Refuse Facilities
11. The house shall have access to suitable and adequate pest- and vermin-proof refuse storage facilities.

Gas, Oil and Electricity Installations
12. Installations for the supply of gas, oil and electricity including pipework, storage facilities and electrical distribution boxes shall be maintained in good repair and safe working order.

Information
13. Sufficient information shall be provided to the tenant about the rented property, the fixed building services, appliances and their routine maintenance requirements so that the occupant can operate them correctly.
See also: ***Housing (Standards for Rented Houses) Regulations 2017; overcrowding***

Housing stock As of Census 2016, Ireland has a housing stock of 2,003,645 houses and ***apartments***. The housing stock excludes non-permanent ***dwellings*** such as caravans and ***mobile homes*** as well as 4,140 communal establishments.

Between 2011 and 2016, the housing stock increased by 0.4 per cent, or 8,800 dwellings. For comparison, between 2002 and 2006, the housing stock increased by 21.2 per cent, or 309,560 dwellings; and between 2006 and 2011, the housing stock increased by 225,232 dwellings or 12.7 per cent.

Census year	Housing stock	Housing stock change	% Housing stock change	Dwellings per 1,000 population	Population
1991	1,160,249			329	3,525,719
1996	1,258,948	98,699	8.5%	347	3,626,087
2002	1,460,053	201,105	16%	373	3,917,203
2006	1,769,613	309,560	21.2%	417	4,239,848
2011	1,994,845	225,232	12.7%	435	4,588,252
2016	2,003,645	8,800	0.4%	421	4,761,865

Table extracted from CSO figures 1991–2016[288]

[288] See: https://www.cso.ie/en/releasesandpublications/ep/p-cp1hii/cp1hii/hs/

Ireland has a dwellings per 1,000 *population* figure of 421. This is -3.2 per cent since 2011; in the same period the population increased by 3.8 per cent.

The 2,003,645 *dwellings* which comprise the Irish housing stock were located in 1,775,475 residential and partly residential buildings in 2016. Over 97 per cent of these buildings had one dwelling only while 49,546 multi-dwelling buildings housed 277,716 units, representing 14 per cent of the housing stock at an average of almost six dwellings per building. The most populated building in Census 2016 contained 372 dwellings and was home to 882 persons. There are 95,013 dwellings with more persons than rooms.

Detached houses comprised 42.1 per cent of the total (715,133 dwellings) and remained the most popular dwelling type. *Semi-detached* dwellings accounted for 471,948 dwellings. Purpose-built *flats* and *apartments* rose from 149,921 in 2011 to 172,096 in 2016, an increase of 14.8 per cent or 22,175 units. More than one in four occupied dwellings in Ireland were built in the period 2001–2010. Of these, just over two-thirds were detached or semi-detached houses, the remainder being *terraced houses*, apartments or flats.[289]

See also: *tenure, vacant dwellings; commune; headship rate; population; density, housing; density, population*

Part V of the *Planning and Development Act 2000* (as amended) and **Housing strategy** the *Urban Regeneration and Housing Act 2015* require that all planning authorities prepare housing strategies and incorporate them into their *development plans*. The housing strategy must include an analysis of demand and supply for the different sectors of the housing market, forecast future requirements and propose strategies to balance demand and supply in a sustainable manner.

The Act specifies that a housing strategy shall:

- Ensure that adequate zoned and serviced lands for residential purposes are available in appropriate locations to meet the requirements of the housing strategy and the existing and future housing demand.
- Ensure that housing is available to people of different income levels and determine the distribution of this housing.
- Ensure that a mixture of house types and sizes is developed to reasonably match the requirements of the different categories of households, including the special requirements of elderly persons and persons with disabilities.
- Counteract undue segregation in housing between people of different social backgrounds.

---

[289] See: https://www.cso.ie/en/media/csoie/releasespublications/documents/population/2017/ Chapter_9_Housing.pdf

- Provide that a specific percentage (not exceeding 10 per cent) of the land zoned in the development plan for residential use or a mixture of residential and other uses shall be reserved for those in need of social or *affordable housing* in the area.

See also: *zoning*

Housing (Traveller Accommodation) Act 1998

The Housing (Traveller Accommodation) Act 1998 requires each local authority to draw up, adopt and implement five-year rolling accommodation programmes to accelerate the provision of accommodation for Travellers. Section 7(4) of the Act provides that the adoption, amendment or replacement of an accommodation programme is a reserved function, meaning that it is a function that is carried out by the elected councillors.

Howard, Ebenezer

See: *garden city; Marino – garden city*

Hubs

Family hubs are group homes for homeless families. Hubs (or 'family hubs') are a new model of accommodation for families experiencing *homelessness*. They are designed to include wrap-around services to help families be in a better position to move into their own homes in the short term.[290]

Hubs are seen as longer-term housing for homeless families, as an alternative to staying in hotel or *bed and breakfast* rooms on a night-by-night basis.[291]

See also: *rough sleeping; Peter McVerry Trust; Respond*

I

iCare

iCare Housing is an *approved housing body* that has been set up specifically to help people in *mortgage* arrears to remain in their family homes. iCare has an agreement in place with Allied Irish Banks, Educational Building Society and Haven Mortgages. iCare Housing buys the house from the bank, writes off the mortgage debt, and gives the household a long-term lease to remain in the home. The price at which iCare buys the house will be listed in the lease and a legally binding option will be given for the original owners to buy back the house at any time over the life of the lease. This is an offering modelled on the Mortgage to Rent Scheme.

See also: *Irish Mortgage Holders Association; Code of Conduct on Mortgage Arrears; Mortgage Arrears Resolution Process*

---

[290] See: https://www.respond.ie/community-services/special-projects/cuan-aileann/
[291] Power, J (2018) 'Over €16m spent renovating 10 homeless family hubs', *Irish Times*, 15 August

An Improvement Notice – issued by a housing authority – sets out the works a *landlord* must carry out, within a set timeframe, to remedy any breach of regulations. Where an Improvement Notice is not complied with, a housing authority may issue a **Prohibition Notice**, which directs a landlord not to re-let a property until the breach of the regulations has been rectified. Failure to comply with an Improvement Notice or a Prohibition Notice is an offence.

See also: **enforcement; unauthorised development; Housing (Standards for Rented Houses) Regulations 2017**

Improvement Notice

Imputed rent (or more precisely, imputed net rent) from housing is derived when the housing costs paid by the household for its dwelling (e.g. owner-occupiers' maintenance costs, insurance, service charges) and interests on the mortgage are deducted from the so-called imputed gross rent.[292] In effect, this means that the rental value of a property is still present even if it is owner-occupied (the rent is 'imputed', or a value assigned).

In Switzerland, **owner-occupiers** pay tax on a theoretical (imputed) rent that their property could achieve. It has been argued that this extra taxation is one of the main drivers of Swiss households renting instead of buying their own homes,[293] leading to a low **home ownership** rate of 38.2 per cent in 2016.[294]

See also: **market rent; economic growth and housing**

Imputed rent

Infill sites are often gaps between buildings, perhaps where one building has been demolished or the space never built upon. They are typically vacant or under-utilised sites. Infill sites usually require no demolition of existing homes, however they sometimes require demolition of ancillary structures such as garages or redundant small commercial and community buildings set within a residential neighbourhood.[295] The use of infill sites is a good way to increase **density**.

Infill can be part of the **urban regeneration** process.

Infill site

Infrastructure is generally considered to be the physical resources and facilities needed for the functional operation of a country. Examples of infrastructure include water, waste, transport and communications. Interestingly, despite being surrounded by infrastructure and dependent on it for provision, housing itself is not considered as infrastructure.

Infrastructure

---

[292] See: https://www.stat.fi/meta/kas/asuntotulo_en.html
[293] Bourassa, S and Hoesli, M (2009) 'Why Do the Swiss Rent?', Working Paper, Université de Genève
[294] Federal Statistical Office (Switzerland) (2018) 'Construction and Housing', available at: https://www.bfs.admin.ch/bfs/en/home/statistics/construction-housing/dwellings/housing-conditions/tenants-owners.html
[295] Future of London (2015) 'Delivering Infill Development – A London 2050 Briefing Paper', Future of London: London

Inheritance tax   See: *capital acquisitions tax* (CAT)

Inner City Helping Homeless   Inner City Helping Homeless (ICHH) was founded in November 2013 as a result of the increased number of people sleeping rough around Dublin city. Members of the local community in the north inner city came together to do a soup run around the city. By 2014 ICHH was operating a seven-night-a-week outreach service all across Dublin city. ICHH offers a seven-day advocacy service assisting homeless individuals and families and educating them on how to navigate through *homelessness*. ICHH is a registered charity, does not receive any government funding and is 100 per cent volunteer run.

See also: *rough sleeping; Peter McVerry Trust*

Institute of Professional Auctioneers and Valuers   The Institute of Professional Auctioneers and Valuers (IPAV) is a representative body for auctioneers and *valuers* in Ireland. The institute is based in Baggot Street in Dublin. Members cover various property functions. A full IPAV member will be an auctioneer, valuer, *estate agent, property managing agent, letting agent* or property professional and have obtained a current relevant licence from the *Property Services Regulatory Authority* (PSRA). A member of IPAV will also have satisfied the national council of IPAV as to their general character, experience and suitability.

See also: *Property Services (Regulation) Act 2011; property services provider*

Institutional landlord   An institutional landlord is a large-scale body (or institution) such as a pension fund, bank, church, or similar organisation with a requirement for a steady, long-term income stream. Institutional landlords are still in their infancy in Ireland, partly due to the lack of suitable accommodation (typically, many units in one block or development) available to purchase.

See also: *landlord; build-to-rent; investment*

Inter-authority transfer   Guidelines on inter-authority movement were introduced in 2017 (Circular 15/2017) to allow for local authorities to facilitate movement of HAP households from one local authority area to another in cases where a *Housing Assistance Payment* (HAP) tenant, currently on a local authority waiting list, wishes to access rented accommodation with HAP support in another local authority area. HAP tenants continue to be dealt with by their originating local authority. However, the rent limits will be those that apply in the local authority where the property is situated. The originating local authority will engage with the relevant new local authority to facilitate eligible requests for inter-authority movement.[296]

---

[296] See: https://www.oireachtas.ie/en/debates/question/2017-07-26/1691/

HAP tenants are still eligible to apply for a transfer or remain on the transfer list for their originating local authority even if availing of the inter-authority movement.

The interest rate is the amount of money charged by a lender to a borrower for the use of its money. It is usually expressed as a percentage of the original sum borrowed. It works two ways: people taking a mortgage are charged an interest rate by the lender; people depositing money in a bank are paid interest by the bank for the use of their deposits.

See also: ***fixed rate mortgage; variable rate mortgage***

                                     Interest rate

Ireland is a party to a number of international legal instruments which protect the right to housing. Ireland is a dualist state and so it is only when Ireland ratifies an international treaty that it becomes part of Irish law. Ireland has ratified the following international agreements, which have provisions protecting the right to housing:

                                 International housing law instruments[297]

The International Covenant on Economic, Social and Cultural Rights (Article 11.1):

The States Parties to the present Covenant recognise the right of everyone to an adequate standard of living for himself and his family, including adequate food, clothing and housing, and to the continuous improvement of living conditions. The States Parties will take appropriate steps to ensure the realisation of this right, recognising to this effect the essential importance of international cooperation based on free consent.

The Convention on the Rights of the Child (Article 27):

1. States Parties recognise the right of every child to a standard of living adequate for the child's physical, mental, spiritual, moral and social development.
2. The parent(s) or others responsible for the child have the primary responsibility to secure, within their abilities and financial capacities, the conditions of living necessary for the child's development.
3. States Parties, in accordance with national conditions and within their means, shall take appropriate measures to assist parents and others responsible for the child to implement this right and shall in case of need provide material assistance and support programmes, particularly with regard to nutrition, clothing and housing.

---

[297] Mercy Law Resource Centre (2018) *The Right to Housing*, Mercy Law Resource Centre: Dublin

4. States Parties shall take all appropriate measures to secure the recovery of maintenance for the child from the parents or other persons having financial responsibility for the child, both within the State Party and from abroad. In particular, where the person having financial responsibility for the child lives in a State different from that of the child, States Parties shall promote the accession to international agreements or the conclusion of such agreements, as well as the making of other appropriate arrangements.

The International Covenant on Civil and Political Rights (Article 17):

1. No one shall be subjected to arbitrary or unlawful interference with his privacy, family, home or correspondence, nor to unlawful attacks on his honour and reputation.
2. Everyone has the right to the protection of the law against such interference or attacks.

The International Convention on the Elimination of All Forms of Racial Discrimination (Article 5):

1. In compliance with the fundamental obligations laid down in article 2 of this Convention, States Parties undertake to prohibit and to eliminate racial discrimination in all its forms and to guarantee the right of everyone, without distinction as to race, colour, or national or ethnic origin, to equality before the law, notably in the enjoyment of the following rights:
   (*e*) Economic, social and cultural rights, in particular:
      a. The right to housing

The UN Convention on the Elimination of All Forms of Discrimination against Women (Article 14):

2. States Parties shall take all appropriate measures to eliminate discrimination against women in rural areas in order to ensure, on a basis of equality of men and women, that they participate in and benefit from rural development and, in particular, shall ensure to such women the right:
   (*h*) To enjoy adequate living conditions, particularly in relation to housing, sanitation, electricity and water supply, transport and communications.

The International Covenant on Economic, Social and Cultural Rights:

Of these international human rights instruments, the International Covenant on Economic, Social and Cultural Rights (ICESCR) provides the most comprehensive protection for the right to housing. Ireland signed up to ICESCR in 1973 and ratified it in 1989. The Optional Protocol to the Convention provides a mechanism to directly enforce the rights under the Convention. The Optional Protocol provides for a complaints mechanism to the UN in relation to the ICESCR where all domestic remedies have been exhausted. Ireland signed the Optional Protocol in March 2012. It has not yet ratified it. Among the countries that have ratified it are Austria, Belgium, Denmark, Finland, France, Germany, Greece, Italy, Luxembourg, Portugal and Spain.

Under the Optional Protocol, complaints of non-compliance with the ICESCR can be made to the UN Committee on Economic, Social and Cultural Rights (UNCESCR). The UNCESCR has emphasised that even in times of financial crisis, states must continue to work towards the protection of rights set out in the Covenant.

In 2015, the United Nations Committee on Economic, Social and Cultural Rights expressed its concern with a number of issues, including:[298]

- The continuing gaps between availability and demand for *social housing*, which result in a long waiting list for social housing
- The increased costs of rental housing and reduced family incomes
- The ineffective social support programmes, such as *Rent Supplement* and the *Housing Assistance Payment*, which do not reflect rent increases
- The increasing number of long-term *mortgage arrears*
- The growing number of families and children who are, or at the risk of being, homeless, as a result of the lack of social housing and the inadequate levels of Rent Supplement
- The lack of effective complaint mechanisms for local authority tenants on tenancy-related issues

The Committee was also concerned at the lack of culturally appropriate accommodation provided to Travellers and Roma and of adequate legal protection for Traveller families at risk of *eviction*.

See also: *Traveller housing; Housing (Traveller Accommodation) Act 1998; European Convention on Human Rights; European Housing Rights Law; European Social Charter*

In housing terms, investment is the purchase of *residential property* to rent in expectation of a steady income stream and future capital value gains (profit) when the property is sold.   **Investment**

---

[298] See paragraph 26: https://www.ihrec.ie/app/uploads/download/pdf/un_committee_on_economic_social_and_cultural_rights_concluding_observations_on_the_third_periodic_report_of_ireland_8_july_2015.pdf

In investment there is a fairly direct relationship between risk and return. The higher the potential return, the greater is the risk and vice versa.[299] A property showing a high *yield* annual return will exhibit more elements of risk than a low yield property, but the returns (income versus expenditure on the property) will be proportionally greater.

See also: *investment value*

Investment value The value of an asset to the owner or a prospective owner for individual *investment* or operational reasons.

See also: *investment*

Irish Association of Self Builders The Irish Association of Self Builders (IAOSB) was established in September 2003 to help people through the self-build journey of planning, finance, contractors, regulations, materials and so forth. The IAOSB website was started in January 2014. The IAOSB has since been run by Shane McCloud and other self-builders on a voluntary basis. The IAOSB has been involved in different areas of self-building, including a campaign started against *S.I. 9 BC(A)R* in 2014.

See also: *Building Control (Amendment) Regulations; S.I. 365 (opt-out); self-build*

Irish Collective Asset-management Vehicle (ICAV) An 'ICAV' (Irish Collective Asset-management Vehicle) is a collective fund *investment* vehicle established by the Irish Collective Asset-management Vehicles Act 2015 (No. 2/2015). ICAVs must be registered with the *Central Bank*. The main perceived benefit of an ICAV is that it is able to elect its classification under the US check-the-box taxation rules. The ability of an ICAV to check-the-box can be helpful to US investors in investment funds, as it allows them to be subject to US tax as if they held the underlying assets in the fund directly.

Some of the main features of an ICAV:

- An ICAV does not have the status of an ordinary Irish company established under the Irish Companies Acts. Instead, it has its own legislative regime to ensure that the ICAV is distinguished from ordinary companies and therefore not subject to those aspects of company law legislation which are not relevant or appropriate to a collective investment scheme.[300] (This should 'future proof' against unintended consequences arising from changes in Irish and European company law.[301])

---

[299] See: https://www.pensionsauthority.ie/en/LifeCycle/Investment_risk_and_reward/
[300] See: https://www.matheson.com/images/uploads/brexit/business/Key_Benefits_and_Features_of_the_ICAV.PDF
[301] See: https://assets.kpmg.com/content/dam/kpmg/pdf/2016/01/fs-the-icav-what-you-need-to-know.pdf

- The board of directors of an ICAV is permitted to elect to dispense with the holding of an annual general meeting by giving written notice to all of the ICAV's shareholders.
- It is possible to prepare accounts per sub-fund. This ensures that investors in a single sub-fund of an umbrella with multiple sub-funds only receive information that is relevant to them and will reduce the costs and time spent by managers in compiling accounts to be provided to shareholders.
- An ICAV is not required to spread risk, unlike an investment company, which is required to do so under the Companies Act.
- An ICAV may be listed on a stock exchange.[302]

The **Central Bank** is responsible for the authorisation and supervision of investment funds established in Ireland, including ICAVs.

The Irish Council for Social Housing (ICSH) is the national *social housing* federation representing over 270 housing associations across Ireland. It was formed in 1982 by housing and hostel organisations in Ireland to act as a national representative, promotional, information and advisory federation. It is a member of *FEANTSA* and *Housing Europe*. The main objectives of the ICSH are: **Irish Council for Social Housing**

- Promotion of non-profit/voluntary housing for the relief of housing need and homelessness
- Acting as a representative body for affiliated members
- Facilitating the exchange of information amongst members in relation to planning, provision and management of social housing
- Provision of information, advice, guidance, education, training and research

See also: *approved housing bodies; Tuath Housing; Clúid Housing; Respond*

The Irish Georgian Society is a membership organisation whose purpose is to promote awareness and protection of Ireland's architectural heritage and decorative arts. The Irish Georgian Society was founded in February 1958 by Desmond and Mariga Guinness. Based in the City Assembly House, the Irish Georgian Society has regional chapters in Cork, Birr, Limerick and London. The organisation has a strong United States membership, generating much of its income, which has its headquarters in Chicago and chapters in Boston, New York and Palm Beach. The Irish Georgian Society has been **Irish Georgian Society**

---

[302] See: https://www.matheson.com/images/uploads/brexit/business/Key_Benefits_and_Features_of_the_ICAV.PDF

more successful in its public image and raising an appreciation for Georgian architecture compared to other heritage charities, mainly through its activities such as tours, publications, lectures, exhibitions and the Guinness Scholarship. The society has saved many historic structures from serious dilapidation over the years, the most notable being the Conolly Folly, Castletown House; Doneraile Court, Co. Cork; and 13 Henrietta Street, Dublin.

See also: *An Taisce; Architectural Conservation Area; Record of Protected Structures*

Irish Home Builders Association The Irish Home Builders Association is a representation body for homebuilders in Ireland and part of the *Construction Industry Federation*.

Irish Mortgage Holders Association The Irish Mortgage Holders Organisation (IMHO) is a not-for-profit organisation which aims to facilitate independent *mortgage*/debt resolution between lenders/creditors and mortgage holders. It was established to provide advocacy for and debt services to those who were in mortgage *arrears*, many of whom could not afford to seek help. The IMHO established a team and sought funding from the banks to provide debt negotiation services, including informal debt and mortgage restructuring, formal arrangements using the insolvency system (the IMHO has an in-house *personal insolvency practitioner*), and a bankruptcy service. All IMHO services are free. Since 2012, the IMHO has restructured 8500 mortgages where 90 per cent have stayed in their home.

The IMHO has appeared before various Oireachtas Committees on a number of occasions, including the Finance Committee and the Housing Committee, where they have challenged the banks' narrative that those in arrears are strategic defaulters who can pay and are choosing not to pay.

The IMHO sees those in mortgage arrears as falling into two categories: one who were eligible for social housing but there was none; and the second and more vulnerable cohort who are ineligible for a mortgage restructure or insolvency arrangement and are not eligible for social housing. To help those in the first category, the IMHO then established *iCare*.

See also: *Mortgage Arrears Resolution Process; Code of Conduct on Mortgage Arrears*

Irish Planning Institute The Irish Planning Institute is the all-island professional body representing professional planners engaged in physical, spatial and environmental planning in Ireland and Irish planners practicing overseas. It was founded in 1975.

See also: *Society of Chartered Surveyors Ireland; Construction Industry Federation; Royal Institute of the Architects of Ireland*

The Ireland Strategic Investment Fund (ISIF), managed and controlled by the **Irish Strategic**
National Treasury Management Agency (NTMA), is an €8.9 billion sover- **Investment Fund**
eign development fund with a statutory mandate to invest on a commercial **(ISIF)**
basis in a manner designed to support economic activity and employment
in Ireland. The fund's predecessor was the National Pensions Reserve Fund
(NPRF).

The ISIF also invests in housing projects. In 2018, it had 'five platforms'
with a pipeline to deliver more than 9,500 homes by 2021; €52 million
infrastructure funding to unlock over 4,000 residential units in Cherrywood
Strategic Development Zone in Dublin; and support for a 3,200-bed student
accommodation project in Dublin City University.[303]

See also: *purpose-built student accommodation*

The trust was founded in 1890 by Edward Cecil Guinness, later First Lord **Iveagh Trust, The**
Iveagh 'to provide housing and related amenities for the labouring poor in
London and Dublin'.[304] In 1903 the Guinness Trust Dublin Fund was amal-
gamated with the Dublin Improvement (Bull Alley Area) Scheme to form the
Iveagh Trust, thereafter managed entirely in Dublin as a separate undertaking
under the name of 'the Iveagh Trust'. Sir Edward gave £50,000 to set up the
Iveagh Trust in Dublin. The original Dublin buildings were funded and built
entirely from the founders' own resources.

Since then, the Iveagh Trust has continued to provide:

* Affordable rented housing for families and single people on low incomes
* Good quality hostel accommodation for homeless men in the Iveagh
  Hostel

Today, the Iveagh Trust owns and manages over 1,400 units of social rented
and hostel accommodation in Dublin city and suburbs.

See also: *Dublin Artisan Dwellings Company*

J

See: *Tenancy in common/Joint tenancy*   **Joint tenancy**

Joint ventures are established where the public and private sector wish to **Joint ventures**
share in the risks and rewards associated with a particular project, and each

---

[303] See: https://isif.ie/wp-content/uploads/2018/07/NTMA-Annual-Report-and-Accounts-2017-
ISIF-Extracts.pdf
[304] See: http://www.theiveaghtrust.ie/?page_id=642

party undertakes the role where it has particular skill and expertise.[305] A joint venture is defined by International Accounting Standard 31 (IAS 31) as a contractual agreement whereby two or more parties undertake an economic activity which is subject to joint control. Joint control represents a contractually agreed sharing of control over an economic activity.[306]

See also: ***public–private partnerships***

K

Kenny Report (1973)

The *Report of the Committee on the Price of Building Land* (1973) is known as the Kenny Report. The Kenny Report advocated a system of ***active land management*** linked to measures to capture the land value uplift, or betterment, arising from economic and social development.[307] The report highlighted the disproportionate rise in the price of building land and the committee recommended that local authorities be given the right to acquire undeveloped lands at existing use value plus 25 per cent by adopting 'Designated Area Schemes'. This financial deal was deemed 'a reasonable compromise between the rights of the community and those of the landowners'.[308] The Kenny Report argued that the official arbitration system used to determine compensation rates for landowners 'tends to inflate land prices'.[309] Thus, it argued that if the free market system continued to be used to determine land prices that the price of building land would continue its upward trajectory.[310]

The Kenny Report was largely ignored at the time for myriad reasons: 'including powerful vested interests and the threat of constitutional challenge around property ownership. Perhaps another reason is that the benefits of implementing such a policy will not accrue to the Minister that chooses to implement it given the length of time such a policy takes for the results to be seen. Ministers are normally in need of quick fixes for problems. In housing there are very few of these.'[311]

See also: ***Compulsory Purchase Order; planning gain***

---

[305] Department of Environment, Heritage and Local Government (2004) *Guidance on the Adoption of a Joint Venture Company Approach for a Public–Private Partnership in Ireland*, Government of Ireland: Dublin

[306] Kirk, R (2008) 'Joint Venture Accounting on the Move', *Accountancy Plus*, June

[307] National Economic and Social Council (2015) *Housing Supply and Land: Driving Public Action for the Common Good – Report 142*, NESC: Dublin

[308] Kenny, J (1973), p. 40

[309] Kenny, J (1973), p. 13

[310] See: http://www.publicpolicyarchive.ie/kenny-report-1973-four-decades-on-the-shelf/

[311] O'Leary, D (2018) 'New housing data highlights the task facing the government', *Irish Times*, 18 July

Teachers, nurses, social workers, police officers and other essential workers are sometimes collectively known as 'key workers'. Many earn too much to qualify for *social housing* support but, as house price increases have far out-stripped wage increases, not enough to purchase their own homes. There is evidence to suggest that housing problems are a source of recruitment issues in these key worker professions.[312] These reduced wages, teamed with an undersupply of affordable accommodation, have made it difficult for many key workers in society to live close to their place of work, and shared accommodation or long commutes are distinctly unattractive to many. There are about 140,000 key workers in Ireland.

Key worker housing

Connecting employment and housing means that housing assistance for key workers has been a particular focus of several European countries. To date, there has been no development of dedicated key worker housing in Ireland.

See also: *affordable housing schemes; affordability*

L

Labour mobility consists of changes in the location of workers both across physical space (geographic mobility) and across a set of jobs (occupational mobility). Geographic mobility can be further subdivided into short-distance and long-distance moves, as well as into voluntary and coerced migration. Labour mobility conveys important economic benefits. At the individual level, mobility allows for improvements in the economic circumstances of those whose skills or aspirations are a poor match for the job or location in which they find themselves.[313] There is a strong relationship between housing and labour mobility.

Labour mobility

Research has shown that at the individual level housing *tenure* is the most powerful factor determining willingness to change residence for employment reasons. Housing tenure has a significant impact on labour migration plans in cases of unemployment and the dynamic impact of regional differences in housing *affordability* on labour mobility is concentrated within the most highly skilled segment of the labour force.[314] A low level of affordability of housing makes labour less mobile.

See also: *regional development; National Planning Framework*

---

[312] Weaver, M (2004) 'Key worker housing: the issue explained', *The Guardian*, 25 May
[313] Long, J and Ferrie, J (2003) 'Labour Mobility', in *Oxford Dictionary of Economic History*, Oxford University Press: Oxford
[314] Lux, M and Sunega, P (2012) 'Labour Mobility and Housing: The Impact of Housing Tenure and Housing Affordability on Labour Migration in the Czech Republic', *Urban Studies*, Vol. 49, No. 3, pp. 489–504

Land[315]

Land is best understood as space and the occupation of that space over time. For most of history, the primary use of land was for agricultural production. But since the birth of modern, capitalist economies other uses have become predominant: first as the site of industrial production, and later as the site of service provision and domestic housing. Today, it is in the housing market that the economic function of land is most visible, as the value of residential property has overtaken the value of land for other purposes (see: **Piketty, Thomas** for more on this).

Land has several specific characteristics. Firstly, land is immobile: land cannot be moved from one place to the other because land is the place itself. Secondly, the supply of land is inelastic or fixed because we cannot make any more of it (bar some minor land reclamation). Thirdly, land is eternal. Outside of some coastal erosion, land will go on forever. Finally, land is essential for all economic activity to take place. Interestingly, these specific characteristics mean that land does not fit well into mainstream economic models where supply can simply increase in response to an increased demand.

The value of land derives from the use it can be put to. This value will also vary depending on the geographical location of the land and its relation to the rest of the economy. In selling a house, the fundamental locational value of the house itself is crucial – everything else can be changed but the location. This can be seen in the often huge discrepancy between the 'replacement cost' of a home calculated for insurance purposes and the actual market value it commands: the difference between the two is essentially the value of the land in that particular place (see: **site/land value tax**). In addition, land values in a particular location reflect the level of wider economic activity in that area. Residential house prices in a thriving city can be many times that of the same house in a remote region because of the economic opportunities that living in a city brings.

The value of land is not only determined by its current use value but, because land is permanent, controlling land is also a means of securing the economic value that holding it will provide in the future. In this respect, land is also an **asset**. Land prices will therefore also reflect people's expectations of future economic activity. Most capital assets tend to depreciate over time, due to natural wear and tear, but land tends to appreciate. This means people are often keen to convert other forms of wealth into land. As such, land is an excellent asset to act as security (collateral) for extending credit and finance.

The ownership of land has become – or always has been – desirable given that land itself is scarce and has played a significant role in the shaping of

---

[315] This entry is an abridged version of a discussion on land in: Ryan-Collins, J, Lloyd, T and Macfarlane, L (2017) *Rethinking the Economics of Land and Housing*, Zed Books: London. This is possibly the best book currently available on land and property.

modern economies. Control over each piece of land is essentially monopolistic so landowners can command returns from those who must use their land based purely on their ownership of it, unrelated to their costs of bringing it into production or any efforts they have expended. This is known as 'economic rent'. This ability to extract economic rent is so powerful it can effectively monopolise much of the growth created in an economy, the vast majority of which will not have been created by the landowners themselves. Therefore, as the economy grows, landowners can increase the *rent* they charge *tenants* to absorb all the additional value that the tenants (shopkeepers, workers, etc.) generate. The ability to extract rent for little effort or risk distorts investment decisions, as it encourages those with capital to over-allocate it to land and property purchases, rather than other productive uses (e.g. setting up a business).

See also: *value; investment; speculation; mortgage*

The Land and Conveyancing Law Reform Act 2009 simplifies property law and conveyancing procedures.

The main components of the Act are:

Land and Conveyancing Law Reform Act 2009

- Joint tenancies may only be severed and converted into a *tenancy in common* now by written consent from all the joint tenants or by court order
- New rules of registration for legal entitlement to *easements*
- There is a right of access to maintain party structures, and financial contributions from the adjoining landowner can be sought
- Beneficial interests in property now pass under contracts to purchase
- New rules apply in respect of when mortgagees can take possession of *dwellings* and principle residences
- Upwards-only rent reviews for new commercial leases are no longer permitted[316]

See also: *Land and Conveyancing Law Reform Act 2013; tenancy; tenure; home ownership*

This Act was enacted to ensure continued application of repealed provisions of the Conveyancing Acts 1881 to 1911 to all mortgages created prior to 1 December 2009 since case law had raised doubts on the issue. The Act also introduced additional protections for borrowers in cases where lending institutions had commenced legal proceedings for the repossession of principal private residences.

Land and Conveyancing Law Reform Act 2013[317]

---

[316] See: http://www.homs.ie/publications/the-land-and-conveyancing-law-reform-act-2009-an-overview/

[317] See: http://www.justice.ie/en/JELR/Pages/Land_and_Conveyancing_Law_Reform_Act_2013

These protections include a provision whereby a court may, where it considers it appropriate or on application by a borrower, adjourn the proceedings to enable the parties to consider whether a ***personal insolvency arrangement*** (PIA) under the Personal Insolvency Act 2012 would be a more appropriate alternative to repossession.[318]

See also: ***Land and Conveyancing Law Reform Act 2009***

Land annuity Land annuities were money that the British government had loaned to Irish farmers before the Government of Ireland Act of 1921 and which the farmers had agreed to repay. Part of the Anglo-Irish Treaty was that the Free State government would collect these debts and return the money to Britain. However, Taoiseach Éamon de Valera abolished the land annuities in 1932.

Britain then imposed a 20 per cent tariff on trade with the Free State. The Irish found that they could no longer sell their beef to Britain or Northern Ireland and so they retaliated by imposing a tariff in the opposite direction. This prevented Britain selling coal to Ireland. However, Britain did not depend on Ireland as much as Ireland did on Britain, and this seriously crippled the Irish economy. After five years, in 1938, the two countries signed an agreement to end the trade war. Under this settlement the Free State give Britain £10,000,000 to pay off the annuities and in return Britain withdrew her naval bases in Ireland.[319]

See also: ***Land Commission; Three Fs; Duffy, Charles Gavan; Davitt, Michael; Tenant Right League***

Landbank A landbank is a supply of land held for future house-building ***development*** achieved through the purchase (and frequently aggregation) of individual parcels of land. The top ten UK housebuilders each have landbanks at any one time for about five years' worth of housing output. As land is used up in supplying housing, further land is acquired to maintain the landbank. Too large a landbank can lead to overexposure to potential risk if the demand for housing stalls or reduces; too small a landbank can mean being exposed to risk by having to purchase land at increased prices and then not being able to build and sell houses at the price range targeted by the company.

'Strategic' landbanks are not always owned by housebuilders, but often held with 'option agreements' with the landowner, which gives the builder the exclusive right to buy the land when they are ready to do so.[320]

'Land banking', i.e. acquiring land for future development, is often conflated with ***land hoarding***.

---

[318] *Ibid.*
[319] See: http://www.wesleyjohnston.com/users/ireland/past/history/19321945.html
[320] Fraser, I (2016) 'Top 10 biggest house builders control land for almost one million homes', *The Telegraph*, 18 December

In 1881 the Irish Land Commission was founded to establish fair rents. In 1885 the Ashbourne Land Act transformed the Commission's main function from fixing rents to breaking up estates and facilitating tenant purchase of their holdings. Between c.1885 and 1920 the Commission oversaw the transfer of 13,500,000 acres. In those days, a 22-acre farm was considered adequate to sustain a family,[321] although it often proved too small to be economical. After feeding themselves, families struggled to produce surpluses to sell for profit on such small holdings.

Land Commission

Following independence, the Commission's records were divided between jurisdictions, and in 1923 the Land Commission was reconstituted to recognise the Free State. After 1923 the Commission continued to acquire and distribute an additional 807,000 acres, but its main business was to administer pre-independence land purchase schemes.

A result of the monumental redistribution of land undertaken by the Land Commission is a significantly dispersed rural housing settlement pattern, which still remains a headache for national and local planning – especially around the provision of infrastructure – to this day. Between 1923 and 1959 the Commission also built 20,000 houses in the Irish countryside based on a standardised design, which was of high quality, but small for the large families that typically inhabited them.[322]

On 31 March 1999 the Land Commission was dissolved, and its historic records were transferred to the Department of Agriculture,[323] having transformed half a million tenants into *fee simple* owners of land in the meantime.

See also: *Land and Conveyancing Law Reform Act 2009; Land and Conveyancing Law Reform Act 2013; land annuity*

The Land Development Agency was established in September 2018 to build 150,000 homes in the period 2018–2038.[324] According to the government, the LDA has two main functions:

Land Development Agency

- Coordinating appropriate state lands for regeneration and *development*, opening up key sites which are not being used effectively for housing delivery
- Driving strategic land assembly, working with both public and private sector land owners to smooth out peaks and troughs of land supply, stabilising land values and delivering increased affordability[325]

---

[321] Barry, J (2012) 'Shadow of the Land Commission still falls on farm sector', *Irish Independent*, 25 July

[322] Kenna, P (2011) *Housing Law, Rights and Policy*, Clarus Press: Dublin

[323] Fitzsimons, F (2014) 'Records of the Irish Land Commission', *History Ireland*, Vol. 22, No. 1

[324] See: https://www.housing.gov.ie/housing/government-launches-eu125bn-land-development-agency-build-150000-new-homes

[325] See: https://merrionstreet.ie/en/News-Room/News/Government_Launches_€1_25bn_Land_Development_Agency.html

Of the 150,000 houses planned for delivery, 30 per cent will be *social housing*, 10 per cent *affordable housing*, and the remainder private housing. 'Affordable' in this context is seen as €320,000 in Dublin, Cork and Galway for a joint income and €250,000 elsewhere.

See also: *affordability*

Land hoarding Land hoarding is the practice of acquiring or holding land that has potential for *development* in the expectation that the value of the land will rise greater than any costs of holding it, and that it can later be sold for significant profit as the scarcity of development land causes prices to rise. Land hoarding avoids having to crystallise development risk as it is essentially trading in land and not engaging in construction.

In the UK, the Letwin Report could find no 'evidence that the major house builders are financial investors of this kind. Their business models depend on generating profits out of sales of housing, rather than out of the increasing value of land holdings; and it is the profitability of the sale of housing that they are trying to protect by building only at the "market *absorption rate*" for their products.'[326]

In Ireland, it remains unclear the extent to which land hoarding occurs. The suspicion that land hoarding was a regular feature of the Irish property market was part of the rationale for the introduction of the *Vacant Sites Register and Levy*. House builders reject the assertion that they are deliberately not developing land in order to see its value rise without having to crystallise development risk by building: e.g. 'Cairn absolutely does not fall into the category of hoarding any of its land.'[327]

Conversely, in 2017, the *National Asset Management Agency* (NAMA) linked the low level of residential development on sites sold by NAMA to land hoarding. Since its inception NAMA had disposed – either through loan sales or asset sales – of land sites with the capacity to deliver 50,000 housing units. However, to that date only 3,700 units had been built or were under construction. In July 2017, Brendan McDonagh, NAMA chief executive, told the Oireachtas Finance Committee: '"There is no doubt that land hoarding is an issue …. For any given site, there is little disincentive to hoarding as long as the owner expects house prices to rise."'[328] The chief executive of Ires *REIT* has also said that his company's bid to secure land for residential development in Dublin and its suburbs was frustrated by private

[326] Letwin, O (2018) *Independent Review of Build-Out Rates*, Ministry of Housing, Communities and Local Government: London
[327] White, D (2017) 'Land hoarding is pushing up the price of new homes', *Irish Independent*, 16 July
[328] McConnell, D (2017) '50 Nama staff on "gardening leave" for more than three months', *Irish Examiner*, 14 July

equity and private owners who were hoarding sites in the expectation that they will increase in value.[329]

Land hoarding often gets confused with **landbanking**.

According to the **Residential Tenancies Act 2004**, a 'landlord' is the person for the time being entitled to receive (otherwise than as agent for another person) the **rent** paid in respect of a dwelling by the **tenant** thereof and, where the context so admits, includes a person who has ceased to be so entitled by reason of the **termination** of the **tenancy**. At the end of 2018, there were 336,890 tenancies, 173,197 landlords and 695,142 occupants in Ireland.[330]

    See also: **private rented sector; tenure; Residential Tenancies Board**

                             Landlord

The Land Registry was established in 1892 to provide a comprehensive and secure system of land registration. The core business of the Land Registry involves examining legal documents and related maps submitted as applications for registration, interpreting the legal effect of such documents and recording their legal impact on the registers and maps. When **title** or ownership is registered in the Land Registry the deeds are filed in the Registry and all relevant particulars concerning the property and its ownership are entered on folios which form the registers maintained in the Land Registry. In conjunction with folios the Land Registry also maintains Land Registry maps.

    The title shown on the folio is guaranteed by the state, which is bound to indemnify any person who suffers loss through a mistake made by the Land Registry. A purchaser therefore can accept the folio as evidence of title without having to read the relevant deeds. The Land Registry identifies properties not **boundaries** and never shows ownership of individual boundary structures such as walls, fences and hedges.

    Since the Irish Land Register is a public record, any person may inspect the folios and maps, on payment of the prescribed fees. Both folios and maps are maintained in electronic form.

    See also: **Registry of Deeds; memorial; General Boundary Rule; cadastre; GeoDirectory**

Land Registry[331]

See: **site value tax**

                             Land value tax

Latent **defects** insurance is a form of insurance taken out in respect of specific new-build premises to provide cover in the event of an inherent defect in the design, workmanship or materials becoming apparent after practical completion. It indemnifies the insured for the cost, up to the total sum insured

                             Latent defects insurance

---

[329] Milne, R (2017) 'More land hoarding claims surface in Ireland', *The Planner*, 8 June
[330] Figures from Residential Tenancies Board, 2019
[331] See: https://www.prai.ie/the-property-registration-authority/

(typically the full **reinstatement cost**), of the repairs to the damage caused by or for repairs to prevent imminent damage by the defect, and is typically available for between eight and twelve years from the date of final certificate or practical completion. The insured can be any party who has an interest in the property such as the owner or developer, but can also be the funder or an incoming tenant with an obligation to repair under the lease.[332]

Several companies offer latent defects insurance in Ireland, and the cost is typically between 0.5 and 1.5 per cent of the construction cost of the building.

See: **Construction Industry Register of Ireland; Pyrite Resolution Board; Homebond**

Lease   A written **tenancy** is known as a lease. There is no legal requirement for a landlord to provide a tenant with a lease, nor is there an obligation on a tenant to sign a lease. A lease is a contract between two or more parties for the right to occupy property (land or buildings) in exchange for payment. A written lease should typically contain the following basic information:

- Name and address of both parties to the lease
- Address of the property
- The period of the tenancy
- The amount of the initial **rent** and how frequently rent is to be paid and in what manner
- When the rent can be reviewed
- The amount of any **deposit** and how and when it will be returned to the tenant (see: **deposit protection scheme**)
- Any costs and which party is responsible for payment (e.g. **service charges**, utility bills)
- The **termination** of lease process
- Contents of the property included in the lease

A lease should not contain terms that contradict the legal rights of either tenants or landlords. If this is the case, the legal rights of a tenant or landlord supersede the terms in the lease. For example, a landlord cannot enter the property at any time without seeking the tenant's permission and giving reasonable notice (e.g. 24 hours). This is the case even if a lease states that the landlord may enter the property at any time. If a lease is signed together with other people, each tenant becomes responsible for all the rent. So, if fellow tenants cannot pay their share of the rent, the remaining tenant may be legally liable for the entire amount.[333]

---

[332] See: https://www.eversheds-sutherland.com/global/en/what/articles/index.page?ArticleID=en/Construction_And_Engineering/Construction_Latent_defect_insurance

[333] See: http://www.citizensinformation.ie/en/housing/renting_a_home/types_of_tenancy.html

Once the lease expires there is no obligation to sign a new lease and a tenant cannot be asked to leave just because they do not sign a new lease. A tenant can make a request to assign or sublet the tenancy to another person. Should a tenant break a lease with no grounds or does not give proper notice of termination, it does not automatically give the landlord the right to keep any **deposit** or make deductions from it. However, landlords may seek to cover costs incurred such as re-advertising, re-letting costs or lost rent.

Depending on the amount of rent payable and the period of the lease, **stamp duty** may need to be paid.

See also: **Deasy's Act; Three Fs: Duffy, Charles Gavan; Rent Pressure Zone; rent review**

Leasehold interest

A leasehold interest is the right to occupy land or buildings for a temporary period. At the end of this period the land or building usually reverts to the owner unless there are rights of renewal. In Ireland, almost all apartments are bought on 999-year leasehold interests. The 999-year **lease** for the **apartment** will also contain specific covenants regarding the use of the property, payment of fees, **service charges** and so forth.

See also: **freehold interest; freehold; fee simple**

Lessee

A lessee is the person who is the subject of a lease, i.e. a **tenant**.

See also: **lessor; leasehold interest; lease**

Lessor

The lessor is the person granting a lease, i.e. a **landlord**.

See also: **lessee; leasehold interest; lease**

Letting agent

A letting agent is a licenced **property services provider** involved in the sourcing of prospective landlords and tenants seeking property to rent ('let') or be rented.

See also: **Property Services (Regulation) Act 2011; Property Services Regulatory Authority; advised letting value**

Licence[334]

A licence can be best described as a permission to enter onto and/or occupy a dwelling (without which a trespass would occur). A licence is not a **tenancy** and therefore, in the main, the **Residential Tenancies Act 2004** (RTA) does not apply to such an arrangement.

A licensee is a person who occupies accommodation under licence. Licensees can arise in all sorts of accommodation but most commonly in the following four areas:

---

[334] Sheehy Skeffington, P (2018) 'The Limited Rights of Residential Licensees in Ireland: A Case for Carefully Targeted Legal Reform', in Sirr, L (ed.), *Administration – special housing edition*, Vol. 66, No. 2

- Persons staying in hotels, guesthouses, hostels, etc.
- Persons sharing a house/apartment with its owner, e.g. under the **Rent-a-Room Scheme** or 'in **digs**'
- Persons occupying accommodation in which the owner is not resident under a formal license arrangement with the owner where the occupants are not entitled to its exclusive use and the owner has continuing access to the accommodation and/or can move around or change the occupants
- Persons staying in rented accommodation at the invitation of the tenant

Sheehy Skeffington has detailed the following types of licensees thus:[335] For the most part, lodgers are contractual licensees. A partner or spouse who has moved into property which his or her partner already owns or rents (whether privately or from a local authority or approved housing body) is generally a licensee of the owner or tenant, unless steps are taken or circumstances arise to alter that position. Partners or spouses who delegate responsibility to the other partner or spouse to negotiate and sign a tenancy agreement may find themselves in the position of a licensee rather than a tenant. Children, including minor children, who live in a parent's home are licensees (except if they are or become an owner or **tenant**, which is unlikely but not impossible prior to a child turning eighteen and obtaining the age of legal majority pursuant to section 2 of the Age of Majority Act 1985).

Each resident of a nursing home or emergency accommodation is likely to reside there as a licensee. Occupants of transitional accommodation provided by an approved housing body can be tenants or licensees: if they are tenants their rights to security of tenure under Part 4 of the RTA are curtailed if their lease is for less than 18 months (section 25(6) RTA). People whose accommodation is supplied by their employer or who live in **purpose-built student accommodation** are in a similar situation: they are most likely licensees, but if their situation amounts to a tenancy their right to security of tenure under Part 4 RTA are curtailed (section 25(4) RTA). A bed for a night or short period in a hotel or hostel is granted on the basis of a contractual licence. Where a person rents one bed in a room with a number of others who similarly have access to that room to use their own bed and they do not share control over when others may be offered bed spaces, the underlying legal arrangement is a licence rather than a tenancy. The occupant's lack of control precludes exclusive possession.

There is no hard and fast rule for determining what agreement is a licence and what is a tenancy. What constitutes a lease as opposed to a licence has been subject of considerable case law, not least because agreements dressed up as licences have been found by the courts to in fact be tenancies, often

---

[335] *Ibid.*

with the intention of limiting occupants' rights to those of licensees rather than tenants. Therefore, the mere fact of calling a letting agreement a 'licence' does not automatically mean it will be considered a licence and not a lease. Neither the ***Residential Tenancies Board*** nor the courts simply accept the title of a document but look instead at the actual terms and substance of the agreement when assessing whether either has jurisdiction to deal with it.

When differentiating between a lease and a licence, the following elements are important to examine:

- ***Exclusive possession***: Where a tenancy is in existence, the tenant will have exclusive occupation of part or all of the dwelling leased by him or her. In certain circumstances a licensee may also have exclusive possession, however in most cases a licensee will not have exclusive possession of the dwelling and the owner will have a right of continuing access to the dwelling or part of the dwelling occupied by the licensee.
- ***Assignment***/Sublease: A licensee cannot usually assign his or her interest in a dwelling. A tenant, however, subject to the landlord's consent (which cannot be unreasonably withheld), can assign or sublet his or her tenancy to a third party.
- ***Termination***: A tenancy can only be terminated in accordance with the Residential Tenancies Act 2004 and the valid terms of any lease agreement. A licence however can be revoked or terminated by the person who grants it provided reasonable notice is given to the licensee. Where a contractual licence exists however, the licence can only be revoked in accordance with the terms of the contract.
- ***Rent***: Rent is an essential element in the creation of a tenancy. A licensee may or may not make payments in respect of their occupation of a ***dwelling***. Payments however which are called something other than rent will not operate to create a licence arrangement when in reality the payments amount to rent.
- Bedsits: The ***Residential Tenancies Act 2004*** applies to self-contained residential units, which includes the form of accommodation more commonly known as a ***bedsit*** (section 4 of the Residential Tenancies Act 2004). An individual who occupies bedsit accommodation is entitled to the full protections of the Residential Tenancies Act 2004 (unless it can be shown for other reasons that the circumstances are such that a licence exists.)
- No contracting out of Part 4 ***tenancy***: Parties cannot contract out of a tenant's entitlement to a Part 4 tenancy (section 54 of the Residential Tenancies Act 2004). Any agreement between two parties which purports to be a licence for the purposes of avoiding the application of Part 4 of the

Residential Tenancies Act 2004 will not operate to deny an individual's right to a Part 4 tenancy.

- Name of contract: Referring to a written document on its face as either a *lease* or a licence does not (in the absence of other criteria) prove the nature of the relationship between the parties.

People living under licence arrangements constitute a significant group in Ireland. Comprising a broad category of people in disparate situations, licensees tend to be the result rather than the focus of policy, regulations and circumstances. Modern statute also confirms the common law position that a licence does not create any estate or legal or equitable interest in the property it relates to (e.g. a freehold or leasehold).[336]

Lien

A lien is the right to hold property or possessions until a debt has been repaid. There are various types of lien, including contractual and statutory. A retaining lien gives a solicitor the right to retain a client's money, documents or other property in their possession until outstanding fees are paid.[337] Liens tend to relate to tangible goods only.

Loan-to-income

Loan-to-income (LTI) is an upper cap or restriction on the amount of money that can be borrowed based on the household income of the applicant(s). The *Central Bank* has set a LTI of 3.5 times the household income (although this can be breached in a percentage of cases).

See also: *mortgage lending rules; loan-to-value*

Loan-to-value

Loan-to-value (LTV) is a ratio used to express the *value* of a loan advanced against the value of the property for which it is being made. For example, a LTV ratio of 70 per cent is the minimum that will be accepted for the government's *Help to Buy* initiative, meaning that the scheme will only be available to applicants borrowing at least 70 per cent of the value of the property.

See also: *mortgage lending rules; Help to Buy; loan-to-income*

Local area plan

A local area plan (LAP) is designed to take a detailed look at a specific area, identifying and analysing the various issues of relevance, before establishing and setting out principles for the future development of an area.[338]

It is mandatory for a *planning authority* to make a local area plan in respect of an area which:

---

[336] Sheehy Skeffington, P (2018) 'The Limited Rights of Residential Licensees in Ireland: A Case for Carefully Targeted Legal Reform', in Sirr, L (ed.), *Administration – special housing edition*, Vol. 66, No. 2

[337] See: http://reidystafford.com/wp-content/uploads/2017/03/LawonSolicitorsLiens.pdf

[338] See: http://www.dublincity.ie/main-menu-services-planning-urban-development-plans/local-area-plans

- Is designated as a town in the most recent census of population
- Has a population in excess of 5,000
- Is situated in the functional area of a planning authority which is a county council[339]

See also: ***development plan***

Local authorities are the 'housing authority' for their area. Local authorities build, acquire, rent and maintain housing on behalf of the members of their community.

Local authorities (role in housing)

They also provide a range of loans and grants for householders under some of the following headings:[340]

- ***Home Renovation Incentive***: Homeowners, landlords and local authority tenants can claim a tax credit on the cost of improvements to residential property.
- Housing Adaptation Grant for People with a Disability: Grants for alterations that need to be made to a home to make it suitable for a person with a physical, sensory or intellectual disability or a mental health difficulty.
- Housing Aid for Older People Scheme: Grants are available to improve the homes of older people so that they can stay in their own homes for as long as possible.
- Mobility Aids Grant Scheme: A grant to help with the cost of works to address mobility problems in the home.
- Improvement works in lieu of local authority housing: Local authorities may improve or extend privately owned houses as an alternative to providing local authority housing.
- Local authority home improvement loans: Local authority loans are available to owner-occupiers towards the cost of necessary works to improve, repair or extend their houses.
- Housing for older people: Schemes and grants for housing and home improvements for older people and people with disabilities.
- Better Energy Homes Scheme: This scheme provides grants to help to increase the energy efficiency of homes, including grants for home insulation.
- Better Energy Warmer Homes Scheme: This scheme aims to increase the energy efficiency and warmth of homes where people on low incomes are living.

---

[339] See: https://www.housing.gov.ie/sites/default/files/migrated-files/en/Publications/Development andHousing/Planning/FileDownLoad,33557,en.pdf
[340] See: http://www.citizensinformation.ie/en/housing/housing_grants_and_schemes/

- Grant scheme to replace lead pipes and fittings: Grants to help low-income households with the cost of replacing domestic water piping that contains lead.
- *Repair and Leasing Scheme*: A new scheme to bring vacant properties into use for social housing

Local authorities used to provide *mortgages* for low-income first-time buyers, one of which was the standard local authority annuity mortgage, and the other for first-time buyers unable to secure adequate loan finance from a bank or building society to purchase a new or second-hand property or build their own home (Home Choice Loan). Both of these have now been replaced by the *Rebuilding Ireland Home Loan* scheme, run by local authorities.[341]

Local authorities have traditionally been the main provider of social (or 'council') housing. In recent years, however, in an effort to keep expenditure off the state accounts, considerable responsibility for delivering housing has been passed to *approved housing bodies* (AHBs). In Ireland, however, a 2018 decision from *Eurostat* put the borrowings of AHBs, on whom the government rely to deliver social housing in increasing numbers, back on the state's balance sheet (see: *social housing*). In 2017, local authorities built 394 houses compared to AHBs which built 799.[342]

See also: *data – housing output issues; council housing; social housing*

Local Authority Extensions Scheme This scheme enables local authorities to extend rented local authority houses to cater for households who would otherwise qualify for inclusion in a housing assessment. The scheme applies to rented local authority houses which can be economically extended to cater for persons accepted as in need of local authority housing. It includes cases where the need is due to *overcrowding*, where an approved applicant not living in the house can be adequately accommodated in the house after it has been extended, and where a tenant or tenant purchaser surrenders a dwelling on being accommodated in the extended house.[343]

Local government 'Local government' is an umbrella term for the range of governance systems for county, city and municipal districts.

There are 31 local authorities in Ireland (26 county councils, two city and county councils, and three city councils), providing a range of services including roads; traffic; planning; housing; economic and community development;

---

[341] See: http://www.citizensinformation.ie/en/housing/owning_a_home/help_with_buying_a_home/local_authority_mortgages.html
[342] See: https://www.housing.gov.ie/sites/default/files/publications/files/ri_report_housing_completions_2017.pdf
[343] See: https://www.housing.gov.ie/housing/social-housing/other/improvements-existing-dwellings

environment, recreation and amenity services; fire services; and maintaining the register of electors. There 949 councillors. The day-to-day management of a local authority is carried out by the executive, i.e. the full-time officials led by the chief executive.[344]

See also: ***local authorities (role in housing)***

The Local Government Management Agency (LGMA) is a state agency established in 2012. The LGMA is an agency of local authorities, primarily funded by local authorities, and operates in the local government sector, reporting on performance as required to the ***Department of Housing, Planning and Local Government***.

The LGMA operates the ***Building Control Management System***.

Local Government Management Agency (LGMA)

The Local Infrastructure Housing Activation Fund (LIHAF) was launched in 2017 to provide public off-site infrastructure to relieve critical infrastructure blockages and enable the accelerated delivery of housing on key development sites in Dublin and in urban areas with high demand for housing.

Local Infrastructure Housing Activation Fund (LIHAF)

A key part of the €200 million scheme was that as part of the deal for receiving state funds to facilitate private development a proportion of 'affordable housing' would be received in return. According to *Dublin Inquirer*: 'a circular from the Housing Department on 26 August [2017] said that the funding would be granted to developers in return for a "minimum 40% of homes delivered, to be available at prices at least 10% below the average cost of market housing including under €300,000 in Dublin". Just weeks later, on 30 September another circular was issued by the department, scrapping that stipulation and saying it is up to local authorities to negotiate individually to get affordable housing.'[345]

It was reported in 2018 that in three developments councils failed to make an agreement with the developers, who would still receive more than €2 million from the fund with no affordable houses for the state. In other cases, deals have been made but with no detail on when the housing would be delivered or at what price. In some cases, the affordable component of a house is a less than 2 per cent price reduction. In Cork, LIHAF funding is being used to facilitate the development of ***build-to-rent*** property, of which the local authority will get an entitlement to rent 40 of the units but there is no indication of a reduced rent. The 40 will be available to rent for 25 years, with no indication of what happens then. Presumably, the units return to the landlord.[346]

---

[344] See: https://www.lgma.ie/en/irish-local-government/
[345] Neylon, L (2017) 'Despite €200 million subsidy for developers, questions over affordable housing', *Dublin Inquirer*, 16 May
[346] Melia, P (2018) 'Taxpayers' return on LIHAF investments is far from clear-cut', *Irish Independent*, 30 March

The second round of LIHAF was replaced and converted into a **Serviced Sites Fund** and the **Urban Regeneration Development Fund**.
See also: *financialisation of housing; land; speculation*

Localism

Localism is an explicit preference for one's own area or locality. A perennial criticism of Irish government policy is that it is formulated through a combination of anecdotal evidence, clientelism and localism, rather than being informed by robust and sound **data**, with an objective analysis of potential outcomes and scenarios.[347]

Local Property Tax

Local Property Tax (LPT) is a self-assessed tax charged on the market value of residential properties in Ireland. Liable persons must pay their LPT liabilities on an annual basis. The tax payable is based on the property's valuation at 1 May 2013. A property is liable for LPT if it was a residential property on the valuation date of 1 May 2013. Following a deferment in reviewing property valuations, the current valuation period runs from 1 May 2013 until 1 November 2020.
In general, tenants are not liable for the LPT, as follows:[348]

- A rent-paying **tenant** with a lease of less than 20 years is not liable for Local Property Tax on that property.
- A rent-paying tenant with a lease of greater than 20 years is liable for LPT on that property.
- If a tenant is renting from a local authority, the local authority is liable to pay the LPT on the property.

Local authorities have the ability to vary the LPT in their areas by 15 per cent so bills may differ from the tax based on the 2013 valuation.

Lodger

A lodger is someone who pays for a place to sleep, and usually for meals, in someone else's house.[349]
See also: *digs; boarding house*

Long-term leasing arrangement

A long-term lease arrangement is where the state (via a local authority or **approved housing body**) rents property from a private owner. They are designed to suit property owners and **landlords** who want to retain property as a long-term investment and have a long-term security of income, but

---

[347] Kitchin, R (2013) 'Making Informed Decisions on Future Housing Policy', *Housing Ireland*, Winter
[348] See: https://www.revenue.ie/en/property/local-property-tax/who-is-liable-for-lpt-and-or-household-charge/are-tenants-liable.aspx
[349] *Cambridge English Dictionary*

who do not wish to retain responsibility for the day-to-day requirements of managing a residential property.

Suitable properties can be leased to the local authority or an AHB for periods of between ten and twenty years. During the term of the *lease*:

- The local authority/AHB will guarantee payments to the owner.
- Payment will continue regardless of *vacancy* periods.
- The local authority/AHB will be responsible for day-to-day property maintenance.

The local authority/AHB will be the landlord to tenants. In addition, property owners who have leased their properties to a local authority will:

- Have no *rent* collection or rent arrears obligations.
- Not incur advertising or administrative overheads.
- Not have to register the tenancy with the *Residential Tenancies Board* (RTB).

Owners will receive a lease amount of approximately 80 per cent of the current *market rent*. *Rent reviews* will be negotiated on a case-by-case basis and will usually be every three to four years.

Under this scheme, a local authority may make housing sites available at low cost to households that have been approved for social housing by the local authority, or local authority tenants or tenant purchasers or certain tenants of voluntary housing associations. *Approved housing bodies* providing houses under the *Capital Assistance Scheme* or Capital Loan and Subsidy Schemes may also avail of the sites scheme, as may persons taking *shared ownership* through a group housing project sponsored by a housing cooperative or local authority.[350]   **Low Cost Sites**

M

A maisonette (from 'little house' in French) is part of a residential building which is occupied separately, usually on more than one floor and having its own outside entrance.[351]   **Maisonette**

See also: *detached house; semi-detached house; bedsit; pied à terre; dwelling; terraced house; condominium; apartment; garden flat; duplex; mews; accessory dwelling unit; granny flat*

---

[350] See: https://www.housing.gov.ie/housing/social-housing/other/improvements-existing-dwellings
[351] *Oxford English Dictionary*

Managing agent   Managing agents are the day-to-day managers of ***multi-unit developments***, and are usually employed by the ***owners' management company*** (OMC). Managing agents' services typically include:

- Inspecting and maintaining ***common areas***
- Organising waste collections
- Collecting management fees from owners
- Administrative duties, such as arranging buildings insurance cover
- Organising meetings between the OMC and owners
- Responding to enquiries from owners

Owners pay the costs of employing the managing agent as a part of their annual ***service charge***. Managing agents are licenced ***property services providers*** and, as such, are regulated by the ***Property Services Regulatory Authority***.

See also: ***letting agent; estate agent***

Marino – garden   The housing scheme at Marino, a north Dublin suburb, was the first sig-
city[352]   nificant development carried out by Dublin Corporation. In 1914 town planners Patrick Geddes and Raymond Unwin prepared a plan for 1,100 houses at Marino on a 96-acre site with a ***density*** of eleven-and-a-half houses per acre (28 houses per hectare, or medium density). The outbreak of World War I put plans for the scheme back for the following four years. In 1919 plans and drawings for the scheme were presented to Dublin Corporation which were inspired by the English ***garden city*** movement.

The significance of the scheme was more than its unique design and high quality; it was the acceptance of the need for financial investment by the state to solve Dublin's housing crisis. Built over three phases, it provided 1,500 working-class homes. This was the beginning of a policy which was contin-ued with vigour by the Fianna Fáil administration in the 1930s and 1940s with the building of large ***housing estates*** at Cabra and Crumlin. As the population of Dublin grew, the garden suburb continued to be the favoured housing solution.

See also: ***Howard, Ebenezer; Geddes, Patrick; World War I housing***

Market rent   The estimated amount for which an interest in real property should be leased on the ***valuation*** date between a willing lessor and a willing lessee on appro-priate ***lease*** terms in an arm's length transaction, after proper marketing and

---

[352] This entry is abstracted from: McCord, R (2011) 'A Garden City – The Dublin Corporation Housing Scheme at Marino, 1924', *The Irish Story*, 7 September, available at: http://www.theirish-story.com/2011/09/07/a-garden-city-the-dublin-corporation-housing-scheme-at-marino-1924/#. W3LxTC17FR0

where the parties had each acted knowledgeably, prudently and without compulsion.
    See also: ***imputed rent; rent***

The estimated amount for which an asset or liability should exchange on the ***valuation*** date between a willing buyer and a willing seller in an arm's length transaction after proper marketing and where the parties had each acted knowledgeably, prudently and without compulsion.
    See also: ***value; valuer***

Market value

See: ***Catholic Church***

McQuaid, John Charles

A memorial is a summary of the ***deeds***.
    See also: ***Registry of Deeds; boundary; Land Registry; cadastre***

Memorial

Mercy Law Resource Centre (MLRC) is an independent law centre, registered charity and company limited by guarantee, founded in 2009. It provides accessible free legal advice and representation to people who are homeless or at risk of ***homelessness*** in the areas of housing law and related social welfare law. It also seeks to advocate change in laws, policies and attitudes which unduly and adversely impact people who are at the margins of society. MLRC provides five key services:

Mercy Law Resource Centre

- Free legal advice clinics in hostels for people who are homeless and in centres that are easily accessible for people facing homelessness
- Legal representation including representation in the superior courts
- Legal support and training to organisations working in the field of housing and homelessness
- Policy work to advocate changes to the laws, policies and attitudes that are particularly harsh for people facing homelessness and people on the margins of our society
- A befriending service for clients who are particularly vulnerable and in need of support

MLRC pursues strategic litigation and casework, seeking through this work to have an impact on broader systemic issues in the area of housing and homelessness. Since its establishment in 2009, MLRC has supported over 6,000 clients.
    Between 2016 and 2018, MLRC published a trilogy of reports in relation to the right to housing: *The Right to Housing* assesses the protection of the right to housing in Irish law and outlines the impact that a constitutional right to housing would have; *Second Right to Housing Report: The Right to*

Housing in Comparative Perspective undertakes a comparative analysis of how the right to housing operates in other jurisdictions; *Children and Homelessness: A Gap in Legal Protection* examines the gap in legal protection in relation to homeless children.

See also: **housing rights approach to housing; UN Special Rapporteur on the Right to Adequate Housing; FIDH; right to housing**

Mews

A mews is a row or street of houses or flats that have been converted from stables or built to look like former stables.

See also: **detached house; semi-detached house; bedsit; maisonette; pied à terre; dwelling; terraced house; condominium; apartment; garden flat; duplex; townhouse**

Micro-home

Micro-homes are primarily an American housing typology. According to the Department of Housing Preservation, a New York City micro-dwelling is defined as an **apartment** with a kitchen, a bathroom, and at least one window that is, by city law, no smaller than 400 square feet (37.16 sqm).[353]

These very small (by traditional standards) **apartments**, leasing at approximately 20 per cent to 30 per cent lower monthly **rent** than conventional units, yet at very high **value** ratios (rent per square foot), have been offered or are being considered in urban and urbanising locales, particularly high-**density**, expensive metropolitan markets such as Boston, New York, San Francisco, Seattle and Washington DC. The target market profile for micro-units is predominantly young professional singles, typically under 30 years of age. Developing and operating a rental apartment community with micro-units is more expensive, but the premium rent per square foot achieved more than makes up for the added cost.[354]

See also: **bedsits; apartment design standards; development**

Millfield Manor fire and report

Millfield Manor is a housing estate in Newbridge, County Kildare. In 2015, a terrace of six timber-frame houses caught fire and burned down within 25 minutes. The then **Minister for Housing** commissioned a report into the fire, due to be published on or before 30 January 2016, which was finally released under Freedom of Information in 2017. The minister who commissioned the report said it was 'not in accordance with the terms of reference.'[355]

The report found neighbouring houses were not in compliance with the building regulations; that there was concern over the potential for the spread

---

[353] See: https://ny.curbed.com/2015/2/23/9989166/what-is-a-micro-home-and-what-does-it-mean-in-new-york
[354] Urban Land Institute (2014) *The Macro View on Micro Units*, ULI: New York
[355] See: https://kfmradio.com/news/26082017-1125/alan-kelly-millfield-manor-report-simply-not-what-i-commissioned

of fire between homes; and highlighted poor workmanship and improper joining of plasterboard to separating walls in attic spaces.[356]

The report was criticised as: the 24-page document that was published largely restates existing regulations and offers advice on how to prevent fires; there is no mention of concerns about timber-frame construction, which accounted for up to 30 per cent of homes built between 2000 and 2008; nor did the report use the houses as a case study, as it was claimed it was supposed to do.[357]

See also: *Fire Safety Notice; Fire Safety Certificate*

The specific minister with responsibility for housing has had various titles since 1919. The following list is of those ministers whose roles included a responsibility for housing, directly or indirectly.

Minister for Housing

Minister	Years	Party
Minister for Local Government		
W.T. Cosgrave	1919–1922	Sinn Féin
Ernest Blythe	1922–1923	Pro-Treaty Sinn Féin
Séamus Burke	1923–1924	Cumann na nGaedheal
Minister for Local Government and Public Health		
Séamus Burke	1924–1927	Cumann na nGaedheal
Richard Mulcahy	1927–1932	Cumann na nGaedheal
Seán T. O'Kelly	1932–1939	Fianna Fáil
P. J. Ruttledge	1939–1941	Fianna Fáil
Éamon de Valera	1941–1941	Fianna Fáil
Seán MacEntee	1941–1947	Fianna Fáil
Minister for Local Government		
Seán MacEntee	1947–1948	Fianna Fáil
Timothy J. Murphy	1948–1949	Labour Party
William Norton (acting)	1949–1949	Labour Party
Michael Keyes	1949–1951	Labour Party
Paddy Smith	1951–1954	Fianna Fáil
Patrick O'Donnell	1954–1957	Fine Gael
Paddy Smith	1957–1957	Fianna Fáil

[356] Baker, S (2017) 'Report into fire that destroyed 6 Kildare houses finds remaining homes not compliant with regulations', *TheJournal.ie*, 1 September, available at: https://www.thejournal.ie/report-into-fire-that-destroyed-six-kildare-homes-finds-houses-not-in-compliance-with-building-regulations-3576979-Sep2017/

[357] Clifford, M (2017) 'Delayed fire safety report an "insult" to residents of estate that lost 6 homes in blaze', *Irish Examiner*, 26 August

Neil Blaney	1957–1966	Fianna Fáil
Kevin Boland	1966–1970	Fianna Fáil
Bobby Molloy	1970–1973	Fianna Fáil
James Tully	1973–1977	Labour Party
Sylvester Barrett	1977–1977	Fianna Fáil
Minister for the Environment		
Sylvester Barrett	1977–1980	Fianna Fáil
Ray Burke	1980–1981	Fianna Fáil
Peter Barry	1981–1982	Fine Gael
Ray Burke	1982–1982	Fianna Fáil
Dick Spring	1982–1983	Labour Party
Liam Kavanagh	1983–1986	Labour Party
John Boland	1986–1987	Fine Gael
Padraig Flynn	1987–1991	Fianna Fáil
John Wilson (acting)	1991–1991	Fianna Fáil
Rory O'Hanlon	1991–1992	Fianna Fáil
Michael Smith	1992–1994	Fianna Fáil
Brendan Howlin	1994–1997	Labour Party
Noel Dempsey	1997–1997	Fianna Fáil
Minister for Environment and Local Government		
Noel Dempsey	1997–2002	Fianna Fáil
Minister for the Environment, Heritage and Local Government		
Martin Cullen	2002–2004	Fianna Fáil
Dick Roche	2004–2007	Fianna Fáil
John Gormley	2007–2011	Green Party
Éamon Ó'Cuív	2011–2011	Fianna Fáil
Minister for the Environment, Community and Local Government		
Phil Hogan	2011–2014	Fine Gael
Alan Kelly	2014–2016	Labour
Minister for Housing, Planning, Community and Local Government		
Simon Coveney	2016–2017	Fine Gael
Minister for Housing, Planning and Local Government		
Eoghan Murphy	2017–	Fine Gael

Mobile home   A mobile home is a large caravan used as permanent or temporary living accommodation. Placing a mobile home on a site requires ***planning permission***, although it can be stored in the garden of a house for up to nine months without planning permission. A mobile home can be used as a ***dwelling*** on a site, for example as a permanent dwelling is being constructed, once it is not connected to any services.

See also: ***household***

Modular housing is prefabricated units where components of the house are **Modular housing** produced off-site in factories and then the modules (bathroom, kitchen, etc.) are assembled on-site. The advantages of modular construction include quality control, as components are produced in factory conditions and not on-site, and time-saving, where assembly of the prefabricated units is much faster than building a house 'ab initio' on site.

See: ***rapid build housing – Poppintree***

The Money Advice and Budgeting Services (MABS) is a state-run, free, con-   **Money Advice** fidential and independent service for people in debt or in danger of getting   **and Budgeting** into debt operating from over 60 offices nationwide. MABS offices operate   **Services (MABS)** an appointment scheduling system and telephone service, and each service is staffed by experienced money advisers who work with clients who are experiencing difficulties with a wide range of personal debts including personal loans, and ***mortgage*** and rent ***arrears***.[358]

See also: ***Mortgage Arrears Resolution Process; Code of Conduct on Mortgage Arrears***

Money laundering is the process by which proceeds of crime are transformed   **Money** into ostensibly legitimate money or other assets. The use of property, includ-   **laundering** ing housing, has been a common method of money laundering. There are several ways to launder money using property, but it is typically done by:

• Purchasing real estate with illegal money and then selling the property or
• Manipulating the price of the property whereby the seller agrees to a contract that under-represents the value of the property and receives criminal proceeds to make up the difference[359]

The Criminal Justice (Money Laundering and Terrorist Financing) Act 2010 identifies 'designated persons' who are obliged to be aware of potential money-laundering activities in their business, including ***property services providers***.

See also: ***politically exposed person***

---

[358] See: https://www.mabs.ie/en/about_us/
[359] See: http://www.antimoneylaundering.gov.ie/en/AMLCU/Pages/Money_Laundering_Terrorist_Financing_Are_you_aware

Mortgage

A mortgage is a loan of money to purchase a property whereby the lender takes charge of the ***deeds*** of the property until the debt is repaid. Mortgages are typically repaid on a monthly basis.

If the mortgage is not repaid according to the terms and conditions of the loan, the lender can repossess the property. Mortgages are governed by the Consumer Credit Act 1995, the Consumer Protection Code, the ***Code of Conduct on Mortgage Arrears***, the ***Money Advice and Budgeting Service/*** Irish Banking Federation (IBF) Operational Protocol and the IBF Pledge.[360] At Census 2016, 31.6 per cent of all households had a mortgage and 36 per cent had no mortgage; 45 per cent of homeowners had a mortgage and 55 per cent had no mortgage.

See also: ***mortgage lending rules; Rebuilding Ireland Home Loan; arrears; split mortgage; housing cost overburden; home ownership; fixed rate mortgage; variable rate mortgage; tracker rate mortgage; interest rate***

Mortgage Allowance Scheme

The Mortgage Allowance Scheme is an allowance paid to local authority tenants who give up their house in order to purchase or build their own home. It was established in 1991 and effectively replaced the ***Surrender Grant***.

Under this scheme applicants can avail of an allowance of up to €11,450 payable over a five-year period. It is paid directly to the lending agency and reduces mortgage payments in each of the first five years: by €3,560 in the first year, €2,800 in the second year, €2,040 in the third year, €1,780 in the fourth year and €1,270 in the fifth year. The allowance paid in any year cannot exceed the amount of the mortgage repayments.

Mortgage Arrears Resolution Process (MARP)

The Mortgage Arrears Resolution Process (MARP) was introduced by the ***Central Bank*** in 2011. The MARP must be used by lenders under the ***Code of Conduct on Mortgage Arrears*** when dealing with borrowers in arrears (or those about to go into arrears). The MARP has four main stages:

1. *Communication*: The borrower must be informed that a third party has been appointed to deal with them; no more than three unsolicited communications with the borrower can be made each month; and the date that arrears began, number of payments missed and amount of arrears must be sent to the borrower, as well as details of fees and charges which apply regarding the arrears.
2. *Financial information*: A statement of financial affairs must be sent to the borrower for completion and once received back must be sent to the Arrears Support Unit to be considered.

---

[360] See: https://www.mabs.ie/en/publications/glossary/m.html

3. *Assessment*: The Arrears Support Unit must assess the financial statement using:
   a. The personal circumstances of the borrower
   b. The overall indebtedness of the borrower
   c. The information in the standard financial statement
   d. The borrower's current repayment capacity
   e. The borrower's previous payment history
4. *Resolution*: Alternative repayment arrangements must include:
   a. An interest-only arrangement for a specified period
   b. An arrangement to pay interest and part of the normal capital element for a specified period
   c. Deferring payment of all or part of the instalment repayment for a period
   d. Extending the term of the mortgage
   e. Changing the type of the mortgage, except in the case of tracker mortgages
   f. Capitalising the arrears and interest
   g. Any voluntary scheme to which the lender has signed up, e.g. Deferred Interest Scheme

Lenders must set up an appeals board to independently review any appeals by borrowers to alternative arrangements recommended.[361]
    See also: ***arrears; Code of Conduct on Mortgage Arrears***

Mortgage broker A mortgage broker is an independent intermediary who gives advice on a range of mortgage products. Mortgage brokers are regulated by the Financial Regulator under the banner of 'Mortgage Intermediary'.[362]
    See also: ***Mortgage Arrears Resolution Process; mortgage lending rules; Code of Conduct on Mortgage Arrears***

Mortgagee The mortgagee is the body (typically a bank or building society) that is lending the money in the form of a mortgage to a ***mortgagor***.

Mortgage interest tax relief[363] Mortgage interest tax relief (MITR) is a tax relief based on the amount of interest that is paid in a tax year on a qualifying mortgage loan. The history of MITR is difficult to trace since it relates to tax revenue forgone so it is

---

[361] See: https://www.lynchsolicitors.ie/mortgage-arrears-resolution-process/
[362] See: https://www.mortgagebrokers.ie/mortgage-information/mortgage-definitions-mortgage-jargon/
[363] See: https://www.revenue.ie/en/property/mortgage-interest-relief/what-is-a-qualifying-mortgage-loan.aspx

not captured in public spending data.[364] According to Baker and O'Brien,[365] MITR has existed since the income tax system was first established, but for many years its cost was limited by the small size of the tenure and low interest rates, and was offset by the taxation of imputed rent on owner-occupied dwellings.

Applicants can claim mortgage interest relief on interest paid by them on a loan used to purchase, repair, develop or improve the home. Applicants can claim mortgage interest relief on interest paid by them on a loan used to purchase, repair, develop or improve the home. Mortgages taken out after 31 December 2012 no longer qualify for mortgage interest relief. Mortgage interest relief was due to be abolished entirely after 31 December 2017, but it was extended to 2020 on a tapered basis for people who were eligible in 2017 (in general, people who took out a qualifying mortgage loan between 2004 and 2012). It will cease entirely from January 2021.

Landlords can deduct mortgage interest during the period their property is let. The amount of interest you can deduct on these mortgages has increased in recent years:

- Prior to 2017, it was 75% of the interest
- In 2017, it was 80% of the interest
- In 2018, it was 85% of the interest
- From January 2019, it is 100% of the interest (as announced in Budget 2019)[366]

See also: *Mortgage Arrears Resolution Process; mortgage lending rules; Code of Conduct on Mortgage Arrears*

Mortgage lending rules[367]

First introduced by the *Central Bank of Ireland* in February 2015, these rules set limits on the size of mortgages that consumers can borrow through the use of *loan-to-value* (LTV) and *loan-to-income* (LTI) limits. The measures are reviewed annually by the Central Bank.

For first-time buyers (FTB), the mortgage is capped at 3.5 times the household income, although 20 per cent of the value of new mortgage lending to FTBs can be above this loan-to-income (LTI) cap. First-time buyers require a minimum of a 10 per cent deposit for the property with a mortgage of 90 per

---

[364] Norris, M (2013) 'Varieties of Home Ownership: Ireland's Transition from a Socialised to a Marketised Policy Regime', UCD Geary Institute Discussion Paper Series, GP2013/06

[365] Baker, T and O'Brien, L (1979) *The Irish Housing System: A Critical Overview*, ESRI: Dublin

[366] See: http://www.citizensinformation.ie/en/money_and_tax/tax/income_tax_credits_and_reliefs/housing_tax_credits_and_reliefs.html

[367] See: https://www.centralbank.ie/financial-system/financial-stability/macro-prudential-policy/mortgage-measures

cent. For second and subsequent buyers (SSB), the mortgage is also capped at 3.5 times the household income, and 10 per cent of the value of new mortgage lending to SSBs can be above the LTI cap. SSBs require a minimum of a 20 per cent deposit for the property with a mortgage of 80 per cent.

For *buy-to-let* mortgages, a deposit of 30 per cent is required, although these mortgages are exempt from LTI limits.

Switcher mortgages are exempt from both LTV and LTI limits.

See also: *arrears; Mortgage Arrears Resolution Process; Code of Conduct on Mortgage Arrears*

The Mortgage to Rent Scheme is a government initiative to help homeowners who are at risk of losing their home. To qualify for the Mortgage to Rent Scheme:

Mortgage to Rent Scheme[368]

- Borrower(s) must have completed the *Mortgage Arrears Resolution Process* (MARP) with their lender
- Must be eligible for *social housing* support in the local authority in whose area the house is located
- Must not own any other property
- Must be living in a property that suits the borrower(s)' needs
- The property must be of a *value* no more than €365,000 for a house and €310,000 for an apartment or townhouse in the areas of Dublin, Kildare, Meath, Wicklow, Louth, Cork and Galway. The maximum values for the remainder of the country are €280,000 for a house and €215,000 for an *apartment* or *townhouse*.
- Income must not exceed €25,000,* €30,000* or €35,000* a year, depending on what part of the country the borrower(s) live in (net household income is the household income after taxes and social insurance (PRSI) have been taken off). (*Additional allowances for children.)
- Cannot have cash assets worth in excess of €20,000
- Must have a long-term right to remain in Ireland[369]

Changes to the scheme were announced in 2017, including allowing private companies purchase the distressed properties (previously it was just *approved housing bodies*, which are registered charities) from the mortgage holder's bank. The first of these private companies was Home for Life, which had a fund of €100 million and an agreement with Permanent TSB in which eligible mortgage holders can apply to it. It is unclear what happens at the end of tenants' 25-year lease agreements (e.g. *security of tenure*).

---

[368] See: https://www.housingagency.ie/Housing-Information/Mortgage-to-Rent-Scheme
[369] See: https://www.housingagency.ie/Housing-Information/Mortgage-to-Rent-Scheme

At the beginning of 2018, there had been 282 successful mortgage to rent cases since 2012.[370]

See also: *iCare*

Mortgagor

A mortgagor is the person borrowing funds in order to purchase a property.

See also: *mortgagee*

Multi-family housing

Multi-family housing is multiple residential units in one building or across several buildings in one *development*. In Ireland, an *apartment* block, or complex, is an example of multi-family housing.

See also: *condominium; detached house; semi-detached house; terraced house; duplex; micro-home; accessory dwelling unit; granny flat; mews*

Multi-Unit Developments Act (MUD) 2011

A multi-unit development is a development in which there are at least five residential units and the units share facilities, amenities and services. In practice, the majority of multi-unit developments are *apartment* blocks, but the Act also covers groups of houses that share common facilities and have an *owners' management company*.[371]

The primary purpose of the Multi-Unit Developments Act 2011 is to reform the law relating to the ownership and management of *common areas* of multi-unit developments and to facilitate the fair, efficient and effective management of *owners' management companies* (OMCs). The Act gives residential unit owners a say in the running of the development and in the amount of annual *service charge* and *sinking fund* contributions which they must pay. The Act also includes a dispute resolution mechanism.[372]

The Act covers four main areas:

- Conditions and obligations relating to the compulsory transfer of the common areas from the developer to the OMC
- Obligations of the developer upon completion of the development stage
- Remedial mechanisms for dealing with disputes
- Regulations, rights and obligations of the owners' management company (OMC) in relation to directorships and voting rights; reporting and information; the calculation, apportionment and recovery of service charges; the provision of a sinking fund; and other related matters.[373]

See also: *service charges; sinking fund; owners' management company*

---

[370] Cogley, M (2018) 'Mortgage-to-rent scheme has helped only 282 families in six years', *The Times, Ireland Edition*, 8 January

[371] See: http://www.citizensinformation.ie/en/housing/owning_a_home/home_owners/management_companies_for_apartment_blocks.html

[372] See: http://www.justice.ie/en/JELR/Pages/Multi-UnitDevelopmentsAct2011

[373] Society of Chartered Surveyors Ireland (n.d.) *A Consumer Guide to Apartment Ownership Under the Multi-Unit Developments (MUD) Act 2011*, SCSI: Dublin

N

The National Asset Management Agency (NAMA) was established as a government body on 21 December 2009 as part of the process of dealing with the property and banking crisis which had then unfolded. It has about 200 employees. According to NAMA, its primary commercial mandate, under section 10 of the NAMA Act, is to preserve and enhance the value of its loans and underlying security and to achieve the best financial return to the state from their management and ultimate sale.[374]

National Asset Management Agency (NAMA)

As a result of the property crash, Irish banks had property development loans secured on property **assets** with a market value far below the amount owed on the loan. NAMA was established as a bank for non-performing loans (effectively a 'bad bank'), acquiring the bad loans from Irish Nationwide Building Society, Bank of Ireland, Allied Irish Banks, Educational Building Society and Anglo Irish Bank. These bad loans were threatening the existence of the banks, as if left with the loans they would not have met their statutory capital requirements (the amount of money that a bank has to hold). The removal of these loans from the banks significantly de-risked their balance sheets.

NAMA ultimately acquired loans worth €26.2 billion from the banks for consideration of €31.8 billion, a 22 per cent premium, providing over €5.6 billion of state aid to Irish banks. In doing so, NAMA acquired more than 12,000 loans across a range of currencies, advanced to over 5,000 debtors (managed as 780 debtor connections) and secured by over 60,000 property units across Irish and international markets. The main factor which determines what NAMA pays for any particular loan is the value of the property securing it. Effectively, NAMA started its existence with a large balance sheet, and was tasked with reducing that balance sheet to zero.[375]

NAMA is also involved in the provision of social housing under its 'Social Initiative'. By 2018, NAMA had identified 6,984 residential properties as being potentially suitable for social housing. Once demand for a property has been confirmed by a local authority, NAMA facilitates contact and negotiation between its debtor or receiver and the local authority or **approved housing body** (AHB) to acquire the property. Contractual arrangements can take the form of a lease or purchase. In general, purchases are completed by AHBs and the properties acquired are then made available to local authorities under a **Payment and Availability Agreement**. Some 2,474 were delivered for social housing use, which is the majority (91 per cent) of all those properties for which demand was confirmed and which remained vacant and available.

---

[374] See: https://www.gov.ie/en/publication/2f5f9e-national-asset-management-agency-nama/
[375] See: https://www.nama.ie/about-us/our-work/loan-acquisition/

Under the NAMA Act 2009, NAMA is a statutorily independent, fully accountable, commercial state organisation, operating under an independent board of directors, which is fully funded from within its own resources. Given this independence, the Minister for Finance does not have a role in NAMA's commercial decisions, nor its day-to-day operations.

NAMA expects to wind down by the end of 2020, although if it has any live projects it may stay active beyond that date.

National Asset Residential Property Services (NARPS)

In 2012, the ***National Asset Management Agency*** (NAMA) established a special purpose (National Asset Residential Property Services 'NARPS') to take direct ownership of properties where there is an established demand and to then lease these properties long-term to an AHB or local authority. In the majority of cases, the properties acquired by NARPS are the remaining incomplete units in unfinished housing estates. In these instances, NAMA funds its debtor or receiver to complete both the properties and the wider common areas of the estate. To date, over half of the properties delivered by NAMA to AHBs/local authorities have been made available through NARPS.

National Association of Building Cooperatives

The National Association of Building Cooperatives (NABCO) was formed in 1973 to represent, promote, inform and train the ***cooperative housing*** movement. It has since become ***Co-operative Housing Ireland***.

National Association of Tenants' Organisations (NATO)

The National Organisation of Tenants' Organisations (NATO) was an umbrella group of 36 tenant representative bodies formed under the leadership of Matt Larkin to resist the modification of the system of ***differential rents*** by local authorities and Dublin Corporation; in particular to ensure that rents paid should be no more than 10 per cent of the household's income.

In late 1972, with an election in the offing, NATO entered an agreement with the potential future government of Fine Gael and Labour, which came to pass later that year. NATO brought many voters with it in supporting the new government so the deal was enacted almost immediately. The transfer of the cost of providing social housing from domestic rates to central government allowed for rates to be abolished in their entirety. This component of the NATO agreement alone has had significant long-lasting effects on housing in Ireland.[376]

National Building Agency

The National Building Agency is now part of the ***Housing and Sustainable Communities Agency***.
See also: ***An Foras Forbartha***

---

[376] Hayden, A (2014) 'Irish Social Housing: The Path to Decline, 1966–1988' in Sirr, L (ed.), *Renting in Ireland: The Private, Voluntary and Social Sectors*, IPA: Dublin

The National Development and Finance Agency (NDFA) was established on 1 January 2003. In its financial advisory role, the NDFA advises state authorities on the optimal financing of priority public investment projects by applying commercial standards in evaluating financial risks and costs. In its procurement role, the NDFA is responsible for all aspects of delivering the procurement of projects (including social housing) and hands them over to the sponsoring body after construction is complete and the asset is operational.[377]

National Development and Finance Agency

The National Development Plan sets out the investment priorities that underpin the successful implementation of the ***National Planning Framework*** (NPF), which guides national, regional and local planning and investment decisions in Ireland over the next two decades to cater for an expected population increase of over 1 million people. The National Development Plan supports the achievement of more ***balanced regional development*** of Ireland's three regions, main cities, other large urban centres, towns and villages, and the north-west of the country.[378]

See also: ***National Spatial Strategy; balanced regional development; regional development***

National Development Plan 2018–2027

The National Economic and Social Council (NESC) is the only state agency under the aegis of the Department of the Taoiseach. The role of the National Economic and Social Council is to advise the Taoiseach (Prime Minister) on strategic policy issues relating to sustainable economic, social and environmental development in Ireland. The members of the council are appointed by the Taoiseach and are representatives of business and employers' organisations, trade unions, agricultural and farming organisations, community and voluntary organisations, and environmental organisations, as well as heads of government departments and independent experts.

National Economic and Social Council (NESC)

Housing policy has been a significant area of NESC's work. Since 2014 NESC has published a series of related reports on the Irish housing system. These reports addressed social housing;[379] the wider rental sector and the role of owner-occupation;[380,381] and housing supply, land, infrastructure

---

[377] See: https://www.ndfa.ie/about

[378] Kilkenny, P and O'Callaghan, D (2018) *Department of Public Expenditure and Reform – Spending Review 2018: Current and Capital Expenditure on Social Housing Delivery Mechanisms*, Department of Public Expenditure and Reform: Dublin

[379] National Economic and Social Council (2014) *Social Housing at the Crossroads: Possibilities for Investment, Provision and Cost Rental – Report 138*, NESC: Dublin

[380] National Economic and Social Council (2015) *Ireland's Private Rental Sector: Pathways to Secure Occupancy and Affordable Supply – Report 141*, NESC: Dublin

[381] National Economic and Social Council (2014) *Homeownership and Rental: What Road is Ireland On? – Report 140*, NESC: Dublin

investment and institutional issues.[382,383] These reports drew on international experience of what has proven effective in regard to housing supply, affordability and sustainable urban development.

Some key perspectives that emerge from NESC's housing policy research are as follows. First, Ireland needs to change its system of urban **development**, land management and housing provision if there is to be a move away from a pattern of boom and bust. Second, **affordability** should be built into policies that are designed to increase the supply of housing. International experience suggests that cost rental is the most effective and fiscally sustainable way of achieving permanent affordability. **Cost rental** uses modest supply-side supports, such as land and finance at favourable rates, to underpin affordability. And third, there is a need for public institutions with the mandate and capacity to drive sustainable urban development.[384]

See also: **active land management**

National Housing Strategy for People with a Disability 2011–2016

The National Housing Strategy for People with a Disability 2011–2016 has been extended to 2020 (under **Rebuilding Ireland**).

The National Housing Strategy for People with a Disability is a framework for delivering housing to people with disabilities through mainstream housing sources. The vision of the strategy is to facilitate access for people with disabilities to the appropriate range of housing and related support services, delivered in an integrated and sustained manner, which promotes equality of opportunity, individual choice and independent living.

Whilst previously many people with disabilities may have had their housing needs met through health-funded service providers, under this strategy people with disabilities will have better access to **social housing** through local authorities.

See also: **access and use (houses)**

National Oversight and Audit Commission

The National Oversight and Audit Commission (NOAC) is a statutory body established in July 2014 to oversee the local government sector. Amongst other things, NOAC is required to:

- Scrutinise performance of any local government body against relevant indicators as selected by NOAC (to include customer service) or as prescribed in ministerial regulations
- Scrutinise financial performance, including value for money, of any local government body in respect of its financial resources

[382] National Economic and Social Council (2015) *Housing Supply and Land: Driving Public Action for the Common Good – Report 142*, NESC: Dublin
[383] National Economic and Social Council (2018) *Urban Development Land, Housing and Infrastructure: Fixing Ireland's Broken System*, NESC: Dublin
[384] *Ibid.*

- Oversee how national local government policy is implemented by local government bodies
- Carry out any additional functions conferred by ministerial order

NOAC has produced housing-related reports including *Review of the Management and Maintenance of Local Authority Housing* (May 2017) and *Rented Houses Inspections – A Review of Local Authority Performance of Private Rented Houses Regulations Functions* (October 2016), both of which highlight the work in housing being done by local authorities, and areas in which they require significant improvement.

See also: ***FIDH; data – housing output issues; National Economic and Social Council; voids***

The ***National Planning Framework*** was launched in February 2018. It is a 'national document that will guide at a high level strategic planning and development for the country over the next 20+ years, so that as the population grows, that growth is sustainable (in economic, social and environmental terms).'[385]

National Planning Framework

The objectives of the NPF are to:

- Guide the future development of Ireland, taking into account a projected 1 million increase in population, the need to create 660,000 additional jobs to achieve full employment and a need for 550,000 more homes by 2040

  Of the 1 million extra people:
  - 25 per cent is planned for Dublin, recognised as the key international and global city of scale and principal economic driver
  - 25 per cent across the other four cities combined (Cork, Limerick, Galway and Waterford), enabling all four to grow their population and jobs by 50–60 per cent, and become cities of greater scale, i.e. growing by twice as much as they did over the previous 25 years to 2016
  - the remaining 50 per cent of growth to occur in key regional centres, towns, villages and rural areas, to be determined in Regional Spatial and Economic Strategies (RSESs)
- Enable people to live closer to where they work, moving away from the current unsustainable trends of increased commuting
- Regenerate rural Ireland by promoting environmentally sustainable growth patterns
- Plan for and implement a better distribution of regional growth, in terms of jobs and prosperity

---

[385] See: http://npf.ie/project-ireland-2040-national-planning-framework/

- Transform settlements of all sizes through imaginative urban regeneration and bring life/jobs back into cities, towns and villages
- Coordinate delivery of infrastructure and services in tandem with growth, through joined-up NPF/National Investment Plan and consistent sectoral plans, which will help to manage this growth and tackle congestion and quality of life issues in Dublin and elsewhere[386]

The NPF does not 'provide every detail for every part of the country'.[387] Instead, it is a 'framework' intended to guide development and investment through a shared set of national objectives and principles. It is then left to the three regional assemblies and the 31 city and county councils to take a lead in refining these into more detailed plans. The NPF 'sets in train a process by which more detailed planning documents must follow: spatial planning, infrastructure planning, social and economic planning'.[388] The central tenet of the NPF is rebalancing growth in the state away from Dublin. Alongside the objective of balance is concentrated growth. In an effort to stem urban sprawl, the government targets the delivery of two-fifths of new housing in **infill** and **brownfield** sites within cities, towns and villages. Outside of the cities, this means capping the prevalence of 'bungalow blight' by reducing one-off dwellings. Councils will be encouraged to concentrate development in rural towns and villages, unless there is a proven 'social and economic need'.[389]

See also: ***National Development Plan; rural housing; regional development; Bungalow Bliss; one-off housing***

National Spatial Strategy 2002–2020

The National Spatial Strategy was launched in December 2002. It was the first national spatial strategy in Europe after the publication of the European Spatial Development Perspective and was considered best practice by other countries. It sought to be inclusive in vision, was underpinned by good intentions and promoted a planned approach to development.[390]

Unfortunately, the National Spatial Strategy 2002, with its focus on **balanced regional development**, was almost immediately torpedoed by the government decentralisation policy introduced in the Budget of 2003, coupled with the subsequent economic collapse and withdrawal of the €400 million 'Gateway Fund'. This central policy thrust of balanced regional

---

[386] See: http://npf.ie/project-ireland-2040-national-planning-framework/
[387] *Ibid.*, p. 5
[388] *Ibid.*, p. 10
[389] Anon. (2018)'The National Planning Framework in Brief', *Eolas*, 29 March
[390] Kitchin, R (2015) 'Why the National Spatial Strategy Failed and Prospects for the National Planning Framework', *Ireland after NAMA*, 24 July, available at: https://irelandafternama.wordpress.com/2015/07/24/why-the-national-spatial-strategy-failed-and-prospects-for-the-national-planning-framework/

development is difficult to achieve as Ireland does not have the resources to promote every location in a 'one for everyone in the audience' approach.[391]

The National Spatial Strategy was withdrawn in 2012.

See also: *regional development; rural housing; National Planning Framework*

National Treasury Management Agency

The National Treasury Management Agency (NTMA) was originally established in 1990 to borrow for the Exchequer and manage the national debt. It now has a range of functions providing financial and risk management services to the government. These include the Ireland Strategic Investment Fund, the *National Development Finance Agency* (NDFA), the State Claims Agency and the *National Asset Management Agency* (NAMA).[392]

National Vacant Housing Reuse Strategy 2018–2021

Pillar 5 of *Rebuilding Ireland* concerns the better utilisation of existing housing, which includes vacant housing. *Rebuilding Ireland* sets out the strategic objective of ensuring that existing housing stock is used to the maximum degree possible – focusing on measures to use vacant stock to renew urban and rural areas. The strategy focuses on all forms of vacant housing, both private and social, and includes vacant individual houses, apartment blocks and individual units within those blocks. In addition, the strategy refers to vacant commercial space, particularly that which may have previously been used as residential accommodation, such as 'over the shop' units, as having the potential to be refurbished or converted for residential use.

The National Vacant Housing Reuse Strategy's vision is to return as many recoverable vacant properties back to viable use as possible, increasing the supply of sustainable housing available, while also revitalising the vibrancy of local communities.

See also: *vacant dwellings; vacancy rate; voids*

Natural property rights theory

Questions about property rights, their origin, and their measure have been at the forefront of serious political discourse since ancient times.[393] The question of whether the right to property ought to be regarded as a fundamental constitutional right has proven controversial.[394]

The intensity of this debate reflects the centrality and uniqueness of the right to property among fundamental rights. Historically, the right to private property has been regarded as the central paradigm for rights in general, and

---

[391] Hughes, B (2018) 'Demography Is Destiny: Strategic Planning and Housing in Ireland', in Sirr, L (ed.), *Administration – special housing edition*, Vol. 66, No. 2, pp. 153–177

[392] See: https://www.nama.ie/about-us/nama-and-the-ntma/

[393] Epstein, RA (2009) 'Property Rights, State of Nature Theory, and Environmental Protection', *New York University Journal of Law and Liberty*, Vol. 4, No. 1, pp. 1–35

[394] Boyce, B (2007) 'Property as a Natural Right and as a Conventional Right in Constitutional Law', *Loyola of Los Angeles International and Comparative Law Review*, Vol. 29, No. 2

the essential precondition for the creation of a private sphere of autonomy that forms the foundation of the pluralistic liberal order. Moreover, to the extent that property rights determine access to the basic means of subsistence, they are the prerequisite to the meaningful exercise of all other rights. But at the same time, the right to property is unique in that the recognition of one person's property rights necessarily implies a restriction on the property rights of others. Indeed, to the extent that the exercise of other rights, such as freedom of speech or the right to a fair trial, may depend on possession of property (as did the right to vote in Ireland less than 100 years ago), recognition of private property rights can have a distorting effect on the exercise of those other rights as well. The greater the inequality in the distribution of private property, the more acute this problem becomes.[395]

Labelling an economic interest a 'fundamental natural right' is a tactic aimed at ending all further argument,[396] particularly regarding its regulation.

See also: ***housing rights approach to housing; Constitution of Ireland (Article 40.3.2, Article 43)***

Negative equity   Negative equity is a situation whereby the ***value*** of a property is worth less than the amount of its outstanding debt (***mortgage***).

According to the ***Central Bank of Ireland***,[397] negative equity remains a prominent, if diminishing, feature of the Irish housing market. Negative equity has adverse consequences for the economy. These include preventing or delaying households from selling their properties, and adverse 'wealth effects' whereby households in negative equity tend to consume less. Furthermore, negative equity matters for mortgage ***default***, with loans in negative equity having a greater probability of default compared to positive equity loans.[398] As well as being of benefit to individual borrowers, a decline in negative equity can be beneficial to overall financial stability, including through positive effects on consumption and consumer confidence and by aiding housing mobility.[399]

See also: ***arrears***

Neoliberalism in Ireland   Neoliberalism is a political and economic philosophy which promotes the 'market' as the key driver of social and financial wellbeing. General principles of neoliberalism include:

---

[395] *Ibid.*

[396] Alexander, GS (2007) 'The Ambiguous Work of "Natural Property Rights"', *Journal of Constitutional Law*, Vol. 9, No. 2, pp. 477–482

[397] Central Bank of Ireland (2017) *Macro-Financial Review – 2017: II*, Central Bank of Ireland: Dublin

[398] Kelly, R and O'Malley, T (2016) 'The Good, the Bad and the Impaired: A Credit Risk Model of the Irish Mortgage Market', *Journal of Financial Stability*, Vol. 22, pp. 1–9

[399] Central Bank of Ireland (2017) *Macro-Financial Review – 2017: II*, Central Bank of Ireland: Dublin

- Privatisation of state assets
- Deregulation of economic sectors
- Openness to investment flows

As MacLaran and Kelly describe it, for almost 30 years governments internationally have become increasingly seduced by an agenda which has sought to place 'the market' at the heart of economic life. According to Brenner and Theodore: 'the linchpin of neoliberal ideology is the belief that open, competitive, and unregulated markets, liberated from all forms of state interference, represent the optimal mechanism for economic development.'[400] Neoliberalism comprises a range of ideas and a theory of economic practices which propose that human wellbeing is best advanced by liberating individual entrepreneurial freedoms and skills within an institutional framework characterised by strong private property rights, free markets and free trade. It is a somewhat unfortunate term because the word 'liberal' is often used in common parlance to describe actions which are socially progressive. Here, however, the term 'liberal' describes the liberalisation of the conditions under which capital is able to operate and profit-seeking facilitated. Neoliberalism does not comprise a specific range of policies, a particular strategy or agenda. Within varying geographical and temporal circumstances, it characterises policies which draw upon fundamental general principles which are then applied to specific economic conditions and social problems.[401]

Ireland has its own particular version of neoliberalism, as outlined by Kitchin et al.:[402] Irish neoliberalism is a mixture of American ideology comprising minimal state intervention; the privatisation of state services; *public–private partnerships*; *developer*-/speculator-led planning; low corporate (and individual) taxation; limited regulation; and clientelism; alongside European social welfarism with its developmental state; social partnership; welfare safety net; high indirect taxation; and EU directives and obligations.

See also: *crisis; economic growth and housing*

New Dwelling Completions is a new quarterly series on the number of new dwellings built in Ireland since 2011 compiled and published by the *Central Statistics Office* (CSO). The CSO's New Dwelling Completions figure does

New Dwelling Completions[403]

---

[400] Brenner, N and Theodore, N (2002) 'Cities and the Geographies of "Actually Existing Neoliberalism"', *Antipode*, Vol. 34, pp. 349–379

[401] MacLaran, A and Kelly, S (2014) 'Neoliberalism: The Rise of a Bad Idea', in MacLaran, A and Kelly, S (eds), *Neoliberal Urban Policy and the Transformation of the City*, Palgrave Macmillan: London

[402] Kitchin, R, O'Callaghan, C, Boyle, M, Gleeson, J and Keaveney, K (2012) 'Placing Neoliberalism: The Rise and Fall of Ireland's Celtic Tiger', *Environment and Planning A*, Vol. 44, pp. 1302–1326

[403] See: https://www.cso.ie/en/releasesandpublications/ep/p-ndc/newdwellingcompletionsq12018/

not include a full range of activity in the housing sector. In particular, there has been a significant level of construction output in the student accommodation sector in recent years which is not included as these are generally connected to the ESB network as commercial connections and are therefore not included in the ESB domestic connections dataset.

See also: *data – housing output issues; purpose-built student accommodation*

NIMBY

A pejorative acronym for Not In My Back Yard, a reference to someone, or a group, who objects to development, particularly of an unpleasant nature, close to their property, but usually has no problem with it being located elsewhere. The extreme version is known as BANANA – Build Absolutely Nothing Anywhere Near Anyone.

See also: *YIMBY*

Notice of termination

A notice of termination of *tenancy* must be in writing, meaning email, text or verbal notification is not valid under the law. A notice of termination may be issued by: being delivered personally; being left at the address where the person ordinarily resides; being posted (there is no special requirement for registered post); affixing to the *dwelling*. In some cases, a *landlord* will be required to submit a statutory declaration with the notice of termination. Where a landlord intends to sell the property within three months of terminating the tenancy, a statutory declaration must accompany the notice of termination confirming this intention. Where a landlord requires the property for their own use or for the use of a family member, a statutory declaration must accompany the notice of termination confirming the intended occupant's identity and (if not the landlord) their relationship to the landlord and the expected duration of the occupation. The statutory declaration must also confirm that the landlord is required to offer a tenancy to the tenant if the dwelling is vacated within a period of one year from the termination date. Grounds for termination of a lease are contained in section 34 of the *Residential Tenancies Act 2004*. The 'slip rule' allows an adjudicator or tribunal to overlook a minor error in a notice of termination, once the error does not prejudice the notice itself, which would otherwise be valid.

For landlords a *fixed term tenancy* can be ended during the period of the fixed term if:

- The tenant has breached one of the conditions of the *lease*.
- The reason for ending a fixed term tenancy is non-payment of rent. The landlord must send a 14-day warning letter allowing time (14 days) to pay the rent *arrears*, before a 28-day notice of termination can be issued (at the end of the 14 days).

- The reason for ending the tenancy is because of a breach of the tenant's responsibilities. In this case, the landlord must state the breach in the warning notice, and in a 28-day notice if one follows.

See also: ***security of tenure; notice periods***

Notice periods

The period of notice before terminating a lease that parties to a tenancy must give depends on the length of occupancy. The tenancy/lease agreement may give a longer period of notice, and a landlord and tenant may also agree a shorter period of notice, but this can only be agreed when a notice has been given. A tenancy can also be ended if both a landlord and tenant agree to terminate a lease. The notice period begins the day after the tenant receives the notice. The notice period for evicting tenants for ***anti-social behaviour*** is seven days. In other cases, landlords and tenants must give the following notice periods:

Length of Tenancy	Landlord to Tenant (days)	Tenant to Landlord (days)
Less than 6 months	28	28
6 months or more, but less than 1 year	90	35
1 year or more but less than 2 years	120	42
2 years or more but less than 3 years	120	56
3 years or more but less than 4 years	180	56
4 years or more but less than 5 years	180	84
5 years or more but less than 6 years	180	84
6 years or more but less than 7 years	180	84
7 years or more but less than 8 years	196	84
8 or more years	224	112

During the first six months of an initial ***Part 4*** tenancy, a landlord may end the tenancy without giving any reason, provided the tenant is given 28 days' notice. A landlord must give one of the grounds for termination in the legislation to end a '***further Part 4***' tenancy in its first six months.

If there is a high and imminent risk of death, serious injury or danger to the structure of the property as a result of the landlord's failure to comply with their obligations, the tenant only has to give seven days' notice. Warning letters do not need to be sent in this situation.

See also: ***Residential Tenancies Act 2004; security of tenure***

Notice to treat

This is a term used in connection with the use of a ***Compulsory Purchase Order*** (CPO). A notice to treat is served on all claimants whose properties are included in the CPO, requesting them to submit detailed claims for compensation within a specified time.[404]

Nyberg Report, The
The Nyberg Report was commissioned by the Irish government in 2011, and conducted by Peter Nyberg, who was a senior civil servant in Finland. His report was entitled *Misjudging Risk: Causes of the Systemic Banking Crisis in Ireland – Report of the Commission of Investigation into the Banking Sector in Ireland*.

See also: **banking crisis; bubble (housing)**

nZEB (near zero energy buildings)[405]
Nearly zero energy building (nZEB) is a term that originated in the EU's 2010 recast of the EU Directive on the Energy Performance of Buildings (the 2002 version of which introduced the requirement for **Building Energy Ratings**). While the 'nearly' prefix may imply bureaucratic compromise, it may also reflect an important recognition about low-energy buildings: any building that uses energy isn't a zero energy building.

While a net zero score can be achieved by adding renewable energy systems to a building, it doesn't change the fact that buildings need energy. The EU's definition of nZEBs recognises this, and states that buildings should have nearly zero energy demand, adding that the very small remaining demand should be met by renewable sources, to the greatest extent possible.

While providing guidance, the EU has left it up to each member state to establish its own definition for nZEB, which all new homes must meet from the start of 2021. In Ireland, the **Department of Housing, Planning and Local Government**'s proposed definition for new homes includes a 70 per cent energy and CO_2 reduction compared to 2005 standards, while requiring high levels of insulation, high-performance windows, **airtightness** and renewable energy systems to meet part of each home's needs.

See also: **Y-value; U-value; thermal bridge**

O

Obsolescence
In housing terms, obsolescence refers to when a building becomes no longer inhabitable and beyond functional use. Houses do not last forever and at some stage will become obsolete; therefore, obsolescence is a normal part of any housing stock.

Rates of natural housing obsolescence vary internationally but are commonly accepted as being between 0.4 and 0.6 per cent of the total

---

[404] Society of Chartered Surveyors Ireland (n.d.) *A Clear Guide to Compulsory Purchase Orders and Compensation*, SCSI: Dublin
[405] Entry courtesy of Jeff Colley of *Passive House Plus* magazine

housing stock. Research for the census periods from 1961 to 2002 found annual housing obsolescence rate ranging between 0.4 and 1 per cent in Ireland.[406] For 2017, using an obsolescence rate of 0.215 per cent (a low rate by national and international standards) the **Department of Housing, Planning and Local Government** added 10,000 houses to their calculation of the national housing stock,[407] out of 14,407 houses being recorded as completed by the CSO.

The causes of obsolescence are many: e.g. physical processes such as material degradation and deterioration over time, ageing, building fatigue, and poor design and construction. It can be caused by buildings not getting the maintenance or adaptations they need throughout their lives. It can also be caused or accelerated by behavioural factors such as maltreatment or overloading the structure, as well as changes in the number of occupants and level of intensity of use of the building. Changes in the surrounding environment can have an impact – nearby construction, traffic, pollution, seismic activity and so forth – and so can alterations in government policy, regulations and standards. The market too plays a role: a lack of demand, depreciation in value and a change in the status of a building's location can affect the amount of maintenance a building receives and hasten its demise.[408]

See also: *data – housing output issues*

Ó Cualann Cohousing Alliance

Ó Cualann Cohousing Alliance CLG is a voluntary housing cooperative, with *approved housing body* status. The alliance is based on the principles of co-housing: 'building communities – not just houses', and envisages developing fully integrated communities where 'owner members' will live side by side with '*tenant* members' in social, voluntary and private rented homes, sharing common amenities.

The Ó Cualann model for mixed tenure, affordable housing was developed by Hugh Brennan and Bill Black in 2013. The Ó Cualann model depends on support from local authorities and other willing land owners who provide land at a discounted rate; *development* and planning levies are waived by the local authority and Ó Cualann substitutes the normal developer's margin with a 5 per cent surplus. This results in houses being delivered at an affordable price to low- and middle-income earners. Houses are pre-sold to members who pay a 10 per cent deposit to Ó Cualann on signing the

---

[406] Fitzgerald, J (2017) 'Understanding why homes are vacant can help solve housing crisis', *Irish Times*, 5 May

[407] See: https://www.housing.gov.ie/housing/statistics/house-building-and-private-rented/private-housing-market-statistics

[408] André, T and van der Flier, K (2011) 'Obsolescence and the End of Life Phase of Buildings', paper presented at Management and Innovation for a Sustainable Built Environment (MISBE) CIB International Conference, 20–23 June, Amsterdam

contract. Owners pay no more than 28 per cent of their net monthly income on their mortgages and there is a '***clawback***' if houses are sold or let within twenty years.

The Ó Cualann model is privately funded by: (a) members who purchase the homes; (b) private individuals who hold loan notes issued by Ó Cualann; and (c) the banks that finance the construction.

The first project in Poppintree in north Dublin was supported by Dublin City Council and construction finance was provided by AIB, which also provided mortgages, through its subsidiaries, to members to purchase the homes. Members' deposits and low-cost loans from private individuals help to reduce bank borrowings. In 2017, 49 A2 energy-rated homes, a mix of two, three and four bedrooms, were built in Poppintree at an average purchase price of €175,000 each.

The Ó Cualann design team takes the projects to planning stage and certifies ongoing payments. The building contractor signs a 'no variation' 'design build' contract and their design team is responsible for all working drawings, energy requirements, etc. Ó Cualann is responsible for the ***assigned certifiers*** and safety consultants.

The Ó Cualann model has support from all political parties in Ireland.

See also: ***deposit (booking); procurement; development contribution scheme; development; developer; community land trust; affordability; affordable housing schemes; rapid build housing – Poppintree***

One-off housing One-off houses are individual houses built on single sites in rural areas. Census 2016 recorded 71.8 per cent of houses in rural areas as being one-off. It is a popular practice in rural Ireland as the houses are often built on land provided for free or cheaply by a family member, thus allowing the owner to construct the house at a more affordable cost. One-off houses typically have their own sewage system (***septic tank***) and are either connected to a private water scheme or have their own well.

One-off housing is not regarded as being good practice by most planning professionals, who look upon them as unsustainable development. The very nature of one-off housing means the development of a large, dispersed settlement pattern. A dispersed settlement pattern increases the cost of providing services such as broadband, electricity and ambulances, and leads to car dependency. It also denude villages and small towns of the critical population needed to ensure the survival of shops and services. This diminishes the social life and viability of rural communities. The ***National Planning Framework*** has recognised that, as a result, many key services have closed, in part due to population decline, leaving more marginalised and vulnerable citizens without access to those services.

In an effort to curb the proliferation of one-off housing, many local authorities had implemented a 'locals only' rule, which effectively meant the development of one-off houses was limited to people who were from the area. In 2013, the European Court of Justice ruled that: 'The condition that there exists a "sufficient connection" between the prospective buyer of immovable property and the target commune (locality) constitutes an unjustified restriction on fundamental freedoms.' This, it was held, contravened article 43 (Freedom of Movement of People) of the Treaty on the Functioning of the European Union, as it discriminated against 'non-locals'.

The ***National Planning Framework*** (NPF) has stipulated that the 'demonstrable economic need to live in a rural area' must be the 'core consideration' to adjudicate on future planning applications for houses in the countryside,[409] although there is no definition of what 'demonstrable economic need' means. The NPF has also categorised rural housing policy by whether the location is under urban or rural influence, thus:

National Policy Objective No.19:

　　Ensure, in providing for the development of rural housing, that a distinction is made between areas under urban influence, i.e. within the commuter catchment of cities and large towns and centres of employment, and elsewhere:

- In rural areas under urban influence, facilitate the provision of single housing in the countryside based on the core consideration of demonstrable economic or social need to live in a rural area and siting and design criteria for rural housing in statutory guidelines and plans, having regard to the viability of smaller towns and rural settlements;
- In rural areas elsewhere, facilitate the provision of single housing in the countryside based on siting and design criteria for rural housing in statutory guidelines and plans, having regard to the viability of smaller towns and rural settlements.[410]

See also: ***rural housing***

Open House Dublin is Ireland's largest architecture festival and delivered by the Irish Architecture Foundation. In 2017, it had 33,000 visits. The idea of Open House is that buildings that aren't usually accessible to the public and buildings of architectural merit open their doors for one weekend, with free tours provided by expert guides. Open House Dublin highlights the

Open House

---

[409] McDonald, F (2018) '"Bungalow Blitz" another nail in the coffin for towns and villages', *Irish Times*, 13 February
[410] See: http://npf.ie/project-ireland-2040-national-planning-framework/

significant role that architecture can, and has, played in the evolving form of our everyday lives.

Dublin was the fourth city to take part in the Open House Worldwide family in 2005. Now there are 44 cities in the family and counting. The rules are that members must value education and awareness, and ensure the initiative is free to the public. It must be delivered in a city of a population of 75,000+.

Open plan   An open plan house is typically where the living, kitchen and dining spaces are all in one. There are few, if any, dividing walls between the different functional areas. According to Tisdall, 'architect Frank Lloyd Wright was an early proponent of open plan design in the late nineteenth century. In Ireland, the mainstream introduction of double-glazed windows in the 1980s and 1990s with their improved draught-proofing and insulation brought increasing desire and opportunity for people to change their homes from multiple smaller rooms with defined functions towards larger multifunctional spaces'.[411]

Overburden   See: *housing cost overburden*

Overcrowding   Section 63 of the *Housing Act 1966* defines 'overcrowding' as follows:

> A house shall for the purposes of this Act be deemed to be overcrowded at any time when the number of persons ordinarily sleeping in the house and the number of rooms therein either—
> (*a*) are such that any two of those persons, being persons of ten years of age or more of opposite sexes and not being persons living together as husband and wife, must sleep in the same room, or
> (*b*) are such that the free air space in any room used as a sleeping apartment, for any person is less than four hundred cubic feet (the height of the room, if it exceeds eight feet, being taken to be eight feet, for the purpose of calculating free air space),
> and 'overcrowding' shall be construed accordingly.

The legislation and definition have been criticised as being out of date and in need of updating. According to *Threshold*, one of the greatest fire safety risks in private rented accommodation is overcrowding, which is not covered under current minimum standards laws.[412]

---

[411] Tisdall, G (2015) 'The problem with open plan …', *Sunday Independent*, 23 November
[412] See: https://www.threshold.ie/news/2017/10/23/government-must-ensure-minimum-housing-standards-a/

Eurostat defines a person as considered as living in an overcrowded household if the household does not have at its disposal a minimum number of rooms equal to:

- One room for the household
- One room per couple in the household
- One room for each single person aged eighteen or more
- One room per pair of single people of the same gender between twelve and seventeen years of age
- One room for each single person between twelve and seventeen years of age and not included in the previous category
- One room per pair of children under twelve years of age[413]

See also: ***Housing (Standards for Rented Houses) Regulations 2017***

Overholding

Overholding is when a ***tenant*** will not leave a property when legally required to. If a valid ***notice of termination*** is not complied with and the tenant does not leave, the only recourse is to refer a dispute to the ***Residential Tenancies Board***. Under no circumstances may the ***landlord*** take the law into his own hands by evicting the tenant.[414]
See also: ***eviction***

Owner-occupied

Dwellings owned by the households that live in them. In Ireland, this includes dwellings that have mortgage debt attached to them (some 31.55 per cent of all households).[415]
See also: ***tenure; home ownership***

Owners' management company (OMC)

An owners' management company (OMC) is a body established under the ***Multi-Unit Developments Act 2011***. It is the legal owner of the ***common areas*** of a development and responsible for their maintenance and upkeep, normally funded through a ***service charge*** and ***sinking fund***. OMCs usually employ a ***property management*** company (or '***managing agent***') to carry out the day-to-day upkeep of the development. An OMC can also establish 'house rules' for a development once they are reasonable and agreed by the owners.
An OMC is established for three reasons:

- To manage and maintain common areas in a multi-unit development
- To be the legal owner of the common areas on behalf of the owners of the units

---

[413] See: https://ec.europa.eu/eurostat/statistics-explained/index.php?title=Glossary:Overcrowding_rate
[414] See: https://www.threshold.ie/download/pdf/illegal_eviction_a_brief_guide.pdf
[415] CSO Census 2016

- To be the legal owner of the beneficial or reversionary interest of each unit. This means that the OMC owns a share in each unit. As such, the OMC is also a party to all sales of units in a development because it 'owns' a share in each property. The OMC cannot legally prevent the sale or purchase of a unit, but it can take action against an owner for non-payment of the ***service charge***.

OMCs have certain specific obligations:[416]

- *Register of members*: The company must supply the buyer of a residential unit with a share or membership certificate and ensure that the register of members is updated.
- *Annual report*: The company must prepare an annual report and hold an annual meeting to discuss the report.
- *Service charges*: The company must establish a scheme for annual service charges to pay for the maintenance, insurance and repair of common areas within its control and for the provision of common services (for example, security) to unit owners.
- *Sinking fund*: Within three years of the transfer of ownership to it, the owners' management company must establish a sinking fund for spending on refurbishment, improvement or maintenance of a non-recurring nature of the multi-unit development.
- *House rules*: The owners' management company may make house rules for the effective operation and maintenance of the multi-unit development.
- *Long-term contracts*: The company may not enter into contracts with providers of goods and services which are to last for more than three years.

OMCs must operate according to the rules of company law that apply to any other commercial company, even though they do not trade for profit. The OMC must hold an AGM at least once a year and all members must be invited to attend. The company must also file an annual return with the Companies Registration Office that must contain certain information about the company and its financial activities.[417]

   See also: ***estate agent; letting agent; managing agent; property services provider; service charge; sinking fund***

---

[416] See: http://www.citizensinformation.ie/en/housing/owning_a_home/home_owners/management_companies_for_apartment_blocks.html#122387
[417] See: https://www.ccpc.ie/consumers/housing/apartments-and-duplexes/owners-management-companies/

P

Charles Stewart Parnell (1846–1891) was an Irish nationalist politician and landlord. Parnell was an advocate of land reform and president of *Michael Davitt*'s Irish National Land League, the principal aim of which was the elimination of landlordism and prevention of *eviction* of *tenant* farmers, alongside helping them own their own land.

Parnell, Charles Stewart

See also: *Tenant Right League; Gavan Charles Duffy; Three Fs*

A Part 4 tenancy refers to Part 4 of the *Residential Tenancies Act 2004* and means that a *tenant* shall, after a period of six months, become entitled to the provision of a 'Part 4' tenancy. The tenants can then stay in the property for a further five-and-a-half years, or three-and-a-half years if the tenancy commenced before 24 December 2016, and subject to certain exceptions for *termination*.

Part 4 Tenancy

Parties to a lease cannot contract out of a tenant's entitlement to a Part 4 tenancy (section 54 of the Residential Tenancies Act 2004). Termination of a Part 4 tenancy is regulated by section 34 of the Residential Tenancies Act 2004. The continuation of a lease after its initial four-/six-year period is known as a *further Part 4 tenancy*.

See also: *notice of termination; security of tenure; tenure; tenure neutrality; private rented sector*

Certain *development* carried out by a local authority requires *planning permission*, and is covered by part 8 of the Planning and Development Regulations 2001.

Part 8, Planning and Development Regulations 2001

Article 80(1) of the Regulations sets out what works are to be assessed under the Part 8 procedure:

- The construction or erection of a house.
- The construction of a new road or the widening or realignment of an existing road, where the length of new road or of the widened or realigned road is 100 metres or more.
- The construction of a bridge or tunnel.
- The construction or erection of a pumping station, treatment works, holding tanks or outfall facilities for waste water or storm water.
- The construction or erection of water intake or treatment works, overground aqueducts, or dams or other installations designed to hold water or to store it on a long-term basis.
- Drilling for water supplies.
- Construction of a swimming pool.

- The use of land, or the construction or erection of any installation or facility, for the disposal of waste – except for development that requires a waste licence or the development of a bring facility which contains not more than five receptacles.
- The use of land as a burial ground.
- The construction or erection of a fire station, a library or a public toilet.
- Any other development the estimated cost of which exceeds €126,000, except the laying underground of sewers, mains, pipes or other apparatus.[418]

Part V social housing

Part V of the ***Planning and Development Act 2000*** introduced a requirement for ***developers*** to allocate 20 per cent of their units for sale in developments of more than five units to the local authority at a reduced price for use as social and/or affordable housing. In 2015, these Part V requirements were reformed. To have a Part V obligation, developments now have to be of ten or more units, and the 20 per cent requirement has been reduced to 10 per cent. The option of buying out the Part V agreement has been removed, as was the option of providing land on alternative sites outside the local authority area. In addition, local authorities can now acquire land from developers at 'existing use value' rather than '***development*** value', the date of ***valuation*** being the date of grant of ***planning permission***.

Options for complying with Part V obligations are now:

- Transfer of land – the default option (for the developer)
- Building and transfer of houses
- Transfer of houses on land off-site
- Grant of a ***lease*** of houses on- or off-site
- A combination of two or more of the options above

Certain developments are exempt from Part V obligations:

- Provision of housing by an approved body for ***social housing*** and/or ***affordable housing***
- The conversion of an existing building or the reconstruction of a building to create one or more dwellings provided that at least 50 per cent of the external fabric is retained
- Carrying out works to an existing house
- Development of houses under a Part V agreement
- If the development is for nine houses or fewer
- Housing on land of 0.1 hectares or less

---

[418] See: https://www.dublincity.ie/councilmeetings/documents/s14416/PART%208%20 PROCEDURE.pdf

Broadly speaking, calculating the compensation paid by the local authority to the developer for the Part V units is done as follows:

- For transferring land from the developer to the local authority, councils will pay existing use value for up to 10 per cent of the land with **market value** being paid for any additional land. The 10 per cent is determined by reference to the number of housing units permitted on the overall development. For instance, if there are ten dwellings permitted on a development, 10 per cent of the land will be determined to equate to one site.
- For transferring a new house from the developer to the local authority, the price to be paid will be calculated by reference to:
  - the existing use value of the site and
  - the cost, including normal construction and development costs and profit (7.5 per cent in Donegal, for example) on those costs, calculated at open market rates that would have been incurred by the local authority had it retained an independent builder to undertake the works, including the appropriate share of any common development works, as agreed between the local authority and the developer
- Where the local authority opts to lease housing from the developer, the rent to be paid will be **market rent** in the area reduced by:
  - discounts in respect of maintenance, management and voids periods specified in the lease, and
  - the net monetary value of the land that the council would receive if the Part V agreement had provided for a transfer of land only[419]

Part V agreements must be in place before a **Commencement Notice** is lodged, and having an agreement in place is typically a condition of any **planning permission** granted.

Soon after the introduction of the original Part V provision in 2000, the obligations were diluted and instead of allocating houses developers could offer alternative land or money to the local authority instead. The effect of this was that instead of delivering 20 per cent social or affordable housing, between 2002 and 2011 less than 4 per cent of all housing built was social housing: this was 9,393 houses in total, only 3,757 (2.7 per cent of the total) of which were for local authorities.[420] A side effect of Part V was that it took pressure off local authorities to fund the construction of social housing. This in turn took pressure off central government to fund social housing construction by local authorities. The scheme also relied heavily on the private

---

[419] See: http://www.donegalcoco.ie/media/donegalcountyc/planning/pdfs/Part%20V%20Guidelines%20for%20Developers.pdf
[420] Brady Shipman Martin (2012) *Review of Part V of the Planning and Development Act, 2000,* The Housing Agency: Dublin

market continuing the construction of houses. When the market collapsed so did the provision of local authority housing just at a time when demand was increasing.

A notable criticism of the Part V mechanism, apart from its reliance on market activity, is that as most developments of ten or more units are built in urban areas, it means that purchasers of these will be paying for social housing provision twice over – once in their own development, and again in taxes to fund social housing in rural areas where most housing developments are small or one-off builds and therefore don't include social housing. This brings the burden back to the local authority again, and nationally to the taxpayer.

Party wall[421]   In semi-detached or terrace houses a shared wall with a neighbour is known as a party wall. It separates buildings belonging to different owners. Where a wall separates two different-size buildings, only the part that is used by both properties is considered to be a party wall. The rest belongs to the person on whose land it stands.

See also: *cadastre; General Boundary Rule; Land Registry; Registry of Deeds; memorial*

Passive house[422]   Passive houses are designed to all but eliminate the need for heating through building a highly airtight and well-insulated building envelope, while recovering heat from stale extract air to preheat incoming fresh air. Passive houses also have targets to meet to prevent overheating. Passive houses can be built for little or no extra construction cost.

The standard is open to all construction approaches, and passive houses can be designed and built by anyone using any materials, provided the building meets its targets. However, it is easier to meet with certified passive house designers, tradespeople and components. Passive houses align well with Ireland's 2011 *Building Regulations* and proposed *nZEB* standard, and offer an important advantage: while other approaches to nZEB are largely unknown and bring attendant risks, the passive house approach has been delivering robust, comfortable, healthy buildings with tiny heating bills for decades. It is the low-risk approach to nZEB targets that all new homes are legally obliged to meet by the end of December 2020.

See also: *thermal bridge; U-value; Y-value; Sustainable Energy Authority of Ireland*

---

[421] Society of Chartered Surveyors Ireland (n.d.) *Boundaries: Procedures for Boundary Identification, Demarcation and Dispute Resolution in Ireland*, second edition, Geomatics Guidance Note, SCSI: Dublin
[422] Entry courtesy of Jeff Colley, of *Passive House Plus* magazine

The Pathway Accommodation and Support System (PASS) is an online system that generates vital information to manage access to accommodation for homeless people. The system provides 'real-time' information in terms of homeless presentation and bed occupancy across the Dublin region. PASS is run by the **Dublin Region Homeless Executive**.

See also: *homelessness*

Pathway
Accommodation
and Support
System (PASS)[423]

A 'Payment and Availability Agreement' means the agreement entered into between an **approved housing body** (AHB) and a local authority in respect of properties whereby the properties will be made available to the local authority for **social housing** purposes.[424] In the context of the delivery of social housing in Ireland, a Payment and Availability Agreement (P&A) is typically an agreement for up to 30 years between a local authority and an approved housing body often associated with the provision of **Capital Advance Leasing Facility** (CALF) finance.

Payment and
Availability
(P&A)
Agreement

A nominal sum of money charged as **rent**. Quite often the rent is so low it is uneconomical to collect. In Dublin, the Guinness brewery pay a rent of £45 per annum on a **lease** of up to 9,000 years. Although a meaningful sum of money when the lease was first signed in 1759, it is today regarded as a peppercorn rent.

See also: *ground rent*

Peppercorn rent

A personal insolvency arrangement (PIA) is an insolvency solution for people with unsecured and secured debts. Secured debt is a debt backed or secured by an **asset** (e.g. a housing loan where a house is mortgaged to secure the loan debt). It is a formal agreement with creditors that will write off some unsecured debt and restructure any remaining secured debt, while keeping the person in their home where possible.

A limit of €3 million applies to the amount of secured debt that can be included in a PIA, unless all secured creditors consent to the inclusion of a higher amount.

Under a PIA, a debtor's unsecured debts will be settled over a period of up to six years (extendable to seven years in certain circumstances) and the debtor will be released from those unsecured debts at the end of that period. Secured debts can be restructured under a PIA (e.g. to provide for payments for a certain period or a write-down of a portion of negative equity). Depending on the terms of the PIA, the debtor may be released from a secured debt

Personal
insolvency
arrangement

---

[423] See: https://www.homelessdublin.ie/info/pass
[424] The Housing Agency (2016) Guidance Note on the Capital Advance Leasing Facility (CALF) for Approved Housing Bodies and Housing Authorities, The Housing Agency: Dublin

at the end of PIA period or the secured debt can continue to be payable by the debtor (although perhaps on restructured terms).

Principal private residence housing loans, investment property loans, **buy-to-let** mortgages/loans and personal guarantees can all be included in a PIA.

See also: ***personal insolvency practitioner***

Personal insolvency practitioner A personal insolvency practitioner (PIP) is a person authorised by the Insolvency Service of Ireland, under part 5 of the Personal Insolvency Act 2012, to act as a personal insolvency practitioner. PIPs liaise between the debtor and their creditors in relation to a ***personal insolvency arrangement*** or debt settlement arrangement. Personal insolvency practitioners are obliged to comply with the Personal Insolvency Act and associated regulations and to demonstrate this to the satisfaction of the Insolvency Service of Ireland.[425]

Peter McVerry Trust Peter McVerry Trust is a charity set up by Fr Peter McVerry SJ to reduce ***homelessness*** and the harm caused by drug misuse and social disadvantage. In 1974 Fr McVerry moved to Summerhill in Dublin's north inner city, where he witnessed firsthand the problems of homelessness and deprivation. In 1979, he opened a small hostel to provide accommodation for homeless boys between the ages of twelve and sixteen. Four years later, in 1983, he officially founded the Arrupe Society, a charity to provide housing and support for young people experiencing homelessness as a response to the growing numbers of individuals becoming homeless in Dublin. In 2005, the name of the charity changed from the Arrupe Society to Peter McVerry Trust.

The trust runs prevention services, housing services, ***Housing First***, drug treatment services, and under-18s residential services.

See also: ***Inner City Helping Homeless***

Pied à terre In French, 'mettre pied à terre' means to dismount. In modern terms, it is a small house or apartment in a city that is owned or rented in addition to a main home, to stay in when visiting that city for a short time.[426]

See also: ***maisonette; mews; duplex; condominium; detached house; semi-detached house; terraced house; apartment; micro-home; accessory dwelling unit***

Piketty, Thomas Thomas Piketty's book *Capital in the Twenty-First Century* was published in 2013, and had a direct relevance for housing analysts. Housing is often the average person's largest source of ***wealth*** and access to housing therefore is a determiner of wealth. 'Wealth and income inequalities shape many of the

---

[425] See: https://www.isi.gov.ie/en/ISI/personal_insolvency_practitioner_information.pdf/Files/personal_insolvency_practitioner_information.pdf
[426] *Cambridge English Dictionary*

spatial segregations and segmented socio-economic structures apparent within housing systems.'[427] The evidence presented in *Capital in the Twenty-First Century* gives even greater significance to housing outcomes as they appear to be a major reinforcer of wealth and income inequalities in some advanced economies. Housing policy-makers show little sign of engaging with the insights of *Capital in the Twenty-First Century*, not least the implication that core housing policies may be reinforcing rather than reducing inequalities within and between generations.[428]

Critics of Piketty's work argue that housing result is based on the rise of only one of the components of capital, namely housing capital, and due to housing prices.[429]

See also: ***economic growth and housing; financialisation of housing***

See: ***Homeless HAP***

Place Finder
Scheme

The Local Government (Planning and Development) Act 1963 was the first planning legislation in Ireland; it became operational in 1964.

**Planning and
Development Act
1963**

Professor Michael Bannon has written extensively on the history of Irish planning: the 1962 Local Government (Planning and Development) Bill was introduced in the Dáil on 12 July 1962. While there was some French and US thinking in the antecedents of the Bill, it was largely based on the Town and Country Planning Act 1962 of England and Wales. The Local Government (Planning and Development) Act 1963 imposed heroic obligations for which Irish society was hopelessly ill-prepared. Indeed, significant interests were downright antagonistic to the very concept of planning and the notion of land management, both in principle and in practice.

The principal sections of the 1963 Act dealt with development plans, ***development control***, amenities, compensation, acquisition of land and miscellaneous provisions. Responsibility for the implementation of the planning process was devolved to 87 independent 'planning authorities'. Each ***planning authority*** was required to prepare a ***development plan*** for the area within its own jurisdiction. Rather than following the procedures of the earlier planning acts, the Local Government (Planning and Development) Act 1963 opted for a 'development-led' rather than a 'plan-led' model, which brought with it a necessity for a major emphasis on ***development control*** and

[427] van Ham, M, Manley, D, Bailey, N, Simpson, L and Maclennan, D (2012) *Neighbourhood Effects Research: New Perspectives*, Springer: Dordrecht
[428] MacLennan, D and Miao, J (2017) 'Housing and Capital in the 21ˢᵗ Century', *Housing, Theory and Society*, Vol. 34, No. 2
[429] Bonnet, O, Bono, PH, Chapelle, G and Wasmer, E (2014) 'Does Housing Capital Contribute to Inequality? A Comment on Thomas Piketty's *Capital in the 21ˢᵗ Century*', *Sciences Po Economics Discussion Papers 2014-07*, Sciences Po Department of Economics

the right to planning appeals, initially to the Minister and post-1976 to an independent appeals board – ***An Bord Pleanála***.[430]

The Planning and Development Act 1963 remained the basis of the Irish planning system until the ***Planning and Development Act 2000***.

See also: ***pre '63***

Planning and Development Act 2000
The Planning and Development Act 2000 consolidated all planning legislation from 1963 to 1999 and codified much of what had grown up in custom and practice during that time, clarifying and simplifying the overall process into one self-contained piece of legislation. The 2000 Act remains the basis for the Irish planning code, setting out the detail of regional planning guidelines, ***development plans*** and local area plans, as well as the basic framework of the development management and consent system. It also provides the statutory basis for protecting natural and architectural heritage, the carrying out of ***Environmental Impact Assessments*** and the provision of social and affordable housing.[431]

'The Planning and Development Act 2000 represented a major enhancement in the scope and relevance of the Irish planning code, and brought Ireland into line with planning thinking … within the EU.'[432] The Act provided for a hierarchy of plans from ***local area plans*** to development plans and regional planning guidelines. Amongst the many innovations introduced by the Act were the preparation of ***housing strategies***, enabling the designation of ***Strategic Development Zones*** and the revision and updating of all facets of the planning code including plan-making procedures, ***development control***, the protection of structures and the enhancement of the role of ***An Bórd Pleanála***.[433, 434]

See also: ***Strategic Environmental Assessment; Record of Protected Structures***

Planning and Development (Housing) and Residential Tenancies Act 2016
The Planning and Development (Housing) and Residential Tenancies Act 2016 is an 'administrative consolidation' of various planning, housing and local government legislation. It includes provisions on ***Strategic Housing Developments***, ***Environmental Impact Assessments*** – screening, miscellaneous constructions, and amendments to the ***Planning and Development Act***

---

[430] Bannon, MJ (2004) 'Forty Years of Irish Planning: An Overview', *Journal of Irish Urban Studies*, Vol. 3, No. 1, pp. 1–16

[431] See: https://www.housing.gov.ie/planning/legislation/planning-legislation

[432] Bannon, MJ (2004) 'Forty Years of Irish Planning: An Overview', *Journal of Irish Urban Studies*, Vol. 3, No. 1, p. 10

[433] Grist, B (2003) 'Planning', in Callanan, M and Keogan, F (eds), *Local Government in Ireland Inside Out*, IPA: Dublin, pp. 22–52

[434] Bannon, MJ (2004) 'Forty Years of Irish Planning: An Overview', *Journal of Irish Urban Studies*, Vol. 3, No. 1, pp. 1–16

2000, amendments to the *Residential Tenancies Act 2004*, amendments to the *Housing Finance Agency* Act 1981, and amendments to the Local Government Act 1998. It was signed into law on 24 December 2016.

The main components of the Act are:

- The introduction of *Rent Pressure Zones* (RPZs)
- The introduction of a maximum 4 per cent increase in rent in RPZs
- To change *Part 4* tenancies to six years from four years
- To restrict landlords from terminating a 'further' *Part 4* tenancy within the first six months on no stated grounds
- To restrict landlords from terminating tenancies when selling more than nine units within the same development within a specified six-month period (the *Tyrrelstown Amendment*)
- The introduction of Strategic Housing Developments
- The potential for a second extension of already extended *planning permissions* for developments comprising twenty or more houses

See also: *notice of termination; purpose-built student accommodation; security of tenure*

Planning and Development Regulations 2001

The principal regulations underpinning the Planning and Development Acts 2000–2015 are the Planning and Development Regulations 2001. They prescribe the detail of the various processes and procedures that make up the planning code.

Since 2001, a number of regulations amending the 2001 Regulations have been made, which, taken together, are collectively cited as the Planning and Development Regulations 2001–2018. Among the provisions made by the Planning and Development Regulations are the classes of *exempted development*, the specific steps required when making an application to a *planning authority* or an appeal to *An Bord Pleanála*, the process which must be followed by local and state authorities when undertaking certain types of *development* and the various fees associated with applications to planning authorities.[435]

See also: *development plan; unauthorised development; Planning and Development Act 1963; Planning and Development Act 2000*

Planning authority

The 'planning authority' is usually the planning department or section in a city or county council which receives applications for *planning permission*.

Planning gain

Planning gain is a mechanism for capturing some of the benefit that has accrued to the developer by reason of the grant of planning permission.

---

[435] See: https://www.housing.gov.ie/planning/legislation/planning-legislation

The logic of planning gain is that by granting **planning permission** the **community** (through its local authority) has created an increase in the value of the land and is therefore entitled to receive some return in the form of a community benefit.[436] Examples of planning gain include the delivery of social and **affordable housing** (e.g. through the **Part V** mechanism), **development contribution** levies, infrastructure, and the provision of specific developments often for the benefit of the local community, such as a swimming pool or other similar recreational facilities.

Planning permission

The main reason planning permission exists is to alert a local authority and neighbours about proposals to build so they can approve, not approve or lodge any concerns about the impact of the proposed **development**. It may be that the plans may conflict with a local authority's **development plan** for the area or limit a neighbour's privacy.[437]

Generally, planning permission is needed for any development of land or property unless the development is specifically exempted from this need. Development includes the carrying out of works (building, demolition, alteration) on land or buildings and the making of a material (i.e. significant) change of use of land or buildings.

Exempted development is development for which planning permission is not required (e.g. domestic extensions under 40 square metres). Categories of exempted development are set out in planning law. There are usually certain thresholds relating to, for example, size or height. Where these thresholds are exceeded, the exemptions no longer apply and planning permission is needed. The purpose of exemptions is to avoid controls on developments of a minor nature.

The most common type of application made is for permission, sometimes referred to as full permission. There are also circumstances when a property owner may want to make an application for 'outline permission'. For example, they may want to see whether the **planning authority** agrees with the proposal in principle before going to the trouble of making detailed plans. If outline permission is obtained, the applicant must obtain full permission before starting work. It is also possible to apply to planning permission after works are completed – see: **retention planning permission**.

Planning permission is obtained from the planning authority for an area, i.e. the local county council, borough council, city council or town council. Forms and information are available from the planning authority.

Once lodged with a local authority, the application will be acknowledged and placed on the planning register in the planning authority offices, for

---

[436] Garnett, D (2015) *The A–Z of Housing (Professional Keywords)*, Macmillan: London.
[437] See: https://www.ebs.ie/blog/2017/08/no-clue-guide-to-planning-permission-in-ireland

public inspection. It will also be included on the lists of planning applications displayed in council offices, public libraries and circulated to certain interest groups. The lists may also be available on the planning authority's website. A planning authority official will usually inspect the development site, and the applicant may be asked to make an appointment to allow access.

If a planning application:

- Lacks any of the required documents
- Lacks the appropriate fee, or
- Is in any other way inadequate (e.g. does not meet the statutory requirements for public notice of your application)

Then the application will be invalid and will be returned to the applicant with the fee.

The statutory eight-week period for deciding the application begins from the time the applicant submits a valid application with the required information in full, pays the correct fee and gives proper public notice of the application. Any person can see a copy of a planning application and make written submissions or observations, on payment of the appropriate fee, to the planning authority on any planning aspect of it. These must be considered by the planning authority when determining an application.

In making the decision on the planning application, the planning authority takes a number of matters into account, including:

- The proper planning and sustainable development of the area (e.g. appropriate land use (*zoning*), road safety, development density, size, location, adherence to established planning and development practices)
- Its own development plan
- Government policy
- The provision of a Special Amenity Area Order
- Any European site (e.g. Special Areas of Conservation, special protection areas)
- Submissions and observations made by members of the public on the application

A planning authority may not take non-planning issues into account, e.g. *boundary* or other disputes, or questions more properly resolved through legal means.

The decision to grant permission, with or without conditions, will be notified to the applicant, and to anyone who commented on the application. What is received is a notice of intention to grant permission. During a period of four weeks beginning on the date of making of this decision, the applicant or anyone else who has made a submission or observation on the application and has paid the appropriate fee may appeal it to ***An Bord Pleanála***, which has an objective of eighteen weeks to decide appeals upon receipt. Where there is no appeal, the planning authority will formally give the grant of permission at the end of the appeal period. Work must not commence until this notification is received.

Planning permission may be subject to certain conditions, which will be listed on the decision. These may require changes to the proposal (e.g. new arrangements for the disposal of surface water, revised height/colour/material for boundary walls, improved landscaping of the site). An applicant may also be required to make a contribution to the local authority for services (e.g. water, sewerage). These contributions differ from place to place and for different types of development. Applicants must comply with all of the conditions attached to the permission and finish work in accordance with them. Even if there is more than one permission for a site, applicants cannot pick and choose the conditions which suits them best.

The standard duration for planning permission (permission or outline permission) is five years from the date of the grant of the permission by the planning authority or An Bord Pleanála. In certain circumstances the planning authority may extend the life of a planning permission.[438]

The following table is a broad timeframe for most planning permission cases.[439]

Stage	Timescale	Action
Public notices		Notice published in newspaper and site notice erected
Receipt of application	2 weeks	Application must be lodged within 2 weeks of publication of newspaper notice
Validation	1–5 days	Application is validated by the planning authority as soon as possible. Current timescale is within 5 days.
Submissions	5 weeks	Submissions/observations can be submitted within the first 5 weeks of receipt of application.
Notice of decision	8 weeks	Submissions/objections (submitted in first 5 weeks) are considered. Planning Authority (PA) issue notice of their decision on the application within 8 weeks of receipt of application. (Alternatively, they may request further information.)

---

[438] See: https://www.housing.gov.ie/sites/default/files/migrated-files/en/Publications/Development andHousing/Planning/FileDownLoad%2C1582%2Cen.pdf
[439] See: www.cavancoco.ie/file/planning/applications/Timeframes-for-Planning-Permission.doc

Stage	Timescale	Action
Further information	6 months	The PA may request further information or clarification of further information, which must be responded to within 6 months (this can be extended by 3 months at the discretion of the PA)
Notice of decision	4 weeks (8 weeks for Environmental Impact Statement)	The PA issue notice of their decision on the application within 4 weeks of receipt of the further information. (Time period is extended to 8 weeks in the case of an application accompanied by an EIS.)
Appeal	28 days	A decision can be appealed to An Bord Pleanála within 28 days of a decision
Final grant	4 weeks + 3 days	If the decision is not appealed to An Bord Pleanála, then the planning authority will issue a final grant of permission

See also: ***unauthorised development***

Planning system The Irish urban planning and development system is essentially based upon development regulation.[440] This typology has three principal elements: a plan-making function, a developmental function involving issues such as land servicing, and a regulatory or control function. These functions can be carried out in distinct departments of a city, regional or national authority (sometimes leading to fragmentation in both the evidence upon which decisions are based and actual decision-making). The planning system in Ireland involves a legally based process, with conflicting views potentially contested at ***development plan*** adoption, planning application, or appeal stages by interested parties.[441] In their work on typologies of European planning systems, Tosics et al. place Ireland within a group where decision-making has a legal basis in English common law, a system of case law which has been gradually built up by decision and precedents.[442] They argue that systems that have their origins in common law are able to combine an empirical slant with an emphasis on past experience and precedent. This can be contrasted with the more managerial and centrally directed approaches of alternative continental European systems.

This common law approach can lead to both a 'development led' and a '***development control***' approach to the planning and development process. In such systems, the property rights of individual owners have a legally protected

---

[440] Newman, P and Thornley, A (1996) *Urban Planning in Europe: International Competition, National Systems and Planning Projects*, Routledge: London

[441] Williams, B, Hughes, B and Redmond, B (2010) 'Managing an Unstable Housing Market', Working Paper Series, 10/02, UCD Urban Institute Ireland: Dublin

[442] Tosics, I, Szemző, H, Illés, D, Gertheis, A, Lalenis, K and Kalergis, D (2010) *EU Plurel Report 2.2.1. National Spatial Planning Policies and Governance Typology*

status. In practice, this means the legal basis for each planning permission can be considered and contested on its own merits and circumstances.

In Ireland, development potential can normally only be fulfilled or created in the presence of infrastructure, transportation and services — all areas controlled directly by political decision-making and public sector policy that are embedded in political processes and require legal and planning consents from public authorities. The general direction of such public and political involvement, which frequently benefits development interest groups, remains a contested issue.

According to Williams,[443] the inevitable tendency in planning and policy-making in urban land markets is that a weak planning system can become involved in a facilitative process to smooth the course of development of the built environment, often in a manner which adopts the requirements of major development and capital interests. This can lead to a dilution of broader aims of planning and development plans. It can also conflict with the aims that planning should be a neutral process of public intervention to secure efficient and equitable patterns of urban and regional development.

Large imbalances exist between the various interest groups involved in the planning of an urban and regional economy and their ability to exert power and influence over the political processes which govern urban development. The existence of such pressure is strongly evident in the nature and processes of planning regulation and development which have evolved in the state (see: *regulatory capture*). Such pressures exist in most market economies and require strong and effective public policy structures to ensure that such influence does not favour sectional interest groups over the common good. Being dependent on development and investment interests for implementation of plans, the state and its planning functions are often seen as following market trends, being too weak to affect them.[444]

See also: *planning permission; planning gain; National Planning Framework; Planning and Development Act 1963*

Plot ratio   Plot ratio is a metric of building density on a site. It is the gross building floor area divided by the gross site area. The gross floor area is the sum of all floor space within the external walls of the buildings, excluding plant, tank rooms and car parking areas. The gross site area is all land within the *curtilage* of the site.[445]

---

[443] Williams, B (2015) 'Public Policy and Urban and Regional Development Markets', in Willams, B and Reynolds-Feighan, AJ (eds), *Urban and Regional Economics*, McGraw-Hill Education: New York

[444] *Ibid.*

[445] See: http://www.kildare.ie/CountyCouncil/Planning/DevelopmentPlans/LocalAreaPlans/RathanganLocalAreaPlan/LinkToDocument,9263,en.PDF

The purpose of plot ratio standards is to prevent the adverse effect of over-development on the layout and amenity of buildings on the one hand and to ensure an adequate sense of enclosure and the efficient and sustainable use of serviced land on the other hand.

Policy can be regarded as: 'implying action in relation to a particular problem which it is intended to solve in pursuit of some objective',[446] or what 'a government ministry hopes to achieve and the methods and principles it will use to achieve them'.[447] From this, policy can be understood to be the government's intentions to achieve objectives, used to inform subsequent implementation.

Policy, housing

Housing policy is usually analysed in economic terms, as a form of market. In theory, markets lead to efficient allocation through a complex process of matching supply and demand. This depends on competition (to bring prices down); good information; the existence of multiple suppliers; and the existence of multiple purchasers. In housing, this theory has limited application.[448] Reasons for market theory's limited application in explaining housing are explained by Barlow and Duncan[449] who point to:

- *Market closure* – housing production and finance are dominated by a few major players (especially after an economic crisis).
- *The impact of space* – location is acutely important in the housing market; there cannot, because of it, be perfect information and full and free competition.
- *Externalities* – housing both affects the environment and is affected by it.
- *Credit allocation* – the housing market is paid for mainly by borrowing, which has to be based on predictions of future value. It is very unlike the market for food.
- *Uncertainty* – because the future is uncertain, so is the housing market. Regulation and intervention are important to reduce uncertainty.
- *Market volatility* – prices are dominated by a limited part of the market – those who are buying and selling property at any one time.
- *The problem of meeting need* – if profitability is the only consideration, people will be left with needs unmet – most obviously, through ***homelessness***.

The government's current 'vision' for housing is: 'Every household should have access to secure, good quality housing suited to their needs at an

---

[446] Malpass, P and Murie, A (1990) *Housing Policy and Practice*, third edition, Macmillan Education: London

[447] Education and Training Unit (2017) 'The Policy and Law Making Process', *ETU*, available at: http://etu.org.za/toolbox/docs/govern/policy.html

[448] Spicker, P (2018) 'Housing and Urban Policy', *An Introduction to Social Policy*, available at: http://spicker.uk/social-policy/housing.htm

[449] Barlow, J and Duncan, S (1994) *Success and Failure in Housing Provision*, Pergamon: London

affordable price in a sustainable community.' Under this heading, 'the Government is helping local authorities and ***developers*** to plan and build better and more houses for people to live in. In this Department, working together with public, private and voluntary bodies [they] are:

- Providing ***social housing*** supports for people who cannot afford to provide a home for themselves.
- Providing an environment that encourages builders to deliver houses for people who wish to buy their own home.
- Ensuring that the building of houses is to the highest standards and is built in areas where it is needed.
- Improving the quality of rented housing and strengthening ***tenant*** and ***landlord*** protection.
- Providing housing support for vulnerable people.
- Supporting and building strong sustainable communities.'[450]

There are also specific policies on providing for vulnerable people:

- Addressing homelessness
- Housing people with disabilities (see: ***access and use (houses)***)
- Housing Travellers (see: ***Traveller housing***)
- Regulating the ***(private) rented sector***
- Regulating ***building control***

A vision is not necessarily a policy. Into the policy space steps ***Rebuilding Ireland***, which can be regarded as an overarching 'policy framework' for housing policy generally.

Rebuilding Ireland is one document in a long line of strategies and plans, which may be regarded as housing policy, evolving as initiatives and contexts change. In June 2002, there were 33 housing strategies and 22 homeless action plans. Policy then and since has applied further layers of actions and strategies leading to a sometimes confusing accrual of policies. *Rebuilding Ireland* (2016) was the third such strategy in four years. Previous publications include: *Housing Policy Framework: A Plan for Social Housing* (1991); *Social Housing: The Way Ahead* (1995); *Building Sustainable Communities* (2005); *Delivering Homes: Sustaining Communities* (2007); *Housing Policy Statement* (2011); *Construction 2020* (2014); and *Social Housing Strategy 2020* (2014).

Within each plan, strategy or policy, there are statements that indicate ministerial thinking on housing, and particularly state involvement in housing provision. 1991's *A Plan for Social Housing* signalled major changes for local

---

[450] See: https://www.housing.gov.ie/housing/housing-policy

authorities: 'The policy measures in this document imply significant changes in the traditional role played by local authorities in the social housing area. The overwhelming emphasis by local authorities on the building of dwellings for rent will be replaced by a wider approach. These additional measures included: shared ownership; improvement of private houses by local authorities; house purchase loans; a subsidised sites scheme; and a new funding scheme for housing associations.'[451] This document effectively established local authorities as both providers (a traditional role) and enablers (a newer role).[452]

Both *A Plan for Social Housing* (1991) and the next policy document, *Social Housing: The Way Ahead* (1995), although confirming a national policy of ensuring access to housing for all households, still afforded a residual or welfare role to social housing in that the majority of people are expected to enter into the private market, albeit with the aid of fiscal incentives, while those who cannot afford to do so may be housed by the local authority or other non-profit (voluntary community) providers. In particular, the use of a points-based housing allocation system to assess housing need (with points 'awarded' for various circumstances, such as family size and composition, overcrowding, income, homelessness, etc.) has contributed to the **residualisation** of social housing and its perception as a 'welfare housing sector'.[453] The **National Development Plan 2000–2006** was Ireland's de facto housing policy in that period, which provided a framework for addressing the shortage of houses available nationally. Relationships such as social partnership also influenced housing policy with an agreed objective to increase the supply of affordable housing by 10,000 units annually.[454] In 2011, the *Housing Policy Statement* increased further the notion of reliance on third-party housing provision when it said: 'a restructuring of the social housing investment programme to allow for the delivery of new social housing through more flexible funding models will provide key sources of delivery in the period ahead. The social housing leasing initiative and, in particular, the **Rental Accommodation Scheme** (RAS), will each play their parts as long-term social housing supports.'[455] This was amplified in 2014's *Social Housing Strategy 2020* which: 'emphasises the State's lead role in building partnerships between Local Authorities and other public, voluntary and private providers of housing in the development of innovative funding mechanisms that do

[451] Brooke, S (2001) 'Social Housing for the Future: Can Housing Associations Meet the Challenge?', *Studies in Public Policy*, No. 8, Policy Institute TCD
[452] *Ibid.*
[453] Redmond, D (2001) 'Social Housing in Ireland: Under New Management?', *European Journal of Housing Policy*, Vol. 1, No. 2
[454] South Dublin Community Platform (2006) 'Housing and Accommodation Thematic Paper'
[455] Department of Environment, Heritage and Local Government (2011) *Housing Policy Statement*, Government of Ireland: Dublin

not increase the General Government Debt, so as to deliver sufficient homes for all our people.' 2016's *Rebuilding Ireland* intensifies the most prominent policy thrust of recent policies, which is the reliance on the private sector: of the 135,000 households whose 'housing needs' are to be met by 2021, 35,000 (26%) of these needs will be met by supplying houses owned by local authorities or *approved housing bodies*; 10,000 (7.4%) subsidised private sector long-term leases; and 88,000 (65%) subsidised short-term leases via the *Housing Assistance Payment* (HAP) and the Rental Accommodation Schemes (RAS).[456] About three-quarters of household need is to be met by the private rented sector and privatised suppliers.

On the private housing policy side, an emphasis on home ownership as the preferred, or normal, *tenure* has been a consistent message, although 'for those priced out of the market or in need of state housing, this emphasis has no relevance'.[457] This has been articulated by statements and actions, in particular by models of *affordable housing*, tax relief on housing debt, *mortgages* for those refused lending elsewhere, and *help-to-buy* incentives. An emphasis on *home ownership* has also been consistently met by support for the provision of housing through various demand-side measures, most recently help-to-buy and the *Rebuilding Ireland Home Loan*.

For occupiers, home ownership 'has been incentivised in recent times through mechanisms such as the availability of tax relief and preferential interest rates on mortgages, particularly for first-time buyers, and the introduction of home-loan insurance. Such incentives reflect the importance that government attaches to home ownership as a driver of economic activity …. Home ownership is generally perceived as an *asset* against which other opportunities for improving socio-economic status and quality of life can be secured.'[458] Support for one category of *households* often comes at the expense of another: households renting therefore subsidise their home-owning peers. As Kenna notes: 'Different stakeholders in the housing system receive subsidy and support according to the political influence of those groups in society.'[459]

As housing is a central feature of so many socioeconomic briefs (e.g. social welfare), it appears directly or indirectly in the remit of several other ministers, including ones with more weight than Housing. It also is affected by the actions of non-governmental external organisations. Therefore, there is a serious question of who exactly is in control of housing policy: the Departments of Social Protection, Public Expenditure and Reform, and, of course,

[456] O'Broin, E (2018) 'It is clear that Rebuilding Ireland has failed', *Irish Times*, 18 July
[457] Focus Ireland (2003) *Housing Access for All: An Analysis of Housing Strategies and Homeless Action Plans*, Focus Ireland: Dublin
[458] Royal Irish Academy Geosciences and Geographical Sciences Committee (2017) *The Dynamics of Housing Markets and Housing Provision in Ireland*, RIA: Dublin
[459] Kenna, P (2011) *Housing Law, Rights and Policy*, Clarus Press: Dublin

Finance all have a say in what happens in housing; as does the ***Central Bank of Ireland***, despite not being part of government. Then there is the ***National Asset Management Agency*** and even more benign bodies such as the ***Sustainable Energy Authority of Ireland***.

The effectiveness of policy can also be tricky to measure. *Rebuilding Ireland*, with its targets for housing output, is beset with issues over the metrics used to measure its success or otherwise and has descended in some ways to a numbers game (see: ***data – housing output issues***). Numbers alone do not always measure the effectiveness of policy. Indeed, social and demographic changes may be much more important than numerical outcomes. And change can happen very fast while it appears the policy-makers sometimes don't notice (see the ***private rented sector*** from 2006 to 2011). A lot of policy is therefore rear-guard action, responding to events that have already happened (as is *Rebuilding Ireland*). The nature of politics too has meant that policy, rather than being a set of long-term, overarching principles to guide delivery, has arguably become a series of short-term political goals that need scoring.

The most noticeable policy trend in housing has been the overt reliance on the private sector to deliver housing that traditionally would have been delivered – very successfully – by the state. In focusing less on state provision of housing and more on inducing the market to provide for state needs, activity, plans and strategies have moved from managing a system (of delivering both private and social housing, for example), to trying to manage a market, which is a far more complicated and expensive objective to which many of the 'laws' of traditional economics do not necessarily apply.

In 2009, Fahey and Norris warned about the 'the multiplicity of [housing] policy instruments that can be used across the various housing sub-markets and the difficulties this poses for recognising them all, not to speak of trying to quantify their scale and impact'[460] – the range of schemes and programmes contained in this book is testament to how right they were.

Across the world, different types of policy approaches to housing have been identified based on a particular balance between market or non-market approaches, reflecting in turn different underlying political ideologies and welfare regimes.[461] Although precise definitions and terminologies vary, distinctions are commonly made between social democratic (usually associated with the Scandinavian countries), corporatist (continental Europe) and liberal (Anglo-American) regimes.[462]

---

[460] Fahey, T and Norris, M (2009) 'Housing and the Welfare State: An Overview', UCD Working Paper Series WP09/09

[461] Drudy, PJ and Punch, M (2002) 'Housing Models and Inequality: Perspectives on Recent Irish Experience', *Housing Studies*, Vol. 17, No. 4, pp. 657–672

[462] Focus Ireland (2003) *Housing Access for All: An Analysis of Housing Strategies and Homeless Action Plans*, Focus Ireland: Dublin

The policy-making process is itself one of mystery in Ireland. There is an inherent secrecy in government decision-making and difficulty in accessing documents to gain insight into 'thinking processes', which severely hamper the examination of policy-making processes.[463, 464, 465] MacCarthaigh remarks that 'a concern about the method and quality of policy-making in Ireland' emerged from the recent economic crisis, maintaining there is no theoretical policy process, little policy analysis, and no induction for civil servants in the 'modes of policy-making' and concludes that we know little about Irish policy-making due to a lack of any fundamental research.[466]

Research[467] has highlighted two overarching deficiencies with housing policy-making in Ireland; two significant observations can be drawn from the research:

- Firstly, housing policy-making in Ireland is typically focused on inputs and outputs, problems and solutions, and not on the process, or 'framework', used for identifying these problems and developing and evaluating appropriate solutions. In other words, there is little focus on *how* policy is developed.
- Secondly, housing policy-making in Ireland is typically focused on the micro tactics, or individual policies, not on the macro purpose, on the societal impact of the combined system of policies, on any long-term vision or 'philosophy'. In other words, there is little focus on *why* policy is developed.

More concrete issues include:

- Early-stage policy-making at Cabinet level is opaque and typically judgement-based.
- Impact assessments are not thorough or systematic and recommendations not actioned.
- Policy is rarely evaluated and there is a lack of evaluation guidance.
- Metrics are often flawed, inconsistent and inadequate.

---

[463] Page, E (2006) 'The Origins of Policy', in Moran, M, Rein, M and Goodin, R (eds), *Oxford Handbook of Public Policy*, Oxford University Press: Oxford

[464] O'Malley, E (2010) 'Political Power and Accountability in Ireland', *Studies: An Irish Quarterly Review*, Vol. 99, No. 393, pp. 43–54

[465] McMahon, N (2012) 'Investigating Policy Processes and Practices in Ireland: Potential Ways Forward', *Irish Journal of Public Policy*, Vol. 4, No. 1

[466] MacCarthaigh, M (2013) 'Reform of Public Policy-making in Ireland', *Journal of the Statistical and Social Inquiry Society of Ireland*, Vol. XLII

[467] Healy, M (2017) 'A Critical Examination of Policy-making Frameworks for Housing Policy in Ireland with Specific Reference to International Better Regulation Frameworks', MSc thesis, Dublin Institute of Technology

- There is no training or independent oversight in the discipline of policy-making.
- Stakeholders are consulted but policies lack transparent linkage with these inputs.
- Policy-makers across government departments are working towards conflicting goals.
- Policy advisors rely on industry players for expertise and are influenced by lobbying.
- Policies are driven by short-term, often local, political agendas.
- There is no over-arching housing philosophy or strategic vision to guide policy-making.

Ultimately, the existing policy-making system is opaque, reactionary, not always evidence-based and bound by political agendas.

See also: ***tenure neutrality; neoliberalism in Ireland; asset-based welfare***

Politically exposed person (PEP)

Studies undertaken by the Financial Action Task Force (Ireland is a member since 1991) and other international organisations identified that the positions held by PEPs are vulnerable to abuse for the purposes of corruption, ***money laundering*** and potentially tax fraud.

Directive (EU) 2015/849 of the European Parliament and of the Council of 20 May 2015 defined a political exposed person (PEP) to include people such as heads of state, ministers and deputy or assistant ministers; members of parliament or of similar legislative bodies; members of supreme courts, of constitutional courts or of other high-level judicial bodies, the decisions of which are not subject to further appeal, except in exceptional circumstances; members of the boards of central banks; members of the administrative, management or supervisory bodies of state-owned enterprises; and 'family members', including the spouse of a politically exposed person; the children and their spouses of a politically exposed person; the parents of a politically exposed person; and 'persons known to be close associates'.

Population

At April 2018, the population of Ireland was estimated at 4,857,000, up 64,500 from April 2017. Population size has significance for housing.

See also: ***household size; housing demand; headship rate***

Practical completion

In the construction of housing, practical completion means: 'the works having been carried to such a stage that they can be taken over and used by the Employer for their intended purpose.'[468] In effect, this typically means

---

[468] Refer to clause 31 of the RIAI standard form of contract, 2017

that the building is safe and ready to occupy, although not necessarily that all the details in the *snag list* have been completed. Practical completion is usually certified by the architect, at which stage insurance for the building moves from the builder's to the owner's.

At practical completion, it is normal for 50 per cent of the *retention withholding money* to be given to the builder.

See also: *self-build*

Pre '63 The term 'pre '63' refers to the introduction of the Local Government (Planning and Development) Act 1963, which brought in regulations for housing and in particular the need to get *planning permission* before dividing up a house into multiple units, usually to rent. A pre '63 house therefore contains flats that may or may not meet modern housing standards (see: *Housing (Standards for Rented Houses) Regulations 2019*). Many contained *bedsits*. In Dublin, these would be typically be found in large two- and three-storey over-basement properties in areas such as the North Circular Road, Rathmines, Drumcondra and Harold's Cross.

See also: *Planning and Development Act 1963*

Prescribed body A prescribed body is an organisation that must be consulted on specified planning matters such as certain planning applications and *development plans*.

The *Planning and Development Act 2000* puts forward where pre-scribed bodies should be notified or referred to; however, the Planning and Development Regulations states individually which specific prescribed bodies are being referred to, as there are several such bodies which are only concerned with specific forms of development only. For example, *An Taisce* is prescribed to be referred in planning applications for the *development* of a dwelling in an *Area of Special Amenity*, whereas this case would not be referred to the Irish Aviation Authority, as it does not necessarily impact on an airport or flight path.[469]

Some prescribed bodies include:

- The Arts Council
- The Heritage Council
- Inland Fisheries Ireland
- Irish Aviation Authority
- Commission for Energy Regulation
- Health Service Executive
- Fáilte Ireland

---

[469] See: http://www.antaisce.org/publications/prescribed-body-role

- Waterways Ireland
- Railway Safety Commission
- ***Environmental Protection Agency***
- Irish Water
- Industrial Development Authority
- Coras Iompair Éireann
- Transport Infrastructure Ireland
- An Taisce
- All local authorities

The purpose of pre-planning is to give an applicant for ***planning permission*** the opportunity to seek advice from the ***planning authority*** on the proposed ***development***.

Pre-planning

Planners are obliged to explain to applicants, and potential applicants, the planning authority's policies in relation to particular areas of the country and the considerations taken into account in dealing with particular classes of applications, e.g. housing. In addition, planners will endeavour to assist in identifying possible alternative locations where a particular proposal on a specific site is considered to be unacceptable. Planners will advise the potential applicant of the issues involved in considering a planning application, including any requirements of the permission regulations, and shall, as far as possible, indicate the relevant objectives of the ***development plan*** and any particular constraints which may have a bearing on the decision of the planning authority. Pre-planning requests should relate to a specific proposal for the land in question.

Price is the amount either asked or paid and can be established as a matter of fact from market evidence. Related measures such as worth and ***value*** are essentially matters of opinion.[470]

Price

An individual's principal private residence at any time is the building or part of a building occupied by the individual as his or her only or main residence.
See also: ***capital gains tax***

Principal private pesidence

Priory Hall is an ***apartment*** development in Donaghmede, north Dublin, built in 2007 by ***developer*** and former IRA hunger-striker Tom McFeely. A fire officer at a hearing in 2009 had reported 'being horrified' by the lack of fire safety in the development.[471] Although officials were aware of the dangers in Priory Hall, the residents were not moved out until 2011. Dublin City

Priory Hall

[470] Dunne, T (2014) 'Words Worth: Price and Value', *Surveyors' Journal*, Autumn
[471] deBurca Butler, J (2013) 'Priory Hall scandal: A century on, the same old story', *Irish Examiner*, 17 May

Council, who had previously removed their own **tenants** from the development, went to the High Court to have an evacuation order put on the development. It was condemned by fire inspectors and evacuated by court order in 2011 as a fire safety hazard.

Dublin City Council subsequently spent about €30 million refurbishing the development and remediating fire safety issues.

See also: ***Fire Safety Notice; Fire Safety Certificate***

Private rented sector

It is worth noting that the term 'private rented sector' is not defined in Irish law despite being an increasing feature of Irish housing policy and of legislation. Norris says: 'the term is commonly used in government policy statements and in popular usage to refer to furnished and unfurnished dwellings rented by private, for-profit landlords'.[472] Between 2011 and 2016, the number of **households** renting in the private rented sector doubled from 9.5 per cent of households to 18.5 per cent. In 2016, some 20.18 per cent of households rented their housing from a private landlord or **approved housing body**. At the end of 2018, there were 336,890 tenancies, 173,197 landlords and 695,142 occupants in Ireland,[473] an average of 2.06 occupants per tenancy and 1.95 tenancies per landlord. Over 85 per cent of landlords have just one or two tenancies; about 1 per cent have twenty or more tenancies.

In the early twentieth century, most of the Irish population rented in the private sector, which was similar to many European countries. In 1946, 42.7 per cent of the population was accommodated in this sector; by 1991 this had dropped to under 8 per cent.[474] An increase in state support for **home ownership** was one reason for this decline, but so too was the development of the **social housing** sector and the abolition of **rent control** from the 1960s to the 1980s.[475] Census 2011 showed a considerable change in the private rented sector, with both the scale and speed of this change being of some surprise. Census 2016 saw a further, but much reduced, increase to over 20 per cent of households. There are a number of specific reasons for this significant increase in the private rented sector numbers (some of which are more social than policy-driven), including: a restriction of entitlement to social housing; the use of the private rented sector by local authorities to house social tenants; difficulty in accessing credit to fund home purchase; a lack of suitable supply of housing in areas where there is demand; potential purchasers awaiting their perception of 'value for money' in house prices; an increase

[472] Norris, M (2011) 'The Private Rented Sector in Ireland', in Scanlon, K and Kochan, B (eds), *Towards a Sustainable Private Rented Sector: The Lessons from Other Countries*, London School of Economics: London, p. 34
[473] Figures from Residential Tenancies Board, 2019
[474] Central Statistics Office (CSO) (various years) Census, CSO: Dublin
[475] Galligan, Y (2005) 'The Private Rented Sector', in Norris, M and Redmond, D (eds), *Housing Contemporary Ireland: Policy, Society and Shelter*, Institute of Public Administration: Dublin

in overseas workers for whom renting is an inherently natural choice and also a practical option given the nature of their work circumstances; and personal choice in opting for renting over home ownership.[476]

According to Norris, the advent and expansion of direct public subsidisation of the private rented sector via use as de facto social housing) is likely to have played a more central role than indirect subsidisation via tax relief in the tenure's recent revival. The contribution of government subsidies to the expansion of private renting increased from 2004 following the establishment of the ***Rental Accommodation Scheme*** (RAS). From this perspective, while housing supports for low-income households of previous decades effected the transfer of social rented tenants and/or dwellings into the social housing sector, in recent decades these targeted housing supports have increasingly achieved the opposite. 'In the short to medium term at least, the Exchequer is unlikely to have the finance to reintroduce the generous subsidies for homeowners or social housing provision that existed in the past. Therefore larger numbers of households are likely to have to rely on private rented accommodation for a longer period of their lives than was the case traditionally in Ireland.'[477]

See also: ***Commission on the Private Rented Residential Sector; tenure; security of tenure; differential rents; Housing (Standards for Rented Houses) Regulations 2008; Housing (Standards for Rented Houses) Regulations 2019; home ownership; Eurostat***

Private Residential Tenancies Board

Established by the ***Residential Tenancies Act 2004*** to register tenancies and also to act as a dispute resolution body between ***landlords*** and ***tenants***. The Private Residential Tenancies Board became the ***Residential Tenancies Board*** (RTB) in 2016.

See also: ***Commission on the Private Rented Residential Sector; private rented sector***

Private treaty

Private treaty is the selling of goods where the price achieved is negotiated between the vendor and the purchaser. If several bidders are interested in the property, the vendor (or their agent) may hold a best and highest offer tender whereby closed written submissions of the final price vendors are willing to pay are submitted by a specific time and date. A vendor in a private treaty sale is not obliged to accept the highest offer. No sale is complete until the final contracts are signed and exchanged (***conveyancing***). This leaves time for

[476] Sirr, L (2013) 'Recession and Renting: The Future of the Private Rented Sector in Ireland', paper presented to the ENHR: European Network for Housing Research Conference, 10–22 June, Tarragona, Spain

[477] Norris, M (2014) 'Policy Drivers of the Retreat and Revival of Private Renting: Regulation, Finance, Taxes and Subsidies', in Sirr, L (ed.), *Renting in Ireland: The Social, Voluntary and Private Sectors*, IPA: Dublin

another bidder to make a further offer and for the vendor to accept it despite having already accepted a negotiated price (***gazumping***).

Private treaty is the most common form of sale for houses in Ireland and is a much slower process than sale by ***auction***.

Procurement Procurement is the process of buying goods or services. The procurement process is a key part of the construction of housing, especially when done by the state (e.g. building local authority housing). There are several different forms of procurement.

- Traditional contract: this is where the client (the person for whom the housing is being built) appoints experts to prepare the drawings and assess the costs of the construction work. Contractors (builders) are then invited to tender for the work. The client usually retains an expert to manage the construction phase of the project on their behalf. Self-build houses often use this form of procurement.
- 'Design and build': this is where a contractor is appointed to both design the housing and build it.
- 'Design, build, finance and operate' (DBFO): this is usually delivered by a contractor with experience in design and building, as well as facilities management and access to funding. Upon construction, the contractor leases the building(s) from the client for a period after which the building(s) reverts to the ownership of the client (e.g. the East Link Bridge returned to ownership of Dublin City Council after its 30-year lease period expired in 2014). Plans to build ***social housing*** via ***public–private partnership*** are also based on the DBFO contract.
- Public–private partnership: these are broad variations on DBFO, comprising all or parts of designing, building, maintaining and operating.

Profit à prendre[478] A *profit à prendre* is the right to take something from another person's land. This could be part of the land itself, such as peat; something growing on it, such as timber or grass (which can be taken by the grazing of animals); or wildlife killed on it, for example by shooting or fishing.

Other rights include:

- Rights of pasture (including cattlegates or beastgates – rights to pasture a specified number of animals)
- Rights of pannage (to turn out pigs to eat acorns, etc.)
- Rights of turbary (turf cutting)

---

[478] See: https://www.prai.ie/registration-of-easements-and-profits-a-prendre-acquired-by-prescription-under-section-49a/

- Rights of estover (to collect wood)
- Rights of piscary (fishing)
- Rights of common in the soil (to take stone, gravel, etc.)

The thing taken must be capable of ownership, so a right to use land in some way, or to take water from a natural feature, cannot be a profit.[479]

See: *Improvement Notice*

**Prohibition
Notice**

Property cycle

The Royal Institution of Chartered Surveyors regard a property cycle as a logical sequence of recurrent events reflected in factors such as fluctuating prices, vacancies, rentals and demand in the property market. There are two different property cycles. The first is the physical cycle of demand and supply which determines vacancy, which in turn drives rents. The second is the financial cycle where capital flows affects prices. Property cycles are international and global forces. Measured by peaks and troughs in performance, property cycles have durations ranging from four to twelve years, with an average of eight years (although some authorities refer to eighteen-year property cycles). Property cycles are usually used as a measure for commercial property, but, where the volatility of the housing market plays an important factor in the economy, the peaks and troughs of the residential market are commonly referred to as boom and bust.[480] Property cycles have been an important feature of Irish economic history. The reasons for their frequency in Ireland may partly be explained by both government intervention (property tax reliefs for example) and, in some cases, a lack thereof.[481]

There are typically several phases to a property cycle:

- Opportunity phase – start of an upward swing
- Growth phase – prices rising; typically in urban areas first
- Peak phase – investment floods in, the busiest phase in the cycle
- Correction phase – values stabilise or drop (crash)

See also: *bubble (housing)*

Property management is the maintenance and operation of real estate. In the Property Services (Regulation) Act 2011, **property management services** are:

**Property
management**

---

[479] HM Land Registry (2018) *Guidance Practice Guide 16: Profits à Prendre*, HM Land Registry: London
[480] Royal Institution of Chartered Surveyors (2012) 'What Is a Property Cycle?', *RICS Modus*, June
[481] Goodbody (2013) *Economic Research – A Detailed Analysis of the Prospects for Irish Property*, Goodbody: Dublin

services in respect of the management of a multi-unit development carried out on behalf of a management body, and such services include—

(*a*) administrative services, and

(*b*) the procurement of or any combination of the maintenance, servicing, repair, improvement or insurance of the development of any part of the development.

Property management does not mean letting services.

Property managers are licenced ***property services providers*** and may also be referred to as ***managing agents***. In ***multi-unit developments***, they are employed by the ***owners' management company***.

See also: ***letting agent; estate agent; Property Services Regulatory Authority***

Property Registration Authority[482] The Property Registration Authority (PRA) is the state organisation responsible for the registration of property transactions in Ireland. It was established under the provisions of the Registration of Deeds and Title Act 2006. The role of the PRA is to provide a system of registration of ***title*** (ownership) to ***land***, which is comprehensive and readily accessible.

The PRA replaced the Registrar of Deeds and Titles as the 'registering authority' in relation to property registration in Ireland. The main functions of the PRA are to manage and control the ***Land Registry*** and the ***Registry of Deeds*** and to promote and extend the registration of ownership of land. The PRA also operates the ***Ground Rents*** Purchase Scheme under the Landlord and Tenant Acts.

See also: ***GeoDirectory; cadastre; deed***

Property services providers Property services providers (PSPs) are persons involved either as corporate bodies, partnerships, sole traders or employees in:

- The purchase or sale, by whatever means, of any estate or interest in land (including buildings) wherever situated
- The auction of private property other than land
- The letting of any estate or interest in land wherever situated
- The provision of property management services

As such, ***auctioneers***, ***estate agents***, ***letting agents*** and property ***managing agents*** must be licensed and regulated by the ***Property Services Regulatory Authority*** (PSRA). This applies to property located in the Republic of Ireland and to transactions in Ireland which relate to property located abroad.

---

[482] See: https://www.prai.ie/the-property-registration-authority/

There are four categories of licence issued by the PSRA. A PSP may hold a single licence covering one or more of the different categories of property service:

- Licence A – the auction of property other than land
- Licence B – the purchase or sale, by whatever means, of land
- Licence C – the letting of land
- Licence D – property management services

The 'Register of Licensed Property Services Providers' comprises a list of property services providers (auctioneers/estate agents, letting agents and management agents) licensed by the authority under the Property Services (Regulation) Act 2011.

According to Leman Solicitors, the Property Services (Regulation) Act 2011 was introduced to address the integrity of property professionals (such as surveyors, *valuers*, *auctioneers*, management companies, *estate agents* and *letting agents*) and to improve the standards in the provision of property services to consumers (prior to 2011 disciplinary proceedings against property professionals were rare).[483] The Property Services (Regulation) Act 2011 provided for the regulation of *property services providers* (e.g. those involved in the sale, letting, or management of property) and the establishment of the *Property Services Regulatory Authority*.

Property Services (Regulation) Act 2011

The Property Services Regulatory Authority was established in 2012 to help restore confidence in the property market and provide greater transparency.[484] The main function of the authority is to control and regulate *property services providers* (i.e. *auctioneers* and *estate agents*, *letting agents* and *managing agents*). This includes the licensing of all such services providers, the establishment of a complaints investigation and redress system for consumers, the setting and enforcement of standards in the provision of property services, the administration of client accounts, the establishment and maintenance of a compensation fund and the creation of three public registers (the 'Register of Licensed Property Services Providers', the '*Residential Property Price Register*' and the 'Commercial Leases Register').

Property Services Regulatory Authority

The regulatory environment provides for:

- A comprehensive licensing system covering all PSPs
- The investigation and adjudication of complaints made against PSPs

---

[483] Leman (2015) 'Has the Property Services Regulatory Authority Regulated?', *Thought Leadership Articles*, 9 April, available at: https://leman.ie/has-the-property-services-regulatory-authority-regulated/
[484] See: http://www.justice.ie/en/JELR/Pages/PR12000092

- The audit/inspection of PSPs operations
- The establishment of minimum qualification standards

Following an investigation, the PSRA has the power to sanction a licensee up to and including the revocation of a licence and may also impose fines of up to €250,000 where a PSP is found to have engaged in 'improper conduct'. All PSPs are required to contribute to the Property Services Compensation Fund. Where a person suffers a loss due to the dishonesty of a PSP the authority may award compensation from this fund.

Protected structure[485] A protected structure is a structure that a local authority considers to be of special interest from an architectural, historical, archaeological, artistic, cultural, scientific, social or technical point of view. Details of protected structures are entered by the local authority in its **Record of Protected Structures**, which is part of the **development plan**. Each owner and occupier of a protected structure is legally obliged to ensure that the structure is preserved.

The obligation to preserve a protected structure applies to all parts of the structure, including its interior, all land around it, and any other structures on that land. The obligation also applies to all fixtures and fittings forming part of the interior of a protected structure or of any structure on land around it.

Many minor works to protected structures are exempted development and do not normally require **planning permission**. However, such works can be carried out without planning permission only if the works would not affect the character of the structure or any element of the structure that contributes to its special interest. Depending on the nature of the structure, planning permission could, for example, be required for interior decorating such as plastering or painting.

Protective Certificate A Protective Certificate is issued by the courts and offers a borrower and their assets protection from legal proceedings by creditors while they are applying for a **personal insolvency arrangement**. In general a Protective Certificate remains in force for 70 days but it may be extended in limited circumstances.[486]

Public housing See: **council housing**

Public–private partnership (PPP) The Department of Public Expenditure and Reform describes public–private partnership (PPP) as an arrangement between the public and private sectors (consistent with a broad range of possible partnership structures) with clear

[485] Dublin City Council (n.d.) *A Guide to Protected Structures*, DCC: Dublin
[486] Insolvency Service of Ireland (2015) *Guide to a Personal Insolvency Arrangement*, ISI: Dublin

agreement on shared objectives for the delivery of public infrastructure and/or public services by the private sector that would otherwise have been provided through traditional public sector procurement.

The World Bank defines a PPP as a: 'long-term contract between a private party and a government entity, for providing a public asset or service, in which the private party bears significant risk and management responsibility, and remuneration is linked to performance'. PPPs typically do not include service contracts or *turnkey* construction contracts, which are categorised as public procurement projects, or the privatisation of utilities where there is a limited ongoing role for the public sector.[487]

A key aspect of the PPP approach is that risk is transferred to the party that is deemed to be able to manage it best.[488] PPPs have been used extensively in Ireland to deliver infrastructure such as motorways. *Social housing* is now to be delivered by PPP (see: *procurement*).

Critics of the PPP model argue that:

- Development, bidding and ongoing costs in PPP projects are likely to be greater than for traditional government procurement processes.
- There is no unlimited risk bearing.
- The private sector will do what it is paid to do and no more than that.
- Government responsibility continues – citizens will continue to hold government accountable for the quality of utility services.
- Government will also need to retain sufficient expertise, whether the implementing agency and/or via a regulatory body, to be able to understand the PPP arrangements, to carry out its own obligations under the PPP agreement and to monitor performance of the private sector and enforce its obligations.
- The private sector is likely to have more expertise and after a short time have an advantage in the data relating to the project.
- Given the long-term nature of these projects and the complexity associated, it is difficult to identify all possible contingencies during project development and events and issues may arise that were not anticipated in the documents or by the parties at the time of the contract (see: *Ballymun*).

Purpose-built student accommodation (PBSA)

Purpose-built student accommodation (PBSA) is housing for students provided by private companies or third-level educational institutions individually or in partnership with a private enterprise. In 2017, the government

---

[487] See: https://ppp.worldbank.org/public-private-partnership/overview/what-are-public-private-partnerships
[488] See: https://www.per.gov.ie/en/public-private-partnerships/

launched the *National Student Accommodation Strategy*, which set a target of 7,000 additional purpose-built student bed spaces to be ready by the end of 2019. The strategy has also set a target of 4,000 students availing of '*digs*' accommodation by 2019. The amount of income that can be earned tax-free from renting a room to a student in a private home has also been increased from €12,000 to €14,000 per annum in 2017.

In facilitating the development of PBSA, amendments were made to planning regulations for planning applications under the **Planning and Development (Housing) and Residential Tenancies Act 2016** (commenced 2017). The fast-track planning procedure for **Strategic Housing Developments** includes student accommodation projects containing 200 or more bed spaces. Student accommodation is not subject to **Part V** requirements for the reservation of 10 per cent of units in the development for **social housing**. Neither is there a requirement to provide car-parking spaces.

There have been issues with PBSA over the high cost to students per academic year and, in particular, significant rent increases from academic year to year, up to 27 per cent in one instance.[489] There is also uncertainty over whether students are occupying the accommodation under a **tenancy** or a **licence**. The **Residential Tenancies (Amendment) Act 2018** brought student housing under the 4 per cent rent cap if such accommodation is in a **Rent Pressure Zone**, and irrespective of whether it is occupied under licence or tenancy.

Pyrite Resolution Board[490]

Since 2013 the Pyrite Resolution Board has run the Pyrite Remediation Scheme, the aim of which is to procure the remediation of certain dwellings with damage caused by pyritic heave of hardcore under-floor slabs. The **Housing and Sustainable Communities Agency** is responsible for the testing of dwellings and the implementation of the remediation process.

The following is a synopsis of the conditions that must be satisfied for a dwelling to be deemed eligible for remediation under the scheme.

- Dwellings must be located within the administrative areas of Dún Laoghaire–Rathdown, Fingal, Kildare, Meath, Offaly or South Dublin County Councils, or Dublin City Council.
- Dwellings must have been constructed and completed between 1 January 1997 and 12 December 2013.
- Dwellings must have been assessed, tested and certified as having a damage condition rating of 2 and it must be verified that damage is attributable to pyrite heave.

---

[489] Bowers, S (2018) 'DCU students protest over 27% rent hike', *Irish Times*, 29 March
[490] See: https://www.pyriteboard.ie/Terms-of-Reference.aspx

- The applicant must be the owner or joint owner of a dwelling. An application can only be made in respect of one dwelling and the dwelling must have been purchased before 12 December 2013.
- The applicant must be able to show, to the satisfaction of the PRB, that he/she does not have available to him or her any practicable option, other than under the scheme or the use of his or her own resources, to remediate or secure the remediation of the dwelling.
- There may be rare exceptional circumstances concerning damage to or from an adjoining dwelling that can be considered by the board.
- An extension, used for habitable purposes, is considered to be a dwelling for the purposes of the Pyrite Resolution Act 2013.

Once a dwelling is deemed eligible for remediation under the Pyrite Remediation Scheme, the following costs will be borne by the scheme:

- The sampling, testing and damage verification
- The preparation of the specification of remediation works in accordance with I.S. 398-2: 2013
- The management of the tender process and implementation of the remediation works
- The remediation of the dwelling as per specification and schedule to the required standard
- The monitoring and inspection of works, snagging and final certification

Q

The standard indicators of the quality of life usually include not only *wealth* **Quality of life**[491] and employment, but also the built environment. Satisfactory accommodation is a major element of people's material living standards and good housing conditions are essential for people's health and childhood development. There are at least three main indicators related to housing and quality of life:

- *Housing quality*: one major element of quality of housing conditions is the availability of sufficient space in the *dwelling*. Having sufficient space is essential to meet people's basic need for privacy and for making home a pleasant place to be. Too many occupants in a dwelling may also have a negative impact on children's health or school performance. Housing quality can also be assessed by looking at other housing deficiencies, such as lack of certain basic sanitary facilities in the dwelling and problems in

---

[491] Streimikiene, D (2015) 'Quality of Life and Housing', *International Journal of Information and Education Technology*, Vol. 5, No. 2, pp. 140–145

the general condition of the dwelling (e.g. a leaking roof or the dwelling being too dark).

• *Housing environment*: housing quality depends not only on the quality of the dwelling itself, but also on the wider residential area. Noise, crime, and the proximity of public services such as schools and hospitals is important indicator of quality of life related with housing.

• *Housing expenditures burden*: the **housing cost overburden** rate is an indicator of housing affordability. It is measured as the percentage of the population living in households where the total housing costs (net of housing allowances) represent 40 per cent or more of their equivalised disposable income. This indicator is thus a measure of the housing costs effectively supported by households.

See also: ***affordability; apartment design standards; micro-home; housing overburden***

Quantitative easing[492]

To help stimulate the economy, central banks use quantitative easing, known in the Euro area as the expanded Asset Purchase Programme (APP). Within the APP, Eurosystem national central banks buy assets from banks. This increases the price of these assets and creates money in the banking system. As a consequence, a wide range of interest rates fall, loans become cheaper and businesses and people are able to borrow more and spend less to repay their debts. As a result, consumption and investment receive a boost. Higher consumption and more investment support economic growth and job creation.

See also: ***Central Bank of Ireland***

R

Radon

Radon is a radioactive gas that can build up to dangerous levels in enclosed spaces such as a house. All homes built since 1 July 1998 must be fitted with a standby radon sump which can be activated at a later stage to reduce any high radon concentrations subsequently found. For homes built in high radon areas, the installation of a radon barrier as well as a standby radon sump is required.[493]

See also: ***defects***

Rapid build housing – Poppintree

Rapid build housing comprises the delivery of housing developments within a programme which shows overall time savings, demonstrated by a combination of savings across contract stages, including appropriate and efficient

[492] See: https://www.centralbank.ie/consumer-hub/explainers/how-does-quantitative-easing-work
[493] See: http://www.epa.ie/mobile/radon/getinformed/faq/#panel60883

construction, resulting in a significant reduction compared with traditional build programmes.[494]

Rapid build (originally referred to as '***modular housing***') was produced as a solution to ***homelessness*** in October 2015. The then Minister for the Environment announced 500 modular houses would be provided as emergency housing for homeless families, with 22 to be in place before Christmas 2015 at a site in Poppintree, ***Ballymun***. A year-and-a-half later, 22 had been occupied for about two months, and no other modular homes had been finished.[495]

Initially proposed as true modular housing (system-built in factories and assembled on site), they turned into 'rapid build' housing, which finally turned out to be standard timber-frame housing. The cost of these units also increased from under €100,000 per modular house to a final total of €243,000 per rapid build house. The actual cost of each house was about €220,000, but Dublin City Council requested and received an allowance of €500,000 for the 28-day project of 22 houses, thus adding €23,000 to the cost of each house.

The contract to build the houses went to Western Building Systems, a Northern Irish company that hadn't advertised its products at the North Strand Fire Station (as other potential tenderers had), and that at the time was selling 205-sq.m. luxury houses in Dungannon for less than the cost of its 92-sq.m. houses in Poppintree. The pre-qualifying threshold for tendering specified an average annual turnover of €10 million, thus excluding nearly every modular housing supplier or builder in Ireland.[496]

Rapid build housing schemes announced for Coolock and the north inner city in 2016 are not due to be finished until 2020.

See also: ***four-stage process; procurement***

Real estate investment trusts (REITs) Real estate investment trusts (REITs) are companies whose income is derived from the rental of commercial and/or residential property. REITs emerged in the 1960s in the US, and were designed to make investments into large-scale, income-producing property available to the ordinary investor, without the need to invest in physical bricks and mortar.[497] Legislation for REITs was introduced in Ireland with the Finance Act 2013.

The following conditions must be met by a REIT or a group REIT by the end of the accounting period in which the company or group elects to be a REIT or group REIT:

---

[494] See: https://www.housing.gov.ie/sites/default/files/publications/files/review_of_delivery_costs_and_viability_for_affordable_residential_developments.pdf

[495] Kelly, O (2017) Government's "rapid-build" schedule in realms of fantasy', *Irish Times*, 1 August

[496] Sirr, L (2017) 'A year of magical thinking when it comes to housing figures', *Sunday Times*, 18 December

[497] Zurich Life (n.d.) *Understanding Irish Real Estate Investment Trusts*, available at: https://www.zurichlife.ie/DocArchive/servlet/DocArchServlet?docId=DOC_9948&docTag=

- It must derive at least 75 per cent of its aggregate income from the property rental business
- It must have at least three properties, the **market value** of no one of which is more than 40 per cent of the total market value of all its properties constituting the property rental business
- It must maintain a property-to-financing-costs ratio of 1.25:1
- At least 75 per cent of the aggregate market value of the assets of the REIT or group REIT must relate to assets of the property rental business
- It must ensure that the aggregate of the specified debt does not exceed 50 per cent of the aggregate market value of the business assets of the REIT or group REIT
- It must have a diversified share ownership and distribute at least 85 per cent of its property income annually on or before the specified date of return for the accounting period in relation to the REIT or the principal company of the group REIT

A company which is either a REIT or a member of a group REIT is not chargeable to corporation tax (CT) on income from its property rental business. Equally, it is not chargeable to **capital gains tax** (CGT) accruing on the disposal of **assets** of its property rental business. However, if a REIT or group REIT acquires an asset and following that acquisition develops that asset to the extent that the cost of **development** exceeds 30 per cent of the market value of the asset at the time the development commenced and the asset is then disposed of within three years of completion of the development then the corporation tax and capital gains tax exemptions applicable to the REIT or group REIT, as the case may be, no longer apply.[498]

Rebuilding Ireland

Rebuilding Ireland is an 'action plan' for housing launched by the government in July 2016. It was the fourth plan in the previous three years. In the absence of a definitive housing policy, *Rebuilding Ireland* is the *de facto* housing policy framework until 2021.

The overarching aim of *Rebuilding Ireland* is to 'ramp up' delivery of housing from its current under-supply across all tenures to help individuals and families meet their housing needs, and to help those who are currently housed to remain in their homes or be provided with appropriate options of alternative accommodation, especially those families in **emergency accommodation**.

The core objectives of *Rebuilding Ireland* are:

- Addressing the unacceptable level of households, particularly families, in emergency accommodation

---

[498] See: https://www.revenue.ie/en/tax-professionals/tdm/income-tax-capital-gains-tax-corporation-tax/part-25a/25a-00-01.pdf

- Moderating rental and purchase price inflation, particularly in urban areas
- Addressing a growing affordability gap for many households wishing to purchase their own homes
- Maturing the rental sector so that tenants see it as one that offers security, quality and choice of tenure in the right locations and providers see it as one they can invest in with certainty
- Ensuring housing's contribution to the national economy is steady and supportive of sustainable economic growth
- Delivering housing in a way that meets current needs while contributing to wider objectives such as the need to support sustainable urban and rural development and communities and maximise the contribution of the built environment to addressing climate change

There are five 'pillars' in *Rebuilding Ireland*, as follows:

- **Pillar 1 – Address Homelessness**
  Provide early solutions to address the unacceptable level of families in emergency accommodation; deliver inter-agency supports for people who are currently homeless, with a particular emphasis on minimising the incidence of *rough sleeping*, and enhance state supports to keep people in their own homes.
- **Pillar 2 – Accelerate Social Housing**
  Increase the level and speed of delivery of *social housing* and other state-supported housing.
- **Pillar 3 – Build More Homes**
  Increase the output of private housing to meet demand at affordable prices.
- **Pillar 4 – Improve the Rental Sector**
  Address the obstacles to greater *private rented sector* delivery, to improve the supply of units at affordable *rents*.
- **Pillar 5 – Utilise Existing Housing**
  Ensure that existing housing stock is used to the maximum degree possible – focusing on measures to use vacant stock to renew urban and rural areas.[499]

The following are the housing output targets from *Rebuilding Ireland*:[500]

- Private house-building: Doubling of output to deliver over 25,000 units per annum on average over the period of the plan (2017–2021), i.e.

---

[499] See: *Rebuilding Ireland: Action Plan for Housing and Homelessness*, available at: http://rebuildingireland.ie

[500] The entry on *data – housing output issues* addresses some of the metrics used to determine whether these targets are being met or not.

125,000 new houses to be built in total. (This figure was subsequently subtly changed to '25,000 units per annum by 2021'.)

- Social housing: 47,000 social housing units delivered by 2021, with a particular focus on an accelerated and expanded social housing construction programme (at which stage some 10,000 units will be delivered on an annual basis). A breakdown of this 47,000 figure was given as follows:[501]

Delivery	Sub-total	Sub-total
Acquired by local authority		11,000 [23.4%]
Leased by local authorities or **approved housing bodies** (5,000 via NTMA Special Purpose Vehicle, and 5,000 via **Repair and Leasing** scheme)		10,000 [21.3%]
Construction Activity		
Local authority new build units	13,189 [28%]	
Refurbishment of social housing derelict and **void** units	3,459 [7.35%]	
Newly constructed units obtained by local authorities under **Part V**	2,070 [4.4%]	
Approved housing bodies new build units	4,698 [10%]	
Newly constructed units obtained under Part V by either local authorities or approved housing bodies	2,620 [5.57%]	
Sub-total of Construction Activity		26,036
TOTAL		**47,036 [increased to 50,000 in 2018]**

(It should be noted here that only approximately half of the 50,000 target are newly built houses, with the remainder coming from existing housing stock through various other methods.)

- ***Homelessness***: Ensure that by mid-2017 hotels are only used in limited circumstances for emergency accommodation for families, by meeting housing needs through the ***Housing Assistance Payment*** (HAP) and general housing allocations, and by providing new supply to be delivered through: an expanded ***rapid build*** housing programme [1,500 units]; and a ***Housing Agency*** initiative to acquire vacant houses (1,600 units)
- Rental sector: A ***build-to-rent*** model that can deliver additional supply towards the overall target supply of 25,000 units per annum. (A further strategy was published in December 2016 – ***Strategy for the Rental Sector***.)

---

[501] See: https://www.kildarestreet.com/wrans/?id=2017-01-17a.1286

Criticisms of the *Rebuilding Ireland* plan include:[502]

- The continuation and expansion of a privatised response to social housing need, through the extended use of rent subsidisation in the private rented sector (despite the rising cost of rents and the insecurity of the sector)
- The reliance on acquisitions from the private market to supply the proposed increase in social housing, thus disadvantaging other potential purchasers
- The proposal that the use of private finance for the construction of new housing by voluntary housing bodies will be 'intensified'
- The policy of meeting social housing need through the use of rent supplementation in the private rental sector is presented as a positive development
- A particularly striking feature of *Rebuilding Ireland* is what might be termed the 'policy-free' narrative adopted to describe the development of the Irish housing system over recent decades. Thus the current housing crisis is attributed solely to the country's economic collapse and the recession, as if policy choices affecting housing made during and indeed prior to this period were of no relevance
- The plan reflects a determination to continue the market-dominated approaches to housing which have prevailed in Ireland for over a quarter of a century with such harmful outcomes for both individuals and the common good

See also: ***Local Infrastructure Hosing Activation Fund (LIHAF); Vacant Housing Strategy; Rebuilding Ireland Home Loan; Rent Pressure Zone; policy, housing***

Rebuilding Ireland Home Loan

A Rebuilding Ireland Home Loan is a government-backed ***mortgage*** for first-time buyers, made available nationwide from all local authorities from 1 February 2018. First-time buyers can apply for a Rebuilding Ireland Home Loan to purchase a new or second-hand property, or to build their own home. The loan is a normal capital and interest-bearing mortgage which is repaid by direct debit on a monthly basis.

Under the scheme, up to 90 per cent of the ***market value*** of a residential property can be borrowed. The maximum market values of the property that can be purchased or self-built are:

- €320,000 in Counties Cork, Dublin, Galway, Kildare, Louth, Meath and Wicklow
- €250,000 in the rest of the country

---

[502] Burns, M, Drudy, PJ, Hearne, R and McVerry, P (2017) 'Rebuilding Ireland: A Flawed Philosophy Analysis of the Action Plan for Housing and Homelessness', *Working Notes*, Issue 80, October

This limits the amount that can be borrowed to no more than €288,000 in Counties Cork, Dublin, Galway, Kildare, Louth, Meath and Wicklow and no more than €225,000 in the rest of the country. Three different interest rates options are offered with the loans:

- 2% fixed for up to 25 years (APR 2.02%)
- 2.25% fixed for up to 30 years (APR 2.27%)
- 2.30% variable (subject to fluctuation) for up to 30 years (APR 2.32%)

To be eligible for a Rebuilding Ireland Home Loan applicants must:

1. Be a first-time buyer
2. Be aged between 18 and 70 years
3. Be in continuous employment for a minimum of two years, as a primary applicant or be in continuous employment for a minimum of one year, as a secondary applicant
4. Have an annual gross income of not more than €50,000 as a single applicant or not more than €75,000 combined as joint applicants
5. Submit two years' certified accounts if self-employed
6. Provide evidence of insufficient offers of finance from two banks or building societies
7. Not be a current or previous owner of residential property in or outside the Republic of Ireland
8. Occupy the property as your normal place of residence
9. Purchase or self-build a property situated in the Republic of Ireland of no more than of 175 square metres (gross internal floor area)
10. Purchase or self-build a property which does not exceed the maximum market value applicable for the county in which it is located
11. Consent to an Irish Credit Bureau check

In order to qualify for a Rebuilding Ireland Home Loan, applicants must have been first rejected by two commercial banks or building societies for lending (no. 6, previous). In other words, applicants must have already been deemed to be unacceptable for income or other reasons to qualify for a mortgage (normally, these are referred to as *sub-prime* borrowers). The second observation is that the Rebuilding Ireland Home Loan circumvents the **Central Bank**'s lending limits of 3.5 times a household income for mortgage borrowing and instead offers a lending limit of up to 5.5 times a household income.[503] Mortgages will be based on borrowers' ability to repay debt rather than household income. Local authorities are able to do this

---

[503] Ryan, S (2018) 'Home truths: Rebuilding Ireland loans: caveat emptor', *Irish Independent*, 6 April

because, as unregulated financial providers, they are not subject to Central Bank rules.[504] Already risky borrowers are thus being permitted to borrow more, all of which is underwritten by the taxpayer. The ability to repay is also an unknown variable for many borrowers over a period of 25–30 years, especially if other debts accrue.

See also: *arrears; home ownership; mortgage lending rules*

Record of Protected Structures

As per Part 4 of the ***Planning and Development Act 2000***, every local authority ***development plan*** must include a record of protected structures (RPS). This record is to protect structures, or parts of structures, which form part of the architectural heritage and which are of special architectural, historical, archaeological, artistic, cultural, scientific, social or technical interest. Local authorities shall record every structure which is, in the opinion of the ***planning authority***, of such interest within its functional area.[505] The planning authority can add and delete structures from its RPS when reviewing its development plan or at any other time.

Inclusion of these structures in the RPS means that their importance is recognised, they are legally protected from harm and all future changes to the structure are controlled and managed through the development control process (for example, ***planning permission)*** or by issuing a declaration under section 57 of the ***Planning and Development Act 2000*** (which asks the local authority to declare what is and is not exempted development for that structure).

See also: ***protected structure***

Record of qualified households

See: ***social housing waiting list***

Redemption, mortgage

Redemption is the repayment of a ***mortgage*** in full. When a mortgage is redeemed the title documents must be returned to the ***mortgagor***. A redemption figure is the amount remaining to be paid off on a mortgage. A redemption fee is a sum likely to be charged by a lending institution to allow a mortgage to be paid off (redeemed) earlier than the agreed mortgage term or to break a ***fixed rate mortgage*** term.

Refurbishment

The Revenue Commissioners use a definition of 'refurbishment' from the Countrywide Refurbishment Scheme (now expired), in which refurbishment means: 'any work of construction, reconstruction, repair or renewal including the provision or improvement of water, sewerage or heating facilities, carried out in the course of the repair or restoration, or maintenance in the nature of

[504] Reddan, F (2018) 'Mortgage scheme: who is eligible and how will it work?', *Irish Times*, 22 January

[505] See: http://www.irishstatutebook.ie/eli/2000/act/30/enacted/en/print#partiv

repair or restoration of the building or for the purposes of compliance with the requirements of the Housing (Standards for Rented Houses) Regulations 1993 (S.I. No. 147 of 1993)'.

See also: ***substantial refurbishment; Rent Pressure Zone; Housing (Standards for Rented Houses) Regulations 2008; Housing (Standards for Rented Houses) Regulations 2019***

Regional development

'Regional development' is a broad term but can be seen as a general effort to reduce regional disparities by supporting (employment- and wealth-generating) economic activities in regions. In the past, regional development policy tended to try to achieve these objectives by means of large-scale ***infrastructure*** development and by attracting inward investment. Past policies have failed to reduce regional disparities significantly and have not been able to help individual lagging regions to catch up, despite the allocation of significant public funding.[506]

A common thread for regional development concerns some kind of economic and social improvement, for example:

- More and better quality infrastructure (soft and hard)
- Improved community services
- Greater and more diverse volume of production
- Lower unemployment
- Growing number of jobs
- Rising average wealth
- Improved quality of life[507]

See also: ***balanced regional development; rural housing; National Planning Framework; National Spatial Strategy***

Registry of Deeds[508]

The Registry of Deeds was established in 1707 to provide a system of voluntary registration for ***deeds*** and conveyances affecting land and to give priority to registered deeds over unregistered registerable deeds. There is no statutory requirement to register a document but failure to do so may result in a loss of priority. The effect of registration is generally to govern priorities between documents dealing with the same piece of land.

As the Register of Deeds is a public register any person may carry out a search to discover the existence of deeds affecting a piece of property filed

---

[506] OECD (2018) *What Is Regional Development?*, available at: http://www.oecd.org/cfe/regional-policy/regionaldevelopment.htm

[507] McCall, T (2010) 'What Do We Mean by "Regional Development"?', Institute of Regional Development, University of Tasmania

[508] See: https://www.prai.ie/the-property-registration-authority/

there. However, a search in the Registry of Deeds will disclose only whether documents have been executed dealing with the land in question – to discover the effect of these documents, the documents themselves (which are not retained by the Registry of Deeds) will have to be examined. Records in the Registry of Deeds date from 1708.

See also: ***Property Registration Authority; ground rents; deeds; memorial***

Regulatory capture is: 'a process by which regulation … is consistently or repeatedly directed away from the public interest and toward the interests of the regulated industry by the intent and action of the industry itself.'[509]

Regulatory capture might manifest itself in various forms, ranging from the blatant (for example, where an official is bribed to make a decision) to the more nuanced types of 'deep' or 'cultural' capture that involve a consanguinity among elite classes of regulators and executives. In the latter situation, regulators and executives might share similar backgrounds, traditions, understandings of the markets and fundamental philosophies, talk to each other frequently and almost exclusively, share implicit understandings: the quintessential 'old boys' club'. Thus an appearance of impartiality on the part of a regulator might belie an inherent bias that, in various subtle ways, systematically favours that part of the industry with which the regulator most closely identifies.[510]

See also: ***speculation***

See: ***replacement cost***

'Renoviction' (a combination of renovation and ***eviction***) is a colloquial term for the illegal ***termination*** of a tenancy under the pretext that the landlord is to substantially refurbish or renovate the dwelling as per section 34 of the ***Residential Tenancies Act 2004***. The landlord subsequently fails to carry out the refurbishment and instead rents the property to new tenants.

The word 'rent' has several different meanings depending on the context in which it is being used. Although the word 'farm' is an archaic term for rent, in contemporary housing usage, 'rent' is used to describe payments made by a ***tenant*** to a ***landlord*** for the temporary right to occupy or use property, land or other similar property. (Many different non-property goods are also

Regulatory capture

Reinstatement value

Renoviction

Rent

[509] Kwak, J (2014) 'Cultural Capture and the Financial Crisis', in Carpenter, D and Moss, D (eds), *Preventing Regulatory Capture – Special Interest Influence and How to Limit It*, Cambridge University Press: Cambridge
[510] Baxter, LG (2012) 'Understanding Regulatory Capture: An Academic Perspective from the United States', in Pagliari, S (ed.), *The Making of Good Financial Regulation: Towards a Policy Response to Regulatory Capture*, Grosvenor House Publishing: London

often rented as opposed to being owned, e.g. mobile phones and cars). Rent is typically a price freely agreed between the parties to the *lease*, although it may be restricted or otherwise limited by legislation (e.g. *Rent Pressure Zones*) or demands of the owner of the asset (e.g. mobile phone company). The rent for a property will usually be agreed based on the type of property, size and condition of accommodation, location, scarcity, and so on. The rent being charged by a landlord to a tenant may or may not bear any relation to the price the landlord may have paid for the property and is often simply the best price they can achieve in the market at that time. What is included in the rent will be set out in the lease. This may, for example, include electricity and gas bills, or service charges if in a *multi-unit development*. Most Irish leases for residential property tend to leave additional expenses such as gas to the tenant.

The setting of rent (how it is set initially) and the setting of rent at any subsequent review of the rent are proscribed in the Residential Tenancies Acts 2004–2018.

Rental Accommodation Scheme (RAS) The Rental Accommodation Scheme (RAS) was introduced in 2004 and targets the provision of housing through the private market for households who have been in receipt of *Rent Supplement* long term (greater than eighteen months) and have been assessed as needing *social housing*. The scheme is delivered by local authorities (LA) who, under the RAS model, source accommodation from the *private rented sector* and, in general, enter into a *tenancy* agreement with the *landlord* and the RAS recipient. There are tenancies which are linked to the current tenant only and there are also agreements based on availability over a defined period. The local authority then makes a monthly payment to the landlord based on *market rates* (guidance is for payment to equate to circa one month's rent less than the market rate over a given 12-month period (i.e. 8 per cent lower than market rate) to represent the level of risk transferred to the LA) and the *tenant* pays a *differential rent* to the LA based on the individual LA's differential rent policy. Each contract includes a periodic *rent review* (typically every two years).[511]

RAS tenants are regarded as having had their housing needs met and are removed from the social housing waiting list. It is intended that *Housing Assistance Payment* will eventually replace the Rental Accommodation Scheme.[512]

See also: *policy, housing; Housing Assistance Payment*

[511] Kilkenny, P and O'Callaghan, D (2018) *Department of Public Expenditure and Reform – Spending Review 2018: Current and Capital Expenditure on Social Housing Delivery Mechanisms*, Department of Public Expenditure and Reform: Dublin
[512] See: http://www.citizensinformation.ie/en/housing/local_authority_and_social_housing/rental_accommodation_scheme.html

See: *Rent Supplement*

The *Strategy for the Rental Sector* was launched in December 2016 as part of Pillar 4 of *Rebuilding Ireland*. In this strategy, the government's vision is for 'a strong, viable and attractive rental sector supported by a policy and regulatory framework that delivers long-term affordable and high quality accommodation solutions to meet diverse *tenant* needs, and a secure, predictable investment environment for *landlords* and accommodation providers.' The strategy contained a series of objectives and measures to achieve this vision. Its three objectives were:

1. Moderating rental and purchase price inflation, particularly in urban areas
2. Maturing the rental sector so that tenants see it as one that offers security, quality and choice of tenure in the right locations and providers see it as one they can invest in with certainty
3. Ensuring housing's contribution to the national economy is steady and supportive of sustainable economic growth

The strategy also focused on four key areas for action:

- Security – bringing greater certainty to tenants and landlords
- Supply – maintaining existing levels of rental stock and promoting additional supply through encouraging new investment and bringing unused capacity to the market
- Standards – improving the quality and management of rental accommodation
- Services – broadening and strengthening the role and powers of the *Residential Tenancies Board* to more effectively provide key services to tenants and landlords

This scheme allows homeowners to rent a room in their house to a private individual on which they are exempt from income tax for earnings below €14,000 per annum ('rent-a-room relief'). The renter of the room within a house is a *licencee* and not a tenant, and is therefore not covered by the provisions of the *Residential Tenancies Acts* and the owner of the room does not have to register as a landlord with the *Residential Tenancies Board*. A self-contained unit, such as a basement flat or a converted garage attached to a home, can qualify for this relief. While renting out a room that is part of a home is not covered by landlord and tenant law, renting out a self-contained unit is covered.[513]

---

[513] See: http://www.citizensinformation.ie/en/housing/owning_a_home/home_owners/rent_a_room_scheme.html

There are certain exclusions to the scheme: no rent-a-room relief can be claimed if:

- The gross income from rent and related services is over €14,000
- The owner is renting the room to their civil partner, son or daughter (but there is no restriction in the case of other family members)
- The owner is an employee or office-holder in a company, and the company pays the owner to allow clients to use the room in their home on an occasional basis
- The owner is renting the room to short-term guests, for example, through an online accommodation booking site[514]

Rent book

A rent book is a record of payments to a landlord. Since 1993, landlords are obliged to provide tenants with a 'rent book' (or other documentation serving the same purpose) at the commencement of a tenancy. This applies to **dwellings** rented by private landlords, **approved housing bodies**, local authorities and employers.

All rent and other payments under the tenancy must be acknowledged in writing by the landlord. In addition, the rent book must contain specific particulars relating to the tenancy including, among other things, the name and address of the landlord and of the landlord's agent (if any), the term of the tenancy, the amount of the rent and of any other payments to be made by the tenant to the landlord, details of any advance rent or deposit paid and an inventory of furnishings and appliances supplied with the house.

See also: **private rented sector**

Rent control

Rent control is a method of regulating **rents**, and particularly their potential increases. There are many variations on rent control (more recently known as 'rent regulation'), but historically, in general, there have been three generations of rent control which Arnott describes:

1. The first was a broad rent freeze (with perhaps an occasional uplift to reflect the impact of inflation). This type of rent control was standard in Europe during the inter-war period and World War II, and lingered on afterwards, in some jurisdictions persisting into the 1980s. In North America, first-generation rent control was applied during World War II but in all jurisdictions except New York City was dismantled by 1950.
2. Second-generation rent control typically allowed rents to be increased annually by a certain percentage automatically (guideline rent increase

[514] See: http://www.citizensinformation.ie/en/housing/owning_a_home/home_owners/rent_a_room_scheme.html

provisions), and contained supplementary provisions which permitted rents to be further increased on a discretionary basis in response to some combination of cost increases (cost pass-through provisions), cash-flow considerations (financial hardship provisions), and profitability concerns (rate of return provisions). In the 1970s and 1980s many European jurisdictions replaced first-generation with second-generation rent control programmes.

3. The third generation of rent control has been more evolutionary than radical, where tenancy has been a gradual convergence to yet another form of rent control whereby rent increases are controlled within a tenancy but are unrestricted between tenancies. This class of rent-control programmes might be termed third-generation rent controls. But since their defining characteristic is the regulation of rent during but not between tenancies, this class of control is more descriptively termed tenancy rent control.[515]

A feature of rent control (where it exists in **Rent Pressure Zones**) in Ireland has been the fact that rents remain regulated between tenancies – in other words, the rent for a new tenant must be based on that of the previous tenant, and cannot revert to **market rent** upon the departure of a tenant.

The Residential Tenancies Act 2004 sets out a function of the **Residential Tenancies Board** of: 'the collection and provision of information relating to the **private rented sector**, including information concerning prevailing **rent** levels'. Every year, the RTB registers approximately 100,000 new tenancies, with annual peaks in activity in September/October. Every quarter, the Residential Tenancies Board (RTB) publishes the authoritative rent report of its kind on the private accommodation sector in Ireland. Compiled by the Economic and Social Research Institute (ESRI), and based on the RTB's own register of tenancies, the Rent Index reveals the actual rents (not asking rents) being paid for rented properties. This extensive database is the largest in the country and is populated with information on rents being paid, location, six categories of dwelling types, accommodation size, number of occupants and tenancy length. The Rent Index is backdated to Q3, 2007.

The Index can also differentiate between **Rent Pressure Zone** (RPZ) and non-RPZ rents. Legislation has allowed the RTB and ESRI to include information at local electoral area level, to help improve the Rent Index. This model provides more granular information on rent prices to **tenants**, **landlords**, **estate agents**, central government, local authorities, and state agencies.

See also: **Daft.ie; private rented sector**

Rent Index (Residential Tenancies Board)

[515] Arnott, R (2003) 'Tenancy Rent Control', *Swedish Economic Policy Review*, Vol. 10, pp. 89–121

Rent Pressure Zone

Rent predictability measures (***rent control***/rent regulation) are provisions enacted under the ***Planning and Development (Housing) and Residential Tenancies Act 2016*** intended to moderate the rise in rents in the parts of the country where rents were highest and rising and where households had greatest difficulties in finding affordable accommodation. They apply until 31 December 2021 when they are to be reviewed.

In these Rent Pressure Zone (RPZ) areas, rents can only rise according to a prescribed formula by a maximum of 4 per cent annually. The existing requirement still applies that the rent set for a property must be in line with local ***market rents*** for similar properties and three examples of rents for comparable properties must be presented to demonstrate this. The following areas are currently RPZs:

1. Cobh, Co. Cork
2. Maynooth, Co. Kildare
3. Ballincollig–Carrigaline, Co. Cork
4. Galway City Central
5. Galway City East
6. Galway City West
7. Celbridge–Leixlip, Co. Kildare
8. Naas, Co. Kildare
9. Newbridge, Co. Kildare
10. Ashbourne, Co. Meath
11. Laytown–Bettystown, Co. Meath
12. Rathoath, Co. Meath
13. Bray, Co. Wicklow
14. Wicklow, Co. Wicklow
15. Dublin City Council
16. South Dublin County Council
17. Dún Laoghaire–Rathdown County Council
18. Fingal County Council
19. Cork City Council
20. Greystones, Wicklow County Council
21. Drogheda, Louth County Council
22. Navan, Co. Meath
23. Limerick City East, Co. Limerick

For an area to be designated a Rent Pressure Zone, rents in the area must be at a high level and they must be rising quickly. Using ***Residential Tenancies Board*** (RTB) data, (i) the rent of a dwelling in the Greater Dublin Area (Kildare, Wicklow and Meath) will now be compared to the average rent across the country, excluding Dublin rents; and (ii) the rent of a dwelling outside of the Greater Dublin Area will be compared to the average rent across the country, excluding the Greater Dublin Area rents.

Not all rental properties are covered by the 4 per cent annual rental restriction. Properties that are new to the rental market and have not been let at any time in the previous two years and properties which have undergone a **substantial change** (significant alterations or improvements which add to the letting value of the property) can be exempted from the measure in setting the initial rent, but are subject to the 4 per cent cap at each rent review thereafter.

Students in **purpose-built student accommodation** are subject to the maximum 4 per cent rent increases in Rent Pressure Zones whether private or belonging to a higher education institution. Obligations and rights under residential tenancies legislation apply to **tenancy** and **licence** agreements in student-specific accommodation (e.g. relevant **termination** provisions, the RTB dispute resolution process, tenancy registration requirements).

Where a landlord is setting the rent in a Rent Pressure Zone the amount cannot be greater than the amount determined by the below formula, the existing requirement that the rent set is not above the local market rents for similar properties still applies and three examples of rents for similar properties in the locality must be presented to demonstrate this.

$$R \times (1 + 0.04 \times t/m)$$

R = the amount of rent last set under a tenancy for the dwelling (the current rent amount)

t = the number of months between the date the current rent came into effect and the date the new rent amount will come into effect.

m = either 24 or 12

For tenancies that are already in existence a review is only permitted 24 months after the tenancy came in to existence or 24 months from the date the rent was last set. In this instance m = 24. For this initial **rent review** after the 24-month period as specified above a maximum rent increase of 4 per cent will apply (this amounts to 2 per cent per annum applied pro-rata for the period since the rent was last increased).

Following on from this initial review after 24 months, a landlord is entitled to review the rent every 12 months. Landlords of all new tenancies within a Rent Pressure Zone commencing on or after 24 December 2016 are entitled to review the rent annually. In this instance m = 12.

If rent reviews take place annually the permissible rent increase in each case will be 4 per cent. If, for example, a landlord opts to review the rent after 18 months (instead of one year) the allowable increase will be 6 per cent (4 per cent per annum pro-rata for one-and-a-half years).

In the case of a new tenancy in a Rent Pressure Zone, a landlord is required to furnish the tenant, in writing, with the following information at the commencement of the tenancy:

- The amount of rent that was last set under a tenancy for the dwelling
- The date the rent was last set under a tenancy for the dwelling
- A statement as to how the rent set under the tenancy of the dwelling has been calculated having regard to the Rent Pressure Zone formula

Rent certainty measures will continue to apply until the next rent review is due to be carried out. Thereafter if the area is not in one of the Rent Pressure Zones then the rent certainty measures will continue to exist, namely that the landlord cannot increase the rent greater than the market rent having given 90 days' notice of the rent increase and having sought three comparable properties advertised within the previous four-week period.

See also: *rent control; security of tenure; policy, housing*

Rent review A rent review is a process where a *landlord* or *tenant* seeks to change the amount of *rent* being charged to a property.[516] It is common for rent reviews in residential property to be annual or biannual (compared to five-yearly rent reviews in commercial property). In Ireland, outside of *Rent Pressure Zones*, rent reviews can be carried out every 24 months; within Rent Pressure Zones, they are permitted on an annual basis.

See also: *rent review notice; Rent Index*

Rent review notice If a *landlord* intends to review the *rent*, they must inform the *tenant* in writing a minimum of 90 days before the new revised rent starts. For the *rent review* notice to be valid it must state:

- The new rent on the property
- When the new rent starts
- That any dispute must be referred to the *Residential Tenancies Board* within 28 days of getting the notice or before the date the new rent starts
- That, in the opinion of the landlord, the new rent is not greater than the *market rent* of properties of a similar size, type and character with similar terms of the *tenancy* in a comparable area
- The rent for three properties of a similar size, type and character and in a comparable area

---

[516] See: https://onestopshop.rtb.ie/during-a-tenancy/

- The date on which the notice is signed
- The notice must be signed by the landlord or their authorised agent

See also: ***notice period; rent review period (rent certainty)***

Outside of ***Rent Pressure Zones*** (RPZ), a ***landlord*** can only review the ***rent*** once in any 24-month period, and cannot review within 24 months of the start of the ***tenancy*** except where there has been a '***substantial change***' in the nature of the accommodation that would cause a change in the letting value of the property. Rents must be in line with current market rent.

Within RPZs, where a tenancy was already in existence prior to 24 December 2016, a landlord may only review the rent 24 months after the start of the tenancy or 24 months from when the rent was last set. Thereafter, rents can be reviewed on an annual basis, but are in the main limited to a 4 per cent increase, again unless the landlord can prove there has been a 'substantial change' in the nature of the accommodation. RPZ rent limits will apply until 31 December 2021, or may be lifted from a designated area earlier by a minister if rent pressure has been alleviated.

See also: ***rent review notice***

Rent review period (rent certainty)

Rent Supplement is a payment to people living in ***private rented sector*** accommodation who cannot afford the cost of their accommodation from their own resources (it is also commonly known as rent allowance). In the past, applicants could apply for Rent Supplement if they were qualified for social housing support and were on the local authority's ***social housing waiting list***. However, people in this situation will now apply for the ***Housing Assistance Payment*** (HAP).[518]

The purpose of Rent Supplement is to help people meet their accommodation costs whilst also receiving a social welfare payment. However, there is no automatic qualification for Rent Supplement because someone is in receipt of a social welfare payment as there are other conditions that must also be met.

All recipients of Rent Supplement must make a minimum contribution towards their rent. The minimum contribution is currently €30 for single people (with or without children) and €40 for couples (with or without children). Other household members with their own income are also liable to contribute towards the rent.

Under the Rent Supplement scheme there is no direct relationship between the Department of Employment Affairs and Social Protection and a landlord. In most cases payment is made to the tenant. However, payment of

Rent Supplement[517]

---

[517] See: http://www.welfare.ie/en/Pages/rent_faq.aspx#q1
[518] See: http://www.citizensinformation.ie/en/social_welfare/social_welfare_payments/supplementary_welfare_schemes/rent_supplement.html

Rent Supplement can be made to the landlord if requested and if the officer dealing with the claims agrees to it. Even if Rent Supplement is paid direct to a landlord, recipients will still have to pay the landlord a minimum of €30 (for single people) or €40 (for couples) per week.

If two offers of social housing from a local authority are refused within a twelve-month period, Rent Supplement will be stopped and recipients will not be allowed to claim Rent Supplement for twelve months.

See also: ***Rental Accommodation Scheme***

Repair and Leasing Scheme

The original Repair and Leasing Scheme was launched in 2017. Due to low uptake, revisions were made to the scheme in 2018. In the same year, 132 agreements to lease were signed out of 1,260 applications received.[519] The details below are for the revised scheme.

The Repair and Leasing Scheme (RLS) is targeted at owners of ***vacant dwellings*** who cannot afford or access the funding needed to bring their properties up to the required standard for rental property. The scheme provides upfront funding for any works necessary to bring the property up to the required standard and in return the property owner agrees to lease the dwelling to the local authority or an ***approved housing body*** (AHB) to be used as ***social housing***. The cost of the repairs is repaid by the property owner by offsetting it against the ***rent***. The maximum cost of repairs allowable under the scheme is €40,000 (including VAT), or €50,000 (including VAT) where the property is a former ***bedsit*** being brought into line with the ***standards for rented houses***.

The local authority or AHB is responsible for internal maintenance and repairs during the term of the lease. At the end of the term, the property will be returned to the owner in good repair, except for fair wear and tear. The owner is responsible for structural insurance, structural maintenance and structural repair. They are also responsible for paying management company ***service charges***, if applicable, and any other charges for which they are liable, such as ***Local Property Tax***. The property can be sold during the lease term with the consent of the AHB or local authority, but the lease agreement must be transferred to the new owner.[520]

The minimum lease term is five years and the maximum term is twenty years at approximately 80 per cent (house) or 85 per cent (apartment) of ***market rent*** with three- or four-yearly ***rent reviews***.[521] Within those limits,

---

[519] See: https://www.housing.gov.ie/housing/social-housing/social-and-affordble/overall-social-housing-provision

[520] See: http://www.citizensinformation.ie/en/housing/housing_grants_and_schemes/repair_and_leasing_scheme.html

[521] Bryne, N/Mason Hayes & Curran (2018) 'Private Sector Delivery Mechanisms', presentation at the Social Housing Seminar, 26 April, Dublin, available at: https://www.mhc.ie/uploads/Social_Housing_Seminar_Slides_for_website.pdf

the length and type of lease can be negotiated with the local authority and the duration may depend on the cost of the upgrade works.

Property owners under the RLS may choose whether to enter into:

- A direct lease: where the owner chooses to enter into a direct leasing arrangement, the local authority or approved housing body will be the landlord of the property; the property owner will have no landlord responsibilities. or
- A rental *availability arrangement* with a local authority: where the owner chooses to enter into a rental availability arrangement with the local authority, the owner of the property will be the landlord to the tenant and carry out the responsibilities of the landlord.

The properties acquired under both arrangements will be offered by the local authority or the AHB as accommodation to households who have been approved by the local authority for social housing.[522]

The replacement cost (or rebuilding/*reinstatement value*) of a house is the price to reconstruct the building at current rates. This is different to the *market value* of the house.

Replacement cost

See also: *land; value; site value tax*

Under the *Code of Conduct on Mortgage Arrears* (CCMA), lenders may only seek repossession of a borrower's *principal private residence* under specific circumstances:

Repossession

a. the lender has made every reasonable effort under the CCMA to agree an alternative arrangement with the borrower or his/her nominated representative; and
b. (i) the period referred to in Provision 45(d) or Provision 47(d), as applicable, has expired;* or
   (ii) the borrower has been classified as not cooperating and the lender has issued the notification required.

*[Provision 45(d): that legal proceedings may commence three months from the date the letter [from a lender outlining why they are not offering an alternative repayment plan] is issued or eight months from the date the arrears arose, whichever date is later, and that, irrespective of how the property is repossessed and disposed of, the borrower will remain liable for the outstanding debt, including any accrued interest, charges, legal, selling and other related costs, if this is the case;

---

[522] See: http://rebuildingireland.ie/repair-and-leasing-scheme/

Provision 47(d): that legal proceedings may commence three months from the date the letter is issued or eight months from the date the arrears arose, whichever date is later, and that, irrespective of how the property is repossessed and disposed of, the borrower will remain liable for the outstanding debt, including any accrued interest, charges, legal, selling and other related costs, if this is the case;]

57. Notwithstanding Provisions 56 [above], where a borrower is in mortgage arrears the lender may apply to the courts to commence legal proceedings for repossession of a borrower's primary residence:

    (*a*) in the case of a fraud perpetrated on the lender by the borrower; or

    (*b*) in the case of breach of contract by the borrower other than the existence of arrears.

58. A lender, or its legal advisors on its behalf, must notify the borrower on paper or another durable medium immediately before it applies to the Courts to commence legal proceedings for the repossession of the primary residence.

59. Where legal proceedings have commenced, a lender must continue to maintain contact with the borrower or his/her nominated representative periodically. If an alternative repayment arrangement is agreed between the parties before an order in relation to the repossession of the property is granted, the lender must seek an order from the court to put the legal proceedings on hold, for the period during which the borrower adheres to the terms of the alternative repayment arrangement.

60. Where a lender has disposed of a property which it has repossessed, the lender must notify the borrower on paper or another durable medium, of the following information and of his/her liability for:

    (*a*) the balance of outstanding debt, if any;

    (*b*) details and amount of any costs arising from the disposal which have been added to the mortgage loan account; and

    (*c*) the interest rate to be charged on the remaining balance, if any.

The information specified above must be provided to the borrower in a timely manner following the completion of the disposal.[523]

Repossessions are regarded by the **Central Bank of Ireland** as a normal part of a functioning housing system, which allows the lender to acquire the underlying asset in cases of non-payment. The number of repossessions is seen as low (c.8,200 since Q3, 2009) in the context of about 728,000 principal dwelling houses (often referred to as PDH) mortgages in Ireland.[524]

See also: ***arrears; Mortgage Arrears Resolution Process***

---

[523] See: https://www.centralbank.ie/docs/default-source/Regulation/consumer-protection/other-codes-of-conduct/24-gns-4-2-7-2013-ccma.pdf?sfvrsn=4

[524] Burke-Kennedy, E (2018) 'Homes of nearly 8,200 Irish mortgage holders repossessed since crash', *Irish Times*, 9 March

A reserve price is the lowest price the vendor will accept if there are no higher bids. The reserve price is not usually disclosed to vendors, and if the property does not achieve the reserve price then the vendor is not obliged to sell it.

See also: ***auction; value; valuer***

Reserve price

Residential care is long-term care given to people in a residential setting outside their own home. In an Irish context, residential care is usually for older people who may be frail and unable to care for themselves at home, but whose care needs are low (i.e. they require limited specialist care or nursing). Such residential care can be funded through the ***Fair Deal Scheme***.

Residential care

Research by the Irish Smart Ageing Exchange (ISAX)[525] has identified eight stages of different types of housing and care needs: family home; adapted family home; regular market (no services); independent living (low level of services); assisted living (medium level of services); specialised living including sub-acute care (high level of services); nursing home; hospital.

ALONE has identified a series of different types of residential care homes that are required in Ireland.

Housing Type	Response	Relevant Considerations
Dedicated social housing for older people	Supportive housing	Limited examples in Ireland. Needs investment and the development of a supportive housing model to ensure consistency across schemes
	Housing with supports	Model needs to be further developed and implemented in Ireland, needs investment and promotion as an alternative to nursing homes
Dispersed housing	Making existing homes more age-friendly	Cost-effective and supportive of ageing in place
Shared housing in the community	Retirement villages	Potential for more private sector development
	Older persons' co-housing communities	Potential for private and social enterprise sectors
	Home sharing	Needs promotion and regulation
	Split housing	Can help in dealing with current general housing crisis
	Boarding out	Requires promotion and regulation
Residential nursing care units	Quality nursing homes developed as part of multi-purpose complexes	Necessary for some; demand can be reduced through more high-support housing and Home Care Packages

---

[525] Amárach Research, Lyons, R, Sirr, L and Innovation Delivery (2016) 'Housing for Older People – Thinking Ahead', ISAX: Dublin

Research findings shows that by 2021:

- The number of people aged 65+ using residential long-term care will rise by 12,270 in Ireland, an increase of 59 per cent since 2006.
- An additional 23,670 older people in Ireland will use home care, up 57 per cent since 2006.
- 2,833 extra people will require residential or formal home care each year in Ireland to 2021.[526]

See also: **downsize**

Residential Landlords Association of Ireland

The Residential Landlords Association of Ireland (RLAI) was formed in March 2013 by **landlords** as a non-profit organisation to provide trusted information for landlords; to advise on best practices in the management of a property rental business; to assist and provide information on housing and **tenancy** issues; and to lobby government and councils on the aims and objectives as proposed by RLAI members.

The aims and objectives of the RLAI are:

- To prevent the introduction of a custodial deposit scheme (**deposit protection scheme**)
- **Local Property Tax** (LPT) to be tax deductible on rental property
- To be consulted at government level on landlord issues
- Policy that **Residential Tenancies Board** penalises landlords and tenants equally
- LPT to be per house and not on individual flats
- Property tax to be totally deductible
- To seek reinstatement of 100 per cent interest relief for rental properties mortgages/loans
- Water charges for complete letting property and not individual units
- Water charges to be deductible if landlords pay
- Better tax regime for landlords
- Tax incentives for landlords to bring properties up to regulation standards
- To promote improved standards for residential letting property stock
- Standardisation of social welfare housing supplement paid to landlord
- Information and contact support for landlords in mortgage **arrears**[527]

---

[526] Wren, M, Normand, C, O'Reilly, D, Cruise, S, Connolly, S and Murphy, C (2012) *Towards the Development of a Predictive Model of Long-Term Care Demand for Northern Ireland and the Republic of Ireland*, Centre for Health Policy and Management: Trinity College Dublin
[527] See: http://www.rlai.ie/#top1_modules

Residential property for ***stamp duty*** purposes means:

- A building, or part of a building, which at the date the instrument (written document) was executed:
  - ◆ was used, or was suitable for use, as a ***dwelling***; or
  - ◆ was in the course of being built, or adapted for use, as a dwelling; or
  - ◆ had been built or adapted for use as a dwelling, and had not since been adapted for any other use; and
- The area attached to the residential property (for example, the garden or yard), excluding the site of the residential property. If this area exceeds one acre, the area in excess of one acre is non-residential property.

Residential property includes a derelict or uninhabitable house.
See also: ***curtilage***

The Residential Property Price Register was established under section 86 of the ***Property Services (Regulation) Act 2011***. It includes the date of sale, price achieved and address of all residential properties purchased in Ireland since 1 January 2010, as declared to the Revenue Commissioners for ***stamp duty*** purposes. It is important to note that the Register is not intended as a 'Property Price Index'. In a small number of transactions included in the Register the price shown does not represent the full market price of the property concerned for a variety of reasons. All such properties are marked **. Where a property is part residential and part non-residential (e.g. living quarters over a shop) the Register will only contain information about the residential part. The date of sale is the date input by the filer of the ***stamp duty*** return as the date of the ***deed*** transferring ownership of the property. The ***Property Services Regulatory Authority*** has acknowledged that there may be errors in the data in the Register. The Register is compiled from data which is filed, for stamp duty purposes, with the Revenue Commissioners. The data is primarily filed electronically by persons doing the ***conveyancing*** of the property on behalf of the purchaser and errors may occur when the data is being filed.
See also: ***value; Rent Index***

The Residential Tenancies Act 2004 was a watershed in the private rented sector in Ireland. The Act provided for reform of residential ***landlord*** and ***tenant*** law, based mainly on the recommendations of the ***Commission on the Private Rented Residential Sector***. The Act outlined obligations for

---

[528] See: https://www.revenue.ie/en/property/stamp-duty/buying-or-transferring-property/residential-property.aspx
[529] See: https://www.propertypriceregister.ie/website/npsra/pprweb.nsf/page/ppr-home-en

both tenants and landlords whether or not there was a written *lease* or agreement. Neither landlords nor tenants could contract their way out of these obligations, although additional ones could be included. The Act:

- Formalised *rent* setting and notice periods for *rent reviews*
- Introduced new *security of tenure* provisions based on a four-year cycle (known as *Part 4*, and subsequently increased to six years)
- Brought in new periods of notice for the *termination* of a tenancy
- Introduced mandatory registration of tenancies
- Established the Private Residential Tenancies Board (see: *Residential Tenancies Board*)
- Put in place a dispute resolution system for landlords and tenants via the Private Residential Tenancies Board

See also: *notice of termination; Residential Tenancies (Amendment) Act 2015*

Residential Tenancies (Amendment) Act 2015

The Residential Tenancies (Amendment) Act 2015 came into effect on 4 December 2015. It had two components of significance, the first of which was to restrict landlords from reviewing the *rent* on their properties to once every 24 months – this had previously been once every 12 months. This restriction was originally legislated for until 3 December 2019 but extended until 31 December 2021. More than half of all tenancies in the country are currently covered by *Rent Pressure Zones* introduced by subsequent legislation; this 24-month rent review restriction applies outside RPZs. The second major change was that *landlords* must give tenants a notice period which has been increased from 28 to 90 days before any new rent can take effect. This Act requires landlords to provide evidence that the new rent is justifiable in terms of local rents.

See also: *rent review; notice periods; notice of termination*

Residential Tenancies (Amendment) Act 2018

The Residential Tenancies (Amendment) Act 2018 contains several components which constitute significant changes to existing legislation, including providing a legal definition of '*substantial change*' in the nature of accommodation provided under *tenancy* in the context of qualifying for an exemption from the rent increase restriction. In addition, the new Act made it compulsory that the *Residential Tenancies Board* be notified of any rent changes and exemptions claimed.

Landlords are now required to register their tenancies on an annual basis on the anniversary of the tenancy commencement date. The fee is €40 for private tenancy and €20 for an *approved housing body* tenancy. This amends section 135 of the *Residential Tenancies Act 2004*, which had provided for registration at the commencement of a tenancy.

The Act also changed *notice periods* for the termination of a tenancy, and introduced a legal definition for substantial change, an amendment to section 19 of the *Residential Tenancies Act 2004*. In addition, a *further Part 4 tenancy* (i.e. a tenancy after the initial six-year period of the tenancy) is not a new tenancy for the purposes of calculating notice periods. In addition, any *Determination Orders* issued by the RTB will be published. In *purpose-built student accommodation*, the Act brought students under the 4 per cent rent cap if the property is in a *Rent Pressure Zone*, irrespective of whether the students are in occupation under a *licence* or tenancy agreement. Students are not entitled to a *Part 4* tenancy, however.

The Act also brought in new criteria for calculating if an area should become a Rent Pressure Zone or not. Landlords are also required to send a copy of the notice of termination to the RTB. The Act also brought in new measures to protect tenants whose tenancies have been terminated:

- Where a landlord terminates a tenancy because he/she intends to sell the property, he/she must enter into a contract for sale within nine months of the termination date and if not, must offer to re-let to a former tenant who provides their contact details.
- Where a landlord terminates a tenancy because he/she needs the property for his/her own occupation or for a family member, that property must be offered back to the former tenant who provides their contact details where it again becomes vacant within one year, rather than six months (as currently provided for in the Act), of the termination date.
- Where a landlord terminates a tenancy because he/she needs to substantially refurbish/renovate the property, that property must be offered back to the former tenant who provides their contact details, upon completion of the works.
- Also a certificate from an architect or surveyor will be required to the effect that the proposed substantial refurbishment/renovation works in question would pose a health and safety risk requiring vacation by the tenants and would require at least three weeks to complete.

The *Private Residential Tenancies Board* became the Residential Tenancies Board (RTB) in 2016 when *approved housing bodies* were brought under its remit alongside private tenancies. It has three main functions: **Residential Tenancies Board**

1. *Tenancy registration*: All private residential landlords and approved housing bodies are obliged to register their tenancies. A public register of tenancies is available on the RTB website which allows members of the public to check if a tenancy is registered with the RTB. The registration of tenancies enables the RTB to collect data on the sector, and is also a

key part of regulating the sector and ensuring **landlords** and **tenants** are aware of their rights and responsibilities.

2. *Dispute resolution*: Since 2004, the RTB has replaced the courts in dealing with the majority of disputes between landlords and tenants through its dispute resolution service. This service offers a choice of resolution types to parties, but primarily mediation or adjudication.

3. *Information, research and education*: The RTB provides information to tenants and landlords as well as to the general public on their rights and obligations, in terms both of living and providing accommodation in the rental sector. It also provides accurate and authoritative data on the rental sector, such as the RTB Rent Index, which allows it to monitor trends in the rental sector, but also allows individuals to check and compare rents in particular locations.

Dispute statistics show that on average tenants take almost two-thirds of cases with landlords almost one-third, and third parties taking about 2 per cent of cases per annum. About 1 per cent of all tenancies end in official dispute, a number that has remained consistent throughout the significant increase in **households** renting.

See also: **Residential Tenancies Act 2004; Residential Tenancies (Amendment) Act 2015; Residential Tenancies (Amendment) Act 2018**

Residual value   The residual is the sum of money available to purchase a site. As such, residual valuations are usually done of **land** with **development** potential. A residual valuation is therefore an assessment of the **value** of the scheme as completed, with a deduction of the costs of development (including developer's profit), to arrive at the underlying land value (the 'residual' sum for which the land can be bought).

A residual valuation can be expressed as a simple equation:

Gross Development Value (end value of completed development)
 – development costs + developer's profit = land value
('residual')[530]

The residual method requires the input of a large amount of data (costs, finance, discounted cash flows, etc.), which is rarely absolute or precise, coupled with making a large number of assumptions. Small changes in any of the inputs can cumulatively lead to a large change in the land value.

See also: **valuer; developer**

---

[530] Royal Institution of Chartered Surveyors (2008) *Value of Development Land*, first edition, RICS: London

'Residualisation' refers to the tendency for the *social housing* sector 'to cater for an increased proportion of deprived people and to cater more exclusively for this group'.[531]

See also: ***approved housing bodies; council housing; social housing***

Residualisation

Respond is an ***approved housing body*** founded in Waterford in 1982. Respond's first housing scheme was in Larchville, Waterford on a piece of land set aside by Waterford City Council. This development contained fifteen houses for older persons, along with a community room. Several housing schemes were developed for young families by Respond Housing Association over the next few years using Respond's own 'Agency Agreement Model' whereby young couples transferred their mortgages to Respond Housing Association which undertook to provide design and project management for fixed-price new houses for them.[532] As well as housing, Respond have also pioneered the development of *hubs* for homeless families.

See also: ***Clúid Housing; Tuath Housing***

Respond

All developments which have been constructed outside the limits of exempted development since 1963, without first seeking *planning permission*, are considered unauthorised and all '*unauthorised developments*' are deemed to be in breach of planning legislation. The *Planning and Development Act 1963* introduced a legislative mechanism for validating structures developed without prior permission. This 'retrospective corrective' is formally known as retention *planning permission*. The original intent of providing this mechanism was partially to avoid controls on developments of a minor nature.[533] (In France, Germany, Italy, Spain, the Netherlands and Luxembourg there is no mechanism for correction when there has been a planning breach.)

In cases where development does not contravene policies in the *development plan* and is not objectionable in principle based on considerations of proper planning and sustainable development, it may be possible to 'regularise' development by a grant of retention permission. It should be noted that:

Retention planning permission

- Retention applications are not given special consideration based on the fact that development has already been carried out.
- Any application to retain development will be assessed based on policies set out in the local authority's development plan and on the principles of sound planning and sustainable development, and on relevant issues raised in third-party observations.

---

[531] Lee, P and Murie, A (1997) Poverty, *Housing Tenure and Social Exclusion*, Policy Press: Bristol

[532] See: https://www.respond.ie/about-us/history/

[533] Harley-Gunning, E (2017) 'Retrospective Corrective: Rethinking Retention Planning Permission in Ireland', MSc thesis, Dublin Institute of Technology

- If retention of an unauthorised development is refused, the unauthorised development must be removed and/or the unauthorised use ceased. 'Repeat' retention applications for developments that have already been refused by the planning authority or **An Bord Pleanála** will not defer enforcement action.[534]

The fees associated with retention applications are typically a multiple of the amount of standard applications per the provision of the planning regulations. Permission for retention does not automatically negate the possibility of prosecution if enforcement action has already been initiated.[535]

Analysis of the retention planning permission statistics across Ireland is hampered by the fact that planning and retention applications are contained under the broader umbrella of standard applications. However, a survey of over 60,000 planning applications showed that retention applications accounted for over 14 per cent of all planning applications. This represents a sizable portion of the market in practice, suggesting there may indeed be a degree of misapplication or overuse. In addition, it is evident that considerable reliance on the retention mechanism still exists.[536]

See also: ***enforcement, planning***

Retention withholding money

This is a sum of money, normally 5–10 per cent of the contract building price, that the client withholds until the works are completed. 50 per cent of the retention withholding money is usually paid to the builder at ***practical completion*** stage and the remainder when the ***snag list*** has been completed.

See also: ***self-build***

Retirement housing

Housing developments of a similar type to ***sheltered housing*** (individual units with some shared services in a communal setting) but typically built for sale.

See also: ***residential care; retirement village***

Retirement village[537]

In the UK in particular, the retirement village is an increasingly popular concept, but lacking any single, clear definition. It is therefore anything from an estate to a full-blown village-sized development of bungalows, flats or houses, intended for occupation by older people. Some retirement villages include a care home alongside independent living and assisted living properties, and most of the larger ones include leisure and hobby facilities as well as restaurants, shops, hairdressing salon, etc.

---

[534] See: http://www.corkcity.ie/en/council-services/services/planning/planning-enforcement/
[535] See: https://www.housing.gov.ie/sites/default/files/migrated-files/en/Publications/DevelopmentandHousing/Planning/FileDownLoad%2C31565%2Cen.pdf
[536] Harley-Gunning, E (2017) 'Retrospective Corrective: Rethinking Retention Planning Permission in Ireland', MSc thesis, Dublin Institute of Technology
[537] See: http://www.housingcare.org/jargon-retirement-village.aspx

To 'retrofit' means to add new or modified parts or components to something that did not have them when first produced. In housing, it usually means the installation of new energy efficiency components (e.g. multi-glazed windows) or insulation (e.g. dry lining) to improve the quality of the structure.

See also: ***Sustainable Energy Authority of Ireland***

Retrofit

To rezone land is to change the planning zone originally assigned to it in a ***development plan*** or ***local area plan***. Rezoning is defined in Irish legislation as: 'a change in the ***zoning*** of land in a development plan or local area plan from a non-development land-use (agricultural, open space, recreational or amenity use or a mixture of such uses) to a development land-use (residential, commercial or industrial uses or a mixture of such uses) or from one development land-use to another, including a mixture of such uses.'

As a change of use from one zoning class to another (e.g. agriculture to residential) is potentially very lucrative for those with an interest in the land, the process of ***zoning*** and rezoning are carefully regulated.

See also: ***windfall gains***

Rezoning

The most common type of ***easement*** is a right of way. A right of way is a right of access or continued passage to one piece of land over a lane or other piece of ground owned by someone else. The Land and Conveyancing Law Reform Act 2009 legislates for the right to acquire a right of way.

Legal title to easements, such as rights of way, will only be acquired by long use if the claimant obtains a court order to this effect and it is registered in the ***Property Registration Authority*** or ***Registry of Deeds***, as appropriate. The person claiming such right must hold at least twelve years uninterrupted use. Accordingly, after twelve years of non-use an easement will be extinguished unless it is registered.[538] If the easement is not registered then the right may be extinguished and the time for re-acquiring that right, twelve years (under the new Act), starts all over again from 1 December 2021 with previous use not being considered.[539]

A public right of way is a right of passage along a road or path, even if the road or path is not in public ownership. There are very few registered public rights of way that are not maintained public roads.[540]

See also: ***profit à prendre***

Right of way

---

[538] Leahy, C (2010) 'The Land and Conveyancing Law Reform Act 2009: An Overview', *Homs Solicitors*, 1 March, available at: http://www.homs.ie/publications/the-land-and-conveyancing-law-reform-act-2009-an-overview/

[539] See: https://www.ors.ie/news/time-running-out-to-register-rights-of-ways/

[540] See: https://www.citizensinformation.ie/en/travel_and_recreation/sport_and_leisure/walking_and_rambling_in_ireland.html

Right to buy   See: *tenant purchase*

Right to   In its 2018 report, *The Right to Housing*, the **Mercy Law Resource Centre**
housing[541]   (MLRC) has written that there is no express right to housing in Irish law.
                          Instead, the basis for protecting rights related to housing often arises out of
                          infringements of other constitutional rights. None of these rights protect the
                          right to housing as such. They may, in certain extreme cases, provide a basis
                          for securing adequate housing. These rights, which have been developed as
                          'unenumerated rights', include: the right to fair procedures, including the
                          right to be heard and to make your case, and the right to an independent and
                          impartial decision-maker; the right to earn a livelihood; the right to privacy;
                          the right to life and bodily integrity; the right to family consortium; the
                          right to dignity and autonomy; the right to equal treatment; the right of the
                          person; and the right to property.

Article 42A of the Constitution obliges the state to protect the interests
of children whose parents, in exceptional cases, have failed in their parental
duties. This protects the child's rights under the Child Care Act 1991 to
adequate shelter, food, clothing, medical care and education.

The United Nations Committee on Economic, Social and Cultural Rights
has noted that the right to adequate housing 'should be seen as the right to
live somewhere in security, peace and dignity.' The Committee has identified the following as key characteristics of the right: legal *security of tenure*;
availability of services; materials, facilities and infrastructure; *affordability*;
habitability; accessibility; location – in a location which allows access to
employment options, healthcare services, schools, childcare centres and other
social facilities; and cultural adequacy. As a social right, under international
human rights law, the right is to be 'progressively realised' by states to the
extent of available resources.

Without a constitutional right to housing, the failure to provide emergency accommodation, for example, cannot be challenged by reference to
an explicit right. A legal right to housing would also mean any state policy
would have to respect that. A cut in funding for homeless accommodation
could lead to a court taking the view that the right to housing had not been
adequately protected.

A right to housing in the Constitution would not mean the right to a
house for everybody. The Mercy Law Resource Centre advises that a constitutional right to housing would require the state, when making policy, to
reasonably protect that right; it would put in place a basic floor of protection;
and it would recognise the home is central to personal dignity.

---

[541] This entry is mainly based on Mercy Law Resource Centre (2018) *The Right to Housing*, Mercy
Law Resource Centre: Dublin

See also: *Constitution of Ireland (Article 40.3.2 and Article 43); housing rights approach to housing; UN Special Rapporteur on the Right to Adequate Housing*

Rockwool is an inorganic material used for insulation and soundproofing. It is made from basalt and chalk (or recycled slag or limestone) heated at high temperatures which is then spun into fibres. It has been around in various forms since the 1800s. **Rockwool**

Section 2 of the Housing Act 1988 defines **homelessness** in Ireland. However, there is no definition in Irish legislation for rough sleeping. In *A Guide to Undertaking a Rough Sleeping Count*, people living rough are defined as: 'living in the streets or public spaces, without a shelter that can be defined as living quarters.'[542] **Rough sleeping**

Rough sleeping is the most extreme form of homelessness. Opinions differ on how people rough sleeping should be counted and how many people are sleeping rough.

See also: *data – housing output issues*

The Royal Institute of the Architects of Ireland (RIAI) is the regulatory body for architects in Ireland. The RIAI is the official registration body under the Building Control Act 2007. RIAI activities are coordinated by a 35-member council, the Institute's governing body, elected by the membership. **Royal Institute of the Architects of Ireland, The (RIAI)**

See also: *Society of Chartered Surveyors Ireland; Construction Industry Federation; Irish Planning Institute*

Rural housing in Ireland is often a fractious issue with much criticism of the environmental, social and economic impact of its dispersed settlement pattern. Supporters claim that rural housing is the lifeblood of rural Ireland. **Rural housing**

Keaveney has written extensively about rural housing in Ireland.[543] According to her, until the early 1970s rural economy and society in Ireland were for many synonymous with farming and farm-related settlement. Transformations brought about by membership of the EU, CAP reforms, a changing global economy, and generations of out-migration culminated in the decline of Irish full-time family farming. Historically, most people who lived in the countryside farmed the land attached to their individual dwelling or worked in employment associated with farming, primary resources or the rural community. It is clear that this situation has changed radically and

---

[542] Gallwey, B (2017) *A Guide to Undertaking a Rough Sleeping Count*, Dublin Region Homeless Executive: Dublin

[543] Keaveney, K (2009) 'Contested Ruralities: Housing in the Irish Countryside', PhD thesis, University of Maynooth

there no longer remains that interdependent relationship between living in the countryside and farming. Transformations in daily rural activities and employment, changing population dynamics, and increased spatial mobility and accessibility have contributed to the shifting geography of rural settlement and housing in Ireland over the past half-century. Specifically, dispersed single rural dwellings have generated much debate in political, planning and popular discourse due to their dominance in the Irish settlement pattern. The geography of rural housing that existed during a more agriculturally reliant era, however, has persisted despite large-scale changes in the rural economy over the last three to four decades. This juxtaposition of a desire to live in the countryside that results in a maintenance and extension of traditional dispersed settlement patterns with the move away from agricultural and rural-based employment is giving rise to tensions about the future of housing in the countryside.

The housing debate strongly contests issues such as who has the right to live in the countryside, how traditional settlement patterns can be sustained into the future – and indeed, what these traditional patterns are to begin with – and what interventions should be made in relation to rural housing developments.

See also: *one-off housing; Bungalow Bliss; S.I. 365 (opt out); septic tank; Land Commission*

Rural Resettlement Ireland

Rural Resettlement Ireland (RRI) was a non-political, voluntary organisation founded in 1990 to help people relocate from the cities to the countryside, particularly in the west of Ireland. Over its lifetime, Rural Resettlement Ireland helped 800 families relocate to rural areas from Dublin. The government reduced its core annual funding for the organisation to €10,000 in 2012, and RRI closed in 2017.

See also: *rural housing*

Rus in urbe

'Rus in urbe' is the illusion – generally created by design – of countryside running through the heart of a city. The concept of bringing the countryside to the city has had a long history from medieval times to the present.

In Ireland, the *Catholic Church* imposed its own version of 'rus in urbe' on newly emerging *housing estates* in Dublin, designed and constructed in the 1920s and 1930s, through their requirement for front and back gardens and the names of the new streets, which if they were not those of saints, were just as likely to be those of rural towns, parishes and counties of Ireland.

See also: *Howard, Ebenezer; garden city; Marino; suburbs; suburbanisation; Simms, Herbert; rural housing*

S

Safe Home Ireland offers a free, confidential information and advice service to assist older qualifying Irish-born emigrants who want to explore the option of returning to secure affordable housing back in Ireland. It also liaises with ***approved housing bodies*** in Ireland to explore appropriate secure housing options for qualifying older Irish emigrants seeking to return to ***social housing***.

Safe Home Ireland

To qualify for assistance from Safe Home Ireland, applicants must be:

- Aged 57+ years
- Capable of independent living
- Living in rented accommodation abroad and unable to provide accommodation for themselves (from their own income/savings) on return to Ireland

Safe Home Ireland is a registered charity and is also supported by the Department of Foreign Affairs and Trade (Emigrant Support Programme).[544]

A scheme dwelling is housing of two or more units. In measuring housing output, the ***Central Statistics Office*** uses the term 'scheme housing' to distinguish between apartments, developments of two or more houses, and single houses.

Scheme dwelling

See also: ***data – housing output issues; one-off housing***

The Seaside Resorts Scheme was aimed at promoting the renewal and improvement of tourist amenities and facilities in certain seaside resorts. The resorts in question were Achill, Arklow, Ballybunion, Bettystown/Laytown/Mosney, Bundoran, Clogherhead, Clonakilty, Courtown, Enniscrone, Kilkee, Lahinch, Salthill, Tramore, Westport and Youghal. The qualifying period for the scheme of reliefs was from 1 July 1995 to 30 June 1998 (extended to 31 December 1999 in certain circumstances). The scheme made provision for various allowances on expenditure for the construction and refurbishment of tourist-related accommodation, as well as rental income.

Seaside Resorts Scheme[545]

The scheme is now terminated, but the impact of heavily subsidised schemes such as this has been criticised as they can end up sucking in local labour, raising house-building costs locally, as well as putting huge strain on infrastructure and sewage treatment.[546]

See also: ***urban regeneration***

---

[544] See: http://www.safehomeireland.com
[545] Taxes Consolidation Act 1997 (Number 39 of 1997), Chapter 4: Qualifying Resort Areas
[546] Kenna, P (2011) *Housing Law, Rights and Policy*, Clarus Press: Dublin

Section 10 funding[547]   Resources for homeless services are derived from two main sources: 1) Section 10 funding from central government (via the **Department of Housing, Planning and Local Government**) to local authorities under the **Housing Act 1988** combined with a 10 per cent contribution of funding directly from each local authority's revenue stream; and 2) the Health Service Executive is a central funder of homeless services provision in addition to its own direct service provision of care and support programmes. In addition, fundraising by voluntary sector service providers and donations received by them are expended on services.

Section 10 of the 1988 Housing Act, while not putting a statutory obligation on local authorities, conferred additional powers on them to respond to homelessness by directly arranging and funding emergency accommodation, making arrangements with a health board or voluntary body for the provision of emergency accommodation and/or making contributions to voluntary bodies towards the running costs of accommodation provided by them. The Department of the Environment, Heritage and Local Government was empowered to recoup local authorities in respect of their expenditure under section 10.[548]

See also: **homesslessness; Peter McVerry Trust; Focus Ireland; Dublin Simon Community; emergency accommodation; Pathway Accommodation and Support System (PASS)**

Section 23 relief   Section 23 relief (contained in the Taxes Consolidation Act 1997) was a tax relief that applied to rented residential property in a tax incentive area. It was available to a person who incurred expenditure on the purchase, construction, conversion or refurbishment of a qualifying property and who let that property, having complied with certain conditions. Relief for expenditure incurred could be set against the **rent** received from that property and other Irish rental income so that the amount of a person's taxable income is reduced.

See also: **urban regeneration**

Section 28 – 'mandatory guidelines'   Section 28 of the **Planning and Development Act 2000** gave ministers powers to issue guidelines to local authorities on planning matters. These guidelines were not mandatory, but local authorities were required to 'have regard' to them. A new form of these section 28 guidelines (Specific Planning Policy Requirements) was introduced by the Planning and Development (Amendment) Act 2015, which made it mandatory for local authorities to apply 'guidelines' in their planning decisions.

---

[547] See: https://www.homelessdublin.ie/info/funding
[548] Department of Environment, Heritage and Local Government (2000) *Homelessness – An Integrated Strategy*, Government of Ireland: Dublin

Section 28 ministerial guidelines do not need the approval of the Dáil to be issued. A section 29 ministerial directive to a local authority, on the other hand, was mandatory to follow, and required 'a resolution of both Houses of the Oireachtas'. These new section 28 'mandatory guidelines' – essentially a conflation of sections 28 and 29 – means: 'the Minister is reaping the benefits of a Section 29 directive in that he is telling elected bodies and *An Bord Pleanála* what to do, but he is doing so without having to go through the legislative requirement of placing that directive before the Dáil and Seanad by dressing it up to resemble a Section 28 guideline.'[549] The first of the new section 28 mandatory guidelines was issued to local authorities in order to compel them to implement the (then) new apartment size standards, which, it was known, many professional planners thought were a retrograde step.[550]

See also: *apartment design standards*

Securitisation is a financing technique by which homogeneous income-generating assets (e.g. *mortgages*) – which on their own may be difficult to trade – are pooled and sold to a specially created third party, which uses them as collateral to issue securities and sell them in financial markets. Although securitisation was not directly responsible for the 2008 financial crisis, it contributed to it and played a role in its amplification.[551]

See also: *financialisation of housing*

Security of tenure refers to the right to remain in a rented property and reasons whereby a *lease* or *tenancy* can be terminated. Security of tenure is a key factor in encouraging stability in the *private rented sector*. In Ireland, security of tenure is primarily provided for in *Part 4* of the *Residential Tenancies Act 2004*.

See: *termination; fixed term lease; Residential Tenancies (Amendment) Act 2015; Tyrrelstown Amendment; Residential Tenancies (Amendment) Act 2018; further Part 4 tenancy*

Self-building is the commissioning of a home to be built on the owner's behalf in its entirety, or total or partial construction by the owner. Around 3,000–4,000 self-build houses are finished each year.

Several companies offer specific 'self-build' *mortgage*s, the main difference being that the sum of money can be drawn down in stages as the building gets completed. Borrowing is therefore done on an 'as needed' basis. Some

---

[549] See: https://the-law-is-my-oyster.com/2016/02/18/the-amendment-of-section-28-of-the-pda-2000/

[550] Kelly, O (2015) 'Studio apartments: Minister defends rules reducing size', *Irish Times*, 22 December

[551] Delivorias, A (2015) *Understanding Securitisation: Background – Benefits – Risks*, European Parliamentary Research Service: Brussels

of these lenders require the borrower to already have a site with planning permission for a dwelling. They may also use the value of the site as a deposit.

Under *S.I. 365* of 2015, people self-building their own home can also choose to opt-out of the requirement to have the design and construction of the building certified under the *Building Control (Amendment) Regulations*.

See also: *Irish Association of Self Builders; S.I. 365 (opt out); house – structural components*

Self-certification, house-building

Self-certification is the process whereby a party confirms that their design or construction complies with standards without being required to have the drawings or the building checked or signed off by an independent third party or a state authority.

From 1990 until 2014, there was no mandatory/statutory requirement for inspection or certification of buildings in Ireland (other than for the design for fire safety and disabled access prior to construction). There was a target for local authorities to inspect a certain number of buildings under construction, but this was not obligatory. Lending institutions and solicitors generally required developers and builders to arrange for a professional to give an 'opinion' that works were compliant when complete, sometimes on the basis of only a single visual inspection when building was completed and works generally covered up.[552] The private house-building industry therefore operated a system of 'self-certification', where the people checked off on their own work.[553] This was a commercially driven process and not a requirement of legislation. Buildings are signed off as having 'substantial compliance', generally for *title* purposes.[554]

From 2014, the *Building Control (Amendment) Regulations* introduced a new system that required owners to make statutory appointments for mandatory inspections by qualified professionals. However, as these professionals can be in the employ of the builder or developer, and individuals can inspect and certify their own work, this is still self-certification. 'The *assigned certifier* [who inspects on site] can be an employee of the *developer*. The assigned certifier is also acting for the developer, not for the purchaser or the state – they do get paid by the end user. They may not act independently. Their position is compromised as once there's a financial link, that leads to a lack of independence.'[555] This means that: 'designers or builders can sign-off on

[552] Isdell, A (2013) 'Building Progress: Building Control Regulations and Their Effect', *Surveyors' Journal*, Summer
[553] Isdell, A (2014) 'Changes to Building Regulations', *Surveyors' Journal*, Spring
[554] Isdell, A (2013) 'Building Progress: Building Control Regulations and Their Effect', *Surveyors' Journal*, Summer
[555] RTÉ (2017) *Morning Ireland* – Kevin Hollingsworth and Cian O'Callaghan in Jackie Fox report on self-certification, 26 May

their own buildings, and owners/developers can dismiss and replace certifiers whenever they choose. This would not be deemed permissible in many other countries in the developed world.'[556]

There are differences of opinion on what constitutes 'self'-certification. The significance lies in the question of independence, with some certifiers taking the view that they are independent by reason of their independent consultant/contractor status, and others (more correctly) taking the view that any certification other than by a public body or a third party without a direct professional or economic relationship with the developer or builder is essentially self-certification and ultimately compromised by conflicts of interest.

The absence of state or independent inspection of construction has led to a significant number of ***defects*** in Irish housing. In 2015, those who chose to ***self-build*** their homes were given the option of 'opting out' from this new process of mandatory certification (see: ***S.I. 365 (opt out)***).

Semi-detached house

A semi-detached house is one half of a pair of dwellings joined to each other. See also: ***terraced house; detached house; maisonette; flat; duplex; garden flat; apartment; condominium; mews; accessory dwelling unit; micro-home***

Septic tank

Septic systems are underground wastewater treatment structures, commonly used in rural areas without centralised sewer systems. They use a combination of nature and proven technology to treat wastewater from household plumbing produced by bathrooms, kitchen drains, and laundry.[557]

The septic container has five functions. It:

- Receives the wastewater from the house
- Separates the solids from the liquids
- Stores the solids
- Decomposes the solids
- Sends the effluent wastewater out to the drain field

Around 500,000 households in Ireland have a septic tank system and 137,000 of these also have a private well for drinking water.[558] A registration and inspection regime was introduced in 2012 for domestic waste water treatment systems, such as septic tanks. The regime aims to protect ground and surface water quality from the risks posed by systems that are not working properly. It was introduced under the Water Services (Amendment) Act 2012 and a related set of regulations.

---

[556] *Ibid.*
[557] See: https://www.epa.gov/septic/how-your-septic-system-works
[558] See: https://www.hse.ie/eng/health/hl/water/drinkingwater/have-you-completed-a-septic-tank-system-check.pdf

Inspections started in 2013, and local authorities arrange for inspections to be carried out. The inspectors are appointed and approved by the ***Environmental Protection Agency***. They concentrate on areas with high risk to the environment and public health where drinking water sources or habitats are at risk from waste water discharges.[559]

See also: ***Bungalow Bliss; one-off housing; rural housing***

Service charge – MUD Act 2011　The obligation to establish and maintain a service charge is contained in section 18(1) of the ***Multi-Unit Developments Act 2011*** (MUD Act).

> 18.— (1) An owners' management company shall, as soon as practicable, establish and maintain a scheme in respect of annual service charges from which the owners' management company may discharge ongoing expenditure reasonably incurred on the insurance, maintenance (including cleaning and waste management services) and repair of the common areas of the multi-unit development concerned and on the provision of common or shared services to the owners and occupiers of the units in the development.

In order to fund maintenance of upkeep of the common areas, an ***owners' management company*** (OMC) levies an annual service charge on owners of properties within the development. It is up to the OMC to set the level of service charge to be levied annually on each property in the development. The obligation on unit owners to pay service charges and the entitlement of management companies to collect them arise from the covenants and obligations which both OMCs and multi-unit property owners enter into in the ***conveyancing*** documents by which they purchase their properties.[560] This is in addition to the general obligations that apply to all OMCs as set out in the MUD Act.

Service charges generate the cash flow that an OMC needs to provide services and maintain a development.[561] Depending on the development, service charges pay for:

- Repair and maintenance of ***common areas***, car parks, footpaths and roads
- Cleaning common areas, windows, carpets/mats, gutters and drains
- Lift repairs and inspections

---

[559] See: http://www.citizensinformation.ie/en/housing/owning_a_home/home_owners/domestic_wastewater_treatment.html
[560] Office of the Director of Corporate Enforcement (2008) *Company Law Handbook on Residential Property Owners' Management Companies*, ODCE: Dublin
[561] Competition and Consumer Protection Commission (2017) 'Owners' Management Companies', CCPC, available at: https://www.ccpc.ie/consumers/housing/apartments-and-duplexes/owners-management-companies/

- Electricity and lighting for common areas
- Landscaping and gardening; pest control
- Security – internal locks and doors, intercoms, external doors and gates
- Safety – smoke alarms, fire extinguishers, health and safety inspections
- Refuse collection and recycling
- Professional charges (for example, block/building insurance, public liability insurance, the OMC's legal/auditor fees)

Service charges in Ireland are calculated in line with the head *lease*, which is the original lease document that the developer's solicitor draws up for each property and is the lease signed by the first purchaser. The head lease outlines how service charges should be calculated, what interest should apply and when they should be paid. These calculations vary from *development* to development, with some calculated on a 'per square footage' basis, others having an equal amount for all units, and others calculated on a percentage basis. It is evident that there is no standard means by which service charges are levied.[562]

Non-payment of service charges will inevitably lead to the deterioration and dilapidation of a development. A lack of funds in the OMC in turn often means these debtors are not pursued. The net effect of not pursuing those who owe service charge money is an increase in service charges for those unit owners who are paying in order to pursue the non-payers through legal mechanisms. Stopping the payment of service charges is a breach of contractual obligations under the terms of the lease under which the property was bought. As such, if an owner does not pay their management fees, they may be liable to legal action and any outstanding debts can be tied to the unit. If the owners' management company does not collect charges, it will run short of money and in time it may not be able to provide even the most basic services. This leads to residents withholding their service charge payment in protest as they are unhappy with the service provided.[563]

See also: *sinking fund*

Serviced Sites Fund

The Serviced Sites Fund was announced in 2017 and is designed to 'support delivery of both off- and on-site infrastructure that can unlock local authority-owned lands to deliver affordable homes.'[564] Funds that had been allocated for the second call under the *Local Infrastructure Housing Activation Fund* (LIHAF) were transferred to the new Serviced Sites Fund.

---

[562] McKeown, A and Sirr, L (2018) 'Service Charge Collection in Multi-Unit Developments', in Sirr, L (ed.), *Administration – special housing edition*, Vol. 66, No. 2
[563] Sirr, L (2010) 'Apartment Living and the Multi-unit Developments Bill', *Public Affairs Ireland*, June
[564] See: https://www.oireachtas.ie/en/debates/question/2018-06-20/32/

Shared ownership is a form of *equity* sharing for people who cannot afford to buy their own homes outright. It is the ownership of the property that is shared between the purchaser and a *landlord*, and not the property itself. Shared ownership is typically offered by local authorities or not-for-profit housing associations. In shared ownership schemes, the purchaser buys a share of the ownership of the property (usually 25–75 per cent) and pays a discounted *rent* for the remaining share. Monthly repayments therefore comprise a *mortgage* repayment and a rent payment. As the purchaser's means improve, they may purchase an increased share of the property (usually offered in 10 per cent increments) until they own it outright within a period of 30 years.

Irish shared ownership had its roots in the Housing (Miscellaneous Provisions) Act 1992, and followed closely its British counterparts. In the Irish scheme, the purchaser bought a 40 per cent equity stake and rented the remainder from the local authority. The equity stake was funded via a local authority loan and the remaining stake was paid for by rent, again to the local authority. The ownership was therefore shared between the purchaser and the local authority.[565] From 2003, the rent was set at a figure of 4.3 per cent, comprising interest of 3.8 per cent of the value of the portion of the property leased from the local authority and an administration charge of 0.5 per cent. As there is rent involved, this shared ownership arrangement was officially deemed to be a lease:

(*a*) granted for a term of more than 20 years but less than 100 years,

(*b*) granted on payment to the lessor of a sum of money being not less than 25 per cent, and not more than 75 per cent, of the market value of the house, and

(*c*) which provides for the right of the lessee to purchase, in one or more transactions, the interest of the lessor in the demised house [demise means to convey title, typically in a lease] at a consideration determined in accordance with the provisions of the lease.[566]

If the shared ownership property was sold within twenty years a proportion of the proceeds from the sale had to be returned to the local authority (known as a '*clawback*' mechanism). The proportion of the proceeds to be repaid will be equal to the percentage discount originally received from the local authority but, similar to the *Affordable Housing Scheme*, this declines annually from years 11 to 20. A difficulty with the scheme was that the terms of the *lease* component were not spelled out in the legislation and therefore

---

[565] Kenna, P (2011) *Housing Law, Rights and Policy*, Clarus Press: Dublin
[566] Section 2, Housing (Miscellaneous Provision) Act 1992

important aspects such as maintenance, rent, repairs and quiet enjoyment are not mentioned.

Since 2011, the shared ownership scheme is no longer operable for new applicants. A written response to a Dáil question in 2017 showed that from 1991 to 2010, a total of 16,492 loans were issued under the scheme, of which 3,777 remained at the end of Q3 2016.[567]

Sheltered accommodation

Sheltered housing (also known as retirement housing) means having a flat or bungalow in a block, or on a small estate, where all the other residents are older people (usually over 55). With a few exceptions, all developments (or 'schemes') provide independent, self-contained homes with their own front doors. Properties in most schemes are designed to make life a little easier for older people – with features like raised electric sockets, lowered worktops, walk-in showers, and so on. They are usually linked to an emergency alarm service to call help if needed. Many schemes also have their own 'manager' or 'warden', either living on-site or nearby, whose job is to manage the scheme and help arrange any services residents need. Managed schemes will also usually have some shared or communal facilities such as a lounge for residents to meet, a laundry, a guest flat and a garden.[568]

In Ireland, local authorities are obliged to provide housing for older people in the same way as they do for the rest of the population. As such, some local authorities provide special accommodation for older people – usually community accommodation with special security features, such as wardens and security cameras. Some *approved housing bodies* also provide specific housing for older people.[569]

See also: *residential care; ALONE*

Short-term leasing for social housing

See: *availability arrangements*

S.I. 9 ('BCAR')

The *Building Control (Amendment) Regulations* 2014 (S.I. no 9 of 2014) came into operation on 1 March 2014.

S.I. 365 (opt out)

Statutory Instrument 365 of 2015 allowed prospective self-builders to submit a Declaration of Intention to Opt-Out of Statutory Certification with the *Commencement Notice* and thereby 'opt out' of the *building control* certification process.

In deciding to opt out, it means owners are not required to lodge statutory undertaking and certificates by the designer, *assigned certifier* and

---

[567] See: https://www.kildarestreet.com/wrans/?id=2017-04-04a.764
[568] See: http://www.housingcare.org/jargon-sheltered-housing.aspx
[569] See: http://www.citizensinformation.ie/en/housing/housing_grants_and_schemes/older_people_housing.html

builder, or lodge an inspection plan. Owners are making the decision to not have a design certifier sign off on the building, and have decided not to have an assigned certifier inspect and oversee the works. Furthermore, they will not be able to register a *Certificate of Compliance on Completion* with their local authority.[570] It is not yet clear if buildings that are opted out of the process will have lower values compared to those that undergo certification.

See also: *self-build; Building Control (Amendment) Regulations*

Simms, Herbert[571]

Herbert George Simms was Dublin Corporation housing architect from 1932 until his death in 1948. He was born in London in 1898, and after training as an architect he came to Dublin. In February 1925 he was appointed temporary architect to Dublin Corporation at a salary of eight guineas per week.[572] In 1926 he was authorised to visit London, Liverpool and Manchester to investigate the latest trends in flat buildings.[573] In 1929–1930 he worked for about a year in India as a town planner in the Punjab, before returning to Dublin. In the early 1930s, a separate housing architects' department was formed with specific responsibility for the design and erection of new dwellings, as distinct from their administration and maintenance. Simms was appointed to the new post of Corporation housing architect.

During the sixteen years he was in office, Simms was responsible for the design and erection of some 17,000 new homes,[574] ranging from striking blocks of flats in the central city, influenced by new apartment blocks by de Klerk in Amsterdam and J.P. Oud in Rotterdam,[575] to extensive suburban housing schemes such as those at Crumlin and Cabra.

When Horace O'Rourke retired in 1945, the post of city architect remained unfilled, which increased the pressure of work on the housing architect. On 28 September 1948 Simms, who had already suffered one nervous breakdown, took his own life by throwing himself onto the railway line at Dún Laoghaire; he was not killed immediately but died later the same day at St Michael's Hospital, Dún Laoghaire. According to the suicide note found on his person, he felt that overwork was threatening his sanity.

A tribute by Ernest F.N. Taylor, the city surveyor, was published in the *Irish Builder*: 'Behind a quiet and unassuming manner there lurked a forceful personality; and Mr Simms could uphold his point of view with a vigour that sometimes surprised those who did not know him well. By sheer hard work

[570] Larkin, N (2017) 'Property Clinic: Should I opt out of costly compliance paperwork?', *Irish Times*, 18 May
[571] See: https://www.dia.ie/architects/view/4969/Simms-HerbertGeorge
[572] Anon. (1925) 'News', *Irish Builder*, Vol. 67, 7 February
[573] McManus, R (2002) *Dublin, 1910–1940: Shaping the City and Suburbs*, Four Courts Press: Dublin
[574] Taylor, EFN (1948) 'Tribute to Herbert Simms', *Irish Builder*, Vol. 90, 16 October
[575] Rothery, S (1991) *Ireland and the New Architecture 1900–1940*, Lilliput Press: Dublin

and conscientious devotion to duty, he has made a personal contribution towards the solution of Dublin's housing problem, probably unequalled by anyone in our time …. It is not given to many of us to achieve so much in the space of a short lifetime for the benefit of our fellow men.'[576]

A single leaf wall consists of just one layer of a building material. Single leaf walls of hollow concrete blocks were the most common form of construction in the greater Dublin area for decades. They are different to the *cavity wall* construction common throughout the rest of the country, which consist of two layers of masonry with a cavity in between.[577]

 See also: *house – structural components*

  Single leaf

Section 19 of the *Multi-Unit Developments Act 2011* (MUD Act) sets out the requirement of an *owners' management company* (OMC) to maintain a sinking fund:

  Sinking fund – MUD Act 2011

> 9.— (1) An owners' management company shall establish a building investment fund (in this Act referred to as a 'sinking fund') for the purpose of discharging expenditure reasonably incurred on—
> (*a*) the *refurbishment*;
> (*b*) improvement;
> (*c*) maintenance of a non-recurring nature; or
> (*d*) advice from a suitably qualified person relating to paragraphs (a) to (c) above
> of the multi-unit development in respect of which the owners' management company stands established.

The sinking fund is a savings pot for capital expenditure within the development such as major structural repairs, refurbishment and redecoration, or the replacement of expensive equipment (e.g. a lift). In effect, it is like a pension fund for a development.[578] Crucially, the sinking fund is part of the *service charge*, paid with the service charge by the members of the OMC and then transferred into a separate bank account at a later date. It is usually intended that a sinking fund will be set up and collected over the whole life of the wasting asset.[579]

 There are two main ways to capitalise a sinking fund: the first is a cash contribution from the owners, usually via the annual service charge. This can

---

[576] Taylor, EFN (1948) 'Tribute to Herbert Simms', *Irish Builder*, Vol. 90, 16 October
[577] See: https://passivehouseplus.ie/single-leaf
[578] Gogan, R (2008) *The Essential Guide to Apartment Living in Ireland*, M1 Publications: Dublin
[579] Royal Institution of Chartered Surveyors (2014) *Sinking Funds, Reserve Funds and Depreciation Charges*, RICS Information Paper, second edition, RICS: London

occasionally be supplemented by the raising of a large, one-off contribution from unit owners (OMC members) at the time the common property capital expenditure is to be made; this is widely referred to as a 'special levy'.[580] Although a once-off levy may seem like a simple solution to any once-off funding requirement, there is always uncertainty over whether owners have the ability or willingness to pay such a levy. At the Beacon South Quarter development in Dublin in 2017 the OMC passed a motion to call on a once-off levy to members for €10,000 each to cover the cost of an expected €10 million bill for safety works and repairs to a water ingress situation.[581]

The second option for financing sinking funds is through loan finance from financial markets or from public authorities. This 'debt financing' refers to the OMC taking up a loan to cover the costs of repairs or other one-off expenditure. The problem with loan financing is that common property does not lend itself to use as loan collateral, as it is not normally possible to separate it from privately owned units.[582] In the Irish context, all unit owners would be required to pledge their property as collateral, and many of those units would have existing borrowings already secured, so this would make it difficult to secure funding from the usual banking sources.[583]

The MUD Act determined that the sinking fund contribution from the service charge should be €200 per member per annum 'or an amount otherwise agreed at an AGM', meaning that OMC members may vote to increase or reduce that sum as they see fit. Ideally, contributions to the sinking fund should be ring-fenced and immediately paid into the sinking fund when payment is made. In the context of most MUDs, €200 is a very small sum per housing unit given the capital-intensive nature of elements such as replacing a lift or repairing a roof. The fact that this amount can be reduced by a vote at an AGM weakens the effectiveness of the legislative requirement even more. Research by Malone[584] has shown that sinking funds are regularly used for ongoing, day-to-day, rather than strategic, expenditure, which is not their aim. This rate of expenditure varied from 5 per cent to 30 per cent of the sinking fund per annum.

The existence and financial health of a sinking fund is something frequently overlooked when purchasing a multi-unit property.

[580] Arkcoll, K, Guilding, C, Lamminamki, D, McManus, L and Warnken, J (2013) 'Funding Common Property Expenditure in Multi-owned Housing Schemes', *Property Management*, Vol. 31, No. 4, pp. 282–296
[581] RTÉ (2017) 'Beacon apartments company to vote on €10k owners' levy', *RTÉ News*, 16 March
[582] Arkcoll, K, Guilding, C, Lamminamki, D, McManus, L and Warnken, J (2013) 'Funding Common Property Expenditure in Multi-owned Housing Schemes', *Property Management*, Vol. 31, No. 4, pp. 282–296
[583] Malone, F (2017) 'Financial Planning in Multi-unit Developments', MSc thesis, Dublin Institute of Technology
[584] *Ibid.*

Site coverage is the ratio of building footprint over the total area of the site. **Site coverage**
     See also: ***plot ratio; density, housing***

The practice of monetising agricultural farmland by selling sites, often with **Site farming**
direct access from the road (road frontage) for residential development, which
is typically for ***one-off housing***.
     See also: ***septic tank; rural housing; Bungalow Bliss***

A site value tax (SVT – sometimes known as a land value tax) is a tax on the **Site value tax**
value of the ***land***, disregarding any improvements (such as a house) on the
land. This allow property owners a return on capital for the improvements
they make, but no excess returns due to increases in the ***value*** of the land.
Proponents of SVT argue that part of what gives land its value is public
goods, and that this value belongs to wider society rather than individuals.[585]
The value of the site is derived from subtracting the ***replacement cost*** of the
house from its ***market value***. The residual is the value of the site. On this
basis, every owner of land would make a contribution to their local authority
based on the value of their site. As property is immobile, evasion is more
challenging. For local authorities, the liability to pay is limited to those who
would receive the benefits of the SVT receipts. In addition, liability for SVT
cannot be passed on to consumers and producers. More significantly, it is
argued that a SVT would militate against property speculation and help
moderate boom and bust cycles. For owners, the system of SVT means that
even if they improve their site (e.g. by developing it) their tax liability would
not increase. Hence, SVT should not be a disincentive to property development. The introduction of the ***Residential Property Price Register*** has
significantly increased the easiness with which a SVT could be facilitated.
     The advantages of a SVT are that:

- It is arguably more equitable than other forms of property taxation
- It counteracts market disincentives to develop the land
- It encourages compact city centre development and productive use of land
- Less information and fewer inspections are needed for the calculations
- Owners who have developed land are rewarded for so doing, while those
  who have not developed valuable land are encouraged to do so[586]

In 2009, the Commission on Taxation looked at site/land value tax and concluded that if a land value tax policy proposal was pursued it would take a

[585] Ozimek, A (2015) 'The Problem With 100% Land Value Taxes', *Forbes*, 29 March,
available at: https://www.forbes.com/sites/modeledbehavior/2015/03/29/the-problem-with-100-
land-value-taxes/#42fd5f305349
[586] Tax Strategy Group (2012) *Taxation of Property*, Department of Finance: Dublin

number of years to become established and would involve a long and sustained challenge for policy-makers to inform the community of its benefits and to implement the proposal. 'We therefore recommend that a land or site value tax should not be pursued at this stage'.[587]

See also: *development contribution scheme; planning gain; stamp duty; local property tax; residual value*

Slum housing   Often informal and illegal, slum housing is characterised by its density, unsafe and unhealthy living conditions, and frequent *overcrowding*.

UN-Habitat defines a slum household as:[588] a group of individuals living under the same roof in an urban area who lack one or more of the following:

1. Durable housing of a permanent nature that protects against extreme climate conditions
2. Sufficient living space which means not more than three people sharing the same room
3. Easy access to safe water in sufficient amounts at an affordable price
4. Access to adequate sanitation in the form of a private or public toilet shared by a reasonable number of people
5. *Security of tenure* that prevents forced *evictions*

See also: *Housing Act 1966; ghetto; tenements*

Snag list   A snag list is a detailed inventory of outstanding details (snags) compiled by the owner of a newly constructed house (or their architect or similar professional) that still have to be rectified or completed. A snag list can range from cosmetic issues to structural faults to breaches of *building regulations*. A good snag list will have a table of numbered snags with details of location, issue, remedy, photographs and a box for the builder to check when the work is done.

Social exclusion   Poverty and social exclusion are often inter-related. The official definition of social exclusion is: 'People are living in poverty if their income and resources (material, cultural and social) are so inadequate as to preclude them from having a standard of living which is regarded as acceptable by Irish society generally. As a result of inadequate income and other resources people may be excluded and marginalised from participating in activities which are considered the norm for other people in society.'[589]

---

[587] Commission on Taxation (2009) *Commission on Taxation Report*, Government Publications Office: Dublin
[588] UN Habitat (2007) *State of the World's Cities 2006–7*, UN Habitat: Nairobi
[589] Government of Ireland (1997) *National Anti-Poverty Strategy – Sharing in Progress 1997–2007*, Government of Ireland: Dublin

There are a number of structural factors that contribute to the existence of poverty. According to Combat Poverty,[590] the uneven distribution of economic resources, including housing, means that not all people have the same opportunities. In terms of housing, people in poverty are more likely to be dependent on the state to meet their housing needs, whether through subsidised private rented accommodation or *social housing*. They are also at greater risk of living in sub-standard accommodation and of becoming homeless.

See also: *homelessness; fuel poverty; transport poverty and equity; affordability*

For information on permanent local authority housing (i.e. not leased), see *council housing*.

Social housing

There are more than 37,000 *households*[591] in the *private rented sector* in receipt of *Housing Assistance Payment* (HAP), a rate that is rising at more than 300 households per week.[592] Some 50,000 households have their housing needs met via HAP and the *Rental Accommodation Scheme* (RAS), and some 40,000 *landlords* or agents are currently in receipt of HAP and RAS payments.[593]

Although social housing began as the provision of state-constructed housing, since the 1990s it has transformed into mostly comprising financial assistance to landlords or tenants to be housed in the private rented sector. This was for several reasons, but included a change in funding mechanisms from central government (from loans to capital grants), and a general lack of funding in local authorities whose stock had been reduced by *tenant purchase* schemes where the revenue from these sales was not sufficient to replace the lost stock. In fact, 'the extent of the rights won by social housing tenants arguably ensured that the sector became increasingly unattractive to the state, and that the longer term future of the social housing system would prove untenable.'[594] The period from 1966 to 1988 was the critical turning point in the shift of Irish housing policy from a period of strong expansion of the social housing stock in Ireland since the early 1930s to an equally strong movement to sell off as much of that same stock as possible to its tenants.

The years 1991–2003 were characterised by local authority housing and housing association renting, with subsidised private renting as a stepping stone to either. This phase comprised a mix of public and private not-for-profit provision, with a gradually declining role for public housing offers

---

[590] See: http://www.combatpoverty.ie/povertyinireland/whatispoverty.htm
[591] See: https://data.gov.ie/dataset/hap-scheme-2014-2018
[592] Burns, S (2018) 'Just 8% of properties affordable for those on rental supports', *Irish Times*, 16 August
[593] See: https://www.oireachtas.ie/en/debates/question/2017-10-26/20/
[594] Hayden, A (2014) 'Irish Social Housing: The Path to Decline, 1966–1988', in Sirr, L (ed.), *Renting in Ireland: The Private, Voluntary and Social Sectors*, IPA: Dublin

combined with a growing stepping stone role for private for-profit providers. From the early 1990s onwards the diversification of the social housing
offer became evident in the sector. A key aspect of a 1991 policy shift was
encouraging higher levels of building by voluntary housing associations (see:
approved housing bodies) and housing cooperatives. At the same time, this
phase was marked by a significant growth in visibility and activity in the
not-for-profit housing association sector. The number of registered housing
associations grew from 75 in the early 1980s to 470 by 2001 (to 500+ in
2018). Output from the sector grew from under 5 per cent of social housing
provision in the 1980s to an average of 33 per cent in the early to mid-1990s
and reached a high point in 2002 with 1,360 units, equating to 21 per cent
of total social housing output that year.[595]

According to Finnerty and O'Connell,[596] the years after 2003 are characterised by the dominance of private for-profit and not-for-profit provision,
in a hybrid and complex provision mix when compared to the previous
phases.[597] The third phase involves a dilution and further diversification of
the social housing offer away from the norms associated with the first and
second phases. The displacement of direct provision by local authorities and
housing associations towards private market-based sources was clearly signalled in 2009, when the then Housing Minister stated that:

> We can no longer rely on the traditional acquisition and construction
> approach to meeting social housing needs. We must embrace every
> opportunity for delivering additional supply through market-based
> mechanisms.[598]

This policy shift was given added impetus in the 2011 government *Housing
Policy Statement*, which envisaged that:

> A restructuring of the social housing investment programme to allow
> for the delivery of new social housing through more flexible funding
> models will provide key sources of delivery in the period ahead.

Driven by the requirement to achieve fiscal consolidation during the
economic crisis, 2009 saw the beginning of major reductions in the allocation

---

[595] O'Connell, C (2007) *The State and Housing in Ireland: Ideology, Policy and Practice*, Nova: New York
[596] Finnerty, J and O'Connell, C (2014) '50 Years of the Social Housing "Offer" in Ireland: The Casualisation Thesis Examined', in Sirr, L (ed.), *Renting in Ireland: The Private, Voluntary and Social Sectors*, IPA: Dublin
[597] O'Connell, C (2007) *The State and Housing in Ireland: Ideology, Policy and Practice*, Nova: New York
[598] Finneran, M (2009) 'Ministerial Address' to Irish Council for Social Housing Annual Confer-ence, Athlone, 16 September

of Exchequer capital investment for the construction of social housing and a switch from capital investment to current expenditure. From a position of accounting for 70 per cent of social housing expenditure in 2008, capital investment's share was almost the same as current expenditure by 2010. Within an increasing current expenditure budget, there was also a shift away from **Rent Supplement** to the consolidation of all housing supports in the local government sector.[599]

This reorientation towards addressing a greater proportion of social housing need through current expenditure delivery mechanisms enabled more needs to be addressed in the short run within the tightened budgetary environment. This approach was facilitated initially by the unprecedented growth and over-supply of housing leading up to the property crash. The *Social Housing Strategy 2020*, published by the government in November 2014, provided a framework for off-balance-sheet delivery of social housing units underpinned by a multi-annual capital and current housing programme. This acknowledged the potential leveraging of off-balance-sheet mechanisms and **public–private partnership** (PPP) **procurement** opportunities to deliver social housing.[600]

In Ireland, low-income households are now almost certainly destined to be accommodated either in a hybrid form of social housing which is predominantly owned by private landlords and leased temporarily by the social landlords (Rental Accommodation Scheme, Housing Assistance Payment or long-term leasing), or in accommodation owned by housing associations and financed through private finance.[601]

In relying increasingly on non-direct state organisations to deliver a supply of social housing, it had been argued that governments were having the best of all worlds: using arms-length private entities whose borrowing – it was assumed – would not appear on the government balance sheet, but at the same time retaining significant control of these bodies. In Ireland, a 2018 decision from **Eurostat** put the borrowings of approved housing bodies (AHBs), on whom the government rely to deliver social housing in increasing numbers, back on the state's balance sheet (this had also happened in England in 2015).[602] The decision to move these bodies onto the state balance sheet relates to the fact that they are almost entirely state-funded and that local

---

[599] Kilkenny, P and O'Callaghan, D (2018) *Department of Public Expenditure and Reform – Spending Review 2018: Current and Capital Expenditure on Social Housing Delivery Mechanisms*, Department of Public Expenditure and Reform: Dublin

[600] *Ibid.*

[601] Finnerty, J and O'Connell, C (2014) '50 Years of the Social Housing "Offer" in Ireland: The Casualisation Thesis Examined', in Sirr, L (ed.), *Renting in Ireland: The Private, Voluntary and Social Sectors*, IPA: Dublin

[602] For more on this see: Gurran, N and Bramley, G (2017) 'The Housing System' in Gurran, N and Bramley, G (eds), *Urban Planning and the Housing Market*, Palgrave Macmillan: London

authorities oversee how houses are allocated and what rates are charged to tenants. In effect, the AHBs are not considered to be 'arms-length' bodies. Eurostat considered that:

> … the AHBs are controlled by government due to several reasons which include the degree of financing, contractual agreement, special regulations and risk exposure (in particular, in the context of the new Payment and Availability Agreement, via the Continuation Agreement) …. As a consequence […] the AHBs, being Non-Profit Institutions controlled by government and not being market producers, should be classified in the government sector.[603]

Recent changes to the social housing offer represent a process of casualisation as they arise from a displacement of local authority provision and its replacement by (minimal) housing association direct provision or long-term leasing, or by subsidised provision by participating for-profit landlords.

Issues with the ongoing use of the private rented sector to house social housing tenants include:

- The lack of *security of tenure* of social housing tenants
- The cost of social housing – both the monthly rental cost to the state and the cost benefit of paying rent instead of constructing housing (it could be argued that a financial benefit with leasing is that maintenance is mainly the responsibility of the landlord, but equally with construction there are no rent reviews)
- The impact on other existing and potential users of the private rented sector (e.g. students, overseas workers) as so much stock is taken up housing rent-supported tenants
- The consequent rise in rents and impact on disposable income and spending power
- The significant transfer of wealth from the state to a relatively small number of landlords

See also: *AirBnB; residualisation; social housing waiting list; National Association of Tenants' Organisations; policy, housing*

Social Housing Capital Investment Programme (SHIP)   The Social Housing Capital Investment Programme (SHCIP) provides funding to local authorities for the provision of social housing by means of construction and acquisition.

---

[603] Extract from letter from Eurostat to CSO, 2 March 2018, available at: https://ec.europa.eu/eurostat/documents/1015035/8683865/Advice-2018-IE-Sector-classification-Approved-Housing-Bodies.pdf/4813b7be-a51b-4952-bbb2-46906aacbbdd

The Social Housing Current Expenditure Programme was extended in November 2009 to allow for the direct provision of *dwellings* for *social housing* purposes by *approved housing bodies* (AHBs). Under the arrangements, approved housing bodies are allowed to procure units in two ways:

- The AHB can *lease* units from a private owner/*developer* and make them available to persons assessed as being in need of social housing support, or
- The AHB can purchase/construct units using private/*Housing Finance Agency* (HFA) finance, which are then made available to meet housing needs in return for an availability payment from the housing authority

In both cases, where proposals are approved, the housing authority enters into a *Payment and Availability* (P&A) agreement directly with the approved body to secure the units for social housing purposes.[604]

The SHCEP (previously referred to as the *Social Housing Leasing Initiative* (SHLI)) recoups to local authorities (LAs) the cost of dwellings sourced under SHCEP to be used for the purposes of providing social housing support. Long-term lease arrangements, entered into by local authorities and AHBs, are secured at 80–85 per cent of the current *market rent* for a minimum of ten years. Availability agreements under *Capital Advance Leasing Facility* (CALF) are secured by LAs with AHBs at 92–95 per cent of the current market rent. The level of discount on market rent that is agreed by the LA is a function of the amount of risk transferred to the AHB regarding responsibility for ongoing maintenance (excluding structural) and responsibility for tenant management.

The units funded under SHCEP come from a number of different sources:

1. The units can be leased directly from the private sector by either a LA or an AHB. These units are privately owned, including from institutional investors. These leases are typically classed as being either long term (typically 10–20 years) or short term (1–10 years). In addition, an *Enhanced Leasing Initiative* was launched in January 2018 and is targeted at private investment and new-build or new to the market properties to be delivered at scale.
2. Units funded under SHCEP can be built or acquired by AHBs, with support available through the Capital Advance Leasing Facility
3. There are a number of other sources of units funded by SHCEP and secured under lease arrangements including units leased to LAs and AHBs from *National Asset Residential Property Services* (NARPS), unsold affordable dwellings managed by AHBs for LAs and the AHB

---

[604] The Housing Agency (2016) *Guidance Note on the Capital Advance Leasing Facility (CALF) for Approved Housing Bodies and Housing Authorities*, The Housing Agency: Dublin

Mortgage to Rent Scheme. Properties that are privately owned but vacant can be remediated and leased with support under the ***Repair and Leasing Scheme*** (RLS) and are also funded by SHCEP.[605]

Social Housing Leasing Initiative (SHLI) In order to increase the availability of properties for social housing provision, the ***Department of Housing, Planning, Community and Local Government*** launched the Social Housing Leasing Initiative in 2009. This involved housing authorities leasing properties from private property owners for the purposes of providing accommodation to households on social housing waiting lists. It was replaced by the ***Social Housing Current Expenditure Programme***.

See also: ***long-term leasing arrangement***

Social housing related programmes – summary The following table provides a summary of some of the various state ***social housing***-related programmes in Ireland.[606]

Programme	Objective
Local Authority Construction & Acquisition (*Social Housing Investment Programme* (*SHIP*))	To provide funding to local authorities (LAs) for the provision of social housing by means of construction and acquisition. It also covers expenditure under the RAPID Delivery programme, *Part V* acquisitions, Land Aggregation Scheme and the Public Safety Initiative in unfinished housing developments.
Capital Assistance Scheme (CAS)	To provide essential funding to AHBs for the provision of accommodation for persons with specific categories of housing need such as homeless and older persons, people with disabilities, returning emigrants and victims of domestic violence.
Returning Vacant Properties to Productive Use (*Voids*)	To provide funding to allow LAs bring back into use long-term vacant social housing units.
Regeneration Programme	To target the country's most disadvantaged communities, including those defined by the most extreme social exclusion, unemployment and *anti-social behaviour*, through the provision of a holistic programme of physical, social and economic regeneration.
Disabled Persons Grants Scheme (DPGs) & Extensions and Improvement Works in Lieu of Local Authority Housing (IWILs)	To provide for the needs of older people or people with a disability living in social housing, who may require chairlifts or the installation of a downstairs bedroom or bathroom and, where necessary, extensions that are needed to address overcrowding (families who outgrow their current dwelling).

[605] Kilkenny, P and O'Callaghan, D (2018) *Department of Public Expenditure and Reform – Spending Review 2018: Current and Capital Expenditure on Social Housing Delivery Mechanisms*, Department of Public Expenditure and Reform: Dublin
[606] Table from *Rebuilding Ireland* (2016)

Estate-wide Remedial Works Scheme	To provide support for LAs to significantly improve run-down estates by improving the layout, addressing issues of anti-social behaviour, improving the housing fabric, and, where possible, addressing issues of social exclusion.
Housing Adaptation Grants for Older People and People with a Disability for private houses	To provide targeted support to private houses, via the Housing Adaptation Grant, Housing Aid for Older People and Mobility Aids Grant, to enable older people and people with disabilities to remain living independently in their own homes for longer and also to facilitate early return from hospital stays.
Energy Efficiency Retrofit Programme for local authority homes	To improve the energy efficiency and comfort levels of older LA homes, benefitting those at risk of fuel poverty, while also making a contribution to Ireland's carbon emissions reduction targets and energy reduction targets for 2020.
Social Housing Current Expenditure Programme (SHCEP)	Under this Programme, LAs are recouped for the cost of long-term lease agreements or rental agreements that they make with private property owners or AHBs. The arrangements are usually for periods of 10–30 years.
Capital Advance Leasing Facility (CALF)	Up-front repayable loan of up to 30 per cent of the relevant capital cost of construction or acquisition projects where units will be made available to the SHCEP. The programme facilitates AHBs raising private finance, including from the *Housing Finance Agency* (HFA).
Rental Accommodation Scheme (RAS)	Targeted scheme for households in receipt of *Rent Supplement* for more than 18 months, and who are assessed by housing authorities as having a long-term housing need.
Housing Assistance Payment (HAP)	New scheme that will replace Rent Supplement and RAS as the support available to households with a long-term housing need who are housed in rented accommodation.

The *social housing* waiting list is officially known as the 'record of qualified households'. It is a list maintained by individual local authorities of people who are qualified for social housing support, but who have not yet received it.

Social housing waiting list

The social housing waiting list comes from the Social Housing Needs Assessment 2018. There were 71,858 *households* on the 'waiting list' as of June 2018.

Key points about the list are:

- The four Dublin local authorities account for over 43 per cent of the list.
- The majority of households qualified for social housing support on the June 2018 count date reside in the private rented sector.

- 54.4 per cent of those qualified for housing support are unemployed.
- Just under half of those on the waiting list are single-person households.
- Being in receipt of **Rent Supplement** is the most commonly cited basis of need for social housing support.
- 17.6 per cent of those on the waiting list have a specific accommodation need from a member(s) having a physical, sensory, mental or intellectual impairment.
- The majority (74.6 per cent) of those qualified for social housing support are Irish citizens; 25.4 per cent were non-Irish nationals, with the main applicant from an EU/EEA country in most of these households.
- Over a quarter of the 71,858 households qualified for support are waiting more than seven years for a social housing support.

See also: *transfer list; private rented sector*

Social justice

Social justice has been described as an 'idea often voiced but rarely understood'.[607] According to Kenna, it is a concept which is often associated with rights, and particularly housing rights. The term is used to demand a greater degree of economic egalitarianism, an income or property redistribution, as well as laws and policies which promote equality of opportunity or equality of outcome for specific groups in society. Social justice (and human rights) perspectives on the housing system view housing as an essential part of the development of human dignity.[608]

Social justice is mentioned in the Constitution in relation to property rights (see: **Constitution of Ireland**) and is recognised as a principle of Irish constitutional law.[609] However, the distinction between 'common good' and 'social justice', with both being mentioned in Article 43 of the Constitution, remains blurred, and both have increasingly been used interchangeably in property-related legal cases.[610] Academic literature suggests that there is a greater degree of the element of 'redistribution' implied in social justice than in 'the greater good'.

See also: **housing rights approach to housing; Social Justice Ireland**

Social Justice Ireland

Social Justice Ireland is a non-profit, non-governmental organisation which focuses on tackling the causes of economic, social, cultural or environmental problems and issues. Formerly known as the Conference of Religious in Ireland (CORI), it was established in 2009 and is an independent think tank and justice advocacy organisation that advances the lives of people and

---

[607] Miller, D (1976) *Social Justice*, Clarendon Press: Oxford
[608] Kenna, P (2011) *Housing Law, Rights and Policy*, Clarus Press: Dublin
[609] *Ibid.*
[610] *Ibid.*

communities through providing independent social analysis and effective policy development to create a sustainable future for every member of society and for societies as a whole. Social Justice Ireland produces a wide range of research reports, and is especially active on **housing policy**. The housing policy objective of Social Justice Ireland is: 'To ensure that adequate and appropriate accommodation is available for all people and to develop an equitable system for allocating resources within the housing sector.'[611]

Social Justice Ireland advocates in respect of the need to increase **social housing** construction in light of spiralling private rents, increasing **homelessness**, households on the **social housing waiting list**, and the issue of long-term mortgage **arrears**, as well as for an off-balance-sheet model of **cost rental** provision in an effort to increase the supply of affordable rental accommodation to the scale required.

The Society of Chartered Surveyors Ireland (SCSI) is the professional body for chartered surveyors in Ireland. The Royal Institution of Chartered Surveyors (RICS) is its partner and equivalent body in the United Kingdom. Members of the chartered surveying profession are typically employed in the construction, land and property markets through private practice, in central and local government, in state agencies, in academic institutions, in business organisations and in non-governmental organisations. Members' services are diverse and can include offering strategic advice on the economics, valuation, law, technology, finance and management of all aspects of the construction, land and property industry.[612] There are twelve professional groups within the SCSI: commercial agency surveyors, property and facilities management surveyors, residential agency surveyors, valuation surveyors, art and antiques surveyors, geomatic surveyors, mineral surveyors, planning and development surveyors, rural surveyors, building surveyors, project management surveyors and quantity surveyors.

Society of Chartered Surveyors Ireland

Chartered surveyors typically need both an appropriate third-level qualification (e.g. a degree in Estate Management, Property Economics, or Quantity Surveying) and completion of the Assessment of Professional Competence (APC), which is a period of on-the-job structured training and assessment. Members of the SCSI are also eligible to join the RICS.

In housing development, speculation is the buying and selling of land in the hope of short-term profit. This is often achieved by buying land, increasing its value by obtaining planning permission, often also lobbying for changes in building standards to accommodate more profitable housing **development**

Speculation

[611] Healy et al. (2018) 'Social Justice Matters: 2018 Guide to a Fairer Society', *Socio-Economic Review 2018*, Social Justice Ireland: Dublin
[612] See: https://www.scsi.ie/about_us/what_is_the_scsi

(e.g. higher buildings, smaller apartment sizes), before selling the land on without ever having crystallised risk by commencing construction.

As land changes hands from speculator to purchaser at increasing sales prices, it increases costs for the next owner should they develop housing to sell. In turn, this then leads to higher sales prices to the public for any housing developed, thereby affecting *affordability* and potentially creating a price *bubble*.

The Adam Smith Institute has examined speculation in land, saying: 'The speculative behaviour of interest in the context of taxation is where the investment motive predominates, where there is heavy reliance on price movements to provide profit, and where considerations of capital growth compete strongly with, or outweigh, any interest in rental income. That speculative activity can ultimately create a bubble in a market is well-attested.'[613]

Speculation is rife in house-building, as Winterbourne describes:[614] In the speculative house-building model, developers sink huge sums of capital into purchasing land. The three ways to gain profit in this model are: waiting on land values to rise; gaining planning permission for housing on a site; and building and selling houses. Land value is central even in the third of these because 70 per cent of a house's financial value is the land it is built upon. Thus, the most important (and risky) part of developers' business models relates to the financial value of land. As a consequence, large housebuilders are in no hurry to build at all. A trickle of housing supply is less likely to have any impact upon land values (see: *absorption rate*). And, in the meantime, this model also crowds out SMEs and custom builders, who cannot compete with the huge capital sums spent by the large developers. This means a competition on the basis of delivering homes as a commodity with use value is largely absent.

Speculation in property is counteracted in many countries through taxation measures such as a tax on second homes, a tax on foreign investors, and capital gains taxes on the sale of *principle private residences* that have been held for less than a specified period (e.g. ten years). These fiscal measures tend to lessen the potential short-term profit that can be made and thus make speculation on the investment less attractive.

Speculation in land and property has been a feature of real estate for over a century. It happens in similar forms in different countries, but is particularly prominent in jurisdictions that have a similar Anglo-Saxon planning and development system to Ireland's (e.g. Australia).

See also: *site value tax; financialisation of housing*

---

[613] Heywood, A and Hackett, P (2013) 'The Case for a Property Speculation Tax', a Smith Institute discussion paper, The Adam Smith Institute: London

[614] Winterburn, M (2018) 'Home Economics: Reversing the Financialisation of Housing', *Journal of Architecture*, Vol. 23, No. 1, pp. 184–193

A split mortgage is where a lender agrees to split a borrower's mortgage loan **Split mortgage**[615] into an affordable mortgage loan, which the borrower continues to repay, and a remaining balance, which is set aside or 'warehoused' until a later date.

See also: ***arrears; Code of Conduct on Mortgage Arrears; Mortgage Arrears Resolution Process***

See: ***adverse possession***   **Squatters' rights**

Squatting is the occupation of property, usually abandoned or disused resi- **Squatting** dential, without the permission of the owner, in order to live there. Squatting is often a 'statement' action or protest. Five main types of squatter have been identified:[616]

1. Deprivation-based squatting: e.g. homeless people squatting for housing need
2. Squatting as an alternative housing strategy: e.g. people unprepared to wait on municipal lists to be housed take direct action
3. Entrepreneurial squatting: e.g. people breaking into buildings to service the need of a community for cheap bars, clubs, etc.
4. Conservational squatting: e.g. preserving monuments because the authorities have let them decay
5. Political squatting: e.g. activists squatting buildings as protests or to make social centres

Ireland has seen various examples of squatting, most famously under the conservational squatting heading with the occupation of Georgian buildings in Hume Street, Dublin in 1970; and political squatting with the occupation of Apollo House, Dublin in 2016 and other houses in 2018 by housing activists and homeless people.

See also: ***adverse possession; homelessness***

Stamp duty is paid on certain written documents (known as 'instruments') **Stamp duty** that transfer ownership of property or are agreements to transfer ownership of property (e.g. when buying a house). The term 'property' includes: land, buildings, business assets (like goodwill), and shares, stocks and marketable securities (both quoted and unquoted). An instrument is liable to stamp duty if it is executed (signed, sealed or both) in Ireland, or outside Ireland if it relates to property in Ireland or something done or to be done in Ireland. Stamp duty is also payable on bank cards, pensions, life and non-life

---

[615] Central Bank of Ireland (2013) *Code of Conduct on Mortgage Arrears*, Central Bank of Ireland: Dublin
[616] Pruijt, HD (2011) 'The Logic of Urban Squatting', *International Journal of Urban and Regional Research*, Vol. 37, No. 1, pp. 19–45

insurance premiums, as well as on transfers of marketable securities or stock where the transfer takes place electronically.

In the conveyancing of residential property, the level of stamp duty payable by the purchaser will be based on the price paid for the property. The rate of stamp duty is 1 per cent on the first €1 million 'consideration' and 2 per cent for consideration in excess of €1 million.

Stamp duty is also paid on certain leases and agreements to *lease*. Stamp duty must be paid on a lease if:

- The lease is in writing
- The rent is at least €40,000 per year (if the lease was executed before 25 December 2017 the annual rent is €30,000), and
- The period of the lease is no longer than 35 years, or is for an indefinite period

There are certain exemptions from the requirement to pay stamp duty. According to the Revenue Commissioners: if an instrument is executed 'to transfer property from: your spouse to you; or your civil partner to you the instrument is exempt from stamp duty. You can claim this exemption even if you and your spouse are separated. You cannot claim the exemption if the transfer involves a third party or sub-sale.' Similarly, 'If you receive property pursuant to an order under section 174 of the Civil Partnership and Certain Rights and Obligations of *Cohabitants* Act 2010, you do not pay stamp duty on the instrument. However, the exemption only applies if there is no third party involved.'[617]

See also: *data – housing output issues*

Standards for rented houses — See: *Housing (Standards for Rented Houses) Regulations 2019*

Step-down housing — Step-down housing is accommodation that can either be institutional or independent for people who have been discharged from hospital or other care and who have ongoing physical or mental health needs but who cannot return home. There is usually on-site care available, sometimes on a 24-hour basis.

See also: *retirement village; downsizing*

Strategic Development Zone (SDZ) — Strategic Development Zones (SDZs) were established in planning legislation in 2000 to enable government to designate certain parcels of land for a fast-track planning process, where the development of those lands is considered to be of strategic national importance (e.g. Dublin Docklands).

[617] See: https://www.revenue.ie/en/property/stamp-duty/working-out-your-stamp-duty/transfers-between-spouses-civil-partners-or-cohabitants.aspx

SDZs are a master planning concept which aim to create sustainable communities. A planning scheme prepared for an SDZ indicates in detail the manner in which a local authority considers the lands should be developed. It has a number of important features that make it distinct from the normal planning system for development:

- A SDZ forms part of the ***development plan*** in force in the area of the scheme and it supersedes any contrary provisions of the development plan.
- There is no appeal opportunity to ***An Bórd Pleánala*** against the decision of the ***planning authority*** on an individual planning application for development within an SDZ.
- The planning authority can use any powers available to it (including ***compulsory purchase order*** procedures) for the purposes of providing, securing or facilitating the provision of the SDZ.
- An authority may enter into agreements with landowners to facilitate the development of the SDZ. It is envisaged that such agreements will form part of the draft planning scheme and will relate to several matters, including the phasing of development.[618]

See also: ***development plan; local area plan***

Strategic Environmental Assessment[619]

Strategic Environmental Assessment (SEA) is the process by which environmental considerations are required to be fully integrated into the preparation of plans and programmes prior to their final adoption. The objectives of the SEA are to provide for a high level of protection of the environment and to promote sustainable ***development***.

The steps involved in SEA are:

- Screening (determining whether or not SEA is required)
- Scoping (determining the range of environmental issues to be covered by the SEA)
- The preparation of an Environmental Report
- The carrying out of consultations
- The integration of environmental considerations into the plan or programme
- The publication of information on the decision (SEA Statement)

See also: ***Environmental Impact Assessment/Environmental Impact Assessment Report***

[618] See: http://buckplanning.blogspot.com/2006/11/strategic-development-zones-and-irish.html
[619] See: http://www.epa.ie/monitoringassessment/assessment/sea/

Strategic Housing Developments

The ***Planning and Development (Housing) and Residential Tenancies Act 2016*** introduced a new category of ***development*** referred to as Strategic Housing Developments (SHD). This allows for planning applications for certain developments to be sent directly to ***An Bord Pleanála*** for decision (note: developments that meet the criteria below must use this process – it is not optional). The measure be applied until 31 December 2019 at which time the period may be extended to 31 December 2021, subject to a review process.

The types of housing development applications which can be made direct to An Bord Pleanála are as follows:

(*a*) the development of 100 or more houses on land zoned for residential use or for a mixture of residential and other uses;

(*b*) the development of student accommodation units which, when combined, contain 200 or more bed spaces, on land the zoning of which facilitates the provision of student accommodation or a mixture of student accommodation and other uses thereon; and

(*c*) development that includes developments of the type referred to in paragraph (*a*) and of the type referred to in paragraph (*b*), or containing a mix of houses and student accommodation or

(*d*) the alteration of an existing ***planning permission*** granted under section 34 (other than under subsection (3A) where the proposed alteration relates to ***development*** specified in paragraph (*a*), (*b*), or (*c*).

There is a two-stage application process for ***developers*** using this route. Stage 1 involves pre-application consultation first with the relevant ***planning authority*** and then with An Bord Pleanála who will form and issue an opinion as to whether documents submitted constitute a reasonable basis for an application or whether further consideration or amendment to the documents are required. Once the pre-planning consultations have taken place, there is no opportunity to submit further information even if merely to rectify or clarify a point. At Stage 2, planning applicants will submit applications for strategic housing directly to An Bord Pleanála. Applications are to be decided within a mandatory 16-week time period (if there is no public hearing). The Bord can be penalised if it fails to meet this deadline.

The public and other persons or bodies can participate in the planning process for Strategic Housing Developments (SHD) at application stage. Members of the public can make a submission or observations on a SHD application to An Bord Pleanála and such submission or observations will be considered by An Bord Pleanála when making a decision on the application. Before an applicant submits an SHD application to An Bord Pleanála they are required to publish a notice of such a proposal in a newspaper circulating in the area of the proposed development.

See: *purpose-built student accommodation*   Student housing

According to *Sustainable Urban Housing: Design Standards for New Apartments – Guidelines for Planning Authorities*,[620] a studio apartment is a small unit with a combined living/sleeping area, generally provided for a single person. The minimum size of a new studio apartment is 37 square metres (which is smaller than the legal size of a New York *micro-home*) to include storage of 3 square metres, leaving a net habitable space of 34 square metres.
    See also: *apartment; apartment design standards; garden flat*   Studio apartment

Subletting occurs when a *tenant* permits another party to *lease* the rental property that the tenant has leased from the *landlord*. The tenant then assumes the position of landlord (known as the head tenant) in relation to his or her subtenant. Subletting can only take place with the consent of the landlord. Subletting is not available in *approved housing body* tenancies.
    See also: *Residential Tenancies Board; notice of termination*   Subletting

A sub-prime ('below' prime) *mortgage* is lending offered to applicants who would be considered to have a poor credit rating and at higher than average risk of mortgage default. Sub-prime borrowers tend to have difficulty in obtaining housing finance from traditional retail banks. Sub-prime mortgages usually have a higher interest rate attached to them due to the increased risk of default.
    As applicants must demonstrate that they had been refused a mortgage from two other lending institutions, the *Rebuilding Ireland Home Loan* scheme therefore exhibits a key attribute of sub-prime lending. By definition, these applicants were considered to be too risky to lend money to, thus exposing the government scheme to a high risk of mortgage default.
    See also: *arrears; Mortgage Arrears Resolution Arrears Process*   Sub-prime mortgage

Rents may be exempt *Rent Pressure Zone* rent limits or rent certainty limits through proving there has been a substantial change in the nature of the accommodation. The changes to the dwelling must be of such a kind and extent that they would have a significant effect on the letting *value* of the   Substantial change[621]

[620] Department of Housing, Planning and Local Government (2018) *Sustainable Urban Housing: Design Standards for New Apartments – Guidelines for Planning Authorities*, Government of Ireland: Dublin
[621] Residential Tenancies Board (2018) *Guidelines for Good Practice On: The Substantial Change Exemption in Rent Pressure Zone Areas*, RTB: Dublin

dwelling. This would be over and above any change in the letting value that would have occurred due to changes in the rental market if the changes to the property had not been made. Substantial changes do not include work required to take a property up to minimum standards and are:

[A] substantial change in the nature of the accommodation provided under the tenancy shall only have taken place where—

(*a*) the works carried out to the dwelling concerned—

    (i) consist of a permanent extension to the dwelling that increases the floor area (within the meaning of Article 6 of the Building Regulations 1997 (S.I. No. 497 of 1997)) of the dwelling by an amount equal to not less than 25 per cent of the floor area (within such meaning) of the dwelling as it stood immediately before the commencement of those works, or

    (ii) result in any three or more of the following:

        (I) the internal layout of the dwelling being permanently altered,

        (II) the dwelling being adapted to provide for ***access and use*** by a person with a disability, within the meaning of the Disability Act 2005,

        (III) a permanent increase in the number of rooms in the dwelling,

        (IV) in the case of a dwelling to which the European Union (Energy Performance of Buildings) Regulations 2012 (S.I. No. 243 of 2012) applies, the BER (within the meaning of those Regulations) being improved by not less than two building energy ratings.

Notification to the ***Residential Tenancies Board*** of rent changes and exemptions is mandatory.

Alterations that do not constitute a substantial change are:

- General upkeep/upgrade repairs and maintenance in line with meeting minimum standards. Indicative examples include:
  - Mandatory repairs and replacements for the maintenance of the interior and fittings
  - Upgrade of electrical installations including smoke alarms
- Modernisation/cosmetic improvement
- Internal upgrades (on an individual basis):
  - Upgrade of kitchen
  - Upgrade of bathroom(s)
  - Painting and decoration
  - Plaster repairs

- Replacement of carpets/flooring
- Painting, tiling, decorating
- External works
  - Works to garden and boundaries

A suburb is a residential area on the edge of a large town or city where people who work in the town or city often live.[622] A suburb usually contains lower density housing than locations closer to the city centre. In the UK, the development of suburbs was facilitated in the nineteenth century by the introduction of train lines which allowed middle-class workers to live further away from their place of work and the often dirty conditions of the city centre. Ireland's suburbs developed in earnest much later.

Living in the suburbs (suburbia) traditionally embodied certain values:

- Desire for the best of country and town (low-density housing in an estate-like setting)
- A belief in the need to protect the domestic realm (women and children) from the dangers of the city
- Faith in progress, science and technology
- A predilection for home ownership

See also: *suburbanisation; garden city; Howard, Ebenezer; Marino; density, housing*

Suburbanisation is the incremental growth of suburbs around the outer fringes of large towns or cities. Suburbanisation is a feature of urbanisation and began to intensify in the twentieth century, and especially post-WWII. Suburbanisation is given expression in single-class, low-density *housing estates* on the peripheries of cities and towns.

See also: *suburbs; garden city; Howard, Ebenezer; Marino*

It is up to each local authority to determine who can succeed an incumbent *tenant* on their death or leaving the local authority property. The following example is from Dublin City Council.[623]

Where death or departure of a tenant takes place, the tenancy will normally be given to a surviving spouse/partner, provided:
- such spouse/partner has been resident in the dwelling for a continuous period of at least two years immediately prior to the death/departure of the tenant.

---

[622] See: https://dictionary.cambridge.org/dictionary/english/suburb
[623] See: http://www.dublincity.ie/sites/default/files/content/Housing/Home/Documents/Housing
AllocationsScheme2013.pdf

On the death or departure of both parents the tenancy will normally be given to a son or daughter, irrespective of number in the household, provided:

- he/she has been living in the dwelling for at least two years immediately prior to the death or departure of the tenant

However, departure of the tenant by way of purchasing or providing own accommodation will not be grounds for a child over 18 years to remain in the dwelling and apply for succession.

Each case will be examined on its merits and where there is more than one member of the household remaining in the dwelling, the tenancy will normally be given to the member who, in the opinion of the Manager, is most likely to keep the household harmoniously together.

A person other than a spouse, partner, son or daughter who has resided in the dwelling for at least five years immediately prior to the death or departure of the tenant may be allowed to succeed where:

- there is no spouse, partner, son or daughter eligible to succeed and
- where the dwelling size is appropriate to his/her needs.

A spouse, partner, son or daughter who was residing at the date of death/departure of the tenant:

- who has not resided for the full two years prior to the death or departure of the tenant
- but has a total of ten years aggregate residence in the dwelling in the previous fifteen years
- is in need of housing accommodation
- is unable to provide accommodation from his/her own resources

may be considered to succeed to the tenancy where the dwelling size is appropriate to his/her needs.

In all cases of claims for succession to tenancy it will be necessary that the applicant(s) have been included in the family household details for rent assessment purposes for the requisite period(s) as outlined above. No application will be considered where this condition is not complied with. In all cases, there must be no alternative suitable accommodation available to the applicant(s) for succession of tenancy.

'Residing' in this case means that the person(s) concerned are entitled to reside and are included in the tenancy for rent assessment purposes.

See also: ***council housing***

Surrender Grant The Surrender Grant was introduced in October 1984. It paid local authority tenants who surrendered their local authority house to their council and built or purchased their own houses a lump sum of £5,000 when their new house was bought and occupied. It was abolished in March 1987.

See also: ***Mortgage Allowance Scheme***

The Sustainable Energy Authority of Ireland (SEAI) is Ireland's national sustainable energy authority. It conducts research into energy and housing (e.g. *Behavioural Insights on Energy Efficiency in the Residential Sector*, 2017), and has a suite of grants available to households for various energy-related projects and upgrades.

Sustainable Energy Authority of Ireland

Under the Better Energy Homes heading, there are the following:

- Insulation grant
- Heat pump system grant
- Solar thermal grant
- Heating controls grant
- ***Building Energy Rating*** (BER)

The Warmer Homes Scheme delivers free energy efficiency upgrades to homeowners who receive certain welfare payments. The Warmth and Wellbeing Pilot Scheme aims to improve the living conditions of vulnerable people living with chronic respiratory conditions making the home warmer and cosier to live in.[624]

T

To 'take in charge' means that the local authority assumes responsibility for certain services located within the common areas and public areas associated with a particular ***housing estate***. When a residential development is completed to the satisfaction of the local authority, the ***developer*** or the majority of homeowners may make a written request to the local ***planning authority*** to have the estate taken in charge. When agreed, any or all of the following facilities that are located within the common areas of that estate shall also be deemed to have been taken in charge, unless those facilities have been expressly excluded in the resolution:

Take in charge

- Roads and footpaths
- Public lighting infrastructure including associated electricity charges
- Fire hydrants and associated networks
- Public water supply, sewerage and storm water networks

---

[624] See: https://www.seai.ie/grants/home-grants/warmth-and-wellbeing/

- Wastewater treatment plants, pumping stations and associated buffer zones (including associated electricity charges)
- Water treatment plants and reservoirs (including associated electricity charges) and any associated protection zones
- Open spaces

Councils will not maintain open spaces, nor lawns and trees. It is recommended that the appropriate level of public liability insurance be at all times maintained by the management company/residents' association. All estates must remain ungated.[625]

Councils will typically not take in charge:

- Apartment blocks
- Gated developments
- Holiday home type developments

Residents of a housing estate may also request that an estate be taken in charge by way of a plebiscite (written ballot) of the majority of residents in an estate.

See also: ***local authority (role in housing)***

Technical guidance documents

Technical guidance documents (TGD) give guidance on building construction so that it meets the requirements of the ***building regulations***. It is not compulsory to follow the TGD guidance, as long as the resulting outcome meets the requirements of the building regulations. If works are carried out in accordance with the TGDs then this is taken as evidence that the building is compliant with the building regulations.

The following are the current TGDs:

- Part A – Structure
- Part B – Fire Safety
- Part C – Site Preparation and Resistance to Moisture
- Part D – Materials and Workmanship
- Part E – Sound
- Part F – Ventilation
- Part G – Hygiene
- Part H – Drainage and Waste Water Disposal
- Part J – Heat-Producing Appliances
- Part K – Stairs, Ladders, Ramps and Guards
- Part L – Conservation of Fuel and Energy
- Part M – ***Access and Use***

---

[625] See: http://www.longfordcoco.ie/Services/Planning/Taking-in-Charge/

See also: *Fire Safety Certificate; Building Control (Amendment) Regulations; septic tank*

A tenancy is an interest or estate in land.[626] This is a property right that imparts exclusive possession, rather than merely a permission to do something in respect of a property (including the generally non-exclusive permission to occupy it). In Ireland, pursuant to section 11 of the **Land and Conveyancing Reform Act 2009**, only two forms of legal estates in land may be created or disposed of: these are *freehold* and *leasehold*. Within the definitions section of that Act, a 'lease' is an instrument that creates a tenancy; a 'tenancy' means the estate or interest which arises from the relationship of landlord and tenant however created, though not including a tenancy at will or sufferance (section 3). The **Residential Tenancies Act 2004** provides a definition of 'tenancy': tenancy includes a periodic tenancy and a tenancy for a fixed term, whether oral or in writing or implied, and, where the context so admits, includes a sub-tenancy and a tenancy or sub-tenancy that has been terminated. The Residential Tenancies Act 2004 applies to every **dwelling** the subject of a tenancy (including a tenancy created before the passing of the Act).

It is significant that the term 'tenancy' includes an oral tenancy, and no contracting out from the terms of the protections is permitted.[627] The effect of this is that no matter what a landlord or tenant agree in a lease, the tenant will always have the protections of the Residential Tenancies Act(s).

In late 2018, there were 336,890 tenancies in Ireland.[628]

See also: *freehold interest; leasehold interest*

Tenancy

Where a property is held by persons as tenants in common, each is the absolute owner of a due proportion of the property. When such a person dies, his due proportion of the property is deemed to be disposed of to his personal representatives.

Joint tenants are distinguished from tenants in common in that, on the death of a joint tenant, the right to the whole property passes to the survivors or survivor. Provided that the joint tenancy has not been severed, the last survivor of joint tenants becomes the absolute owner of the property.[629]

Tenancy in common/Joint tenancy

The **Residential Tenancies Act 2004** provides a definition of a 'tenant' as: 'the person for the time being entitled to the occupation of a dwelling under a **tenancy** and, where the context so admits, includes a person who has ceased

Tenant

[626] Wylie, JCW (2014) *Landlord and Tenant Law*, third edition, Bloomsbury Professional: Dublin
[627] *Ibid.*
[628] Figures from Residential Tenancies Board, 2019
[629] Revenue (2007) *Tenants in Common and Joint Tenants*, Revenue Commissioners: Dublin

to be entitled to that occupation by reason of the termination of his or her tenancy.'

See also: ***security of tenure***

Tenant purchase Tenant purchase means the right of a local authority ***tenant*** to purchase their property. The sale of local authority housing to its tenants is governed by the Housing (Sale of Local Authority Houses) Regulations 2015.

The latest iteration of tenant purchase came into being in January 2016. Under the Tenant (Incremental) Purchase Scheme 2016 a local authority tenant living in a local authority house that is available for sale under the scheme and who meets the eligibility criteria can apply to purchase their house.[630] However, there are a number of types and uses of houses not eligible under the scheme, such as:

- ***Apartments*** (a separate purchase scheme for apartments applies)
- Houses that have been specifically designed for occupation by elderly persons
- Houses that have been specifically designed in a group setting for occupation by members of the Travelling community
- Houses in a private ***development*** transferred to the local authority by the ***developer***

There are eligibility criteria: local authority tenants living in a local authority house included in the scheme can apply to buy the house. They must however be in receipt of some form of social housing support for at least a year, and must have a minimum gross annual income of €15,000, as determined by the local authority, in accordance with the rules of the scheme. They will pay the ***market value*** of the house – less a discount which, depending on income, will vary between 40 per cent and 60 per cent. The local authority will also place a charge on the house called an 'incremental purchase charge'. This charge will be equal to the discount received on the price of the house and will remain in place for 20, 25 or 30 years (depending on the discount given). Each year, the local authority will reduce the charge by 2 per cent. At the end of the 20, 25 or 30 years, the charge will be zero as long as the purchaser obeys the terms and conditions of the scheme. They must live in the house as their normal place of residence and get agreement from their local authority if they want to sell, let or sublet the house. They will be able to resell the house at any time if the local authority agrees. However, if the property is sold before the end of the 20, 25 or 30 years, they will have to pay back the value of the outstanding charge on the house to their local authority.

---

[630] See: https://www.housing.gov.ie/housing/home-ownership/tenant-purchase-scheme/tenant-purchase

Like all homeowners, the new owners will be responsible for maintaining and carrying out repairs on their house from the date of purchase. They will also have to acquire and keep adequate property insurance on the house. The local authority can refuse to sell the house in particular circumstances such as to tenants or household members involved in ***anti-social behaviour*** or with rent ***arrears***.

The right to buy a local authority house by its tenant was initially established in the Labourers' Act of 1935, but only applied to rural social (i.e. council) housing tenants. Between the 1920s and the late 1950s social housing output accounted annually for between a third and a half of total house-building. A major spin-off of land reform for social housing – its conversion into a route to home ownership – emerged in the 1930s. A government commission set up to examine the right of rural social tenants to buy their dwellings concluded that 'it is scarcely necessary to argue the advantages of ownership' for rural social tenants 'since the freedom and security that go with ownership ... we regard as basic and essential in any Christian state that bases social order on justice'.[631] O'Connell points out that over time the assumption that dwellings would be bought by tenants was gradually factored into arrangements for social housing finance and management. For instance, the traditional reliance on loans for capital funding was gradually scaled back and replaced by direct central government grant aid. This enabled local authorities to sell dwellings at discount without having to service a loan on the associated losses.[632] The Housing Act 1966, which unified the urban and rural housing codes, in the process applied the right-to-buy provisions of the rural code to the urban social housing sector. The result was that Irish social tenants enjoyed a universal right to purchase their homes. In urban areas, take-up of this right was limited at first, but it rose dramatically from the mid-1970s, when particularly generous discounts for purchasers were introduced.

According to Hayden,[633] in early 1972, following the rejection of their proposals for the reform of the ***differential rent*** structure, the ***National Association of Tenants' Organisations*** (NATO) sanctioned a rent strike and some 40,000 of the 105,000 tenants in local authority social housing homes refused to pay rent, at a cost to local authorities of £120,000 in rent and rates foregone. However NATO's attentions were not confined to the differential rents structure. Hand in hand with their demands for reduced rents, NATO

---

[631] Saorstát Eireann (1933: 23) *Final Report of the Commission of Inquiry into the Sale of Cottages and Plots Provided Under the Labourers (Ireland) Acts*, cited in Fahey, T and Norris, M (2011) 'From Asset Based Welfare to Welfare Housing? The Changing Function of Social Housing in Ireland', UCD policy paper

[632] O'Connell, C (2007) *The State and Housing in Ireland: Ideology, Policy and Practice*, Nova: New York

[633] Hayden, A (2014) 'Irish Social Housing: The Path to Decline, 1966–1988', in Sirr, L (ed.), *Renting in Ireland: The Private, Voluntary and Social Sectors*, IPA: Dublin

demanded more favourable tenant purchase terms. Nobody, the Minister claimed, could claim 'that these terms [in the Housing Act 1966] are less than generous to the tenants concerned'. However, discontent with the terms of the scheme enacted was expressed by both opposition politicians and tenants alike. In a letter to NATO, the Minister argued that by selling houses, local authorities lessen their ability to provide decent accommodation for those who cannot afford to buy since 'the more houses they sell the less they will have available for letting to persons in need'. He stated that the prices being offered to tenant purchasers 'compare favourably with prices of similar houses sold in the open market'. NATO however demanded further benefits for tenant purchasers, including that: the purchase price be based on the market value of the house when it was built and not the current market value; that they be granted the normal remission of rates applicable to new private houses; that some allowance be made for rent paid; and that the government grant on new houses be deducted from the purchase price.

In the end, NATO mostly got their way, and the result was that by the 1980s two-thirds of the dwellings built by local authorities had been sold to tenants and they accounted for a quarter of the owner-occupied stock. In the period 1973–1991 a total of 67,000 dwellings were sold to sitting tenants. Tenant purchase not only raised the rate of home ownership in Ireland to one of the highest in western Europe, it also effected a relatively even distribution of ***home ownership*** and housing wealth across the social class spectrum.[634] The construction of social housing was supported by all parties and was seen by government not just as a central mechanism for meeting housing needs but also as a means of stimulating employment, particularly in periods of economic decline.[635] It was viewed by parties of both the centre-left and centre-right as a progressive form of wealth distribution which was quite compatible with welfare state principles.

See also: ***council housing; social housing***

Tenant Right League   The Tenant Right League was formed by ***Charles Gavan Duffy*** and Frederick Lucas in 1850 with the objective of seeking the ***Three Fs***: fixity of ***tenure***, fair ***rent***, and free sale of the tenant's interest.

See also: ***Davitt, Michael***

Tenement   A tenement is usually a large building divided into individual residences which may be ***flats***, or in some instances merely a room or two. Tenements are generally associated with poor quality accommodation in run-down areas.

[634] Finnerty, J and O'Connell, C (2014) '50 Years of the Social Housing "Offer" in Ireland: The Casualisation Thesis Examined', in Sirr, L (ed.), *Renting in Ireland: The Private, Voluntary and Social Sectors*, IPA: Dublin
[635] O'Connell, C (2007) *The State and Housing in Ireland: Ideology, Policy and Practice*, Nova: New York

Some of Dublin's most architecturally impressive buildings also housed some of its worst accommodation.

The National Archive has interesting records and information on tenements in Dublin: Tenements in inner-city Dublin were filthy, overcrowded, disease-ridden, teeming with malnourished children and very much at odds with the elite world of colonial and middle-class Dublin. The decay of Dublin was epitomised by Henrietta Street in the north inner city, which had once been home to generations of lawyers, but was, by 1911, overflowing with poverty. An astonishing 835 people lived in 15 houses. There were members of nineteen different families living in Number 7 Henrietta Street. Among the 104 people who shared the house were charwomen, domestic servants, labourers, porters, messengers, painters, carpenters, pensioners, a postman, a tailor, and a whole class of schoolchildren. Out the back were a stable and a piggery. The death rate in the city was not helped by the unsanitary conditions in inner-city tenements, where livestock were kept in dairy yards and cattle yards and down side lanes. People living in tenements were failed by Dublin Corporation, the city authority, which did not develop a meaningful policy to improve tenement life. A Housing Inquiry in 1914 found that sixteen members of the corporation owned tenements and it was clear that corporation members intervened to foil the enforcement of regulations against their properties.[636]

There were several disasters with tenement buildings collapsing and killing some of the inhabitants. The most well-known was in Church Street, Dublin when on 2 September 1913 two tenement homes collapsed to the ground, killing seven working-class Dubliners, with children among the dead. While this tragedy did spark a very significant housing inquiry, tenement collapses remained all too common in Dublin in the decades that followed. Two tenements collapsing within weeks of each other in June 1963 forced Dubliners to re-examine the housing situation in the city, and sparked a huge inquiry into housing in the city which delivered many shocking finds. It also saw hundreds of families moved out of their homes at short notice, for fear further collapses could be imminent.[637]

The development of local authority *housing estates* in the 1950s and 1960s (including *Ballymun*) was partly as a result of trying to eradicate tenements in Dublin, and providing alternative accommodation for those who lived in them.

See also: *ghetto; slum*

Tenure comes from the French word 'tenir', which means to hold. Different tenures refer to the various ways in which people occupy or possess their

Tenure

---

[636] See: http://www.census.nationalarchives.ie/exhibition/dublin/poverty_health.html
[637] See: https://comeheretome.com/2013/08/26/the-tenement-crisis-in-dublin-1963/

homes, each of which has varying levels of rights and security.[638] The main tenure types in Ireland are ***freehold*** (outright ownership) with ***mortgage*** or without; renting – either in the private or public (social) sector; and ***licence***.

As of Census 2016, ***home ownership***, with or without a loan, in Ireland was at 67.6 per cent (82 per cent in rural areas, 59.2 per cent in urban areas); renting from the private sector or an ***approved housing body*** at 20.18 per cent; and renting from a local authority at 8.85 per cent. Renting has overtaken both home ownership categories to become the predominant tenure status in the urban towns and cities, rising from a share of 27 per cent in 2006 to 36 per cent in 2016. Just over 53 per cent of all homeowners have no mortgage. The age at which home ownership became the majority tenure category was 35 years in 2016. Prior to that age, more householders were renting than owning their home. Households which were occupied by a husband and wife only were the most likely type of household to be owned outright, along with half of one-person households. Around 55 per cent of households comprising a husband and wife with children had an existing loan or mortgage. Rented households were more common for couples, while around 45 per cent of one-parent households were paying rent. Among households consisting of unrelated persons, four out of every five homes were rented.[639]

See also: ***home ownership; tenancy***

Tenure neutrality Tenure neutrality is the situation in which the consumer is financially indifferent between owning and renting a dwelling. This means that the method of financing how a household decides to accommodate itself and the tax system do not distort consumer choices between renting and owning.[640]

Kemeny defined tenure neutrality as being based on the principle that governments should balance subsidies between tenures and maximise comparability between the social-legal status of households in different tenures. He also identified a 'unitary' housing system that operates in Germany, Sweden, the Netherlands, Switzerland, Austria, Denmark and France.[641] Here, housing policy is 'tenure neutral'; that is, each tenure is afforded similar levels of government support.[642]

Ireland's *Housing Policy Statement* of 2011 was built upon a tenure-neutral approach. The then Minister, Willie Penrose, said: 'We will not prioritise one form of housing over another, or stampede people into housing solutions that

---

[638] Dukelow, F and Considine, M (2017) *Irish Social Policy: A Critical Introduction*, second edition, Bristol University Press: Bristol

[639] See: https://www.cso.ie/en/releasesandpublications/ep/p-cp1hii/cp1hii/tr/

[640] Bergenstråhle, S (2013) 'The Right to Housing and Need for Tenure Neutrality', *Global Tenant*, April

[641] Kemeny, J (1995) *From Public Housing to the Social Market: Rental Policy Strategies in Comparative Perspective*, Routledge: London

[642] Norris, M and Winston, N (2011) 'Does Home Ownership Reinforce or Counterbalance Income Inequality? Trends in Western Europe 1997–2007', UCD Working paper WP19

do not match their personal or financial circumstances.' Given the subsequent considerable financial support for home ownership, it is arguable that tenure neutrality is no longer a mainstay of Irish housing policy.

See also: ***tenure; Minister for Housing; Help-to-Buy***

Where a tenancy has lasted less than six months, a landlord does not have to give a reason for terminating the lease but must serve a valid written ***notice of termination***, allowing a minimum 28-day notice period (only seven days' notice is required in the first six months for ***anti-social behaviour***). **Termination of a lease**[643]

Grounds for termination of a tenancy are set out in section 34 of the ***Residential Tenancies Act 2004***. If a tenancy has lasted less than six months, the landlord does not have to give a ground as to why the tenancy is ending. If a tenancy lasts six months or more (known as a '***Part 4***' tenancy), the landlord must give a reason as to why a tenancy is ending which must be one of the following:

1. The tenant has not complied with their responsibilities, despite being notified of this in writing by the landlord and being given reasonable time to remedy the matter(s).
2. The property no longer suits the needs of the tenant, for example, it may be too small. In this case, a statement as to why it is no longer suitable for the needs of the tenant must also be given with the notice of termination. The statement must also specify the bed spaces in the dwelling.
3. If the landlord requires the property for personal or family use,* the tenancy can be ended. In this case, a statutory declaration providing 'specific details' must be included in the notice of termination or given with the notice of termination stating this. (This does not apply to ***approved housing bodies***.) These specific details are:
   * The intended occupant's identity
   * Their relationship to the landlord
   * The expected duration of their occupation
4. The tenancy can be ended if the landlord intends to sell the property within three months of the termination date. If this happens, a statutory declaration must also be given with the notice of termination confirming the landlord's intention to sell.

   Since January 2017 the '***Tyrrelstown Amendment***' applies to landlords terminating tenancies who want to sell ten or more units within a single development within six months. Usually, tenants will be allowed to remain in their rented dwelling during and after the sale of the property unless:

---

[643] See: https://onestopshop.rtb.ie/ending-a-tenancy/how-a-landlord-can-end-a-tenancy/landlords-grounds-for-ending-a-tenancy/

- by selling at market value the dwelling is more than 20 per cent below the market value that could be obtained for the dwelling if there was no one living in the units; and
- to restrict the sale would be unduly difficult or would cause hardship to the landlord.

5. A tenancy can be terminated where the landlord intends to carry out **substantial refurbishment** of the property.* The notice must contain or be accompanied by a written statement specifying the nature of the intended works to be carried out and, where **planning permission** is required, a copy is to be provided. Where no planning permission is required the statement must name the contractor (if any), the dates when the works are to be carried out and the proposed duration of the works. The statement must also say the tenant will be offered first refusal to take up the tenancy of the property if it becomes available to rent again within a period of six months from the termination date.

6. A tenancy can be ended if the landlord intends to change the use of the property,* for instance, the landlord intends to change from a residential to commercial letting. In this case, the notice of termination must include, or be accompanied by, a statement setting out the intended use of the property, a copy of planning permission (if relevant), details of any work to be carried out, the name of the contractor, and the dates and proposed duration of the works.

    * The termination notice must also say that the tenant will be offered first refusal to take up tenancy of the property if the property becomes available to rent again.

See also: ***notice periods; Residential Tenancies (Amendment) Act 2018***

Terraced house   A terraced house or a terrace house is one of a row of similar houses joined together by their side walls.[644] An 'end of terrace' house is the last house at either end of the terrace. Terraced housing quite often has no front gardens, although suburban Dublin terraced housing of the 1920s and 1930s had both front and back gardens (e.g. local authority housing in Drimnagh or Cabra). Both the Victorian and Georgian eras developed terraces of large three- or four-storey houses.

See also: ***detached house, semi-detached house; bedsit; maisonette; pied à terre; dwelling; mews; condominium***

Thermal bridge   In a house, heat makes its way from the heated space towards the outside. In doing so, it follows the path of least resistance. A thermal bridge can therefore

---

[644] From *Collins English Dictionary*

be described as a localised area of the building envelope where the heat flow is different (usually increased) in comparison to adjacent areas,[645] forming a 'bridge' between the heated and unheated spaces through the materials of the building (as opposed to through gaps between the materials).

The heat loss from thermal bridging is measured as linear thermal transmittance or ψ-value with units of W/m²K (watts per metre squared Kelvin) or k-value.[646]

See also: ***Y-value; U-value; passive house***

The Three Fs are: fixity of ***tenure***, fair ***rent***, and free sale of the tenant's interest.

See also: ***Duffy, Charles Gavan; Davitt, Michael; Tenant Right League***

Three Fs

Threshold was founded in 1978. Threshold is a national housing charity providing frontline advice and advocacy services for people with housing problems and people at risk of ***homelessness*** for over forty years. Threshold owes its origins to the development of the Flat Dwellers' Chaplaincy, established in 1974 by Fr Donal O'Mahony in response to the scale and diversity of housing problems at that time when discrimination in terms of access to rented accommodation, illegal ***evictions*** and poor living conditions were widespread.

Threshold

Threshold works by:

- Campaigning for suitable housing delivered on a rights-based approach
- Analysing existing problems and seeking innovative approaches and solutions through quality research
- Providing independent advisory and advocacy services
- Working in collaboration with others for those disadvantaged by the housing system
- Providing long-term solutions for people who are homeless

Threshold also works with ***landlords*** to find solutions to landlord–***tenant*** problems, and delivers training on housing and housing law.

See also: ***housing rights approach to housing***

A timber-frame house is one in which the framing structure is made of heavy timber. There are various different forms of timber-frame housing. Timber frames can be a suitable choice if the structural shell is required quickly, if the ground conditions are particularly poor, or if the design does not include

Timber-frame housing

[645] See: https://elearning.passivehouse.com/mod/book/tool/print/index.php?id=294
[646] Little, J (2011) 'Thermal Bridging', *Passive House Plus*, 27 July

very large structural spans. Timber-framed houses are typically constructed off-site and put together once they reach the site of the house.

The main advantages of timber-frame construction are seen as:

- Speed of on-site build: a prefabricated structure can be assembled on-site quicker than traditional brick and block construction. However, the time for the design and manufacture of the frame in the factory must be taken into account.
- Quality: off-site construction means that it is possible to achieve higher levels of build quality in controlled factory conditions.
- Sustainability: timber-frame construction is regarded as more sustainable than traditional forms of house construction.
- Costs: the ability to control costs is significant with timber-frame housing once there is a high quality set of tender documents.[647]

See also: *Millfield Manor fire and report*

Title[648]

'Title' in relation to property means not only the documents that show who owns the property but also guarantees that no one else can come along and say that they own the property. There are two types of title in Ireland, known as **Land Registry** title (registered) and **Registry of Deeds** title (unregistered).

The owner of a property that is registered in the Land Registry will have a numbered folio. This document records the name and address of the owner, a description of the property and a map of the property known as the file plan. A folio is conclusive evidence of the person's ownership of the property. When Land Registry property is being sold the folio must be produced in order to sell.

A Registry of Deeds title is that which is registered with the Registry of Deeds. This occurs where the title has built up over a number of years. These documents can include Deeds of Conveyance used to transfer *freehold* unregistered land or Deeds of Assignment used to transfer *leasehold* unregistered land.

See also: *deed map; deeds; title plan*

Title plan[649]

A large-scale location plan, usually printed at a scale of 1:1,000 for urban areas, 1:2,500 for suburban areas or 1:5,000 for rural areas, which shows the approximate position of the general *boundaries* of the property in red, in relation to the surrounding properties.

---

[647] See: https://www.designingbuildings.co.uk/wiki/Advantages_and_disadvantages_of_timber_frame_buildings

[648] Burns, M (n.d.) '10 Legal Steps to Buying a House in Ireland', *Lawyer.ie*, available at: https://www.lawyer.ie/property/buying-a-house/

[649] Society of Chartered Surveyors Ireland (n.d.) *Boundaries: Procedures for Boundary Identification, Demarcation and Dispute Resolution in Ireland*, second edition, Geomatics Guidance Note, SCSI: Dublin

See also: *cadastre; deed map; General Boundary Rule*

'Townhouse' has two separate meanings. The first is a modern-style house, typically tall and narrow with a small footprint and multiple floors. The second refers to a house in the city belonging to someone who also has a house in the country.

Townhouse

See also: *pied à terre; detached house, semi-detached house; bedsit; maisonette; dwelling; terraced house; condominium; duplex*

In 2017 RTÉ produced an explainer of the ***tracker rate mortgage*** scandal: as far back as 2006 tracker customers began asking their banks to switch to a ***fixed rate mortgage*** for a period (usually around three years). There had also been reports of banks encouraging some tracker customers to move to fixed rate options, with the logic being that fixed rates for a period would offer customers a degree of certainty with regard to repayments. In the majority of cases, the understanding on the customers' end was that when the fixed rate period of their mortgage was finished, they would be moved back onto their original tracker mortgage rate. However, in many instances banks would not return customers to their original tracker rates, instead putting them on higher fixed rate and ***variable rate*** loans; and in many cases where customers were put back on trackers by their banks this was done so at a higher rate than the original tracker agreement. With more and more cases emerging, it became clear lenders were denying customers their legal right to a tracker mortgage. The effect of this was that people ended up, in many cases, paying hundreds of Euro more than they had to on a monthly basis to service their mortgages. This resulted in extensive financial strain being unnecessarily put on people, with a number of people having their homes repossessed.[650] More than 33,000 bank customers were affected by the scandal.[651]

Tracker mortgage scandal and examination

In 2015 the ***Central Bank of Ireland*** decided to carry out an industry-wide review of tracker mortgage accounts. Since 2010 it had been identifying and pursuing some lenders in relation to tracker-related issues, including borrowers who switched from their tracker rate and/or lost their right to revert to a tracker rate when they came to the end of a fixed rate period on their mortgage. The examination requires all lenders to examine the extent to which they have been meeting their contractual obligations to customers. It also includes the transparency of their communications with customers in relation to tracker-related issues. The examination covers all lenders who may have sold tracker mortgages in the past, including those no longer selling

---

[650] Cox, A (2017) 'Explainer: The Tracker Mortgage Scandal', *RTÉ News*, 27 October, available at: https://www.rte.ie/news/business/2017/1025/915149-explainer-the-tracker-mortgage-scandal/
[651] Quinn, E and McConnell, D (2017) 'Total bill for tracker scandal could hit €1 billion', *Irish Examiner*, 21 December

mortgages. It also covers mortgages that have been redeemed or switched to another lender.[652]

Tracker rate mortgage[653]

According to the Central Bank, a tracker rate *mortgage* is 'a type of home loan where the interest rate charged on the loan tracks that of another publicly available rate, typically the interest rate set by the European Central Bank'.[654]

Trade down

In housing terms, to 'trade down' means to buy a similar, but smaller, property. It can also be referred to as '*downsizing*'.

Transfer list

Local authorities operate transfer lists for people who want to move to another local authority home. If a tenant is already living in a local authority home and wishes to move to another local authority home, then they can generally apply for a 'transfer' to another local authority property in the same housing authority area. The applicant is then placed on a 'transfer list'. This can take a considerable period of time depending on availability of homes in the area requested. In order to qualify for the transfer list, applicants will need to meet criteria, such as:

- Having lived in their home for a minimum number of years
- Not have any rent arrears, and
- The home must be in good condition[655]

Each council operates its own policies in relation to their housing transfer list. Some councils facilitate mutual transfers where two tenants apply to swap dwellings. The criteria for entry on the transfer list in South Dublin County Council is shown below:[656]

1. Exceptional medical/compassionate grounds (regard to be had for report from council's medical advisors/housing welfare officers as appropriate)
2. On grounds of *anti-social behaviour* where a Garda superintendent has stated that there is a risk to personal safety
3. Older persons (aged 65 or over) downsizing accommodation
4. Tenants downsizing to the specific unit size of accommodation that matches their need
5. Overcrowding

---

[652] See: https://www.centralbank.ie/consumer-hub/explainers/tracker-mortgage-examination---faq
[653] Central Bank of Ireland (2013) *Code of Conduct on Mortgage Arrears*, Central Bank of Ireland: Dublin
[654] See: https://www.centralbank.ie/consumer-hub/explainers/what-is-the-tracker-mortgage-examination
[655] See: https://www.housingagency.ie/housing-information/what-is-social-housing/can-i-transfer-to-another-local-authority-home.aspx
[656] See: https://www.sdcc.ie/en/services/housing/finding-a-home/transfers/

6. Tenants other than those in categories (3) and (4) above downsizing accommodation to make better use of housing stock
7. To facilitate incremental purchase, where the authority has consented to such a purchase

See also: ***housing needs assessment; social housing waiting list***

Transitional accommodation refers to a dwelling let by a housing association for periods not longer than eighteen months. Transitional accommodation usually serves a specific purpose and can include homeless services, domestic violence services, and specific services for people with disabilities, amongst others. Landlords (normally ***approved housing bodies***) must register transitional accommodation with the ***Residential Tenancies Board***. The accommodation must also be designated as transitional with the relevant local authority and the minister. By designating a tenancy as 'transitional', Part 4 of the Act will not apply, i.e. the tenant will not acquire the four-/six-year security of tenure protections after the initial six-month period (unless the eighteen-month period elapses). If a ***notice of termination*** is not served within the specified time limits, then tenants of transitional housing can acquire ***Part 4 tenancy*** rights and ***security of tenure***.

Transitional housing[657]

The links between transport and housing are complex and multifarious. The public benefits at a local and regional level when transportation and housing work cooperatively. 'Finding ways to accomplish a mutually supportive relationship between these two community drivers from a spatial, technical, practical, and politically feasible standpoint'[658] is challenging. If governments get it right, then the benefits include less traffic congestion and air pollution, lower costs for both housing and transportation, lower labour costs for employers and reduced expenses for families, preservation of open space and heritage, mitigation of the jobs/housing mismatch, more efficient and environmentally friendly land uses, and greater choices in development patterns, housing types and transportation services.

Transport and housing

Achieving these outcomes is difficult because quite often transport and housing develop along their own trajectories with little, or not enough, regard for each other (although attempts to link the two are improving). The results on the ground can be unsustainable and expensive housing alongside expensive, congested, time-consuming and polluted commuting journeys. One of the biggest problems is that whereas 'transportation is planned at both the regional and the local level, primarily by the public sector, housing, on

---

[657] See: https://www.icsh.ie/sites/default/files/3_guidance_note_for_transitional_accommodation_-august_2017.pdf
[658] Eisenberg, A (n.d.) *The Housing Transportation Connection: Building Better Communities Through Better Housing and Transportation*, US Millennial Housing Commission: Washington DC

the other hand, is almost entirely a local and private affair.'[659] In a primarily development-led, rather than plan-led, planning system, as in Ireland, linking transport and housing can be a costly after-the-fact affair. Transport, when done well, is a system; housing, given its disparate, unconnected nature, never comes close to being a system.

See also: ***development contribution scheme; transport poverty and equity; rural housing***

Transport poverty and equity

The term 'transport poverty' has been used by some transport campaign organisations, media and regional government to raise awareness that some households and individuals are struggling or unable to make the journeys they need. However, it should be noted that the term is about more than access to a car.[660]

Recent research has shown that the newer the year of construction of the house (especially since 1991), the less sustainable the mode of transport used to travel to and from school and college. It is also evident that low- and middle-income households are experiencing the longest commutes. In addition, those without cars felt they experienced significant barriers to employment opportunities compared to those with cars. There is also a clear correlation between lack of active travel and obesity in Ireland.[661]

The principles of transport equity have much potential to shape the future development of housing (especially principle no. 4):

1. Transport should not be a barrier to equity of opportunity to key life chances.
2. Groups vulnerable to transport disadvantage should be given special consideration in plans and projects (e.g. lower income, children, elderly, lone parents, mobility and sensory impaired).
3. People are entitled to use walking, cycling and public transport as an effective, safe and efficient mode of transport.
4. People should be able to have zero car ownership in urban areas, and be able to reach key local and strategic destinations (at least) by effective walking, cycling or public transport.[662]

See also: ***transport and housing***

Traveller housing

Industrialisation and increased mechanisation on farms in the 1960s had a profound impact on Travellers' nomadic lifestyles. It took until the Housing Act 1988 before the housing needs of Travellers was specifically mentioned,

---

[659] *Ibid.*

[660] Titheridge, H, Christie, N, Mackett, R, Oviedo Hernández, D and Ye, R (2014) *Transport and Poverty: A Review of the Evidence*, University College London: London

[661] Rock, S (2017) 'Transport Inequity and Car Dependency: A Self-Reinforcing Relationship', paper presented at the TASC Conference, 21 June, Dublin

[662] *Ibid.*

while housing arrangements for other specific groups in society such as Irish speakers, newly-weds, sufferers of TB, elderly and disabled people, and those in unfit and overcrowded accommodation had appeared regularly in reports and legislation.[663]

As at Census 2016, there were 30,987 people in Ireland who identified themselves as belonging to the Traveller community. Nearly 40 per cent of these are under 15, compared to 21.4 per cent of the rest of the population. Almost 50 per cent of Traveller women aged 40–49 have given birth to five or more children.

According to the Census, Travellers are more urbanised than the general population, with almost eight in ten living in cities or towns (of 1,500 or more), compared with 62.4 per cent of the total population. Dublin city and suburbs had the largest number of Irish Travellers with 5,089 persons. This was followed by Galway city and suburbs with 1,598 persons and Cork city and suburbs with 1,222. Among towns with 1,500 or more persons, Tuam had the highest number of Irish Travellers with 737 persons, followed by Longford with 730 persons. Navan, Mullingar, Dundalk and Ballinasloe all had 500 or more Irish Travellers in 2016.[664]

As of the end of 2017, there were 11,116 Traveller families in all forms of accommodation. Of this:

- 6,234 were accommodated by or with the assistance of a local authority
- 585 were on unauthorised sites
- 795 were housed from their own resources
- 2,387 were housed in the *private rented sector*
- 1,115 were sharing housing[665]

To date, Traveller accommodation targets have not been met at any point since they were made mandatory on local authorities in the Traveller Accommodation Act 1998.[666]

Túath Housing

Túath is a not-for-profit company, limited by guarantee, incorporated in the Republic of Ireland and an *approved housing body*. Túath is run by a board of management drawn from volunteers. The association was first established in 2000 and is approved for voluntary housing, under section 6 of the Housing (Miscellaneous Provisions) Act 1992, for the purposes of the

---

[663] Kenna, P (2011) *Housing Law, Rights and Policy*, Clarus Press: Dublin
[664] CSO Census 2016
[665] Holland, K (2018) 'Travellers on roadside or in overcrowded homes increased 66 per cent in 5 years', *Irish Times*, 27 July
[666] Holland, K (2017) 'Traveller housing targets have not been met in 18 years', *Irish Times*, 14 September

Housing Acts 1966–2009. The association is a member of the ***Irish Council for Social Housing***.

Túath's aim is to provide long-term, safe, quality housing at best value whilst locally building sustainable communities. Túath is primarily a service organisation, housing people in need and managing homes whilst responding to, engaging with and involving people to make ***social housing*** work. Its core business is managing social homes in a sustainable way, which leads people and families to peacefully enjoy, live and settle within communities. Túath has a staff of over 70 and manages over 4,000 homes nationwide with four offices located in Dublin, Galway, Cork and Dundalk, Co. Louth.

Turnkey

A turnkey development is one that is constructed to be sold as a complete development (i.e. ready to occupy). Turnkey projects involve authorities going to the market to procure a total social (or mixed) housing solution (land, design and construction) to meet an identified ***social housing*** need. In local authority contracts to deliver turnkey housing, the contractor takes full responsibility for the completed project being 'fit for purpose'. There are two main contractual approaches to delivering turnkey housing for the state.

A proportion of social housing is delivered by local authorities in Ireland via turnkey schemes agreed with builders. Local authority 'new build' output figures consolidate all local authority new unit construction activity, including units delivered by traditional construction, ***rapid build***, turnkey, regeneration and ***Part V*** units,[667] making calculation of the actual number of turnkey and council houses delivered each year difficult.

Approved housing bodies also use the turnkey arrangement to have new social homes constructed. In some cases, turnkeys can involve the completion of unfinished developments, and potentially provide early construction delivery and tackle remaining ***unfinished estates*** around the country.

See also: ***data – housing output issues***

Tyrrelstown Amendment

The 'Tyrrelstown Amendment' is a colloquial term for section 35(A) of the ***Planning and Development (Housing) and Residential Tenancies Act 2016***. The amendment was brought in after attempts were made to evict large numbers of ***tenants*** from a housing development in Tyrrelstown, Dublin in 2016 using the provision in the ***Residential Tenancies Act 2004*** that allows for the termination of a ***tenancy*** if the ***landlord*** wishes to sell the property. The amendment to the legislation attempts to prevent landlords from evicting tenants where they are selling ten or more units in the one development within a six-month period.

---

[667] Kilkenny, P and O'Callaghan, D (2018) Department of Public Expenditure and Reform – Spending Review 2018: Current and Capital Expenditure on Social Housing Delivery Mechanisms, Department of Public Expenditure and Reform: Dublin

Section 35(A) of the Planning and Development (Housing) and Residential Tenancies Act 2016 now says:

A Part 4 tenancy shall not be terminated by the landlord on the ground specified in paragraph 3 of the Table to section 34 [grounds for termination] where the landlord intends to enter into an enforceable agreement—
(*a*) in respect of **dwellings** situated within the development concerned,
(*b*) for the transfer to another, for full consideration, of the whole of his or her interest in 10 or more of those dwellings, each being the subject of such a tenancy, and
(*c*) to so transfer during a relevant period of time.

There is, however, an exception to this amendment. The rule does not apply if the landlord can show:
(i) that the price to be obtained by selling at **market value** the dwelling that is the subject of an existing tenancy to which Part 4 applies is more than 20 per cent below the market value that could be obtained for the dwelling with **vacant possession**, and
(ii) that the application of that subsection would, having regard to all the circumstances of that case—
(I) be unduly onerous on that landlord, or
(II) would cause undue hardship on that landlord.

See also: **renoviction; termination of a lease; Part 4 tenancy**

U

The U-value of a material or construction element is the rate of heat loss through that material, taking account of both thermal conductivity and thickness. The lower the U-value of a material, the less heat can pass through it and the better it is at insulating. Homes built to the passive house standard in Ireland or the UK typically include a wall U-value of $0.15W/m^2K$ or better. A 2016 analysis by *Passive House Plus* of data from **Sustainable Energy Authority of Ireland**'s National **Building Energy Rating** research tool revealed that the average U-values for new Irish homes have been dramatically improved as a consequence of tightening building regulations.
See also: **passive house; thermal bridge; Y-value**

U-value[668]

---

[668] See: https://passivehouseplus.ie/u-value

Unauthorised development[669]

Any development which requires *planning permission* and does not have that permission, or which is going ahead in breach of the specific conditions set out in its planning permission, is classed as 'unauthorised development'.

The term '*development*' potentially covers a wide range of activities, such as:

- Change of use of a property (for example converting a shop to an office)
- Erection of signs or advertisements
- Works on a building that is protected because of its historic or architectural value

Where any activities need planning permission and don't have it, or if the work is not being carried out in accordance with the permission that was previously granted, then it is an unauthorised development. The carrying out of unauthorised development is an offence and any person who has carried it out may be subject to *enforcement* proceedings. Enforcement is the *planning authority*'s way of making sure that unauthorised development becomes compliant with planning law.

A planning authority can apply to the Circuit Court or the High Court for an injunction to prevent an unauthorised development from being carried out, or from beginning. Individuals or groups can also apply for an injunction, even if the planning authority hasn't taken this step.

Underfloor heating

With underfloor heating, heat is distributed through pipes laid evenly in loops under the floor in a room through which heated water runs. The pipes are laid at sub-floor level and attached to insulation boards. Electricity-based underfloor heating systems are more suitable for smaller rooms and work independently from the central heating system. Water-based systems work off the existing heating system. Underfloor heating systems are more economic to run than traditional central heating systems as they heat the water to a lower temperature and retain the heat for longer.

Unfinished estates

A rather 'one-dimensional and simplistic'[670] approach to housing policy and supply led to a significant oversupply of housing when *mortgage* lending dried up in 2008. This oversupply was evident in the 620 estates in which 50 per cent or more of the housing units were unoccupied, under development or unfinished. These were known as 'ghost estates' due to the lack of occupants; 86 of these developments had 50 or more housing units.[671]

---

[669] See: https://www.housing.gov.ie/sites/default/files/migrated-files/en/Publications/Development andHousing/Planning/FileDownLoad%2C31565%2Cen.pdf

[670] Kenna, P (2011) *Housing Law, Rights and Policy*, Clarus Press: Dublin

[671] Kitchin, R and Gleeson, J, Keaveney, K and O'Callaghan, C (2010) 'A Haunted Landscape: Housing and Ghost Estates in Post-Celtic Tiger Ireland', (NIRSA) Working Paper Series, No. 59, NIRSA – National Institute for Regional and Spatial Analysis

There were several reasons why Ireland ended up with an oversupply of housing, most of it in areas of diminishing or no demand, and the biggest reason was poor planning practice by local authorities. According to Kitchin et al.,[672] what happened is a pattern of *development* that ran counter to what one would have expected or hoped for. Essentially, a number of local authorities did not heed good planning guidelines and regional and national objectives; conduct sensible demographic profiling of potential demand; or take account of the fact that much of the land zoned for residential development lacked essential services such as water and sewerage treatment plants, energy supply, public transport or roads. Instead, permissions and zoning had been facilitated by the abandonment of basic planning principles by elected representatives on the local and national stage and driven by the demands of local people, *developers* and speculators. Further, central government not only failed to adequately oversee, regulate and direct local planning, but actively encouraged its excesses through tax incentive schemes and the flaunting of its own principles as set out in the *National Spatial Strategy* through policies such as decentralisation.

The highest proportions of 'empty' unoccupied developments are in western and midland counties. Counties such as Cork, Leitrim, Longford, Sligo and Roscommon had particularly high rates of housing oversupply in comparison to their populations.

Planning permissions for housing developments may contain conditions requiring the lodgement with the *planning authority* of a security for the purposes of providing funding for the satisfactory provision of public *infrastructure* (not the development) in case of default by the developer. In many instances this security is in the form of a cash deposit, an insurance policy or a construction bond. Since 2011, local authorities across the country obtained approximately €63 million from such securities to complete essential public infrastructure within unfinished housing developments including roads, water services, public lighting and amenity areas, and where breaches of planning conditions have occurred.

There have been numerous knock-on effects of the phenomenon of unfinished estates. Many of the builders of these estates were not professional *developers*, but tradespeople who emigrated to find work elsewhere, leaving the estate incomplete. These tradespeople are now in high demand in Ireland as a labour shortage threatens a house-building recovery. The rehabilitation of unfinished housing in these estates also caused house-building completion numbers to be artificially inflated as houses built, in some instances many years previously, were finally connected to the electricity grid and thus counted as new houses (see: *data – housing output issues*). The artificial

---

[672] *Ibid.*

inflation of house-building completions – in part caused by unfinished estates – has caused the counting methodology to be reviewed and the GDP figure for 2017 was called into question as more accurate completion statistics became available.

See also: ***data – housing output issues; housing stock***

United Nations Special Rapporteur on the Right to Adequate Housing

In 2000, the UN Commission on Human Rights decided to appoint a Special Rapporteur whose mandate was to focus on adequate housing as a component of the right to an adequate standard of living. The current Rapporteur is Leilani Farha, a Canadian lawyer.

The scope of the mandate as established now consists of the following elements:

- To promote the full realisation of adequate housing as a component of the right to an adequate standard of living
- To identify best practices as well as challenges and obstacles to the full realisation of the right to adequate housing, and identify protection gaps in this regard
- To give particular emphasis to practical solutions with regard to the implementation of the rights relevant to the mandate
- To apply a gender perspective, including through the identification of gender-specific vulnerabilities in relation to the right to adequate housing and land
- To facilitate the provision of technical assistance
- To work in close cooperation, while avoiding unnecessary duplication, with other special procedures and subsidiary organs of the Human Rights Council, relevant United Nations bodies, the treaty bodies and regional human rights mechanisms
- To submit a report on the implementation of the present resolution to the General Assembly and to the Council

See also: ***housing rights approach to housing***

Urban regeneration

Urban regeneration – sometimes called urban renewal – is the attempt to improve the physical structure and, more importantly and elusively, the economy of areas of industrial decline, poor housing and unemployment. In all regeneration programmes, public money is used as an attempt to pump prime private investment into an area. Earlier projects tended to focus on physical regeneration, usually housing, whereas later programmes have attempted to stimulate social and economic regeneration.[673]

---

[673] Weaver, M (2001) 'Urban regeneration – the issue explained', *The Guardian*, 19 March

Property ***development*** remained the most common strategy used to address economic and population decline in these districts. Urban regeneration in Ireland was operationalised mainly using fiscal incentives, rather than direct public spending.[674],[675] Irish urban regeneration intervention of recent decades typically encompassed a package of fiscal incentives – e.g. the Urban Renewal Scheme, Town Renewal Scheme – and has also been property-led.[676]

See also: ***Urban Regeneration and Housing Act 2015; Vacant Sites Register and Levy; section 23; Urban Regeneration Development Fund***

Urban Regeneration and Housing Act 2015

There are two main components to the Urban Regeneration and Housing Act 2015. The first significant element is that changes were made to ***Part V*** provisions. The Part V requirement to reserve 20 per cent of a residential scheme for social and affordable housing was reduced to 10 per cent ***social housing*** (removing the ***affordable housing*** element) and only on developments with more than nine units. The option of providing a cash payment in lieu of social housing was removed, as was the option of providing sites, either on the land the subject of the planning application or elsewhere. However, the Act gave ***developers*** the option of transferring completed units on land which is not the subject of the planning application, rather than the current option to enter into an agreement to build units and transfer them on completion. This was intended to allow social housing units to be delivered in another location in the event that the development under negotiation does not meet the social housing needs of the local authority. The Act also permitted developers to fulfil their Part V obligations either within the development the subject of the planning application or on other land through long-term leasing of units or rental accommodation ***availability arrangements***. These new Part V arrangements may be applied retrospectively to existing ***planning permissions*** where works have not commenced, provided that:

- All parties to the agreement consent
- The Part V agreements are amended prior to lodgement of the Commencement Notice
- The amended agreement complies with the new statutory requirements

The second significant component of the Act was the introduction of a ***Vacant Sites Register and Levy***.

---

[674] Adair, A, Berry, J and McGreal, S (2003) 'Financing Property's Contribution to Regeneration', *Urban Studies* Vol. 40, Nos. 5–6, pp. 1065–1080

[675] Jones, P and Evans, J (2008) *Urban Regeneration in the UK*, Sage: London

[676] Norris, M, Gkartzios, M and Coates, D (2013) 'Property-led Urban, Town and Rural Regeneration in Ireland: Positive and Perverse Outcomes in Different Implementation Contexts', UCD Discussion Paper Series WP2013/11

Finally, the Act provided that if a new ***development contribution scheme*** is made by a ***planning authority*** the new scheme will have retrospective effect on the parts of the development that has not yet commenced.

Urban Regeneration Development Fund

This is a fund introduced in 2018 to which public-sector-led bids for projects which will transform an area can be made. There is a minimum bid of €2 million in rural towns and €10 million in metropolitan areas. Proposals are eligible under the headings of:

- Active land management – strategic relocations to facilitate re-purposing of areas and places
- Addressing vacancy, building refurbishment, redevelopment
- Public realm/place-making/recreation/community facilities
- Housing affordability measures
- Tackling social disadvantage
- Infrastructure – physical and social – sustainable mobility
- Transition to a low-carbon and climate-resilient society

Applications for funding must demonstrate a minimum of a 100 per cent return on monies received (i.e. a €10 million bid must demonstrate at least an additional €10 million in new development or economic activity).

See also: ***Local Infrastructure Housing Activation Fund (LIHAF); Serviced Sites Fund***

Urban sprawl

Urban sprawl is the expansion of an urban area to accommodate its growing population.[677]

See also: ***suburbanisation; suburbs; sustainable development***

V

Vacancy rate

The overall vacancy rate in Census 2016, including holiday homes, was 12.3 per cent. If holiday homes are excluded from the housing stock the vacancy rate drops to 9.4 per cent.[678] A vacancy rate of between 2.5 per cent and 6 per cent is considered normal in a properly functioning housing market. This vacancy rate allows for dwellings under renovation, in between tenancies (in both public and private housing stock) and those dwellings left vacant while being sold.[679]

---

[677] United Nations Statistical Division (1997) *Glossary of Environment Statistics*, Studies in Methods, Series F, No. 67, United Nations: New York
[678] CSO Census 2016
[679] Department of Housing, Planning and Local Government (2018) *National Vacant Housing Reuse Strategy 2018–2021*, Government of Ireland: Dublin

See also: ***National Vacant Housing Reuse Strategy 2018–2021; vacant dwellings***

According to the CSO, some 12.3 per cent of the 2,003,645 dwellings that formed the Irish housing stock were vacant in Census 2016. The 2011–2016 period recorded a 15 per cent drop in vacancy to 245,460 dwellings in 2016.

Vacant dwellings[680]

Within this the number of holiday homes had increased between 2011 and 2016, from 59,395 to 62,148. There were 203,048 empty buildings in April 2016, of which the vast majority (98.4 per cent) were single-dwelling units. A total of 3,308 multi-dwelling buildings containing 11,680 duplexes, flats or apartments were completely vacant. Mixed occupied and vacant buildings numbered 15,768 and within these buildings 34,040 units were vacant while 126,154 were either occupied or temporarily absent on Census night.

Of the total 245,460 vacant dwellings, 62,148 were identified as holiday homes. There were 183,312 other vacant dwellings in April 2016, of which 140,120 were houses and 43,192 were apartments. The majority of houses were detached, accounting for 44 per cent of vacant dwellings.

When examining the vacancy rates within each dwelling type, one in ten of all detached and terraced houses were recorded as being empty. For semi-detached houses the vacancy rate dropped down to just over 5 per cent. Among purpose-built apartments the percentage of vacant homes stood at 13.5 per cent. The highest rates of vacancy were within flats in converted buildings where around 30 per cent were classified as vacant.

The lowest number of empty dwellings (excluding holiday homes) relative to population size was in South Dublin, followed by Fingal and Kildare, while in Leitrim for every 1,000 people in that county there were 112 vacant homes. Longford recorded the largest fall, dropping from 96 vacant per 1,000 population to 69 in 2016. Of the 183,312 vacant houses and apartments, 117,381 were located within the 873 settlements (cities, towns and villages) identified in Census 2016. In 2016, there were 54 towns in Ireland where there were over 25 per cent of dwellings vacant.

The methodology used to categorise a dwelling as vacant is important. In identifying vacant dwellings, enumerators were instructed to look for signs that the dwelling was unoccupied, e.g. no furniture, no cars outside, junk mail accumulating, overgrown garden, and to find out from neighbours whether it was vacant or not. It was not sufficient to classify a dwelling as vacant after one or two visits. Similar precautions were also taken when classifying holiday homes. Dwellings under construction and derelict properties are not included in the count of vacant dwellings. In order to be classified as

---

[680] CSO Census 2016

under construction, the dwelling had to be unfit for habitation because the roof, doors, windows or walls had not yet been built or installed.

The main reasons for vacancy are: dwelling for sale; occupant deceased; vacant long term; rental property; occupant in nursing home; renovation; new build; occupant emigrated; dwelling boarded up – habitable; occupant in hospital; occupant with relatives; other personal use; abandoned farm house; and 'other'.

See also: ***National Vacant Housing Reuse Strategy 2018–2021; vacancy rate***

Vacant possession

Despite the ubiquity of the term, 'vacant possession' is not defined in legislation. According to legal experts,[681] there have been a number of cases in the UK where the meaning of vacant possession has been discussed. Simply put, vacant possession means that the relevant person, whether that is a purchaser or landlord, is in a position to enjoy the property undisturbed. If a seller or tenant continues to use the property in a manner that is inconsistent with vacant possession or if there is an impediment, physical or otherwise, to enjoying the property, vacant possession may not have been delivered.

See also: ***adverse possession***

Vacant Sites Register and Levy

Under the ***Urban Regeneration and Housing Act 2015***, each local authority must compile a register of lands in its area that are suitable for housing but are not coming forward for development. The Act defines vacant sites for residential and regeneration purposes:

(1) A site is a vacant site if –
(*a*) In the case of a site consisting of residential land –
  (i)   The site is situated in an area in which there is a need for housing,
  (ii) The site is suitable for the provision of housing, and
  (iii) The site, or the majority of the site, is vacant or idle,
and
(*b*) In the case of a site consisting of regeneration land –
  (i) The site, or the majority of the site, is vacant or idle, and
  (ii) The site being vacant or idle has adverse effects on existing amenities or reduces the amenity provided by existing public infrastructure and facilities (within the meaning of section 48 of the Act of 2000) in the area in which the site is situated or has adverse effects on the character of the area.

---

[681] See: https://www.mhc.ie/latest/insights/real-estate-update-vacant-possession-what-does-it-mean

In the Act, 'site' means any area of land exceeding 0.05 hectares identified by a ***planning authority*** in its functional area but does not include any structure that is a person's home; 'home', in relation to a person, means a ***dwelling*** in which the person ordinarily resides (notwithstanding any periods during which the dwelling is vacant) and includes any garden or portion of ground attached to and usually occupied with the dwelling or otherwise required for the amenity or convenience of the dwelling. It should be noted that, according to section 5(*b*) of the Act, residential sites depending on investment in public ***infrastructure*** and facilities (e.g. road infrastructure and/or water services) to facilitate ***development*** are not deemed to be vacant sites.

Sites on the Vacant Sites Register are charged a 3 per cent levy in 2019 on their value in 2018. This rises to 7 per cent in the following year until the site is no longer vacant. The levy shall be payable in arrears each year beginning in 2019 by the owner of the vacant site that is entered on the register on 1 January of that year. The levy shall be payable within two months of a demand being made by the authority. Arrangements can be made for paying by instalments. Any levy not paid remains as a charge on the property until paid. As per section 15(2) of the Act, a vacant sites levy shall not be payable in respect of any land in respect of which the derelict sites levy within the meaning of the ***Derelict Sites Act 1990*** is payable in accordance with that Act.

Local authorities must apply the vacant sites levy irrespective of ownership, meaning councils can end up fining themselves if their land appears on the register.

There are exemptions to the levy, for example if the site has loans attached to it which are greater than the value of the site. Section 16(2) says that if the amount of the loan is:

(*a*) greater than the ***market value*** of the vacant site, vacant site levy in respect of that site is 0 per cent;

(*b*) greater than 75 per cent, but less than 100 per cent, of the market value of the vacant site, vacant site levy in respect of that site is 0.75 per cent; and

(*c*) greater than 50 per cent, but less than 75 per cent, of the market value of the vacant site, vacant site levy in respect of that site is 1.5 per cent of such market value.

Section 17 provides an exemption to the levy in circumstances of death of the owner or a change of ownership. It says that where there is a change in ownership of a site on the register, the amount of vacant sites levy to be charged in respect of that site for that year, and for the preceding year, will be zero. This exemption does not apply for transfers between associated companies or connected persons (other than where ownership of the site devolves on the death of the owner) or transfers for the sole or principal purpose of avoiding the obligation to pay the levy.

If a vacant site on the Vacant Sites Register is also on the register of derelict sites under the Derelict Sites Act 1990, only the vacant sites levy will still be payable.

In relation to temporary uses, section 6(7) of the Urban Regeneration and Housing Act 2015 provides that 'In determining … whether a site was vacant or idle for the duration of the 12 months concerned, a planning authority, or the Board on appeal, shall not have regard to any unauthorised development or unauthorised use.'

According to the Department of Housing, Planning and Local Government,[682] in effect, therefore, where a site has been vacant for a while (for more than the preceding twelve months) and is now suddenly put to use, for example as a car park, for the purposes of avoiding the levy on the basis that it is no longer vacant or idle, if that use has not been authorised by way of a *planning permission* then the use is unauthorised and the site is therefore liable to the levy. However if that use has been authorised by way of a planning permission, then the levy does not apply to the site. Similarly, if the site owner commences development on a site further to obtaining planning permission for such development, the levy does not apply but if the owner commences some development on the site without planning permission, then the levy does apply. It comes down to whether the use or development is authorised or unauthorised.

See also: *National Vacant Housing Reuse Strategy 2018–2021; vacancy rate*

Valuation   A valuation is an estimation or subjective assessment of the *value* of an interest in a property to the holder of the interest. The valuation will be arrived at through the valuer's professional knowledge of market conditions and transactions. The valuation of a particular interest in *land* is normally made by reference to its *tenure*, its use and its income-producing capacity.[683] It may also be regarded as the art of expressing opinions in a mathematical form in order to arrive at the value of a particular interest in a particular piece of property at a given moment of time.[684] In effect, a valuation is the advised prediction of price that the property may be expected to achieve in the market given its condition, location, tenure, and so forth.

See also: *valuer, advised market value; advised letting value*

[682] Department of Housing, Planning and Local Government, personal communication, 2018
[683] Scarrett, D (2014) *Property Valuation – The Five Methods*, Routledge: London
[684] Millington, AF (2000) *An Introduction to Property Valuation*, Estates Gazette: London

There are several definitions of 'value'. The International Valuation Standards Council (IVSC) define 'market value' as: 'the estimated amount for which a property should exchange on the date of valuation between a willing buyer and a willing seller in an arm's length transaction after proper marketing wherein the parties had each acted knowledgeably, prudently and without compulsion.'

The Royal Institution of Chartered Surveyors have a more detailed definition, which is broadly along the same lines as the IVSC:

the open market value ('OMV') is the best price obtainable in a transaction completed on the valuation date based upon the following assumptions:

i.   a willing seller (a hypothetical owner who is neither eager nor reluctant i.e. not forced but not at a price which suits only him/her).
ii. prior to the valuation, a reasonable period to market the property and complete all the necessary legal formalities was available.
iii. during this period, the state of the market was the same as at the date of valuation.
iv. any bid from a special purchaser is excluded.
v.   all parties acted knowledgeably, prudently and without compulsion.

Irish valuers give an '***Advised Market Value***' (AMV). This term has a statutory basis in the ***Property Services (Regulation) Act 2011***. The advised market value, in relation to land valued for sale by a licensee, means the valuer's reasonable estimate, at the time of such valuation:

i.   of the amount that would be paid by a willing buyer in an arm's length transaction after proper marketing where both parties act knowledgeably, prudently and without compulsion; or
ii. of the relevant price range within which would fall the amount that would be paid by a willing buyer in an arm's length transaction after proper marketing where both parties act knowledgeably, prudently and without compulsion.

In relation to land valued for sale or letting, 'relevant price range' means a price range where the difference between the upper limit of such valuation and the lower limit of such valuation is not more than 10 per cent of such lower limit.

The intention of this legislation is to ensure that the quoted price is as close to the final selling price as possible, so that interested parties are not unduly or deliberately misled into believing that a property might be sold close to the quoted price, when both the agent and vendor are expecting a far higher price. When advertising a property, the agent responsible must not quote a price that is less than the AMV. They must also be able to demonstrate how they arrived at this value.[685]

Valuer

A valuer is a licenced professional (see: ***property services providers***) who is often a member of a professional body such as the ***Society of Chartered Surveyors Ireland***, whose role is to appraise the ***value*** of property for different purposes. They will typically be involved in the preparation of valuations and ***valuation*** advice for property for sale, purchase or letting.

Valuers will use various methods to assess the value of the property in question, including:

- Direct comparison
- Investment method
- Profits/accounts method
- Residual method
- Contractors method
- Discounted cash flow method

Variable rate

Variable rate mortgages are those where the ***interest rate*** is set at a margin above the European Central Bank's lending rate. As the ECB rates fluctuate, the interest rate on the mortgage varies too.

See also: ***fixed rate mortgage***

Vesting Certificate

When a Vesting Certificate is issued it vests the ***fee simple*** and any intermediate titles free from incumbrances in an applicant. Vesting Certificates are issued by the ***Property Registration Authority*** under section 22(1) of the Landlord and Tenant (Ground Rents) Act 1978. A Vesting Certificate will be issued when an applicant buys out their ***ground rent***, for example.

See also: ***memorial; Land Registry; Registry of Deeds***

Voids

A void is an empty local authority or ***approved housing body*** property. A certain number of voids in housing is to be expected each year as properties are vacated and remain empty awaiting refurbishment or new tenants, and managing voids is a core function of both these bodies. Voids become problematic when they become 'long-term' voids (i.e. more than 27 weeks) rather than merely a temporary hiatus. Reasons for long-term voids can include: the units are included in a planned regeneration or remedial works scheme; units have been vacated by the tenant for the purpose of enabling works to

---

[685] Carey, E (2016) 'When estate agents quote misguiding prices', *Irish Times*, 6 April

be carried out that require vacant possession; units are for sale; or units have been refused by successive potential tenants.[686]

The measurement of voids is worth noting. When local authorities tell the **Department of Housing, Planning and Local Government** how many voids they have, they do not include units that are not being offered to waiting-list applicants because they need substantial refurbishment works or are intended to be demolished.[687] The **Housing Agency** has argued that the reported figures should include all housing that is empty[688] for more effective **asset management**. For example, Dublin City Council has reported their **social housing** void rate at around 1.5 per cent, which is units awaiting re-letting.[689] However, if they reported all voids then the void rate jumps to 6.29 per cent of their housing stock (as at 1 December 2015).[690]

See also: **National Oversight and Audit Commission; data – housing output issues**

A vulture fund is a colloquial term for various types of pension and private **Vulture funds** equity funds that, as part of their investment strategies, buy up debt (loans owed), and often distressed debt, i.e. loans owed but which are under- or non-performing. Many institutions, particularly banks, are not willing to write down debt and have sold off portfolios of performing, under-performing and non-performing debt, often in the form of household **mortgages**, to international vulture funds at a considerable discount in order to get them off their books. The purpose of a vulture fund is to acquire these loans and, in the case of under- or non-performing mortgages, to get possession of the underlying **asset** (the house) in order to sell it to cover the cost of the debt owed on it and make a profit.

Most vulture funds are not regulated to do business in Ireland, mainly due to the fact that they have acquired rather than gave the loans, but will employ local, regulated forms to operate on their behalf, known as **credit servicing firms**. Unlike banks, neither do they have a presence on the high street.

Cerebus, Pepper, Lone Star Capital, Blackstone, Oaktree Capital, Starwood Capital and King Street Capital are some of the companies colloquially known as vulture funds that are operating in Ireland.[691]

See also: **sub-prime**

---

[686] National Oversight and Audit Commission (2017) *A Review of the Management and Maintenance of Local Authority Housing – Report No. 12*, NOAC: Dublin
[687] National Oversight and Audit Commission (2018) *Performance Indicators in Local Authorities 2016 – Report No. 14*, NOAC: Dublin
[688] Neylon, L (2016) 'How should we count the number of council voids?', *Dublin Inquirer*, 21 December
[689] See: http://www.dublincity.ie/dublin-city-councils-position-relation-vacant-local-authority-dwellings
[690] Neylon, L (2016) 'How should we count the number of council voids?', *Dublin Inquirer*, 21 December
[691] Pope, C (2016) 'Vulture funds and why they can act with virtual impunity', *Irish Times*, 14 March

W

Wayleave

A wayleave is a *right of way* across land or property usually for the provision of services or infrastructure such as gas pipelines or electricity pylons. They can be created by express grant, by reservation or by statute. Where a wayleave is being acquired over agricultural land, it is normal practice to agree compensation by way of a once-off payment per linear metre; or a sum equating to a percentage of the agricultural value of the land affected. Payment is also usually made for disturbance and crop loss, with the acquiring authority responsible for restoration/remediation works (e.g. replacing topsoil, reseeding, stone removal, temporary fencing). The acquiring authority is also responsible for the payment of professional fees (e.g. legal, *valuer*, agronomist). Infrastructure bodies such as the ESB and Bord Gais will usually have their own codes of practice, which will have been agreed with farmers' groups over may years.

Problems can arise when a wayleave is taken through land with high *development* potential. *Density* may be affected, as it is not normally permitted to construct buildings on, under or within a certain distance of the permanent wayleave (pipeline, cable, etc.). Even if the wayleave scheme improves the value of the farmer's *land*, the acquiring authority must still fund it (e.g. the installation of mains water drainage scheme to which future development could be connected).

See also: *easements; right of way*

Wealth

Wealth is something that is owned (i.e. any form of property/*assets*), and which can be traded on an open market. It is a stock rather than a flow, and can be either publicly or privately owned. The stock of wealth in a country is the total *market value* of all the financial and non-financial assets in that country. This is often expressed as a percentage of national income. If a country's total stock of wealth is equal to seven times national income, then it is 700 per cent of GDP. The most dominant form of wealth is in the form of currency savings or in a property (house).

Wealth is the result of past earnings and income, but it is also affected by inheritance and decisions relating to investment, savings and consumption. The assets that constitute wealth can be divided into real assets and financial assets. The *Central Bank of Ireland* defines 'total net worth' as the difference between a stock of total assets and liabilities. Assets include *land*, real estate, business equity, agricultural assets, vehicles, cash savings, life assurance reserves, pension fund equity, and personal property. Liabilities are debts. Assets give value to the person who holds that asset. Housing and cars provide use value. Most assets can appreciate in value, which can give financial security. Assets can lead to participation in society, status, access to power and influence, economic freedom, and psychological benefits. In other words, wealth provides substantial benefits to the holder of wealth above and beyond the monetary income generated from that wealth.[692]

The net worth of Irish households rose to €727 billion at the end of 2017. Household net worth, calculated as the sum of housing and financial assets minus their liabilities, is the equivalent of €151,657 per person.[693]

See also: ***household debt; wealth inequality; Piketty, Thomas; asset-based welfare***

Wealth inequality is a core aspect of economic inequality. Highly unequal societies are typified by high levels of wealth concentration, where wealth is held by very few people. Wealth tends to be distributed more unequally than income and a highly unequal distribution of wealth causes problems for both the economy and society.[694]

Housing has a significant role to play in wealth inequality. Research shows that unsustainable housing prices can cause significant macroeconomic instability, drive wealth inequality, and accelerate households' accumulation of debt.[695] ***Piketty*** demonstrated that wealth inequality is rising in all the advanced capitalist democracies, and in particular Anglo-Saxon economies, and other scholars have pointed out that these dynamics are increasingly shaped by the price effect of housing. It is also argued that, if it is the case that rising house prices is a determinant of wealth inequality within OECD countries then future comparative capitalism research would be well placed to analyse this relationship between housing capital and inequality.[696]

See also: ***wealth; asset-based welfare***

Wealth inequality

The welfare state is a system whereby the state undertakes to protect the health and wellbeing of its citizens, especially those in financial or social need, by means of grants, pensions, and other benefits. This includes the provision of housing to those who need it.

The welfare state modifies the impact of the market by providing some sort of minimum guarantee (mitigating poverty); covering a range of social risks (security); and providing certain services (health care, child and elder care, etc.) at the best standards available. Welfare states differ as regards the

Welfare state

---

[692] O'Connor, N and Staunton, C (2017) *Cherishing All Equally: Economic Inequality in Ireland*, TASC: Dublin

[693] Burke-Kennedy, E (2018) 'Irish households now wealthier than during the boom', *Irish Times*, 4 May

[694] O'Connor, N and Staunton, C (2017) *Cherishing All Equally: Economic Inequality in Ireland*, TASC: Dublin

[695] Fuller, G, Johnston, A and Regan, A (2018) 'Bringing the Household Back In: Comparative Capitalism and the Politics of Housing Markets', UCD Geary Institute Discussion Papers, WP2018/07

[696] *Ibid.*

level of ambition and the mix between these aspects: coverage may include a broad or narrow range of risks and services, and minima may alleviate poverty or aim at providing equality.[697]

According to a narrow definition, the welfare state comprises two types of government spending arrangements: (i) cash benefits to households (transfers, including mandatory income insurance) and (ii) subsidies or direct government provision of human services (such as child care, pre-schooling, education, health care, and old-age care). By broader definitions, the welfare state may also include price regulation (such as *rent control* and agricultural price support), housing policies, regulation of the work environment, job security legislation, and environmental policies.[698]

The origins of the UK's welfare state are to be found in the Beveridge Report of 1942, *Social Security and Allied Services*, which outlined the expansion of the welfare state after World War II. Although this report was widely read by Irish policy-makers, and influenced future policy, most of the Irish reforms were modest compared to the UK: the 1952 Social Welfare Act extended access to social security benefits but still excluded large sections of the population from cover; the Health Act of 1953 established a mixed system of public and private health care in which most of the population still had to pay for services; and free second-level education was not introduced until 1967.[699] Instead, Ireland promoted a system of property-based welfare through land redistribution, subsidised home ownership, and government-provided mortgages.[700]

See also: *asset-based welfare; policy, housing*

Windfall gain A windfall gain is a large, and often unexpected, profit (e.g. a lottery win). In housing and planning terms, windfall gains are often due to changes in the *zoning* of land from one designation to another more valuable one (e.g. from an agriculture to residential zoning class). From 2010 to 2014, there was an 80 per cent windfall gain tax on 'profits or gains arising from certain land disposals following a relevant planning decision (*rezoning* or a decision to allow a material contravention of a *development plan*)'.[701] This tax was abolished in 2014 in an effort to encourage development. It has been argued,

---

[697] Goul Andersen, J (2012) 'Welfare State and Welfare State Theory', Centre for Comparative Welfare Studies Working Paper, Department of Political Science, Aalborg University

[698] Lindbeck, A (2006) 'The Welfare State – Background, Achievements, Problems', IFN Working Paper Series 662, Research Institute of Industrial Economics: Stockholm

[699] Carey, S (2007) *Social Security in Ireland 1939–1952: The Limits to Solidarity*, Irish Academic Press: Dublin; and McCashin, T (2004) *Social Security in Ireland*, Gill and Macmillan: Dublin; both cited in Norris, M (2017) *Property, Family and the Irish Welfare State*, Palgrave Macmillan: London

[700] Norris, M (2017) *Property, Family and the Irish Welfare State*, Palgrave Macmillan: London

[701] See: https://www.revenue.ie/en/tax-professionals/tdm/income-tax-capital-gains-tax-corporation-tax/part-02/02-02-01.pdf

however, that such windfall taxes help to mitigate the typical boom and bust periods in a ***property cycle***.

See also: ***rezoning; population; land; speculation***

The Irish Land (Provision for Soldiers and Sailors) Act 1919 ('Homes fit for heroes') provided for the construction of houses for ex-World War I servicemen throughout Ireland. The scheme included the 200,000 Irishmen who volunteered for British Army service during the Great War, of whom 100,00 returned to Ireland. The largest of these, at 289 houses, was at Killester, in north Dublin.[702]

The Act empowered the Irish ***Land Commission*** to provide housing for any men who had served in the British forces. The Act did not stipulate how the project would be funded, how many houses would be built or terms for those who would receive housing. Significant developments, with between 40 and 80 houses in each, were built to the outskirts of Dublin at Cabra (1932–1934), Glasnevin (1928–1931), Ballinteer (1931–1932), Kimmage (1931–1933) and Sandymount (1923). Numerous smaller developments were built, for example in Dún Laoghaire, Sallynoggin, Castleknock, Dundrum, Palmerstown, Clontarf, Raheny and Drimnagh. There is considerable variety of house styles between and within these developments. Substantial concentrations of approximately 50–60 houses were built at Charleville, County Cork; Limerick; Clonmel; Thurles; Athlone; Mullingar; and Bray. Elsewhere, they were isolated or in small groups of perhaps two to eight, occurring widely both in the countryside and in towns. However, concentrations averaging 10–35 houses are more characteristic and normally located in or on the edge of towns.[703]

World War I housing

X

X-inefficiency is when a lack of effective/real competition in a market or industry means that average costs are higher than they would be with competition.

X-inefficiency

---

[702] O'Sullivan, J (2012) 'Houses for Heroes: Life in the Killester Colony 1919–1945', in *Dublin Historical Record*, Vol. 65, No. 1/2, pp. 2–33
[703] Aalen, F (1988) 'Homes for Irish Heroes: Housing under the Irish Land (Provision for Soldiers and Sailors) Act 1919, and the Irish Sailors' and Soldiers' Land Trust', *The Town Planning Review*, Vol. 59, No. 3, pp. 305–323

Y

Y-value   A Y-value is used to show how much heat is lost through the junctions of a building. Normal results for a residential house will be in the range of 0.15–0.02 W/m²K, with the latter score indicating that there are very few ***thermal bridges*** in the house.[704]

See also: ***U-value***

Yield   A yield is a measurement of future income on an ***investment***. It is generally calculated annually as a percentage, based on the asset's (or investment's) cost or ***market value***. Gross yield is the annual rental income from the property expressed as a percentage of the capital value (cost) of the property. Net yield is calculated using gross rental income minus expenses.

There are several different types of yield:

- *All risks yield*: Implies that the investor had considered all the risks and potential reward in arriving at a purchase price which is then reflected in the yield.
- *Equated yield*: Describes the yield on a property investment which takes into account growth in future income.
- *Indicative yield*: Estimates the annual dividend yield; it is only a forecast and can go up or down. Initial yield is the annualised rent of a property expressed as a percentage of the property value.
- *Prime yield*: Describes the remunerative rate of interest appropriate at the date of a valuation if the property is to be let at its full market rental value. Considered as a benchmark to compare against other properties.
- *Reversionary yield*: Is the anticipated yield to which the initial yield will rise and fall.

See also: ***capital value; land***

YIMBY   Yes In My Back Yard. This is a pro-***development***, pro-growth grassroots movement, originating in San Francisco, as an opposition to the more commonly known ***NIMBY***. It aims to encourage development in order to bring more ***affordability***, especially in housing. It is often regarded as a developer-led, anti-planning, pro-deregulation movement.

---

[704] See: https://www.energistuk.co.uk/knowledge-bank/blog/y-value.php

Z

Zoning is a town planning tool whereby specific parts of a local authority's area are designated for specific uses (e.g. industrial, amenity, residential). This is illustrated on a map as part of the authority's ***development plan***. The main objective of zoning is to promote the orderly ***development*** of a local authority area by eliminating potential conflicts between incompatible land uses and to establish an efficient basis for investment in public ***infrastructure*** and facilities.[705]

Zoning tends to be used as a guideline for development, rather than an absolute, and other factors will influence the decision to grant or otherwise a planning application (e.g. factors such as making the most efficient use of land, ***density***, ***height***, massing, traffic generation, public health regulations, design criteria, visual amenity and potential nuisance by way of noise, odour or air pollution are also of importance in establishing whether or not a development proposal conforms to the proper planning and sustainable development of an area).[706]

Within each zoning, there will be different categories of development that are permitted (or permitted in principle), open for consideration, or not permitted. When land is zoned for a particular type of development in the development plan this is a clear indication that a planning permission for this form of development may be obtained. Zoning may also indicate restrictions on development (e.g. a low number of houses per hectare; certain types of industry only) and permitted development will be limited accordingly.[707]

For example, within the Fingal local authority area, zoning objective 'RS' (residential), the objective is to: 'Provide for new residential communities subject to the provision of the necessary social and physical infrastructure'.[708] Permitted in principle under residential area zoning are:

* Bed and breakfast
* Childcare facilities
* Community facilities
* Education
* Guest house
* Office ancillary to permitted use

Zoning

---

[705] Fingal County Council (2017) 'Chapter 11: Land Use Zoning Objectives', *Draft Development Plan 2017–2023*, Fingal County Council: Dublin

[706] Dún Laoghaire–Rathdown County Council (2004) *County Development Plan 2004–2010*, DLR: Dublin

[707] See: https://www.housing.gov.ie/sites/default/files/migrated-files/en/Publications/Development andHousing/Planning/NationalSpatialStrategy/FileDownLoad%2C1589%2Cen.pdf

[708] See: https://consult.fingal.ie/en/consultation/draft-fingal-development-plan-2017---2023-stage-2/chapter/chapter-11-land-use-zoning

- Open space
- Residential
- Residential care home/retirement home
- Retirement village
- Traveller community accommodation
- Utility installations

Not permitted are such uses as:

- Abattoir
- Betting office
- Caravan park
- Dancehall/nightclub
- Exhibition centre
- Food, drink and flower preparation/processing
- Garden centre
- Heavy vehicle park
- Logistics
- Plant storage
- Retail warehouse
- Taxi office
- Vehicle sales outlet – small vehicles
- Waste disposal and recovery facility

See also: ***unauthorised development; retention planning permission; speculation; land***

Leabharlanna Poiblí Chathair Baile Átha Cliath
Dublin City Public Libraries

Bibliography

Aalbers, M (2016) *The Financialisation of Housing: A Political Approach*, Routledge: London

Aalen, F (1988) 'Homes for Irish Heroes: Housing under the Irish Land (Provision for Soldiers and Sailors) Act 1919, and the Irish Sailors' and Soldiers' Land Trust', *The Town Planning Review*, Vol. 59, No. 3, pp. 305–323

Adair, A, Berry, J and McGreal, S, (2003) 'Financing Property's Contribution to Regeneration', *Urban Studies*, Vol. 40, Nos. 5–6, pp. 1065–1080

Alexander, GS (2007) 'The Ambiguous Work of "Natural Property Rights"', *Journal of Constitutional Law*, Vol. 9, No. 2, pp. 477–482

Allen, J, Barlow, J, Leal, J, Maloutas, T and Padovani, L (2004) *Housing and Welfare in Southern Europe*, Blackwell: London

ALONE (2018) *Housing Choices for Older People in Ireland: Time for Action*, ALONE: Dublin

Amárach Research, Lyons, R, Sirr, L and Innovation Delivery (2016) 'Housing for Older People – Thinking Ahead', ISAX: Dublin

André, T and van der Flier, K (2011) 'Obsolescence and the End of Life Phase of Buildings', paper presented at Management and Innovation for a Sustainable Built Environment (MISBE) CIB International Conference, 20–23 June, Amsterdam

Anon. (1925) 'News', *Irish Builder*, Vol. 67, 7 February

Anon. (1927) 'News', *Irish Builder*, Vol. 69, 19 March

Anon. (1932) *Irish Builder and Engineer*, Vol. 73, p. 110

Anon. (2001) 'Getting to grips with the chaos in planning', *Irish Times*, 7 March

Anon. (2018) 'The National Planning Framework in Brief', *Eolas*, 29 March

Arkcoll, K, Guilding, C, Lamminamki, D, McManus, L and Warnken, J (2013) 'Funding Common Property Expenditure in Multi-owned Housing Schemes', *Property Management*, Vol. 31, No. 4, pp. 282–296

Arnott, R (2003) 'Tenancy Rent Control', *Swedish Economic Policy Review*, Vol. 10, pp. 89–121

Bacon, P (1998) *An Economic Assessment of Recent House Price Developments – A Report Submitted to the Minister for Housing and Urban Renewal*, Government of Ireland: Dublin

Bacon, P (1999) *The Housing Market: An Economic Review and Assessment – A Report Submitted to the Minister for Housing and Urban Renewal*, Government of Ireland: Dublin

Bacon, P (2000) *The Housing Market in Ireland: An Economic Evaluation of Trends and Prospects – A Report Submitted to the Minister for Housing and Urban Renewal*, Government of Ireland: Dublin

Bacon, P (2009) *Evaluation of Options for Resolving Property Loan Impairments and Associated Capital Adequacy of Irish Credit Institutions: Proposal for a National Asset Management Agency (NAMA) – Abridged Summary of Report*, Government of Ireland: Dublin

Baker, S (2017) 'Report into fire that destroyed 6 Kildare houses finds remaining homes not compliant with regulations', *TheJournal.ie*, 1 September, available at: https://www.thejournal.ie/report-into-fire-that-destroyed-six-kildare-homes-finds-houses-not-in-compliance-with-building-regulations-3576979-Sep2017/

Baker, T and O'Brien, L (1979) *The Irish Housing System: A Critical Overview*, ESRI: Dublin

Bannon, MJ (1978) 'Patrick Geddes and the Emergence of Modern Town Planning in Ireland', *Irish Geography*, Vol. 11, No. 2, pp. 141–148

Bannon, MJ (2004) 'Forty Years of Irish Planning: An Overview', *Journal of Irish Urban Studies*, Vol. 3, No. 1, pp. 1–16

Barlow, J and Duncan, S (1994) *Success and Failure in Housing Provision*, Pergamon: London

Barry, J (2012) 'Shadow of the Land Commission still falls on farm sector', *Irish Independent*, 25 July

Battye, F, Bishop, B, Harris, P, Murie, A, Rowlands, R and Tice, A (2006) *Evaluation of Key Worker Living: Final Report*, DCLG Publications: West Yorkshire

Baxter, LG (2012) 'Understanding Regulatory Capture: An Academic Perspective from the United States', in Pagliari, S (ed.), *The Making of Good Financial Regulation: Towards a Policy Response to Regulatory Capture*, Grosvenor House Publishing: London

BBC (2010) 'Who, What, Why: How do you count rough sleepers?', *BBC Magazine*, 16 August

BDO (2014) *Health's Ageing Crisis: A Time for Action – A Future Strategy for Ireland's Long-term Residential Care Sector*, BDO Ireland: Dublin

Berens, G, Haney, R and Miles, ME (1996) *Real Estate Development: Principles and Process*, Urban Land Institute: Washington DC

Bergenståhle, S (2013) 'The Right to Housing and Need for Tenure Neutrality', *Global Tenant*, April

Bland, P (2009) *Easements*, second edition, Thomas Reuters (Professional) Ireland Limited: Dublin

Bonnet, O, Bono, PH, Chapelle, G and Wasmer, E (2014) 'Does Housing Capital Contribute to Inequality? A Comment on Thomas Piketty's *Capital in the 21st Century*', *Sciences Po Economics Discussion Papers 2014-07*, Sciences Po Department of Economics

Bourassa, S and Hoesli, M (2009) 'Why Do the Swiss Rent?', Working Paper, Université de Genève

Bowers, S (2018) 'DCU students protest over 27% rent hike', *Irish Times*, 29 March

Boyce, B (2007) 'Property as a Natural Right and as a Conventional Right in Constitutional Law', *Loyola of Los Angeles International and Comparative Law Review*, Vol. 29, No. 2, pp. 201–290

Brady Shipman Martin (2012) *Review of Part V of the Planning and Development Act, 2000*, The Housing Agency: Dublin

Brenner, N and Theodore, N (2002) 'Cities and the Geographies of "Actually Existing Neoliberalism"', *Antipode*, Vol. 34, pp. 349–379

Brooke, S (2001) 'Social Housing for the Future: Can Housing Associations Meet the Challenge?', *Studies in Public Policy* No. 8, Policy Institute TCD

Burke-Kennedy, E (2018) 'Homes of nearly 8,200 Irish mortgage holders repossessed since crash', *Irish Times*, 9 March

Burke-Kennedy, E (2018) 'Irish households now wealthier than during the boom', *Irish Times*, 4 May

Burns, M (n.d.) '10 Legal Steps to Buying a House in Ireland', *Lawyer.ie*, available at: https://www.lawyer.ie/property/buying-a-house/

Burns, M, Drudy, PJ, Hearne, R and McVerry, P (2017) 'Rebuilding Ireland: A Flawed Philosophy Analysis of the Action Plan for Housing and Homelessness', *Working Notes*, Issue 80, October

Burns, S (2018) 'Just 8% of properties affordable for those on rental supports', *Irish Times*, 16 August

Byrne, D (1999) 'Ireland: Housing and Mortgage Markets and the Single Currency', *Housing Finance International*, March, pp. 25–28

Byrne, N/Mason Hayes & Curran (2018) 'Private Sector Delivery Mechanisms', presentation at Social Housing Seminar, 26 April, Dublin, available at: https://www.mhc.ie/uploads/Social_Housing_Seminar_Slides_for_website.pdf

CABE and Corporation of London (2004) *Better Neighbourhoods: Making Higher Densities Work*, CABE: London

Carey, E (2016) 'When estate agents quote misguiding prices', *Irish Times*, 6 April

Carey, S (2007) *Social Security in Ireland 1939–1952: The Limits to Solidarity*, Irish Academic Press: Dublin

Carswell, S (2018) 'Why David Drumm cooked the books at Anglo Irish Bank', *Irish Times*, 25 June

Case, K and Shiller, R (2003) 'Is there a Bubble in the Housing Market?', *Brookings Papers on Economic Activity*, Vol. 34, No. 2, pp. 299–362

Central Bank of Ireland (2013) *Code of Conduct on Mortgage Arrears*, Central Bank of Ireland: Dublin

Central Bank of Ireland (2017) *Macro-Financial Review – 2017: II*, Central Bank of Ireland: Dublin

Central Bank of Ireland (2018) *Residential Mortgage Arrears and Repossessions Statistics: Q3 2018*, Central Bank of Ireland: Dublin

Chartered Institute of Housing/Housing Agency (n.d.) *A Guide to Choice-Based Lettings*, available at: http://www.cih.org/resources/PDF/Republic%20of%20Ireland/A%20guide%20to%20choice-based%20lettings.pdf

Chartered Institute of Housing (2017) *Housing First in the UK and Ireland*, CIH: Coventry

Clifford, M (2017) 'Delayed fire safety report an "insult" to residents of estate that lost 6 homes in blaze', *Irish Examiner*, 26 August

Coffey, C (2016) 'What are your rights when you buy at auction?', *RTE*, available at: https://www.rte.ie/lifestyle/living/2016/1018/825059-what-are-your-rights-when-you-buy-at-auction/

Cogley, M (2018) 'Mortgage-to-rent scheme has helped only 282 families in six years', *The Times, Ireland Edition*, 8 January

Commission on the Private Rented Residential Sector (2000) *Report of the Commission on the Private Rented Residential Sector*, Department of Environment and Local Government: Dublin

Commission on Taxation (2009) *Commission on Taxation Report*, Government Publications Office: Dublin

Cooperative Housing Ireland (2016) *Strategy for the Rented Sector*, available at: https://cooperativehousing.ie/rentalsectorstrategy/

Coppock, J (ed.) (1977) *Second Homes, Curse or Blessing?*, Pergamon: Oxford

Cox, A (2017) 'Explainer: The Tracker Mortgage Scandal', *RTÉ News*, 27 October, available at: https://www.rte.ie/news/business/2017/1025/915149-explainer-the-tracker-mortgage-scandal/

Crotty, R (1969) 'Regional Planning for Ireland: The Buchanan Report', *Studies: An Irish Quarterly Review*, Vol. 58, No. 231 (Autumn), pp. 225–239

Cullen, P (2012) 'Law lets householders use reasonable force', *Irish Times*, 13 January

Daly, M (2006) *The Slow Failure: Population Decline and Independent Ireland, 1920–1973*, University of Wisconsin Press: Madison

deBurca Butler, J (2013) 'Priory Hall scandal: A century on, the same old story', *Irish Examiner*, 17 May

Delivorias, A (2015) *Understanding Securitisation: Background – Benefits – Tisks*, European Parliamentary Research Service: Brussels

Department of Communications, Energy and Natural Resources (2011) *Warmer Homes – A Strategy for Affordable Energy in Ireland*, Government of Ireland: Dublin

Department of Environment, Community and Local Government (2014) *Code of Practice for Inspecting and Certifying Buildings and Works, Building Control Regulations*, Government of Ireland: Dublin

Department of Environment, Community and Local Government (2015) *Sustainable Urban Housing: Design Standards for New Apartments – Guidelines for Planning Authorities*, Government of Ireland: Dublin

Department of Environment, Heritage and Local Government (2000) *Homelessness – An Integrated Strategy*, Government of Ireland: Dublin

Department of Environment, Heritage and Local Government (2004) *Guidance on the Adoption of a Joint Venture Company Approach for a Public–Private Partnership in Ireland*, Government of Ireland: Dublin

Department of Environment, Heritage and Local Government (2007) *Circular N16/2007 – Arrangements for Provision of Social Housing through Turnkey Projects*, Government of Ireland: Dublin

Department of Environment, Heritage and Local Government (2007) *Sustainable Development: A Strategy for Ireland*, Government of Ireland: Dublin

Department of Environment, Heritage and Local Government (2009) *Guidelines for Planning Authorities on Sustainable Residential Development in Urban Areas (Cities, Towns & Villages)*, Government of Ireland: Dublin

Department of Environment, Heritage and Local Government (2010) *National Survey of Ongoing Housing Developments*, Government of Ireland: Dublin

Department of Environment, Heritage and Local Government (2011) *Housing Policy Statement*, Government of Ireland: Dublin

Department of Environment, Heritage and Local Government (2011) *Social Housing Support – Household Means Policy*, Government of Ireland: Dublin

Department of Housing, Planning and Local Government (2017) *Circular Letter PL 10/2017 – Guidance on Planning Applications for Short-term Lettings*, Government of Ireland: Dublin

Department of Housing, Planning and Local Government (2018) *Sustainable Urban Housing: Design Standards for New Apartments*, Government of Ireland: Dublin

Department of Housing, Planning and Local Government (2018) *Sustainable Urban Housing: Design Standards for New Apartments – Guidelines for Planning Authorities*, Government of Ireland: Dublin

Department of Housing, Planning and Local Government (2018) *National Vacant Housing Reuse Strategy 2018–2021*, Government of Ireland: Dublin

Department of Public Expenditure and Reform (2014) *A Report on the Implementation of the Agency Rationalisation Programme*, Government of Ireland: Dublin

Dixon, T and Eames, M (2013) 'Scaling Up: The Challenges of Urban Retrofit', *Building Research & Information*, Vol. 41, No. 5

Doling, J and Ford, J (2007) 'A Union of Home Owners, Editorial', *European Journal of Housing and Planning*, Vol. 7, No. 2, pp. 113–127

Doling, J and Ronald, RJ (2010) 'Home Ownership and Asset-based Welfare', *Housing and the Built Environment*, Vol. 25, pp. 165–173

Douglas, J (2006) *Building Retrofit*, Butterworth Heinemann: Oxford

Drudy, PJ and Punch, M (2002) 'Housing Models and Inequality: Perspectives on Recent Irish Experience', *Housing Studies*, Vol. 17, No. 4, pp. 657–672

Dublin City Council (n.d.) *A Guide to Protected Structures*, DCC: Dublin

Duffy, D, Byrne, D and Fitzgerald, J (2014) 'Alternative Scenarios for New Household Formation in Ireland', *Quarterly Economic Commentary*, ESRI: Dublin

Duffy, PJ (1983) 'Rural Settlement Change in the Republic of Ireland – A Preliminary Discussion', *Geoforum*, Vol. 14, No. 2

Duffy, PJ (2000) 'Trends in Nineteenth- and Twentieth-Century Settlement', in Barry, T (ed.), *A History of Settlement in Ireland*, Routledge: London

Dukelow, F and Considine, M (2017) *Irish Social Policy: A Critical Introduction*, second edition, Bristol University Press: Bristol

Dún Laoghaire–Rathdown County Council (2004) *County Development Plan 2004–2010*, DLR: Dublin

Dunne, T (2014) 'Words Worth: Price and Value', *Surveyors' Journal*, Autumn

Education and Training Unit (2017) 'The Policy and Law Making Process', *ETU*, available at: http://etu.org.za/toolbox/docs/govern/policy.html

Edwards, B and Turrent, D (eds) (2000) *Sustainable Housing: Principles and Practices*, Taylor and Francis: London

Eisenberg, A (n.d.) *The Housing Transportation Connection: Building Better Communities Through Better Housing and Transportation*, US Millennial Housing Commission: Washington DC

Epstein, RA (2009) 'Property Rights, State of Nature Theory, and Environmental Protection', *New York University Journal of Law and Liberty*, Vol. 4, No. 1, pp. 1–35

Evans, A (2004) *Economics, Real Estate and the Supply of Land*, Blackwell Publishing: Oxford

Fahey, T and Norris, M (2009) 'Housing and the Welfare State: An Overview', UCD Working Paper Series WP09/09

Fahey, T and Norris, M (2011) 'From Asset Based Welfare to Welfare Housing? The Changing Function of Social Housing in Ireland', UCD policy paper

Fáilte Ireland (2018) 'Accommodation Capacity in Ireland 2018', available at: http://www.failteireland.ie/FailteIreland/media/WebsiteStructure/Documents/3_Research_Insights/3_General_SurveysReports/Accommodation-Capacity-in-Ireland-2018.pdf?ext=.pdf

Fingal County Council (2017) 'Chapter 11: Land Use Zoning Objectives', *Draft Development Plan 2017–2023*, Fingal County Council: Dublin

Finnerty, J and O'Connell, C (2014) '50 Years of the Social Housing "Offer" in Ireland: The Casualisation Thesis Examined', in Sirr, L (ed.), *Renting in Ireland: The Private, Voluntary and Social Sectors*, IPA: Dublin

Fitzgerald, C and Murray, S (2018) 'Hundreds more people removed from homeless figures over "categorisation issue"', *TheJournal.ie*, 30 May, available at: https://www.thejournal.ie/miscategorisation-homeless-figures-4045054-May2018/

Fitzgerald, J (2017) 'Understanding why homes are vacant can help solve housing crisis', *Irish Times*, 5 May

Fitzsimons, F (2014) 'Records of the Irish Land Commission', *History Ireland*, Vol. 22, No. 1

Focus Ireland (2003) *Housing Access for All: An Analysis of Housing Strategies and Homeless Action Plans*, Focus Ireland: Dublin

Foley-Fisher, N and McLaughlin, E (2015) 'Capitalising on the Irish Land Question: Land Reform and State Banking in Ireland, 1891–1938', *Discussion Papers in Environmental Economics*, Paper 2015-03

Fraser, I (2016) 'Top 10 biggest house builders control land for almost one million homes', *The Telegraph*, 18 December

Fuller, G, Johnston, A and Regan, A (2018) 'Bringing the Household Back In: Comparative Capitalism and the Politics of Housing Markets', UCD Geary Institute Discussion Papers, WP2018/07

Future of London (2015) 'Delivering Infill Development – A London 2050 Briefing Paper', Future of London: London

Gallent, N, Mace, A and Tewdwr-Jones, M, (2005) *Second Homes: European Perspectives and UK Policies*, Ashgate: Aldershot

Gallent, N, Schucksmith, M and Tewdwr-Jones, M (eds) (2003) *Housing in the European Countryside: Rural Pressure and Policy in Western Europe*, Routledge: London

Galligan, Y (2005) 'The Private Rented Sector', in Norris, M and Redmond, D (eds), *Housing Contemporary Ireland: Policy, Society and Shelter*, Institute of Public Administration: Dublin

Gallwey, B (2017) *A Guide to Undertaking a Rough Sleeping Count*, Dublin Region Homeless Executive: Dublin

Garnett, D (2015) *The A–Z of Housing (Professional Keywords)*, Macmillan: London

Glass, R (1964) 'Introduction: Aspects of Change', in Centre for Urban Studies (ed.), *London: Aspects of Change*, MacKibbon and Kee: London

Glossop, C (2008) 'Housing and Economic Development: Moving Forward Together', *Centre for Cities*, November, available at: http://www.centreforcities. org/wp-content/uploads/2014/09/08-11-06-Housing-and-economic-development.pdf

Gogan, R (2008) *The Essential Guide to Apartment Living in Ireland*, M1 Publications: Dublin

Goodbody (2013) *Economic Research – A Detailed Analysis of the Prospects for Irish Property*, Goodbody: Dublin

Goul Andersen, J (2012) 'Welfare State and Welfare State Theory', Centre for Comparative Welfare Studies Working Paper, Department of Political Science, Aalborg University

Gould, P (1998) *The Unfinished Revolution: How the Modernisers Saved the Labour Party*, Little Brown: London

Government of Ireland (1997) *National Anti-Poverty Strategy – Sharing in Progress 1997–2007*, Government of Ireland: Dublin

Government of Ireland (2016) *Rebuilding Ireland: Action Plan for Housing and Homelessness*, available at: http://rebuildingireland.ie

Greenstein, R and Sungu-Eryilma, Y (2005) 'Community Land Trusts: Leasing Land for Affordable Housing', *Land Lines*, Lincoln Institute, April

Grimes, L (n.d.) *Limited Interests, Some Taxation Implications*, Certified Public Accountants: Dublin

Grist, B (2003) 'Planning', in Callanan, M and Keogan, F (eds), *Local Government in Ireland Inside Out*, IPA: Dublin

Grotti, R, Russell, H, Fahey, E and Maître, B (2018) *Discrimination and Inequality in Housing in Ireland*, IHREC: Dublin

Gurney, C (1999) 'Pride and Prejudice: Discourses of Normalisation in Private and Public Accounts of Home Ownership', *Housing Studies*, Vol. 14, No. 2, pp. 163–183

Gurran, N and Bramley, G (2017) 'The Housing System', in Gurran, N and Bramley, G (eds), *Urban Planning and the Housing Market*, Palgrave Macmillan: London

Hall, M and Müller, M (eds) (2004) 'Introduction: Second Homes, Curse or Blessing? Revisited', in Hall, M and Müller, M (eds), *Tourism, Mobility and Second Homes: Between Elite Landscapes and Common Ground*, Channel View Publications: Clevedon

Harley-Gunning, E (2017) 'Retrospective Corrective: Rethinking Retention Planning Permission in Ireland', MSc thesis, Dublin Institute of Technology

Harris, R and Arku, G (2006) 'Housing and Economic Development: The Evolution of an Idea since 1945', *Habitat International*, Vol. 30, No. 4, pp. 1007–1017

Hay, C (1999) *The Political Economy of New Labour: Labouring under False Pretences*, Manchester University Press: Manchester

Hayden, A (2014) 'Irish Social Housing: The Path to Decline, 1966–1988', in Sirr, L (ed.), *Renting in Ireland: The Private, Voluntary and Social Sectors*, IPA: Dublin

Hayden, A and Norris, M (2018) *The Future of Council Housing: An Analysis of the Financial Sustainability of Local Authority Provided Social Housing*, Community Foundation

Healy, M (2017) 'A Critical Examination of Policy-making Frameworks for Housing Policy in Ireland with Specific Reference to International Better Regulation Frameworks', MSc thesis, Dublin Institute of Technology

Healy, S, Bennett, C, Bourke, S, Leahy, A, Murphy, E, Murphy, M and Reynolds, B (2018) 'Social Justice Matters: 2018 Guide to a Fairer Society', *Socio-Economic Review 2018*, Social Justice Ireland: Dublin

Hearne, J (2017) 'New build homes face emerging crisis', *Passive House Plus*, 6 April

Henckel, T (2017) 'What economics has to say about housing bubbles', *The Conversation*, 2 April, available at: http://theconversation.com/what-economics-has-to-say-about-housing-bubbles-74925

Heywood, A and Hackett, P (2013) 'The Case for a Property Speculation Tax', a Smith Institute discussion paper, The Adam Smith Institute: London

HM Land Registry (2018) *Guidance Practice Guide 16: Profits à Prendre*, HM Land Registry: London

Holland, K (2017) 'Traveller housing targets have not been met in 18 years', *Irish Times*, 14 September

Holland, K (2018) 'Travellers on roadside or in overcrowded homes increased 66 per cent in 5 years', *Irish Times*, 27 July

Hoolachan, J, McKee, K, Moore, T and Soaita, AM (2017) '"Generation Rent" and the Ability to "Settle Down": Economic and Geographical Variation in Young People's Housing Transitions', *Journal of Youth Studies*, Vol. 20, No. 1, pp. 63–78

Housing Agency, The (2016) *Guidance Note on the Capital Advance Leasing Facility (CALF) for Approved Housing Bodies and Housing Authorities*, The Housing Agency: Dublin

Housing Agency, The (2017) *Annual Report 2016*, The Housing Agency: Dublin

Housing Finance Agency (2018) *Annual Report 2017*, HFA: Dublin

Hughes, B (2018) 'Demography Is Destiny: Strategic Planning and Housing in Ireland', in Sirr, L (ed.), *Administration – special housing edition*, Vol. 66, No. 2, pp. 163–177

Hynes, L (2016) 'Focus on downsizing: When small is beautiful', *Irish Independent*, 3 April

Indecon (2012) *Indecon's Assessment of the Feasibility of a Tenancy Deposit Protection Scheme in Ireland*, Indecon review submitted to the Department of the Environment, Community and Local Government/Housing Agency and the PRTB, available at: https://onestopshop.rtb.ie/images/uploads/forms/indecons-assess-ment-of-the-feasibility-of-a-tenancy-deposit-protection-scheme-in-ireland.pdf

Insolvency Service of Ireland (2015) *Guide to a Personal Insolvency Arrangement*, ISI: Dublin

Isdell, A (2013) 'Building Progress: Building Control Regulations and Their Effect', *Surveyors' Journal*, Summer

Isdell, A (2014) 'Changes to Building Regulations', *Surveyors' Journal*, Spring

Jones, P and Evans, J (2008) *Urban Regeneration in the UK*, Sage: London

Joint Committee on Housing, Planning and Local Government (2017) *Safe As Houses? A Report on Building Standards, Building Controls and Consumer Protection*, Government of Ireland: Dublin

Kapila, L (2017) 'Might Dublin see its first community land trust?', *Dublin Inquirer*, 12 July

Keaveney, K (2009) 'Contested Ruralities: Housing in the Irish Countryside', PhD thesis, University of Maynooth

Kelly, F (2018) 'Six-storey apartments "are optimal height for affordability"', *Irish Times*, 13 April

Kelly, O (2015) 'Studio apartments: Minister defends rules reducing size', *Irish Times*, 22 December

Kelly, O (2017) Government's "rapid-build" schedule in realms of fantasy', *Irish Times*, 1 August

Kelly, R and O'Malley, T (2016) 'The Good, the Bad and the Impaired: A Credit Risk Model of the Irish Mortgage Market', *Journal of Financial Stability*, Vol. 22, pp. 1–9

Kemeny, J (1995) *From Public Housing to the Social Market: Rental Policy Strategies in Comparative Perspective*, Routledge: London

Kenna, P (2011) *Housing Law, Rights and Policy*, Clarus Press: Dublin

Kenny, J (1973) *Committee on the Price of Building Land: Report to the Minister for Local Government*, Government Publications Office: Dublin

Kilkenny, P and O'Callaghan, D (2018) *Department of Public Expenditure and Reform – Spending Review 2018: Current and Capital Expenditure on Social Housing Delivery Mechanisms*, Department of Public Expenditure and Reform: Dublin

Kirk, R (2008) 'Joint Venture Accounting on the Move', *Accountancy Plus*, June

Kitchin, R (2013) 'Making Informed Decisions on Future Housing Policy', *Housing Ireland*, Winter

Kitchin, R (2015) 'Why the National Spatial Strategy Failed and Prospects for the National Planning Framework', *Ireland after NAMA*, 24 July, available at: https://irelandafternama.wordpress.com/2015/07/24/why-the-national-spatial-strategy-failed-and-prospects-for-the-national-planning-framework/

Kitchin, R and Gleeson, J, Keaveney, K and O'Callaghan, C (2010) 'A Haunted Landscape: Housing and Ghost Estates in Post-Celtic Tiger Ireland', (NIRSA) Working Paper Series No. 59, NIRSA – National Institute for Regional and Spatial Analysis

Kitchin, R, O'Callaghan, C, Boyle, M, Gleeson, J and Keaveney, K (2012) 'Placing Neoliberalism: The Rise and Fall of Ireland's Celtic Tiger', *Environment and Planning A*, Vol. 44, No. 6, pp. 1302–1326

Kreilkamp, V (2006) 'The Novel of the Big House', in Wilson Foster, J (ed.), *The Cambridge Companion to the Irish Novel* (Cambridge Companions to Literature, pp. 60–77), Cambridge: Cambridge University Press

Kwak, J (2014) 'Cultural Capture and the Financial Crisis', in Carpenter, D and Moss, D (eds), *Preventing Regulatory Capture – Special Interest Influence and How to Limit It*, Cambridge University Press: Cambridge

Larkin, N (2017) 'Property Clinic: Should I opt out of costly compliance paperwork?', *Irish Times*, 18 May

Law Reform Commission (1999) *Report on Gazumping*, LRC: Dublin

Law Reform Commission (2003) *Consultation Paper on General Law of Landlord and Tenant*, LRC: Dublin

Leahy, C (2010) 'The Land and Conveyancing Law Reform Act 2009: An Overview', *Homs Solicitors*, 1 March, available at: http://www.homs.ie/publications/the-land-and-conveyancing-law-reform-act-2009-an-overview/

Lee, P and Murie, A (1997) *Poverty, Housing Tenure and Social Exclusion*, Policy Press: Bristol

Lees, L, Slater, T and Wyly, E (2008) *Gentrification*, Routledge: Oxford

Le Grand, J (2003) *Motivation, Agency and Public Policy: Of Knights and Knaves, Pawns and Queens*, Oxford University Press: Oxford

Leman (2015) 'Has the Property Services Regulatory Authority Regulated?', *Thought Leadership Articles*, 9 April, available at: https://leman.ie/has-the-property-services-regulatory-authority-regulated/

Letwin, O (2018) *Independent Review of Build-Out Rates*, Ministry of Housing, Communities and Local Government: London

Lindbeck, A (2006) 'The Welfare State – Background, Achievements, Problems', IFN Working Paper Series 662, Research Institute of Industrial Economics: Stockholm

Litman, T (2018) *Evaluating Transportation Equity: Guidance for Incorporating Distributional Impacts in Transportation Planning*, Victoria Transport Policy Institute

Little, J (2011) 'Thermal Bridging', *Passive House Plus*, 27 July

Lock, D (2000) 'Housing and Transport', in Edwards, B and Turrent, D (eds), *Sustainable Housing: Principles and Practices*, Taylor and Francis: London

Long, J and Ferrie, J (2003) 'Labour Mobility', in *Oxford Dictionary of Economic History*, Oxford University Press: Oxford

Lund, B (2015) '"It's Politics Stupid": A Public Choice Analysis of Housing Policy', paper delivered at the Housing Studies Association Conference, 8–10 April, York

Lux, M and Sunega, P (2012) 'Labour Mobility and Housing: The Impact of Housing Tenure and Housing Affordability on Labour Migration in the Czech Republic', *Urban Studies*, Vol. 49, No. 3, pp. 489–504

MacCarthaigh, M (2013) 'Reform of Public Policy-making in Ireland', *Journal of the Statistical and Social Inquiry Society of Ireland*, Vol. XLII

MacLaran, A and Kelly, S (2014) 'Neoliberalism: The Rise of a Bad Idea', in MacLaran, A and Kelly, S (eds), *Neoliberal Urban Policy and the Transformation of the City*, Palgrave Macmillan: London

MacLennan, D and Miao, J (2017) 'Housing and Capital in the 21ˢᵗ century', *Housing, Theory and Society*, Vol. 34, No. 2

MacMahon, T (2017) 'The Emergence of Build to Rent', *Eolas Magazine*

Malone, F (2017) 'Financial Planning in Multi-unit Developments', MSc thesis, Dublin Institute of Technology

Malpass, P and Murie, A (1990) *Housing Policy and Practice*, third edition, Macmillan Education: London

Marcuse, P and Keating, W (2006) *The Permanent Housing Crisis: The Failures of Conservatism and the Limitations of Liberalism*, Temple University Press: Philadelphia

Martens, K (2011) 'Substance Precedes Methodology: On Cost–benefit Analysis and Equity', *Transportation*, Vol. 38, No. 6, pp. 959–974

McCall, T (2010) 'What Do We Mean by "Regional Development"?', Institute of Regional Development, University of Tasmania

McCartney, J (2018) 'How many houses do we really need?', *Irish Times*, 1 June

McCartney, R (2017) 'Airbnb becomes flash point in the District's hot debate over gentrification', *Washington Post*, 1 November

McCashin, T (2004) *Social Security in Ireland*, Gill and Macmillan: Dublin

McConnell, D (2017) '50 Nama staff on "gardening leave" for more than three months', *Irish Examiner*, 14 July

McConnell, D (2019) 'Extra charges set for Airbnb homes in clampdown on regulations', *Irish Examiner*, 12 April

McCord, R (2011) 'A Garden City – The Dublin Corporation Housing Scheme at Marino, 1924', *The Irish Story*, 7 September, available at: http://www.theirishstory.com/2011/09/07/a-garden-city-the-dublin-corporation-housing-scheme-at-marino-1924/#.W3LxTC17FR0

McDonald, F (2018) '"Bungalow Blitz" another nail in the coffin for towns and villages', *Irish Times*, 13 February

McKeown, A and Sirr, L (2018) 'Service Charge Collection in Multi-Unit Developments', in Sirr, L (ed.), *Administration – special housing edition*, Vol. 66, No. 2, pp. 135–152

McMahon, N (2012) 'Investigating Policy Processes and Practices in Ireland: Potential Ways Forward', *Irish Journal of Public Policy*, Vol. 4, No. 1

McManus, R (2002) *Dublin, 1910–1940: Shaping the City and Suburbs*, Four Courts Press: Dublin

Melia, P (2018) 'Taxpayers' return on LIHAF investments is far from clear-cut', *Irish Independent*, 30 March

Melia, P (2018) 'Death of the semi-D as height limits scrapped', *Irish Independent*, 8 December

Mercy Law Resource Centre (2018) *The Right to Housing*, Mercy Law Resource Centre: Dublin

Miller, D (1976) *Social Justice*, Clarendon Press: Oxford

Millington, AF (2000) *An Introduction to Property Valuation*, Estates Gazette: London

Milne, R (2017) 'More land hoarding claims surface in Ireland', *The Planner*, 8 June

Montgomerie, J (2015) 'Housing-based welfare strategies do not work and will not work', *LSE Blog*, 30 January, available at: http://blogs.lse.ac.uk/politicsandpolicy/homeownership-and-the-failures-of-asset-based-welfare/

Morrison, N and Monk, S (2006) 'Job–housing Mismatch: Affordability Crisis in Surrey, South East England', *Environment and Planning*, Vol. 38, No. 1115–1130

National Economic and Social Council (2004) *Housing in Ireland: Performance and Policy*, NESC: Dublin

National Economic and Social Council (2014) *Social Housing at the Crossroads: Possibilities for Investment, Provision and Cost Rental – Report 138*, NESC: Dublin

National Economic and Social Council (2014) *Homeownership and Rental: What Road is Ireland On? – Report 140*, NESC: Dublin

National Economic and Social Council (2015) *Ireland's Private Rental Sector: Pathways to Secure Occupancy and Affordable Supply – Report 141*, NESC: Dublin

National Economic and Social Council (2015) *Housing Supply and Land: Driving Public Action for the Common Good – Report 42*, NESC: Dublin

National Economic and Social Council (2018) *Urban Development Land, Housing and Infrastructure: Fixing Ireland's Broken System*, NESC: Dublin

National Oversight and Audit Commission (2017) *A Review of the Management and Maintenance of Local Authority Housing – Report No. 12*, NOCA: Dublin

National Oversight and Audit Commission (2018) *Performance Indicators in Local Authorities 2016 – Report No. 14*, NOAC: Dublin

National Records of Scotland (2018) *Population Density, 2011*, National Records of Scotland: Edinburgh

Needham, B (2014) *Dutch Land-use Planning: The Principles and the Practice*, Routledge: Oxon

Newman, P and Thornley, A (1996) *Urban Planning in Europe: International Competition, National Systems and Planning Projects*, Routledge: London

Neylon, L (2016) 'How should we count the number of council voids?', *Dublin Inquirer*, 21 December

Neylon, L (2017) 'Despite €200 million subsidy for developers, questions over affordable housing', *Dublin Inquirer*, 16 May

Niskanen, WA (1973) *Bureaucracy: Servant or Master?*, Institute of Economic Affairs: London

Norman, J, MacLean, H and Kennedy, C (2006) 'Comparing High and Low Residential Density: Life-cycle Analysis of Energy Use and Greenhouse Gas Emissions', *Journal of Urban Planning and Development*, Vol. 132, No. 1

Norris, M (2011) 'The Private Rented Sector in Ireland', in Scanlon, K and Kochan, B (eds), *Towards a Sustainable Private Rented Sector: The Lessons from Other Countries*, London School of Economics: London

Norris, M (2013) 'Varieties of Home Ownership: Ireland's Transition from a Socialised to a Marketised Policy Regime', UCD Geary Institute Discussion Paper Series, GP2013/06

Norris, M (2014) 'Policy Drivers of the Retreat and Revival of Private Renting: Regulation, Finance, Taxes and Subsidies', in Sirr, L (ed.), *Renting in Ireland: The Social, Voluntary and Private Sectors*, IPA: Dublin

Norris, M (2017) *Property, Family and the Irish Welfare State*, Palgrave Macmillan: London

Norris, M, Gkartzios, M and Coates, D (2013) 'Property-led Urban, Town and Rural Regeneration in Ireland: Positive and Perverse Outcomes in Different Implementation Contexts', UCD Discussion Paper Series WP2013/11

Norris, M, Paris, C and Winston, N (2010) 'Second Homes within Irish Housing Booms and Busts: North–South Comparisons, Contrasts and Debates', *Environment and Planning C: Politics and Space*, Vol. 28, No. 4

Norris, M and Winston, N (2004) *Housing Policy Review, 1990–2002*, Government Stationery Office: Dublin

Norris, M and Winston, N (2011) 'Does Home Ownership Reinforce or Counterbalance Income Inequality? Trends in Western Europe 1997–2007', UCD Working paper WP19

Nyberg, P (2011) *Misjudging Risk: Causes of the Systemic Banking Crisis in Ireland – Report of the Commission of Investigation into the Banking Sector in Ireland*, Government of Ireland: Dublin

O'Broin, E (2018) 'It is clear that Rebuilding Ireland has failed', *Irish Times*, 18 July

O'Connell, C (2007) *The State and Housing in Ireland: Ideology, Policy and Practice*, Nova: New York

O'Connell, S (2018) 'The full Irish: how B&Bs bounced back', *Irish Times*, 17 March

O'Connor, D (1988) 'Housing in Dublin 1887–1987', *Irish Architect*, Vol. 67, June/July/August

O'Connor, N and Staunton, C (2017) *Cherishing All Equally: Economic Inequality in Ireland*, TASC: Dublin

Office of the Director of Corporate Enforcement (2008) *Company Law Handbook on Residential Property Owners' Management Companies*, ODCE: Dublin

O'Leary, D (2018) 'New housing data highlights the task facing the government', *Irish Times*, 18 July

O'Malley, E (2010) 'Political Power and Accountability in Ireland', *Studies: An Irish Quarterly Review*, Vol. 99, No. 393, pp. 43–54

O'Reilly, N and Shine, P (2013) 'Beyond the Bounds: Resolving Boundary Disputes', *Surveyors' Journal*, Autumn

O'Sullivan, E (2014) 'Bigger and Better', paper presented at the Future of Private Renting in Northern Ireland Conference, 6 November, Belfast

O'Sullivan, F (2018) 'Barcelona Finds a Way to Control Its Airbnb Market', *Citylab*, 6 June

O'Sullivan, F (2018) 'Berlin Just Canceled Its Airbnb Ban', *Citylab*, 23 March

O'Sullivan, J (2012) 'Houses for Heroes: Life in the Killester Colony 1919–1945', *Dublin Historical Record*, Vol. 65, No. 1/2, pp. 2–33

Ozimek, A (2015) 'The Problem With 100% Land Value Taxes', *Forbes*, 29 March, available at: https://www.forbes.com/sites/modeledbehavior/2015/03/29/the-problem-with-100-land-value-taxes/#42fd5f305349

Page, E (2006) 'The Origins of Policy', in Moran, M, Rein, M and Goodin, R (eds), *Oxford Handbook of Public Policy*, Oxford University Press: Oxford

Paris, C (2006) 'Multiple "Homes": Dwelling and Hyper-mobility and Emergent Transnational Second Home Ownership', paper presented to the European Network for Housing Research Conference, 2–5 July, Ljubljana

Paris, C (2008) 'Re-positioning Second Homes within Housing Studies: Household Investment, Gentrification, Multiple Residence, Mobility and Hyper-consumption', *Housing, Theory and Society*, Vol. 25, pp. 1–19

Pennington, M (2002) *Liberating the Land: The Case for Private Land Use Planning*, Institute of Economic Affairs: London

Pew Trusts (2014) *Links between Health and Housing*, The Pew Charitable Trusts: Philadelphia

Pope, C (2016) 'Vulture funds and why they can act with virtual impunity', *Irish Times*, 14 March

Power, J (2018) 'Over €16m spent renovating 10 homeless family hubs', *Irish Times*, 15 August

Pruijt, HD (2011) 'The Logic of Urban Squatting', *International Journal of Urban and Regional Research*, Vol. 37, No. 1, pp. 19–45

Quinlan, R (2018) 'Investors have €5bn available for Irish build-to-rent housing schemes', *Irish Independent*, 1 March

Quinn, B (2004) 'Dwelling through Multiple Places: A Case Study of Second Home Ownership in Ireland', in Hall, M and Müller, M (eds), *Tourism, Mobility and Second Homes: Between Elite Landscapes and Common Ground*, Channel View Publications: Clevedon

Quinn, E (2018) 'Banks tap huge margin on buy-to-lets', *Irish Examiner*, 8 March

Quinn, E and McConnell, D (2017) 'Total bill for tracker scandal could hit €1 billion', *Irish Examiner*, 21 December

Rae, A (2018) 'Think your country is crowded? These maps reveal the truth about population density across Europe', *The Conversation*, 23 January, available at: https://theconversation.com/think-your-country-is-crowded-these-maps-reveal-the-truth-about-population-density-across-europe-90345

Reception and Integration Agency (2018) *Monthly Report, June*, Department of Justice and Equality: Dublin

Reddan, F (2018) 'Mortgage scheme: who is eligible and how will it work?', *Irish Times*, 22 January

Redmond, D (2001) 'Social Housing in Ireland: Under New Management?', *European Journal of Housing Policy*, Vol. 1, No. 2, pp. 291–306

Regling, K and Watson, M (2010) *A Preliminary Report on the Sources of Ireland's Banking Crisis*, Government Publications Office: Dublin

Residential Tenancies Board (2018) *Guidelines for Good Practice On: The Substantial Change Exemption in Rent Pressure Zone Areas*, RTB: Dublin

Revenue (2007) *Tenants in Common and Joint Tenants*, Revenue Commissioners: Dublin

Rock, S (2017) 'Transport Inequity and Car Dependency: A Self-Reinforcing Relationship', paper presented to TASC Conference, 21 June, Dublin

Rogers, D and Power, E (2017) 'Explainer: The financialisation of housing and what can be done about it', *The Conversation*, 23 March, available at: https://theconversation.com/explainer-the-financialisation-of-housing-and-what-can-be-done-about-it-73767

Ronald, R (2008) *The Ideology of Home Ownership: Homeowner Societies and the Role of Housing*, Palgrave Macmillan: London

Rothery, S (1991) *Ireland and the New Architecture 1900–1940*, Lilliput Press: Dublin

Rowley, E (2015) 'The Architect, the Planner and the Bishop: The Shapers of "Ordinary" Dublin, 1940–60', *FOOTPRINT*, No. 17, Autumn/Winter, pp. 69–88

Royal Institution of Chartered Surveyors (2008) *Value of Development Land*, first edition, RICS: London

Royal Institution of Chartered Surveyors (2012) 'What Is a Property Cycle?', *RICS Modus*, June

Royal Institution of Chartered Surveyors (2014) *Sinking Funds, Reserve Funds and Depreciation Charges*, RICS Information Paper, second edition, RICS: London

Royal Irish Academy Geosciences and Geographical Sciences Committee (2017) *The Dynamics of Housing Markets and Housing Provision in Ireland*, RIA: Dublin

RTÉ (2017) '26 residential buildings served fire safety notices this year', *RTÉ News*, 4 July

RTÉ (2017) 'Beacon apartments company to vote on €10k owners' levy', *RTÉ News*, 16 March

RTÉ (2017) *Morning Ireland* – Kevin Hollingsworth and Cian O'Callaghan in Jackie Fox report on self-certification, 26 May

RTÉ (2018) 'No money paid out in State house building scheme', *RTÉ News*, 16 April

Ryan, S (2018) 'Will 2018 be the year of the credit union mortgage?', *Irish Independent*, 20 January

Ryan, S (2018) 'Home truths: Rebuilding Ireland loans: caveat emptor', *Irish Independent*, 6 April

Ryan-Collins, J, Lloyd, T and Macfarlane, L (2017) *Rethinking the Economics of Land and Housing*, Zed Books: London

Sadasivam, K and Alpana, S (2009) 'Sustainable Development and Housing Affordability', *International Journal of Justice and Sustainability*, Vol. 16, No. 9, pp. 1–9

Scarrett, D (2014) *Property Valuation – The Five Methods*, Routledge: London

Sheehy Skeffington, P (2018) 'The Limited Rights of Residential Licensees in Ireland: A Case for Carefully Targeted Legal Reform', in Sirr, L (ed.), *Administration – special housing edition*, Vol. 66, No. 2

Shelter (2008) *Housing First: Good Practice*, Shelter: London

Sirr, L (2010) 'Apartment Living and the Multi-unit Developments Bill', *Public Affairs Ireland*, June

Sirr, L (2013) 'Recession and Renting: The Future of the Private Rented Sector in Ireland', paper presented to the ENHR: European Network for Housing Research Conference, 10–22 June, Tarragona, Spain

Sirr, L (2014) (ed.) *Renting in Ireland: The Private, Voluntary and Social Sectors*, IPA: Dublin

Sirr, L (2017) 'A year of magical thinking when it comes to housing figures', *Sunday Times*, 18 December

Sirr, L and Xerri, K (2015) 'Ireland – A Northern European Country with a Southern European Housing Ethos', paper presented at the ENHR Conference, 28 June–1 July, Lisbon

Smith, M (2018) '(S)height', *Village Magazine*, December

Smith, N (1982) 'Gentrification and Uneven Development', *Economic Geography*, Vol. 58, No. 2, pp. 139–155

Smith, N (2000) 'Gentrification', in Johnston, RJ, Gregory, D, Pratt, G and Watts, M (eds), *The Dictionary of Human Geography*, fourth edition, Blackwell: Oxford

Society of Chartered Surveyors Ireland (n.d.) *A Consumer Guide to Apartment Ownership Under the Multi-Unit Developments (MUD) Act 2011*, SCSI: Dublin

Society of Chartered Surveyors Ireland (n.d.) *Boundaries: Procedures for Boundary Identification, Demarcation and Dispute Resolution in Ireland*, second edition, Geomatics Guidance Note, SCSI: Dublin

Society of Chartered Surveyors Ireland (n.d.) *A Clear Guide to Compulsory Purchase Orders and Compensation*, SCSI: Dublin

Society of Chartered Surveyors Ireland (2014) *Disability Access in Buildings – Part M of the Building Regulations*, SCSI: Dublin

Society of St Vincent de Paul (2015) 'Energy Poverty – Experienced by One Parent Families in the Republic of Ireland', *Policy Links*, Edition No. 1, January

Somerville-Woodward, R (2002) *Ballymun: A History*, Volumes I and II, Ballymun Regeneration Limited: Dublin

South Dublin Community Platform (2006) 'Housing and Accommodation Thematic Paper'

Spicker, P (2018) 'Housing and Urban Policy', *An Introduction to Social Policy*, available at: http://spicker.uk/social-policy/housing.htm

Stead, N (2000) 'Unsustainable Settlements', in Barton, H (ed.), *Sustainable Communities: The Potential for Eco-neighbourhoods*, second edition, Earthscan: London

Streimikiene, D (2015) 'Quality of Life and Housing', *International Journal of Information and Education Technology*, Vol. 5, No. 2, pp. 140–145

Taxes Consolidation Act 1997 (Number 39 of 1997), Chapter 4: Qualifying Resort Areas

Tax Strategy Group (2012) *Taxation of Property*, Department of Finance: Dublin

Taylor, EFN (1948) 'Tribute to Herbert Simms', *Irish Builder*, Vol. 90, 16 October

Tisdall, G (2015) 'The problem with open plan …', *Sunday Independent*, 23 November

Titheridge, H, Christie, N, Mackett, R, Oviedo Hernández, D and Ye, R (2014) *Transport and Poverty: A Review of the Evidence*, University College London: London

Tosics, I, Szemző, H, Illés, D, Gertheis, A, Lalenis, K and Kalergis, D (2010) *EU Plurel Report 2.2.1. National Spatial Planning Policies and Governance Typology*

Tuininga, M (2012) 'Aquinas and Calvin believed property rights were subject to the rights of the poor', *Christian in America*, 19 September, available at: https://matthewtuininga.wordpress.com/2012/09/19/aquinas-and-calvin-believed-property-rights-were-subject-to-the-rights-of-the-poor/

UN Habitat (2007) *State of the World's Cities 2006–7*, UN Habitat: Nairobi

United Nations Human Rights Council (2017) *Report of the Special Rapporteur on Adequate Housing as a Component of the Right to an Adequate Standard of Living, and on the Right to Non-Discrimination in this Context*, United Nations General Assembly: New York

United Nations Statistical Division (1997) *Glossary of Environment Statistics*, Studies in Methods, Series F, No. 67, United Nations: New York

Urban Land Institute (2014) *The Macro View on Micro Units*, ULI: New York

van Ham, M, Manley, D, Bailey, N, Simpson, L and Maclennan, D (2012) *Neighbourhood Effects Research: New Perspectives*, Springer: Dordrecht

Wachsmuth, D, Chaney, D, Kerrigan, D, Shillolo, A and Basalaev-Binder, R (2018) *The High Cost of Short-Term Rentals in New York City*, Urban Politics and Governance Research Group School of Urban Planning, McGill University

Wallace, A, Bevan, M, Croucher, K, Jackson, K, O'Malley, L and Orton, V (2005) *The Impact of Empty, Second and Holiday Homes on the Sustainability of Rural Communities: A Systematic Literature Review*, Centre for Housing Policy: York

Walsh, K (2015) 'What are squatters' rights, exactly?', *Irish Examiner*, 22 January.

Ward, N (2018) 'Balanced Regional Development: Issues and Insights', University of East Anglia: Kent

Weaver, M (2004) 'Key worker housing – the issue explained', *The Guardian*, 25 May

Weaver, M (2001) 'Urban regeneration – the issue explained', *The Guardian*, 19 March

Western Development Commission (2015) 'Balanced Regional Development – what does it mean?', *WDC Insights*, 11 May, available at: https://wdcinsights.wordpress.com/2015/05/11/balanced-regional-development-what-does-it-mean/

Wheeler, S (2004) *Planning for Sustainability: Creating Liveable, Equitable, and Ecological Communities*, Routledge: Oxford

White, D (2017) 'Land hoarding is pushing up the price of new homes', *Irish Independent*, 16 July

White, T (2018) 'Build-to-rent: how developers are profiting from Generation Rent', *The Guardian*, 11 April

Whitehead, C and Scanlon, K (2007) *Social Housing in Europe*, London School of Economics and Political Science: London

Wilkinson, S (2012) 'Analysing Sustainable Retrofit Potential in Premium Office Buildings', *Structural Survey*, Vol. 30, No. 5

Williams, B (2015) 'Public Policy and Urban and Regional Development Markets', in Williams, B and Reynolds-Feighan, AJ (eds), *Urban and Regional Economics*, McGraw-Hill Education: New York

Williams, B, Hughes, B and Redmond, B (2010) 'Managing an Unstable Housing Market', Working Paper Series, 10/02, UCD Urban Institute Ireland: Dublin

Winston, N (2012) 'Sustainable Housing: A Case Study of the Cloughjordan Eco-village, Ireland', *Enterprising Communities: Grassroots Sustainability Innovations Advances in Ecopolitics*, Vol. 9, pp. 85–103

Winterburn, M (2018) 'Home Economics: Reversing the Financialisation of Housing', *Journal of Architecture*, Vol. 23, No. 1, pp. 184–193

Woods, E (2012) 'Economies of Reuse', MSc Architecture thesis, University of Cincinnati

Wren, M, Normand, C, O'Reilly, D, Cruise, S, Connolly, S and Murphy, C (2012) *Towards the Development of a Predictive Model of Long-Term Care Demand for Northern Ireland and the Republic of Ireland*, Centre for Health Policy and Management: Trinity College Dublin

Wylie, JCW (2010) *Irish Land Law*, fourth edition, Bloomsbury Professional: Dublin

Yeang, LD, Alan Baxter and Associates, and studioREAL (2013) *The Urban Design Compendium*, third edition, English Partnerships: London

Zurich Life (n.d.) *Understanding Irish Real Estate Investment Trusts*, available at: https://www.zurichlife.ie/DocArchive/servlet/DocArchServlet?docId=DOC_9948&docTag=